W0055467

Advances in Computing Science

Advisory Board

R. F. Albrecht, Innsbruck
Z. Bubnicki, Wroclaw
R. E. Burkard, Graz
A. G. Butkovskiy, Moscow
C. H. Cap, Zürich
M. Dal Cin, Erlangen
W. Hackbusch, Kiel
G. R. Johnson, Fort Collins
W. Kreutzer, Christchurch
W. G. Kropatsch, Wien
I. Lovrek, Zagreb
G. Németh, Budapest
H. J. Stetter, Wien
Y. Takahara, Chiba
W. Törnig, Darmstadt
I. Troch, Wien
H. P. Zima, Wien

F. Solina
W. G. Kropatsch
R. Klette
R. Bajcsy (eds.)

Advances
in Computer Vision

SpringerWienNewYork

Prof. Dr. Franc Solina

Faculty of Computer and Information Science, University of Ljubljana,
Ljubljana, Slovenia

Prof. Dr. Walter G. Kropatsch

Abt. Mustererkennung und Bildverarbeitung, TU Wien,
Vienna, Austria

Prof. Dr. Reinhard Klette

Computer Science Department, Auckland University,
Auckland, New Zealand

Prof. Dr. Ruzena Bajcsy

Computer and Information Science, GRASP Laboratory,
University of Pennsylvania, Philadelphia, USA

This work is subject to copyright.
All rights are reserved, whether the whole or part of the material is concerned, specifically
those of translation, reprinting, re-use of illustrations, broadcasting, reproduction by
photocopying machines or similar means, and storage in data banks.

© 1997 Springer-Verlag/Wien

Typesetting: Camera-ready by authors

Graphic design: Ecke Bonk

Printed on acid-free and chlorine-free bleached paper

SPIN: 10631594

With 96 Figures

ISSN 1433-0113

ISBN-13:978-3-211-83022-2   e-ISBN-13:978-3-7091-6867-7

DOI: 10.1007/978-3-7091-6867-7

Preface

Computer vision used to be a rather small and exclusive research area focused mainly on theoretical issues and on solving problems for large and wealthy costumers such as manufacturing companies and the military who could afford the high costs. But expensive special image capture and computing hardware is now no longer required. Low cost video cameras, powerful personal computers and highspeed computer networks are making images ubiquitous in every possible application domain. Besides more traditional application domains such as manufacturing, robotics, medicine and security, newer ones such as virtual reality, tele-presence and image databases are in vogue. Computer vision solutions used to be very specific and difficult to adapt to other or even unforeseen situations. The current development is calling for simple to use yet robust applications that could be employed in various situations. This trend requires the reassessment of some theoretical issues in computer vision. A better general understanding of vision processes, new insights and better theories are needed.

This volume contains a selection of papers presented at the eight overall "Theoretical Foundations of Computer Vision" meeting and the second in the castle of Dagstuhl in March 1996. The aim of this meeting was to bring together scientists in computer vision from the West and from the former eastern block countries. The organizers believed that there was still a certain ignorance of each other's work and that such face to face meetings are beneficial to all participants and to the whole computer vision field. The organizers feel that this goal was achieved and that the road to more direct contacts and exchanges between researchers and students is now open.

Due to this goal the meeting covered a broad variety of computer vision topics. As the title of the meeting suggests most of the papers have a strong theoretical flavor but with some very real world implications. It was not easy to organize them in a linear fashion. The volume starts with papers dealing with 2D images (scale space, morphology, segmentation, neural networks, Hough transform, texture, pyramids) followed by papers on recovering the 3D structure (shape from shading, optical flow, 3D object recognition). Finally, the last few papers are on how vision is integrated into a larger task-driven framework (hand-eye calibration, navigation, perception-action cycle).

March 1997

Franc Solina, Walter G. Kropatsch, Reinhard Klette, Ruzena Bajcsy

Contents

VIII

A semidiscrete nonlinear scale-space theory and its relation to the Perona–Malik paradox

Joachim Weickert and Brahim Benhamouda

1 Introduction

Although much effort has been spent in the recent decade to establish a theoretical foundation of certain partial differential equations (PDEs) as scale-spaces, it is almost never taken into account that, in practice, images are sampled on a fixed pixel grid[1]. For nonlinear PDE-based filters, usually straightforward finite difference discretizations are applied in the hope that they reflect the nice properties of the continuous equations. Since scale-spaces cannot perform better than their numerical discretizations, however, it would be desirable to have a genuinely discrete nonlinear framework which reflects the discrete nature of digital images. In this paper we discuss a semidiscrete scale-space framework for nonlinear diffusion filtering. It keeps the scale-space idea of having a continuous time parameter, while taking into account the spatial discretization on a fixed pixel grid. It leads to nonlinear systems of coupled ordinary differential equations. Conditions are established under which one can prove existence of a stable unique solution which preserves the average grey level. An interpretation as a smoothing scale-space transformation is introduced which is based on an extremum principle and the existence of a large class of Lyapunov functionals comprising for instance p-norms, even central moments and the entropy. They guarantee that the process is not only simplifying and information-reducing, but also converges to a constant image as the scale parameter t tends to infinity.

This semidiscrete framework gives an answer to one of the central problems related to nonlinear diffusion scale spaces: the surprising practical success of the Perona–Malik (PM) filter in spite of its theoretical doubtfulness (*Perona–Malik paradox* [13]). Recently Kichenassamy [12, 13] has made significant contributions to the understanding of this phenomenon for the *continuous* PM equation. In our paper we contrast these results by applying our *(semi-)discrete* theory for explaining this effect. In particular, we shall see that the PM equation – whose continuous formulation is generally regarded to be ill-posed – leads to a well-posed semidiscrete scale-space. Within its stability range, an explicit (Euler forward) time discretization inherits these semidiscrete well-posedness and scale-space properties to the fully discrete setting. Moreover, we prove that its 1-D variant is monotonicity preserving. Thus, a sigmoid-like edge cannot develop oscillations, and the practically observed instabilities are restricted to staircasing effects.

The paper is organized as follows: Section 2 explains the continuous PM filter and presents an m-dimensional semidiscrete formulation. In Section 3 we discuss a

---

[1]One exception is Lindeberg's semidiscrete linear diffusion scale-space [14].

semidiscrete well-posedness and scale-space theory for nonlinear diffusion filters, which we apply in Section 4 for establishing well-posedness of the semidiscrete PM scale-space. Section 5 is devoted to fully discrete results, especially the proof of monotonicity preservation. The paper concludes with a summary in Section 6.

2   The Perona–Malik filter

2.1   Continuous formulation

We consider an m-dimensional rectangular image domain $\Omega = (0, a_1) \times \cdots \times (0, a_m)$ with boundary $\partial\Omega$, and a (grey-value) image which is given by a bounded mapping $f : \Omega \to \mathbb{R}$. In order to avoid the blurring and localization problems of linear diffusion filtering, Perona and Malik proposed a nonlinear diffusion method [16]. Their nonuniform process (which they name anisotropic[2]) reduces the diffusivity at those locations which have a larger likelihood to be edges, since they reveal larger gradients. Perona and Malik obtain a filtered image $u(x, t)$ as solution of a nonlinear diffusion equation with the original image as initial condition and reflecting boundary conditions (∂_n denotes the derivative normal to the image boundary $\partial\Omega$):

$$\partial_t u = \text{div}\left(g(|\nabla u|^2)\, \nabla u\right) \quad \text{on} \quad \Omega \times (0, \infty), \tag{1}$$

$$u(x, 0) = f(x) \quad \text{on} \quad \Omega, \tag{2}$$

$$\partial_n u = 0 \quad \text{on} \quad \partial\Omega \times (0, \infty). \tag{3}$$

Among the diffusivities they propose is[3]

$$g(|\nabla u|^2) = \frac{1}{1 + |\nabla u|^2/\lambda^2} \quad (\lambda > 0). \tag{4}$$

The experiments of Perona and Malik were visually impressive [16]: edges remained stable over a very long time. It was demonstrated that edge detection based on this process clearly outperforms the linear Canny edge detector.

However, the PM approach reveals some serious problems: It is not hard to see [16] that the PM equation is of forward parabolic type only for $|\nabla u| \leq \lambda$. Regions with $|\nabla u| > \lambda$ are identified as edges, where it may act like a backward diffusion equation across the edge. The forward–backward diffusion behaviour is explicitly intended in the PM method, since it gives the desirable result of blurring small fluctuations and sharpening edges.

On the other hand, backward diffusion is well-known to be an ill-posed process where the solution (if it exists) is highly sensitive even to the slightest perturbations of the initial data.

---

[2]In our terminology the PM filter is regarded as an isotropic model, since it uses a scalar-valued diffusivity and not a diffusion tensor. For models with a diffusion tensor, see e.g. [19, 20].

[3]For smoothness reasons we write $g(|\nabla u|^2)$ instead of $g(|\nabla u|)$.

The current understanding of the PM process is not complete, but there is very much theoretical and practical evidence that such forward–backward processes are ill-posed as well [18, 6, 10, 15, 4, 2, 7, 3, 17]. As one possibility to understand the behaviour of this process it has been suggested to study regularizing approximations where the regularization parameter tends to zero [17, 8, 9]. In this field, however, conjectures are still dominating over established convergence results.

Recently Kichenassamy [12, 13] proved that the PM filter does not even have weak solutions. He introduced a notion of generalized solutions to the PM process, which are piecewise linear and contain jumps, and he analyzed their moving and merging. The current opinion is that, for these solutions, one should neither expect uniqueness nor stability with respect to the initial image [4, 17, 13].

Interestingly, all practically observed instabilities are less severe than one would expect from theory: The main observed instability in simple implementations is the so-called *staircasing effect*, where a smoothed step edge evolves into piecewise linear segments which are separated by jumps. Contributions to the explanation and avoidance of staircasing can be found in [23, 3, 1, 5, 12, 13]. In particular, it should be noted that Kichenassamy's generalized solutions are in accordance with these numerical results.

The staircasing effect, however, is mainly visible for fine spatial discretizations and for slowly varying ramp-like edges. Under practical situations, this is hardly observed, and it is an experimental fact that discretizations of the PM are not very unstable. To find an explanation for this phenomenon, let us now investigate a spatially discretized version of this process.

2.2 Semidiscrete formulation

A discrete m-dimensional image can be regarded as a vector $f \in \mathbb{R}^N$, whose components f_i, $i \in J := \{1, ..., N\}$ display the grey values at the N pixels. Pixel i represents the location x_i. Let h_l denote the grid size in l direction. By u_i and g_i we denote approximations to $u(x_i, t)$ and $g(|\nabla u(x_i, t)|^2)$, respectively. Then, a consistent[4] spatial discretization of the PM equation with reflecting boundary conditions can be written as

$$\frac{du_i}{dt} = \sum_{l=1}^{m} \sum_{j \in \mathcal{N}_l(i)} \frac{g_j + g_i}{2h_l^2} (u_j - u_i),$$ (5)

where $\mathcal{N}_l(i)$ consist of the two neighbours of pixel i along the direction l (boundary pixels may have only one neighbour) and

$$g_i := g \left(\frac{1}{2} \sum_{l=1}^{m} \sum_{p,q \in \mathcal{N}_l(i)} \left(\frac{u_p - u_q}{2h_l} \right)^2 \right)$$ (6)

---

[4]The originally in [16] proposed scheme is not consistent, which may cause severe deviations from rotational invariance, as can be seen in [15].

uses a gradient approximation by central differences. In vector–matrix notation (5) becomes

$$\frac{du}{dt} = \sum_{l=1}^{m} A_l(u)\, u \tag{7}$$

where the matrix $A_l(u) = a_{ijl}(u)$ is given by

$$a_{ijl} := \begin{cases} \frac{g_i+g_j}{2h_l^2} & (j \in \mathcal{N}_l(i)), \\ -\sum_{l=1}^{m} \sum_{k \in \mathcal{N}_l(i)} \frac{g_i+g_k}{2h_l^2} & (j = i), \\ 0 & (\text{else}). \end{cases} \tag{8}$$

We observe that a semidiscrete PM process creates a nonlinear system of ordinary differential equations. Let us now study a general well-posedness and scale-space framework for problems of this type.

3   A semidiscrete scale-space theory

Recently a continuous scale-space interpretation has been established for regularized variants of the continuous PM process [4, 19, 20]. In addition to invariances such as the preservation of the average grey value, it has been shown that – in spite of its contrast-enhancing potential – these equations create smoothing scale-spaces: the obey a maximum–minimum principle, have a large class of smoothing Lyapunov functionals, and converge to a constant steady state [19].
Of course, it is desirable to find discrete approximations which also reveal these qualities *exactly*. To this end, criteria have been identified under which one can guarantee that a semidiscrete scheme of type

$$\frac{du}{dt} = A(u)\, u, \tag{9}$$
$$u(0) = f, \tag{10}$$

possesses such properties [20, 21]. All one has to check are the following criteria for $A(u) = (a_{ij}(u))$:

(S1) Smoothness: $\qquad\qquad\qquad\qquad\qquad\qquad\qquad\qquad A \in C^1(\mathbb{R}^N, \mathbb{R}^{N \times N})$.

(S2) Symmetry: $\qquad\qquad\qquad\qquad\qquad\qquad\qquad a_{ij} = a_{ji} \quad \forall i, j \in J$.

(S3) Vanishing row sums: $\qquad\qquad\qquad\qquad\qquad \sum_{j \in J} a_{ij} = 0 \quad \forall i \in J$.

(S4) Nonnegative off-diagonals: $\qquad\qquad\qquad\qquad a_{ij} \geq 0 \quad \forall i \neq j$.

(S5) Irreducibility:
We can connect any two pixels by a path with nonvanishing diffusivities. Formally: For any $i, j \in J$ there exist $k_0, ..., k_r \in J$ with $k_0 = i$ and $k_r = j$ such that $a_{k_p k_{p+1}} \neq 0$ for $p = 0, ..., r-1$.

Under these prerequisites the filtering process satisfies the following properties [20, 21]:

(a) *Well-posedness:*
The considered problem has a unique solution for all $t > 0$, which depends continuously on the initial value and the right-hand side of the ODE system.
This is of significant practical importance, since it guarantees stability under parameter variations and under perturbations of the original image. Such a property is desirable when considering stereo images, image sequences or slices from medical CT or MR sequences, since we know that similar images remain similar after filtering. It is remarkable that a process which may be edge-enhancing reveals such well-posedness properties.

(b) *Average grey level invariance:*
The average grey level $\mu := \frac{1}{N}\sum_{j\in J} f_j$ is not affected by the semidiscrete diffusion filter: $\frac{1}{N}\sum_{j\in J} u_j(t) = \mu$ for all $t > 0$.
This invariance is useful for scale-space based segmentation algorithms and for all applications where grey values are related to physical qualities, for instance in medical imaging.

(c) *Extremum principle:*

$$\min_{j\in J} f_j \leq u_i(t) \leq \max_{j\in J} f_j \qquad \forall i \in J, \quad \forall t \in [0, \infty).$$

This property is much more than a stability result which forbids under- and overshoots. Since it also ensures that iso-intensity linking towards the original image is possible, it states an important causality property, cf. [11].

(d) *Smoothing Lyapunov functionals:*
In spite of some possible edge enhancement, the considered processes are simplifying, information-reducing transformations with respect to many aspects: The p-norms $\|u(t)\|_p := (\sum_j |u_j(t)|^p)^{1/p}$ are decreasing in t for all $p \geq 2$, all even central moments $M_{2n}[u(t)] := \frac{1}{N}\sum_j (u_j(t) - \mu)^{2n}$ are decreasing in t, and the entropy $S[u(t)] := -\sum_j u_j(t) \ln u_j(t)$, a measure of uncertainty and missing information, is increasing in t (if f_j is positive for all j).

(e) *Convergence to a constant steady state:*
The scale-space evolution tends to the most global image representation that is possible: a constant image with the same average grey level as f:

$$\lim_{t\to\infty} u_i(t) = \mu \quad \forall i \in J.$$

These semidiscrete results are part of a more general framework which includes also a continuous and fully discrete theory [21]. Full details with proofs can be found in [20], where it is also shown that it is possible to derive semidiscrete

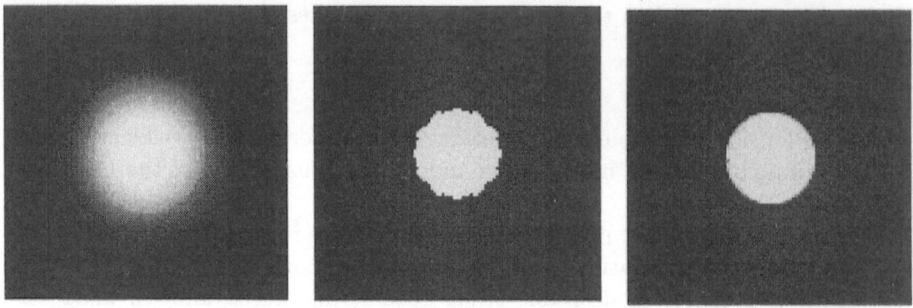

Figure 1: Nonlinear diffusion of a Gaussian-like image. (a) LEFT: Original image, $\Omega = (0, 101)^2$. (b) MIDDLE: Processed with the PM filter, $\lambda = 9$, $t = 250$. (c) RIGHT: Regularized PM filter [4], $\lambda = 9$, $\sigma = 0.7$, $t = 250$.

scale-spaces from spatial discretizations of continuous scale-spaces. Due to its ill-posedness, however, the continuous PM equation cannot be treated within this continuous scale-space framework.

4 Application to the semidiscrete Perona-Malik process

Interestingly, it is not hard to verify that the semidiscrete PM process satisfies the well-posedness and scale-space requirements (S1)–(S5).

(S1) Since $g \in C^\infty(\mathbb{R})$, it follows from (8) that $A := \sum_l A_l \in C^\infty(\mathbb{R}^N, \mathbb{R}^{N \times N})$.

(S2) The symmetry of A follows directly from (8) and the symmetry of the neighbourhood relation $(i \in \mathcal{N}_l(j) \iff j \in \mathcal{N}_l(i))$.

(S3) By the construction of A it is also evident that all row sums vanish.

(S4) Since g is positive, it follows that $a_{ij} \geq 0$ for all $i \neq j$.

(S5) In order to show that A is irreducible, let us consider two arbitrary pixels i and j. Then we have to find $k_0,...,k_r \in J$ with $k_0 = s_1$ and $k_r = s_2$ such that $a_{k_q k_{q+1}} \neq 0$ for $q = 0,...,r-1$. If $i = j$, we know already from (8) that $a_{ii} < 0$. In this case we have the simple path $i = k_0 = k_r = j$. For $i \neq j$, we may choose any arbitrary path $k_0,...,k_r$, such that k_q and k_{q+1} are neighbours for $q = 0,...,r-1$. Then,

$$a_{k_q k_{q+1}} = \frac{g_{k_q} + g_{k_{q+1}}}{2h_l^2} > 0$$

for some $l \in \{1,...,m\}$. This completes the proof of (S5).

We observe that – despite the fact that the PM filter is regarded to be ill-posed in the continuous setting, its semidiscrete approximation on a fixed grid satisfies

(S1)–(S5) and, thus, reveals all the beforementioned well-posedness and scale-space properties. Hence, the spatial discretization causes an implicit regularization[5]. It is caused by the fact that the extremum principle limits the modulus of discrete gradient approximations.

The grid regularization, however, is certainly not the best regularization strategy. Experiments show that grid refinement leads to more staircasing [15, 7, 3]. Moreover, grid regularization may cause artefacts which reflect the grid structure (Fig 1(b)). One can avoid these problems by introducing the regularization explicitly in the continuous PM model, for instance by a Gaussian smoothing of ∇u within the diffusivity [18, 4, 15, 23, 19, 20]. Figure 1(c) illustrates that – as soon as the standard deviation σ of the Gaussian reaches the pixel size – this regularization dominates over the pixel regularization and avoids their artefacts. Moreover, since it bounds the gradient already in the continuous formulation, it leads to continuous models which satisfy similar well-posedness and scale-space properties as in the semidiscrete case [19, 20]. Last but not least, it makes the filter more robust against noise [4] and reduces staircasing [15, 7, 3]. Thus, such regularizations are generally recommendable.

5 Fully discrete results

We have seen that a spatial discretization is sufficient to make the PM filter well-posed. Of course, in practice, one has to apply a temporal discretization as well. If we consider a time step size $\tau > 0$ and denote by u_i^k an approximation of $u(x_i, k\tau)$, then the simplest fully discrete PM equation is given by the explicit scheme

$$\frac{u_i^{k+1} - u_i^k}{\tau} = \sum_{l=1}^{m} \sum_{j \in \mathcal{N}_l(i)} \frac{g_j^k + g_i^k}{2h_l^2} (u_j^k - u_i^k). \tag{11}$$

In [20] it is shown that such a scheme inherits its well-posedness and scale-space properties from the semidiscrete one if the time step size satisfies the stability restriction[6] $\tau < 1/\sum_{l=1}^{m} \frac{2}{h_l^2}$. So we do not have to worry that we loose the nice semidiscrete results by the temporal discretization.

Finally, we prove an important property which is responsible for the fact that – apart from the grid artefacts depicted in Fig. 1 – staircasing is essentially the only practical instability that is observed when implementing the PM equation: the one-dimensional discrete PM process is *monotonicity preserving* [3]: if the grey values are increasing (decreasing) from left to right, then they remain increasing (decreasing) after filtering. Together with the extremum principle, this property explains why over- and undershoots and the creation of other oscillations are not possible.

---

[5]Such a regularizing effect has already been conjectured in [4].
[6]Much more efficient absolutely stable schemes are proposed in [22].

Proposition 1 *For $\tau < \frac{h_1^2}{2}$, the 1-D explicit PM scheme is strictly monotonicity preserving. For a consecutive pixel numbering this means that*

$$u_i^k < u_{i+1}^k \quad \forall i \quad \implies \quad u_i^{k+1} < u_{i+1}^{k+1} \quad \forall i.$$

Proof: Consider some arbitrary inner pixel $i \in \{2, ..., N-2\}$. From

$$u_i^{k+1} = \tau\, a_{i,i+1}\, u_{i+1}^k + (1 - \tau\, a_{i,i+1} - \tau\, a_{i,i-1})\, u_i^k + \tau\, a_{i,i-1}\, u_{i-1}^k$$

$$u_{i+1}^{k+1} = \tau\, a_{i+1,i+2}\, u_{i+2}^k + (1 - \tau\, a_{i+1,i+2} - \tau\, a_{i+1,i})\, u_{i+1}^k + \tau\, a_{i+1,i}\, u_i^k$$

and the symmetry of A we obtain

$$u_{i+1}^{k+1} - u_i^{k+1} = \tau\, a_{i+1,i+2}\, (u_{i+2}^k - u_{i+1}^k) + (1 - 2\tau a_{i,i+1})\, (u_{i+1}^k - u_i^k) + \tau\, a_{i-1,i}\, (u_i^k - u_{i-1}^k).$$

Let $\tau < \frac{h_1^2}{2}$ and $u_j^k < u_{j+1}^k$ for all j. Since $0 < a_{j,j+1} \leq 1/h_1^2$ for all j, we know that all summands of the RHS are positive. Thus, it follows that $u_i^{k+1} < u_{i+1}^{k+1}$ for $i \in \{2, ..., N-2\}$. It is easy to see that the same reasoning is applicable to the modified equations arising at the boundaries when $i = 1$ or $N-1$.   q.e.d.

6   Conclusions

In this paper we have discussed a genuinely semidiscrete nonlinear theory for nonlinear diffusion scale-spaces. As one example for the importance of such a theory we have applied it in order to explain the well-posedness of the semidiscrete Perona–Malik scale-space. These results also carry over to the fully discrete setting, where a monotonicity preserving property has been proved. They explain that observed instabilities of PM discretizations are restricted to staircasing effects and grid artefacts affecting the rotational invariance. These effects may be tamed by introducing a grid independent spatial regularizations already in the continuous equation [18, 4, 15, 20].

Acknowledgments

This work has been funded by *Stiftung Innovation des Landes Rheinland–Pfalz, Deutscher Akademischer Austauschdienst*, and the *Real World Computing Partnership*. The paper was written while J.W. was with the Image Sciences Institute of Utrecht University.

References

[1] Acton, S.T.: Edge enhancement of infrared imagery by way of the anisotropic diffusion pyramid. Proc. IEEE Int. Conf. Image Processing (ICIP–96, Lausanne, Sept. 16–19, 1996), Vol. 1, 865–868 (1996).

[2] Barenblatt, G.I., Bertsch, M., Dal Passo, R, Ughi, R.: A degenerate pseu-doparabolic regularization of a nonlinear forward–backward heat equation arising in the theory of heat and mass exchange in stably stratified turbulent shear flow. SIAM J. Math. Anal. 24, 1414–1439 (1993).

[3] Benhamouda, B.: Parameter adaptation for nonlinear diffusion in image processing. M.Sc. thesis, Dept. of Mathematics, University of Kaiserslautern, P.O. Box 3049, 67653 Kaiserslautern, Germany (1994).

[4] Catté, F., Lions, P.-L., Morel, J.-M., Coll, T.: Image selective smoothing and edge detection by nonlinear diffusion. SIAM J. Numer. Anal. 29, 182–193 (1992).

[5] Cong, G., Ma, S.D.: Nonlinear diffusion for early vision. Proc. 13th Int. Conf. Pattern Recognition (ICPR 13, Vienna, Aug. 25–30, 1996), Vol. A, 403–406 (1996).

[6] Dzhu Magazieva, S.K.: Numerical study of a partial differential equation. U.S.S.R. Comput. Maths. Math. Phys. 23, No. 4, 45–49 (1983).

[7] Fröhlich, J., Weickert, J.: Image processing using a wavelet algorithm for nonlinear diffusion. Report No. 104, Laboratory of Technomathematics, University of Kaiserslautern, P.O. Box 3049, 67653 Kaiserslautern, Germany (1994).

[8] De Giorgi, E.: Congetture riguardanti alcuni problemi di evoluzione – a paper in honor of John Nash. Preprint CV-GMT-96040102, Math. Dept., Scuola Normale Superiore, Piazza dei Cavalieri, 56126 Pisa, Italy, 1995 (in English).

[9] De Giorgi, E.: Su alcuni problemi instabili legati alla teoria della visione. Paper in honour of C. Ciliberto, Math. Dept., Scuola Normale Superiore, Piazza dei Cavalieri, 56126 Pisa, Italy (in Italian).

[10] Höllig, K.: Existence of infinitely many solutions for a forward–backward heat equation. Trans. Amer. Math. Soc. 278, 299–316 (1983).

[11] Hummel, R.A.: Representations based on zero-crossings in scale space. Proc. IEEE Comp. Soc. Conf. Computer Vision and Pattern Recognition (CVPR '86, Miami Beach, June 22–26, 1986), IEEE Computer Society Press, Washington, 204–209 (1986).

[12] Kichenassamy, S.: Nonlinear diffusions and hyperbolic smoothing for edge enhancement. In Berger, M.-O., Deriche, R., Herlin, I, Jaffré, J., Morel, J.-M. (eds.): ICAOS '96: Images, wavelets and PDEs. London: Springer 1996 (Lecture Notes in Control and Information Sciences, vol. 219, pp. 119–124).

[13] Kichenassamy, S.: The Perona–Malik paradox. SIAM J. Appl. Math., to appear.

[14] Lindeberg, T.: Scale-space theory in computer vision. Boston: Kluwer 1994.

[15] Nitzberg, M., Shiota, T.: Nonlinear image filtering with edge and corner enhancement. IEEE Trans. Pattern Anal. Mach. Intell. 14, 826–833 (1992).

[16] Perona, P., Malik, J.: Scale space and edge detection using anisotropic diffusion. IEEE Trans. Pattern Anal. Mach. Intell. 12, 629–639 (1990).

[17] Perona, P., Shiota, T., Malik, J.: Anisotropic diffusion. In ter Haar Romeny, B.M. (ed.): Geometry-driven diffusion in computer vision. Dordrecht: Kluwer 1994 (pp. 72–92).

[18] Posmentier, E.S.: The generation of salinity finestructure by vertical diffusion. J. Phys. Oceanogr. 7, 298–300 (1977).

[19] Weickert, J.: Theoretical foundations of anisotropic diffusion in image processing. Computing, Suppl. 11, 221–236 (1996).

[20] Weickert, J.: Anisotropic diffusion in image processing. Ph.D. thesis, Dept. of Mathematics, University of Kaiserslautern, Germany, 1996. Revised version to be published by Teubner Verlag, Stuttgart.

[21] Weickert, J.: Nonlinear diffusion scale-spaces: From the continuous to the discrete setting. In Berger, M.-O., Deriche, R., Herlin, I, Jaffré, J., Morel, J.-M. (eds.): ICAOS '96: Images, wavelets and PDEs. London: Springer 1996 (Lecture Notes in Control and Information Sciences, vol. 219, pp. 111–118).

[22] Weickert, J.: Recursive separable schemes for nonlinear diffusion filters. In ter Haar Romeny, B., Florack, L., Koenderink, J., Viergever, M. (eds.): Scale-space theory in computer vision. Berlin: Springer 1997 (Lecture Notes in Computer Science, vol. 1252, pp. 260–271).

[23] Whitaker, R.T., Pizer, S.M.: A multi-scale approach to nonuniform diffusion. CVGIP: Image Understanding 57, 99–110 (1993).

Topological approach

to mathematical morphology

Ulrich Eckhardt and Eckart Hundt

1 Introduction

For low–bit–rate coding of video sequences, specifically in the context of the MPEG–4 proposal, morphological approaches proved to be highly attractive (see e.g. [16]). During a series of coding experiments performed at Siemens Research Laboratory in München [9] the authors felt that there are some deficiencies of theory which need investigation. The aim of this paper is to sketch a theory which allows to understand the relationships between three classes of discrete concepts, namely discrete topology, discrete morphology and discrete metrics.

Mathematical morphology is based on topologies for systems of subsets of a set [13]. The topology of the underlying set enters only indirectly. Therefore such concepts as connectedness of sets can cause difficulties if treated purely morphologically. These conceptual difficulties became especially apparent, when structures and algorithms were used practically which simultaneously involve both subset topologies and connectedness of subsets as is the case e.g. in watershed segmentation [16].

The picture is completely different in the discrete formulation. Mathematical morphology depends on "structuring elements" of fixed size and so only details of a certain minimal size can be treated. This means that morphology is in its essence discrete. On the other hand topology, being basically a continuous (i.e. nondiscrete) concept, cannot be canonically translated into a discrete setting. There are numerous approaches to discrete topology, specifically for the discrete plane $\mathbb{Z}^2$ consisting of the set of all points in the plane having integer coordinates (4–, 6–, 8–, 4/8–topology [15], Alexandroff–Hopf–topology [1, Erster Teil, erstes Kapitel, §1.1, Beispiel 4°], Khalimsky–topology [7], Kovalevsky–topology [8], Marcus–Wyse–topology [12]) Most of these approaches are not topologies for the digital plane in the strict sense, the axioms of topology have to be weakened in a specific way. There exist in the literature many proposals for topological structures ("discrete topologies") based on reduced topological axiom systems (see for example [14]). It is investigated here what connections exist between some of them and how they relate to mathematical morphology.

A fundamental computational tool are discrete metrics. These arise in all applications where relations between different objects are found by means of sequential propagation processes. One example are watershed algorithms which are based on geodetic distances. Morphological operators and also topological concepts can sometimes be based in a quite natural way on certain metric concepts which depend on the notion of "path–connectedness". One of the main results of this paper is that for so–called symmetric semi–topological spaces of character 1 these concepts coincide.

As a result of our investigation we can state that discrete topology and discrete morphology present two different aspects of digital sets. Topological operators (closure and kernel) lead to concepts such as connectedness or continuity but they do not have nontrivial "root images" which are sets having "nice" properties. On the other hand, it is fundamentally not possible to formulate such concepts as connectedness of a set in the morphological context, however, morphological operators (opening, closing) have a large set of root images.

There remain many open questions, for example concerning the relations between discrete and continuous concepts. Some fundamental results concerning this subject can be found in the forthcoming book of Latecki [11].

The results of this paper are given without proofs. Most of the proofs, however, are rather straightforward. Some of them are included in [4]. Computational results of our experiments were published elsewhere [9].

2 Generalized Topological Spaces

There exist numerous generalizations of topological structures. In recent years there was a growing interest in such "discrete" topologies which was mainly caused by applications in information processing. Nevertheless, this subject was treated since the begin of the century by many authors (see [14] for a bibliography). Our main topic here are pre–topological spaces as introduced by Brissaud [2] for modelling sitations in economics and semi–topological spaces which were used by Latecki [10] for modelling spatial relations in artificial intelligence.

2.1 Pre–Topological Spaces

A *pre–topological space* (X, a) consists of a nonempty set X and a *closure operator* a which associates to each subset $S \subseteq X$ its *closure* $a(S) \subseteq X$ such that the following axioms are fulfilled

PT1 $S \subseteq a(S)$ for all $S \subseteq X$,

PT2 $a(\emptyset) = \emptyset$,

PT3 $a(S_1) \subseteq a(S_2)$ for all subsets S_1 and S_2 in X with $S_1 \subseteq S_2$.

The *kernel operator* i is the dual operator to a: $i(S) = (a(S^c))^c$. Here S^c denotes the set–theoretic complement of the set S.

A pre–topological space fulfilling the stronger third axiom (the so–called *finite Čech property*)

PT3′ $a(S_1 \cup S_2) = a(S_1) \cup a(S_2)$ for all subsets S_1, S_2 of X

is termed a *closure space* [3, Chapter 14] or *nearness space* (see [14, 6]. A pre–topological space is said to have the *infinite Čech property* if

PT3″ $a\left(\bigcup_\alpha S_\alpha\right) = \bigcup_\alpha a(S_\alpha)$ for each system of subsets $\{S_\alpha\}$.

2.2 Semi–Topological Spaces

A *semi–topological space* $(X, \mathcal{B})$ consists of a nonempty set X and a system $\mathcal{B}$ of subsets of X such that for each point $x \in X$ there is a system $\mathcal{B}(x)$ of sets with $x \in B$ for all $B \in \mathcal{B}(x)$ [10]. $\mathcal{B}(x)$ is termed the *system of point bases* of the point x. All members of $\mathcal{B}$ are considered to be *open sets*. Moreover, open sets are constructed by the following two axioms:

ST1 X and $\emptyset$ are open sets,

ST2 Any union of open sets is always an open set.

The members of $\mathcal{B}(x)$ are termed *neighborhoods* of x.
Given a nonempty set X and a closure operator a which defines a pre–topology on X. Let further a semi–topology be given on X by a system of point bases $\mathcal{B}$. a and $\mathcal{B}$ are termed *compatible* if

Com1 For each $x \in X$ and each $B \in \mathcal{B}(x)$ is $x \in i(B)$,

Com2 For each subset $S \subseteq X$ and each $x \in i(S)$ there is a $B \in \mathcal{B}(x)$ such that $B \subseteq S$.

Further we define

$$i_{\mathcal{B}}(S) = \{x \in X \mid B \subseteq S \text{ for a } B \in \mathcal{B}(x)\},$$

or equivalently

$$a_{\mathcal{B}}(S) = \{x \in X \mid B \cap S \neq \emptyset \text{ for all } B \in \mathcal{B}(x)\}.$$

Similarly,

$$\mathcal{B}_a(x) = \{B \subseteq X \mid x \in i(B)\}.$$

The system $\mathcal{B}_a$ is sometimes termed a *pre–filter* belonging to (X, a) (see [2]). The following Theorem states that semi–topological spaces and pre–topological spaces are equivalent in a certain sense.

Theorem 1 *Let X be a nonempty set which is equipped with a pre–topology a and a semi–topology $\mathcal{B}$ such that a and $\mathcal{B}$ are compatible.*
1. $a_{\mathcal{B}}$ and $\mathcal{B}$ are compatible.
*2. If a fulfills (**Com1**), then $a(S) \subseteq a_{\mathcal{B}}(S)$ for all $S \in X$. This means that $a_{\mathcal{B}}$ is the coarsest pre–topology on X having property (**Com1**).*
3. $\mathcal{B}_a$ and a are compatible.
4. $a_{\mathcal{B}_a} = a$.
5. Given two semi–topologies $\mathcal{B}_1$ and $\mathcal{B}_2$, both compatible to a. Then for each $B_1 \in \mathcal{B}_1(x)$ there exists a $B_2 \in \mathcal{B}_2(x)$ such that $B_2 \subseteq B_1$.
6. $B \in \mathcal{B}(x) \implies B \in \mathcal{B}_a(x)$.

The semi–topological space $(X, \mathcal{B})$ is *(locally) stable with respect to finite inter-sections* or simply *(locally) f–i–stable*, if for each point $x \in X$ and for any finite number of sets $B_1, B_2, \cdots B_n$ such that $B_i \in \mathcal{B}(x)$ for all $i = 1, 2, \cdots, n$ there exists a set $B \in \mathcal{B}(x)$ such that

$$B \subseteq \bigcap_{i=1}^{n} B_i.$$

Theorem 2 *Given a nonempty set X which is equipped with a pre–topology a and a semi–topology $\mathcal{B}$ such that a and $\mathcal{B}$ are compatible.*
(X, a) has the finite Čech property $\iff$ $(X, \mathcal{B})$ is f–i–stable.

2.3 Spaces of Character 1

Following Engelking [5, Chapter 1.1], we define the *character $\chi(x)$* of a point x in a semi–topological space $(X, \mathcal{B})$ as the cardinality of $\mathcal{B}(x)$.
The character of space X is

$$\chi(X) = \sup_{x \in X} \chi(x).$$

A semi–topological space $(X, \mathcal{B})$ is termed a space of *character 1* if $\chi(X) = 1$.

Theorem 3 *1. A pre–topological space (X, a) which is compatible to a semi–topological space $(X, \mathcal{B})$ of character 1 has the infinite Čech property.*
2. If (X, a) has the infinite Čech property then there exists a semi–topological space $(X, \mathcal{B})$ of character 1 which is compatible with a.

Corollary 1 *Given two semi–topological spaces $(X, \mathcal{B})$ and $(X, \mathcal{B}_0)$, both compatible to (X, a). Let furthermore be $(X, \mathcal{B}_0)$ be of character 1.*
Then $(X, \mathcal{B})$ is ∞–i–stable in the following sense: For each $x \in X$ and for any system $\{B_\alpha\}$ with $B_\alpha \in \mathcal{B}(x)$ there exists a set $B \in \mathcal{B}(x)$ such that

$$B \subseteq \bigcap_{\alpha} B_\alpha.$$

In Table 1 the hierarchy of topologies is given indicating the mutual relations between pre–topological and semi–topological concepts and presenting structures of growing richness.

3 Connectedness

3.1 B–, $\mathcal{T}_s$– and L–Connectedness

According to Brissaud [2] we define connectedness in a pre–topological space as follows:
A subset S of a pre–topological space (X, a) is *not connected in the sense of Brissaud)* if there exist two subsets F and G in X having the properties

Table 1: Hierarchy of topologies. In the left column the pre–topological concepts are given, the right column contains their semi–topological equivalents. The structures at the bottom of the table are richer than those at the top.

Pre–Topological Space (Brissaud 1975) (X, a) $a(\emptyset) = \emptyset, \qquad a(X) = X$ $S \subseteq a(S)$ for all $S \subseteq X$	
Inclusion Property $S_1 \subseteq S_2 \Longrightarrow a(S_1) \subseteq a(S_2)$ $\Longleftrightarrow$	**Semi–Topological Space** (Latecki 1992) $(X, \mathcal{B})$ Open Sets: $\emptyset$, X, $\forall x \in X \; \exists \, B(x) \neq \emptyset :$ $B \in \mathcal{B}(x) \Longrightarrow x \in B$ and B open, Unions of open sets are open.
Finite Čech Property (Čech 1966) $\Longleftrightarrow$ $a(S_1) \cup a(S_2) = a(S_1 \cup S_2)$	**Finite Local Intersection Property** $\forall x \in X \; \forall B_1, B_2 \in \mathcal{B}(x)$ $\exists \, B \in \mathcal{B}(x) : B \subseteq B_1 \cap B_2$
Infinite Čech Property $\bigcup_{\alpha} a(S_\alpha) = a\left(\bigcup_{\alpha} S_\alpha\right)$ $\Longleftrightarrow$	**Infinite Local Intersection Property** $\forall x \in X \; \forall B_\alpha \in \mathcal{B}(x)$ $\exists \, B \in \mathcal{B}(x) : B \subseteq \bigcap_{\alpha} B_\alpha$ $\Longleftrightarrow$ X has **Character 1**: $\forall x \in X \; : \; |\mathcal{B}(x)| = 1$

$$F = \bigcup_{j=1}^{m} F_j, \quad G = \bigcup_{j=1}^{n} G_j,$$

$$S \subseteq F \cup G,$$

$$S \cap \bigcup_{j=1}^{m} a(F_j) \neq \emptyset, \quad S \cap \bigcup_{j=1}^{n} a(G_j) \neq \emptyset,$$

$$S \cap \bigcup_{j=1}^{m} a(F_j) \cap \bigcup_{j=1}^{n} a(G_j) = \emptyset,$$

Latecki [10] defines connectedness in semi–topological spaces in a somewhat different way which can be interpreted as Brissaud's definition with $m = n = 1$. In the language of semi–topological spaces, Latecki's definition amounts to:
A subset S of a semi–topological space $(X, \mathcal{B})$ is *not connected in the sense of Latecki)* if there exist two subsets F and G in X having the properties

$$S \cap F = S \cap i(F) \text{ and } S \cap G = S \cap i(G),$$

$$S \subseteq F \cup G,$$

$$S \cap F \neq \emptyset \text{ and } S \cap G \neq \emptyset.$$

A subset of a pre– or semi–topological space which is connected in the sense of Brissaud's definition will be termed *B–connected* and it will be termed *L–connected* if it is connected by Latecki's definition.
We introduce a third connectedness definition. For this reason we equip a semi–topological space with a topology:
Let $(X, \mathcal{B})$ be a semi–topological space. The *topology of strictly open sets* $\mathcal{T}_s$ is the topology generated by all sets S having the property $x \in S \implies B \subseteq S$ für some $B \in \mathcal{B}(x)$. Such sets are termed *strictly open sets*. For f–i–stable semi–topological spaces the system $\mathcal{T}_s$ of strictly open sets is a topology.
A subset S of a (f–i–stable) semi–topological space $(X, \mathcal{B})$ is *strictly connected* or $\mathcal{T}_s$–*connected* if it is connected in the topology $\mathcal{T}_s$.
From the definitions it follows immediately that any B–connected set is $\mathcal{T}_s$–connected and any $\mathcal{T}_s$–connected set is L–connected.

Theorem 4 *Let $(X, \mathcal{B})$ be an f–i–stable semi–topological space and $S \subseteq X$. Then B–connectedness coincides with $\mathcal{T}$– and L–connectedness.*

3.2   Path– and Arc–Connectedness

A *path* in a semi–topological space $(X, \mathcal{B})$ is a finite set $\{x_0, x_1, \cdots, x_n\}$ such that for each $j = 0, 1, \cdots, n-1$ there is a neighborhood $B \in \mathcal{B}(x_j)$ such that $x_{j+1} \in B$ or there is a neigborhood $B \in \mathcal{B}(x_{j+1})$ such that $x_j \in B$.
A subset S of a semi–topological space $(X, \mathcal{B})$ is *path–connected* if there exists for any two points x and y in S a path $\{x_0, x_1, \cdots, x_n\}$ which is completely contained in S such that $x_0 = x$ and $x_n = y$.

Lemma 1 *Every L–connected set is path–connected.*

3.3 Spaces of Character 1

Semi–topological spaces of character 1 have a remarkable property:

Theorem 5 *Given a semi–topological space* $(X, \mathcal{B})$ *of character 1.*
Let $\{S_\sigma\}$ *be a system of strictly open sets. Then* $\bigcap S_\sigma$ *is also strictly open.*

The assertion of the Theorem means that in a semi–topological space of character 1 the strictly open sets induce a topology having the *Alexandroff–property* that all intersections of (strictly) open sets are (strictly) open.
Semi–topological spaces of character 1 have the following important property:

Theorem 6 *In semi–topological spaces of character* 1 *L–connectedness coincides with path–connectedness.*

3.4 Symmetry and Arc–Connectedness

A semi–topological space $(X, \mathcal{B})$ is termed *symmetric* if for each $x \in X$, for each neighborhood $B_x \in \mathcal{B}(x)$ and for each $y \in B_x$ there exist a $B_y \in \mathcal{B}(y)$, such that $x \in B_y$.

Theorem 7 *A symmetric semi–topological space* $(X, \mathcal{B})$ *of character 1 is not L–connected if and only if it contains a nonempty strict subset which is strictly open.*

Let $\mathbb{Z}$ be the set of all integers, equipped with the *standard semi–topology* given by the neighborhood system

$$O(n) = \{n - 1, n, n + 1\}, \qquad \text{for all } n \in \mathbb{Z}.$$

For given $x, y \in \mathbb{Z}$ the set $[x, y] := \{z \in \mathbb{Z} \mid x \leq z \leq y\}$ with the relative topology induced by the standard semi–topology of $\mathbb{Z}$ is termed an *interval*.
A subset Y of a semi–topological space $(X, \mathcal{B})$ is termed an *arc* if Y is homeomorphic to an interval.
A semi–topological space $(X, \mathcal{B})$ is *arc–connected* if for any two points x and y in X there exists an arc in X containing x and y.
Given a symmetric semi–topological space $(X, \mathcal{B})$ of character 1.
A subset $W := \{x_0, x_1, \cdots, x_n\}$ in X is an arc if and only if it is a simple path (i.e. $x_i \in B$ for a neighborhood $B \in \mathcal{B}(x_j)$ for $x_i, x_j \in W$, $i \neq j$ implies $i = j + 1$ or $i = j - 1$).
We can state the following Theorem:

Theorem 8 *In a symmetric semi–topological space of character 1 the concepts of B–, $\mathcal{T}_a$–, L–, path– and arc–connectedness coincide.*

4 Morphological Spaces

4.1 Introduction

The concept of *mathematical morphology* is due to Matheron [13] and was propagated by Serra [17, 18].

Given a pre–topological space (X, a). Then the closure operator a and its dual interior operator i have the following properties:

Theorem 9 *Given a pre–topological space* (X, a). *Then*
1. $a(S_1) \cup a(S_2) = a(S_1 \cup S_2)$ *for all* $S_1, S_2 \subseteq X$ $\iff$ $i(S_1) \cap i(S_2) = i(S_1 \cap S_2)$ *for all* $S_1, S_2 \subseteq X$
2. Let $S \subseteq X$, $x \in a(S) \setminus S$. *Then* $i(\{x\}) = \emptyset$.
3. $x \in S - i(S) \iff x \in a(S^c) \setminus S^c \iff x \in a(S^c) \cap S \implies i(\{x\}) = \emptyset$.

4.2 Morphological Operators

The *closing* of a set $S \subseteq X$ is defined by $c(S) = i(a(S))$ and the *opening* by $o(S) = a(i(S))$.

The following assertions hold:

Theorem 10 *1.* $o(S) = (c(S^c))^c$. *This means that the two operators* o *and* c *are dual to each other.*
2. $S \subseteq c(S)$ *for all* $S \subseteq X$ $\iff$ $o(S) \subseteq S$ *for all* $S \subseteq X$.
3. $S_1 \subseteq S_2 \implies i(S_1) \subseteq i(S_2)$. *This means that the operators* a *and* i *are growing or isotone. The same holds for the operators* c *and* o.
4. The opening operator o *is* anti–extensive *(i.e.* $o(S) \subseteq S$ *for all* $S \subseteq X$*) if and only if the closing operator is* extensive *(i.e.* $S \subseteq c(S)$*).*
5. If there exist a nontrivial strictly open set $S \subseteq X$ *(i.e. neither* $S = \emptyset$ *nor* $S = X$*), and if the opening is anti–extensive, then* X *is not connected.*
6. $S \subseteq i(a(S))$ *for all* $S \subseteq X$ $\iff$ $x \in i(a(\{x\}))$ *for all* $x \in X$.
7. Let $x \in i(a(\{x\}))$ *for all* $x \in X$.
Then for each set $S \subseteq X$

$$o(a(S)) = a(S), \qquad c(i(S)) = i(S).$$

4.3 Morphological Spaces

The pre–topological space (X, a) is termed a *morphological space* if

$$x \in i(a\{x\}) \qquad \text{for all } x \in X.$$

The set $i(a(\{x\})$ is usually termed the *structuring element* (centered at x).

Theorem 11 *Let* (X, a) *be a morphological space. Then*
1. $i(S) \subseteq o(S) \subseteq S \subseteq c(S) \subseteq a(S)$ *for all* $S \subseteq X$.

2.

$$c(i(S)) = i(S) \quad \text{and} \quad o(a(S)) = a(S)$$
$$\text{and} \quad a(c(S)) = a(S) \quad \text{and} \quad i(o(S)) = i(S),$$
$$\text{specifically} \quad c(c(S)) = c(S) \quad \text{and} \quad o(o(S)) = o(S) \quad \text{for all } S \subseteq X.$$

3. $S_1 \subseteq S_2 \implies c(S_1) \subseteq c(S_2)$ and $o(S_1) \subseteq o(S_2)$ for all subsets S_1, S_2 of X.

In a morphological space (X, a) the closing operator c has all properties of a pre–topological closure operator. This means that (X, c) is again a pre–topological space. The operation $(X, a) \longrightarrow (x, c)$ is termed *morphologization* of (X, a). Morphological spaces are characterized by the following Theorem:

Theorem 12 (X, a) *is a morphological space if and only if X is symmetric with character* 1.

In spaces of character 1 there exists exactly one basic neighborhood Ox for each point x. The next result is somewhat counterintuitive:

Corollary 2 *In a morphological space is $a(\{x\}) = Ox$.*

Given a morphological space (X, a). We now investigate some of the properties of this space. First we pose the question whether it is possible to repeat the morphologization process.

Lemma 2 *Given a morphological space (X, a) and its associated space (X, c). The semi–topological space which is generated by the system of basic neighborhoods*

$$B_c(x) = \{Oy \mid y \in Ox\}.$$

is compatible to (X, c).

Remark This answers the question whether the morphologization process can be repeated. The pre–topological space (X, c) is of character 1 if and only if $Ox = \{x\}$ for all $x \in X$. This means that (X, a) was equipped with a trivial topology.

At a first glance, the properties of (X, c) seem not to be attractive. For example, in (X, c) only sets consisting of single points are connected. On the other hand, (X, c) contains a lage number of "nice" sets, namely all sets S with $c(S) = S$ or $o(S) = S$. Such sets are useful for algorithms in pattern recognition or image processing. These sets can be considered as "root signals" of the closing operator. In nontrivial pre–topological spaces, in contrast, the closure operator has the only root signals $\emptyset$ and X.

References

[1] Alexandroff, P., Hopf, H.: Topologie, Berlin: Springer 1935.

[2] Brissaud, M.: Les espaces prétopologiques. Comptes rendus, Paris, Série A 280, 705–708 (1975).

[3] Čech, E.: Topological Spaces. London: Wiley Interscience 1966.

[4] Eckhardt, U., Latecki, L.: Digital topology. Hamburger Beiträge zur Angewandten Mathematik, Reihe A, Preprint 89, Oktober 1994.

[5] Engelking, R.: General Topology. Warszawa: Polish Scientific Publ. 1977.

[6] Herrlich, H.: A concept of nearness. General Topology and its Applications 4, 191–212 (1974)

[7] Khalimsky E., Kopperman, R., Meyer, P.R.: Computer graphics and connected topologies on finite ordered sets. Topology and its Applications 36, 1–17 (1990).

[8] Kovalevsky, V.A.: Finite topology as applied to image analysis. Computer Vision, Graphics, and Image Processing 45, 141–161 (1989).

[9] Lakämper, R., Seytter, F.: Manipulation objektbasiert codierter Bilder als Anwendungsbeispiel neuer Videostandards. Proc. DAGM, Braunschweig, 1997.

[10] Latecki, L.: Digitale und Allgemeine Topologie in der bildhaften Wissensrepräsentation. St. Augustin: infix 1992.

[11] Latecki, L.J.: On the Relation between Spatial Objects in $\mathbb{R}^2$ ($\mathbb{R}^3$) and their Discrete Representations in $\mathbb{Z}^2$ ($\mathbb{Z}^3$). Dordrecht: Kluwer 1997.

[12] Marcus, D., Wyse, F. et al.: A special topology for the integers. Amer. Math. Monthly 77, 85, 1119 (1970).

[13] Matheron G.: Random Sets and Integral Geometry. New York: Wiley 1975.

[14] Naimpally, S.A., Warrack. B.D.: Proximity Spaces. Cambridge: University Press 1970.

[15] Rosenfeld, A.: Digital topology. American Mathematical Monthly 86, 621–630 (1979).

[16] Salembier, P., Brigger, P., Casas, J.R., Pardás, M.: Morphological operators for image and video compression. IEEE Transactions on Image Processing 5, 881–898 (1996).

[17] Serra, J.: Image Analysis and Mathematical Morphology. London: Academic Press 1982.

[18] Serra, J. (ed.): Image Analysis and Mathematical Morphology, Volume 2: Theoretical Advances. London: Academic Press 1988.

Segmentation by watersheds: definition and parallel implementation

Jos B.T.M. Roerdink and Arnold Meijster

1 Introduction

In the field of grey scale mathematical morphology the watershed transform, originally proposed by Digabel and Lantuéjoul, is frequently used for image segmentation [1,9,11]. It can be classified as a region-based segmentation approach. The intuitive idea underlying this method is that of flooding a landscape or topographic relief with water. Basins will fill up with water starting at local minima, and at points where water coming from different basins would meet, dams are built. When the water level has reached the highest peak in the landscape, the process is stopped. The set of dams thus obtained partitions the landscape into regions or 'catchment basins' separated by dams. These dams are called watershed lines or simply *watersheds*. A sketch is given in Fig. 1.

2 Watersheds by immersion

Although a definition for the continuous case is possible [6, 8], we restrict ourselves here to discrete images. First an algorithmic definition of the watershed is presented following Vincent & Soille [11].

Consider a digital grey scale image $f : D \longrightarrow \mathbb{N}$, where $D \subseteq \mathbb{Z}^2$ is the domain of the image and $f(p)$ denotes the grey value of pixel $p \in D$. Let G denote the pixel grid, i.e. G is a subset of $\mathbb{Z}^2 \times \mathbb{Z}^2$. A *path* P of length l between two pixels p and q is an $l + 1$-tuple $(p_0, p_1, \dots, p_{l-1}, p_l)$ such that $p_0 = p$, $p_l = q$ and $\forall i \in [0, l) : (p_i, p_{i+1}) \in G$. A set of pixels M is called *connected* if and only if for every pair of pixels $p, q \in M$ there exists a path between p and q which only passes through pixels of M. A *connected component* is a nonempty connected set of pixels of maximal size. A *regional minimum* (minimum, for short) of f at altitude h is a connected component of pixels p with $f(p) = h$ from which it is impossible to reach a point of lower altitude without having to climb.

Before going to the algorithm for computing watersheds, we need a few more definitions.

Definition 1 Let $A \subseteq \mathbb{Z}^2$, and a, b two points in A. The *geodesic distance* $d_A(a, b)$ within A is the minimum of the lengths of all paths from a to b in A. If B is a subset of A, define $d_A(a, B) = \mathrm{MIN}_{b \in B}(d_A(a, b))$.

Definition 2 Let $A \subseteq \mathbb{Z}^2$. Let $B \subseteq A$ be partitioned in k connected components $B_i, i = 1, \dots, k$. The *geodesic influence zone* of the set B_i within A is defined as

$$iz_A(B_i) = \{p \in A \mid \forall j \in [1..k] \setminus \{i\} : d_A(p, B_i) < d_A(p, B_j)\}$$

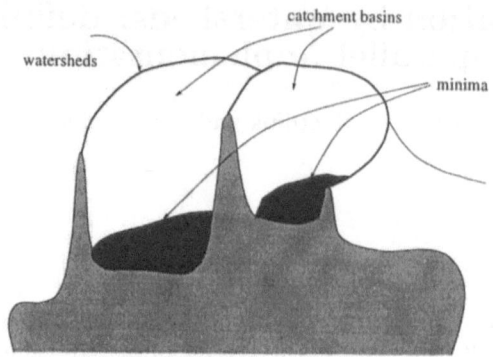

Figure 1: *Minima, catchment basins, and watersheds.*

Definition 3 Let $A \subseteq \mathbb{Z}^2$, $B \subseteq A$. The set $IZ_A(B)$ is defined as the union of the geodesic influence zones of the connected components of B, i.e.,

$$IZ_A(B) = \bigcup_{i=1}^{k} iz_A(B_i)$$

The complement of the set $IZ_A(B)$ within A is called the SKIZ (*'skeleton by influence zones'*) of A:

$$\mathrm{SKIZ}_A(B) = A \backslash IZ_A(B)$$

So the SKIZ consists of all points which are equidistant (in the sense of the geodesic distance) to at least two connected components.

2.1 Recursive algorithm

A recursive algorithm for computing the watershed transform was given by Vincent and Soille [10, 11].
The set $T_h = \{p \in D \mid f(p) \le h\}$ is called the *threshold set* of f at level h. Let h_{min} and h_{max} respectively be the minimum and maximum grey level of the digital image. Let MIN_h denote the union of all regional minima at altitude h.

Definition 4 (Recursive watershed) Define the following recurrence:

$$X_{h_{min}} = \{p \in D \mid f(p) = h_{min}\}$$

$$X_{h+1} = X_h \cup \mathrm{MIN}_{h+1} \cup (IZ_{T_{h+1}}(X_h) \backslash T_h), \qquad h \in [h_{min}, h_{max}) \quad (1)$$

The *watershed transform* $Wshed(f)$ of f is the complement of $X_{h_{max}}$ in D:

$$Wshed(f) = D \cap (X_{h_{max}})^c$$

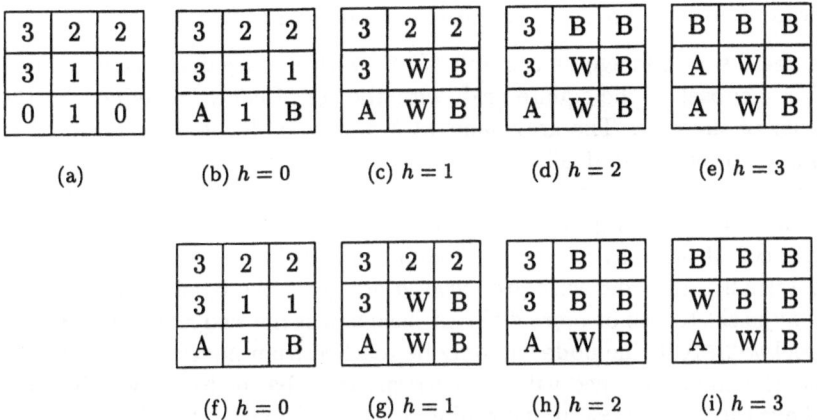

Figure 2: *Watershed on the 4-connected grid. (a): Original image; (b)-(e): labelling steps based on Eq. 1; (f)-(i): labelling steps based on Eq. 2.*

The recursion (1) is based upon the relation between X_h and X_{h+1}. A connected component of T_{h+1} can be either a new minimum, or an extension of the basin X_h: in the latter case one computes the geodesic influence zone of X_h within T_{h+1}. By adding the '$\setminus T_h$' term in (1), we make sure that at level $h+1$ only pixels with grey value $h+1$ are added to existing basins. It should be noted that the SKIZ is not necessarily connected, and that a set of pixels equally distant from two connected components may be thicker than one pixel. Most algorithms for computing watersheds are direct translations of the recursive relation (1).

Remark 5 In the original definition of Vincent & Soille [11], Eq. 1 has the form

$$X_{h+1} = X_h \cup \text{MIN}_{h+1} \cup IZ_{T_{h+1}}(X_h), \qquad h \in [h_{min}, h_{max}) \qquad (2)$$

This allows that pixels which at earlier levels $h' < h+1$ are equidistant to at least two connected components of the set of basins, and thus are provisionally classified as watershed pixels, are relabelled as belonging to some basin. In (1) this is prevented by the '$\setminus T_h$' term. In fact, the implementation described in [11] based on queue data structures actually corresponds to (1), *not* to (2) (at step $h+1$ only pixels with grey value $h+1$ are put in the queue). A simple example is given in Fig. 2, for a 3×3 discrete image on the square grid with 4-connectivity. The labelling according to (1) is shown in Fig. 2(b)-(e). There are two local minima (the zeroes), so there will be two basins whose pixels are labelled A, B. Watershed pixels are labelled by W. Figure 2(f)-(i) shows the phenomenon of relabelling of watershed pixels when using (2): the pixel in the second row, second column is first labelled W, then B. When using the modified definition (1) this pixel remains labelled as W.

2.2 Sequential implementation of the recursive algorithm

Consider the discrete image as a graph (F, E) with nonnegative vertex values, where F is a subset of the square grid, with the set of edges E defined by the connectivity of the grid. The grey value at a node v is denoted by $f(v)$. Also, assume for the moment that all neighbouring pixels in the image have different grey values. The implementation of the recursive definition can be easily formulated on such a graph [4, 11]. The algorithm assigns a label lab to each minimum and its associated basin by iteratively flooding the grid using a breadth first algorithm. Initially, all nodes with grey level h are given the label MASK. If some node v is adjacent to two or more different basins, it is marked a watershed node by the label WSHED. If the node can only be reached from nodes which have the same label the node is merged with the corresponding basin. Nodes which at the end still have the value MASK are new minima, and get a new label. If the restriction of distinct neighbouring grey values does not hold, additional processing is necessary to partition the plateaus (regions of constant grey value) into regions belonging to different minima. This corresponds to the computation of influence zones during every iteration of the algorithm.

2.3 Alternative algorithm

A straightforward parallel implementation of the above algorithm is difficult when plateaus occur. Therefore, an alternative approach was developed, in which the image is first transformed to a graph with distinct neighbour values. Then the graph algorithm described above is directly applicable. This observation leads us to a three-stage watershed algorithm [4].

Step 1. Transform the image f to a directed valued graph $f^* = (F, E)$, called the *components graph of f*. The vertex set F represents maximal connected sets of pixels with the same grey values, called 'level components' or 'flat zones'. A pair of level components (v, w) is an element of the edge set E if and only if $\exists (p \in v, q \in w : (p, q) \in G \wedge f(p) < f(q))$, cf. Fig. 3.

Step 2. Compute the watershed of the directed graph, resulting in a graph with labelled vertices.

Step 3. Transform the labelled graph back to an image. Pixels corresponding to a watershed node are coloured white, the other pixels black. This yields a binary image with plateaus representing watersheds of the original image. Thin watersheds can be obtained by computing a skeleton of this image, for which different skeleton algorithms can be used.

2.4 Parallelization of the alternative algorithm

The runtime performance of the sequential algorithm proposed in the previous subsection turns out to be approximately the same as that of the algorithm described in [11]. However, since all pixels which are in the same level component

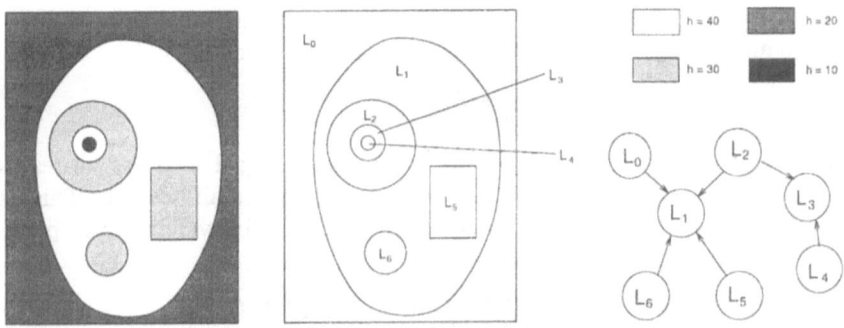

Figure 3: *(a) input image. (b) labelled level sets. (c) components graph.*

are clustered in one single node of the components graph, we can decide locally whether a node is a watershed node by looking at the adjacent nodes. In contrast to the traditional algorithm, the graph algorithm can be parallelized rather easily, see Meijster & Roerdink [3, 4]. Assume a ring network of N processors, where each processor can communicate directly with both neighbouring processors. The programming style we use is called SPMD (single program multiple data), meaning that every processor runs exactly the same program, performing operations on its own data space.

Level components labelling. Labelling of level components is performed by a single processor on the entire image. After labelling, this processor distributes the input image and the labelled image over the processors in the network. To each processor is assigned an (approximately) equal slice of consecutive scanlines. Consecutive slices are assigned to neighbouring processors, with one scanline overlap so that it can be decided whether level components are shared with neighbouring processors.

Parallel watershed of a graph. After labelling every processor builds a local components graph for its own slice of the image. Since some level components are shared between several processors the graphs on the processors are not disjoint. Next every processor performs an adapted version of the flooding algorithm, taking special care of vertices which are shared between two or more processors. At the end of the flooding process each processor transforms its local components graph back to an image slice, as in the sequential case.

3   Watershed definition by shortest paths

Meyer [6] gives a definition of the watershed of a continuous (see also [8]) or digital grey value image in terms of shortest paths with respect to a certain distance function. We confine ourselves here to the digital case.

The *lower slope* of a grey value image f, which is the maximal slope linking a pixel p to any of its neighbours of lower altitude, is defined as

$$LS(p) = \underset{q \in \{p\} \cup N_E(p)}{\text{MAX}} (f(p) - f(q)),$$

where $N_E(p)$ is the set of neighbours of pixel p on the grid E. Here we restrict ourselves to the case where distances between neighbours all equal 1. This can be generalized, e.g. to chamfer distances [6]. The *cost* for walking from pixel p to a neighbouring pixel q is defined as

$$cost(p, q) = \begin{cases} LS(p) & \text{if } f(p) > f(q) \\ LS(q) & \text{if } f(p) < f(q) \\ \frac{LS(p) + LS(q)}{2} & \text{if } f(p) = f(q) \end{cases}$$

Denote the set of all paths from p to q by $p \rightsquigarrow q$. The *topographical distance* between p and q *along a path* $P = (p_0, \dots, p_{l(P)})$ of length $l(P)$ is defined as

$$T_f^P(p, q) = \sum_{i=0}^{l(P)-1} cost(p_i, p_{i+1}).$$

The *topographical distance* between points p and q is the minimum of the topographical distances along all paths between p and q:

$$T_f(p, q) = \underset{P \in p \rightsquigarrow q}{\text{MIN}} T_f^P(p, q).$$

The topographical distance between a point $p \in D$ and a set $A \subseteq D$ is defined as $T_f(p, A) = \text{MIN}_{a \in A} T_f(p, a)$. It is assumed that values of pixels in all the local minima of f have been reset to 0.

The set of lower neighbours p' of p (i.e. $f(p) \geq f(p')$), for which the slope $f(p) - f(p')$ is maximal is denoted by $\Gamma(p)$. We call $\pi = (p_0 = p, p_1, \dots, p_n = q)$ a *path of steepest descent* from p to q if, for each $i = 0, \dots, n-1$, $p_{i+1} \in \Gamma(p_i)$. The topographical distance has the following property, on which the watershed definition crucially depends.

Proposition 6 *There exists a path π of steepest descent from p to q if and only if $T_f(p, q) = f(p) - f(q)$. In all other cases, $T_f(p, q) > f(p) - f(q)$.*

This proposition implies that lines of steepest descent are the geodesics (shortest paths) of the topographical distance function. In fact, T_f is not exactly a distance, since for pixels p, q in the interior of a plateau $T_f(p, q) = 0$. So an auxiliary order relation is necessary to separate them.

Let $(m_i)_{i \in I}$ be the collection of minima of f. The *catchment basin* of a minimum m_i, denoted by $CB(m_i)$, is defined as the set of points $p \in D$ that are topographically closer to m_i than to any other minimum m_j:

$$CB(m_i) = \{p \in D \mid \forall j \in I \setminus \{i\} : T_f(p, m_i) < T_f(p, m_j)\}.$$

The watershed of a function f is the set of points of its domain which do not belong to any catchment basin:

$$Wshed(f) = D \cap (\cup_{i \in I} CB(m_i))^c.$$

3.1 Computation of the watershed based on Dijkstra's algorithm

In order to obtain the watershed of an image, the distance of each pixel to each minimum has to be computed. Using the function *cost* as the weight function associated with the edges of the grid, Dijkstra's algorithm [2] for finding shortest paths in a graph can be used to compute the topographical distances.

Given an undirected graph $G = (V, E)$, and a weight function $w : E \to \mathbb{N}$, that assigns a length to each edge of the graph, the goal is to find for each $v \in V$ the length of the shortest path from a source node s to v. In Dijkstra's algorithm, one initializes for each node $v \in V \setminus \{s\}$ the distance $d[v]$ between v and s to infinity, while the distance $d[s]$ between s and itself is set to zero. Next, a wavefront starting in s is propagated through the graph along the edges. During the propagation one keeps track of the distance the wavefront has travelled so far. When a node is reached by the wavefront and the distance travelled is smaller than the current value stored in this node, this value is updated. Propagation stops when all nodes of the graph have been reached.

Instead of applying this algorithm separately for each minimum, one may modify the function d in Dijkstra's algorithm as follows [5]. Store for each $v \in D$ in the first coordinate of $d[v]$ the index of the nearest minimum, and in the second coordinate the distance to this minimum. The range of the function d is $\mathcal{R} = (I \cup \{\text{WSHED}\}) \times \mathbb{N}$. This leads to the implementation in Algorithm 1. In each minimum a wavefront is initiated, labelled with the index of the minimum it started in. If wavefront i reaches a node v after it has propagated over a distance l, and l is less then the value of the second coordinate of $d[v]$ (denoted by $snd(d[v])$), the value l is placed in the second coordinate of $d[v]$, while the first coordinate $fst(d[v])$ is set to i. If a node v is reached by another wavefront that has propagated over the same distance, the first coordinate of v is set to the artificial value WSHED, designating that v is a watershed pixel.

Algorithm 1 Sequential watershed algorithm based on shortest paths

---

procedure *SeqWshed* $(E : D \times D;\ cost : E \to \mathbb{N};\ \textbf{var } d : D \to \mathcal{R})$;
var $u : D$;
begin forall $v \in D$ **do** $d[v] := (0, \infty)$;
      forall $i \in I$ **do**
       forall $v \in m_i$ **do** $d[v] := (i, 0)$;
      while $D \neq \emptyset$ **do**
      begin $u := GetMinDist(D)$; (∗ find $u \in V$ with smallest d-value ∗)
          $D := D \setminus \{u\}$;
            forall $v \in D$ **with** $(u, v) \in E$ **do**
            if $snd(d[u]) + cost[u, v] < snd(d[v])$
            then $d[v] := (fst(d[u]), snd(d[u]) + cost[u, v])$;
            else if $snd(d[u]) + cost[u, v] = snd(d[v])$
               then $d[v] := (\text{WSHED}, snd(d[v]))$;
     end
end;

28

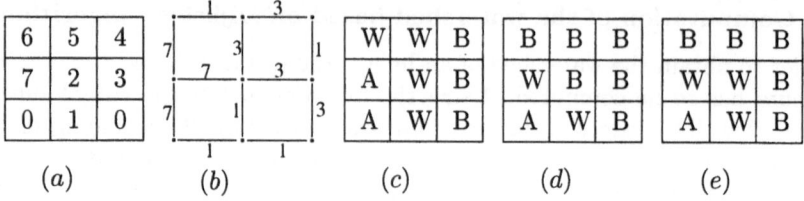

(a)   (b)   (c)   (d)   (e)

Figure 4: *Watershed on the 4-connected grid. (a): original; (b): cost function on the edges; (c): watershed according to topographical distances; (d): watershed according to Eq. 2; (e): watershed according to Eq. 1.*

In Fig. 4 an example is given of the computation of the watershed of a digital image via topographical distances. For comparison we also show the result of the Vincent-Soille definition (2), as well as our modification (1). Note that all three results are different.

Implementation using ordered queues. The function *GetMinDist* in Algorithm 1 can be implemented such that it has time complexity which is linear in the number of pixels of the image. This can be realized with a priority queue of fifo-queues, also called a 'hierarchical' or 'ordered' queue [1].

With each fifo-queue is associated the distance that a wavefront still has to travel before it will reach the pixels in this queue. These distances are used as the priority values in the priority queue. Pixels which are located in the interior of a plateau are ordered in this queue according to another distance function which measures how far pixels are away from the boundary of the plateau. It is clear that, using this data structure, *GetMinDist* runs in $O(1)$ time, since it simply returns (and removes) the pixel at the front of the first fifo-queue in the priority queue. Insertion in the queues can also be done in $O(1)$ time, if we keep track of the first and last position in each fifo-queue.

3.2   Parallelization

The algorithm has been implemented on a Cray J932, a shared memory computer [5]. Computing the lower slope and the cost function in parallel is easy, since the computations are independent for different pixels. Detection of minima is a time-consuming step, since local minima can be huge plateaus, and as a result one cannot decide whether a pixel is located in a regional minimum by just inspecting its value and those of its neighbours. The algorithm for detecting local minima was adapted from [7], but research on faster algorithms is currently going on. Computation of the watershed on the graph can also easily be parallelized. Each processor computes the catchment basins of an (approximately) equal number of minima. Since we use shared memory, concurrent references to the same memory locations have to be synchronized using critical sections.

Performance Results.   The speedup for computing lower slope and cost function is almost linear in the number N of processors. The same holds for minima detection, although the influence of concurrent references to the same memory locations starts to play a major role if we use many processors. If the number of minima is smaller than N, no speed is gained by using more processors. In practice, however, the number of minima is usually much larger than N. Load imbalance as a result of different sizes of the catchment basins is a much more serious cause of decrease in speedup, see the timing results in [5].

4   Conclusions

We have reviewed various existing definitions of watersheds based on recursive thresholding [11] or shortest paths with respect to a certain distance function [6]. We also made a modification of the definition in [11] to avoid 'leaking watersheds', i.e., relabelling of watershed pixels. Some examples were presented which show that the various definitions in principle give different answers. Of course, in practical applications the differences may be small. For both watershed definitions, a sequential and a parallel implementation was described. The original watershed algorithm [11] is very hard to parallelize because of its inherently sequential nature. A parallel implementation of this algorithm was based upon splitting the computation in three consecutive stages involving the transformation to a components graph. The watershed on this graph is easy to parallelize because of its local nature [4]. The distance-based definition [6] allows computing watersheds in parallel using a simple adaptation of Dijkstra's shortest path algorithm [5]. The problem of load imbalance due to unequal sizes of catchment basins will be the subject of future study.

References

[1] Beucher, S., Meyer, F.: The morphological approach to segmentation: the watershed transformation. In: Dougherty E. R. (ed.): Mathematical Morphology in Image Processing. New York: Marcel Dekker 1993 (chapter 12, pp. 433–481).

[2] Dijkstra, E.W.: A note on two problems in connexion with graphs. Numerische Mathematik 1, 269–271 (1959).

[3] Meijster, A., Roerdink, J. B. T. M.: The implementation of a parallel watershed algorithm. In: van Vliet J.C. (ed.): Proc. Computing Science in the Netherlands, 27-28 November, Utrecht. Amsterdam: Stichting Mathematisch Centrum 1995 (pp. 134–142).

[4] Meijster, A., Roerdink, J. B. T. M.: A proposal for the implementation of a parallel watershed algorithm. In: Hlaváč V., Šára R. (eds.): Computer

Analysis of Images and Patterns. New York Heidelberg Berlin: Springer-Verlag 1995 (Lecture Notes in Computer Science, vol. 970, pp. 790–795).

[5] Meijster, A., Roerdink, J. B. T. M.: Computation of watersheds based on parallel graph algorithms. In: Maragos P., Shafer R. W., Butt M. A. (eds.): Mathematical Morphology and its Applications to Image and Signal Processing. Dordrecht: Kluwer Acad. Publ. 1996 (pp. 305–312).

[6] Meyer, F.: Topographic distance and watershed lines. Signal Processing 38, 113–125 (1994).

[7] Moga, A.N., Viero, T., Dobrin, B.P., Gabbouj, M.: Implementation of a distributed watershed algorithm. In: Serra J., Soille P. (eds.): Mathematical Morphology and its Applications to Image Processing. Dordrecht: Kluwer Acad. Publ. 1994 (pp. 281–288).

[8] Najman, L., Schmitt, M.: Watershed of a continuous function. Signal Processing 38, 99–112 (1994).

[9] Serra, J.: Image Analysis and Mathematical Morphology. New York: Academic Press 1982.

[10] Vincent, L.: Algorithmes Morphologiques a Base de Files d'Attente et de Lacets. Extension aux Graphes. PhD thesis. Fontainebleau: Ecole Nationale Supérieure des Mines de Paris 1990.

[11] Vincent, L., Soille, P.: Watersheds in digital spaces: an efficient algorithm based on immersion simulations. IEEE Transactions on Pattern Analysis and Machine Intelligence 13(6), 583–598 (1991).

A graph network for image segmentation

Herbert Jahn

1 Introduction

Image segmentation as one of the oldest problems in image processing and computer vision is, despite of various attempts to solve it [1], not yet solved satisfactorily. Having in mind the huge capability of the human visual system, highly parallel and pipelined computation seems to be necessary for success in this field. According to Uhr [2] parallel-serial layered architectures are best suited for image analysis. In this sense, a new Layered Graph Network (LGN) was developed [3], which is presented and applied to the processing of simulated and real world images.

Segmentation is understood here as "partial segmentation" in the sense of Levine [4], i.e. the found segments do not necessarily correspond to the objects in the picture, but only to more or less homogeneous regions, which are the basis for the subsequent process of "complete segmentation", where segments correspond to objects. Crucial for this purpose is the definition of the partial segments, which according to Pavlidis [5] must have a certain uniformity and which part the image into disjoint nonempty subsets. Looking at certain segments in outdoor scenes, e.g. the foliage of a tree, it becomes obvious that segments can have a complicated structure with many holes inside. Because of shading and other effects, also non-closed edges can be part of a segment.

To cope with such structures a graph representation of images [5] seems adequate. In such a graph a segment is considered as a connected component. To define the graph each pixel must have a connection to some (0,...,4) pixels of its 4-neighborhood, e.g. as a node adjacency list. Analogous to the Region Adjacency Graph (RAG) one could call such a graph a Pixel Adjacency Graph (PAG). Crucial for the construction of the graph is the criterion of adjacency of two (4-neighbored) pixels. If this criterion depends only on the gray value distribution of some local neighborhood of the pixels then, because of noise, many bridges between visually separate segments will occur, and the inherent image structure will be destroyed. Averaging over sub-segments is needed, and this can be accomplished by a special layered structure which will be presented in this paper.

The structure is similar to the well-known pyramid structure [6], but with the differences that, first, each layer represents a graph and averaging is carried out over the connected components of these graphs and that, secondly, the number of sub-segments of layer l-1 belonging to a segment of layer l is not fixed.

The criterion of adjacency of pixels or sub-segments used here depends on the standard deviation of the gray values of neighboured pixels or sub-segments. Therefore one can generate segments corresponding to image regions with slightly varying and noisy gray value distribution.

It is essential that the LGN presented here does not use any a priori information about objects or segments in the images being processed. It is not tailored to a special class of images and should be applicable to a big diversity of images. Furthermore, it is essential that no pixels (and no sub-segments in the higher layers of the network) are distinguished from the others. There are no seed points as in some other merging methods (region growing) and thus the sub-segment formation in the network layers can be highly parallelized which is necessary for efficient computation. Of course, the simulation of the network on a conventional von Neumann machine is very non-efficient and can be used only for demonstration of the ability of the method.

In section 2 the method is explained in more detail. Results demonstrating the power of the approach are given in section 3.

2 The PAG and the LGN Structure

Let the image be represented by an image region of N x N pixels (i,j) $(i,j = 0,...,N-1)$ with the gray values $g_{i,j}$ and $N = 2^n$. To constitute the PAG we consider each image point (i,j) and its 4-neighbours $(i+1,j)$, $(i-1,j)$, $(i,j+1)$, $(i,j-1)$. Be (i_1,j_1) one of the 4-neighbours of (i,j). Then it must be decided whether (i_1,j_1) is adjacent to (i,j) or not by using an appropriate criterion. If they are adjacent then the points (i,j) and (i_1,j_1) (which correspond to the nodes of the graph) will be connected by a branch. A suitable description of the graph is given by the node adjacency list [5] where every node (i,j) has a list of its adjacent nodes. Now a segment of the image is defined as a connected component of the graph. Such a kind of graph definition was used in the clustering of dot patterns [7], and one can interpret the segmentation method presented here as a method of clustering the data. Crucial for the graph structure to be generated is the criterion of adjacency of points (i,j) and (i_1,j_1). Node (i,j) and node (i_1,j_1) are adjacent, if their gray values fulfill the condition

$$\left| g_{i,j} - g_{i_1,j_1} \right| \leq F \tag{1}$$

Here F is some adaptive threshold which depends on the gray values in some neighbourhood of the points (i,j) and (i_1,j_1). To specify F we start with the following consideration: The visual separation of two neighboured pixels (i,j) and (i_1,j_1) is more difficult if there is a big variation of the gray values in their neighbourhood. Therefore F should be proportional to a measure of this variation. A simple measure, which gives good results, is the standard deviation σ of the gray values in a neighbourhood N of (i,j) and (i_1,j_1).

To simplify the computation, it is useful to attach to each pixel (i,j) a value $\sigma_{i,j}$. It turned out that the computation of σ in the 8-neighbourhood N_8 of (i,j) is sufficient. Therefore,

$$F = t_1 \bar{\sigma}(i,j;i_1,j_1) \quad . \tag{2}$$

Here, t_1 is a threshold, and

$$\bar{\sigma}(i,j;i_1,j_1) = \frac{1}{2}(\sigma_{i,j} + \sigma_{i_1,j_1}).$$

(3)

The threshold (2) which increases with noise but vanishes if the grey values in the 8-neighbourhoods of (i,j) and (i$_1$,j$_1$) are constant is not sufficient.

In order to assess the segmentation results by visual inspection using a computer screen, the properties of this screen and that of the human visual system must be taken into account. Looking at such a screen one can not discriminate pixels with

$$\left|g_{i,j} - g_{i_1,j_1}\right| \le t_2.$$

(4)

In general, the threshold t_2 depends on the brightness but here we use only constant values of t_2. Now, combining (2) and (4), the adjacency criterion for level $1 = 1$ is

$$\left|g_{i,j} - g_{i_1,j_1}\right| \le MAX\{t_1\bar{\sigma}(i,j;i_1,j_1), t_2\}.$$

(5)

In principle, one could apply the adjacency criterion (5) to the whole image. Then one would obtain a graph in one step (i.e. without a layered processing structure). But this has the drawback that only local information contributes to the graph and no sufficient noise reduction takes place. Single noisy image points then can connect visually separate segments, and one generally obtains too large segments. In graph theory such connections between connected components are called bridges.

To avoid (or to minimize the number of) such bridges, averaging over adequate regions is necessary, and this can be done using a layered processing structure. In order to generate such a layered structure one divides the image i,j $= 0,1,...,N$-1 ($N = 2^n$) in every layer (or level) l ($l=1,...,l_{max}$) into sub-regions Reg(l,k$_1$,k$_2$) each containing 2^l x 2^l image points:

Reg(l,k$_1$,k$_2$) (k$_1$, k$_2$ = 0,...,2^{n-l}-1): $\quad 2^l k_1 \le i \le 2^l(k_1 +1)$ -1
$\qquad\qquad\qquad\qquad\qquad\qquad\qquad\qquad 2^l k_2 \le j \le 2^l(k_2 +1)$ -1

Figures 1b,c,d show the regional partition (marked by dashed lines) for l $= 1,2,3$ and N $= 8$ (n $= 3$).

Let's consider first the layer l=1. Applying (1) to all pixels inside a 2 x 2 region Reg(1,k$_1$,k$_2$) one can attach to every pixel (i,j) a node adjacency list NAL(1,i,j) which contains all pixels from the same region which are adjacent to the pixel (i,j). In the image plane i,j $= 0,...,N$-1 the node adjacency list NAL defines a graph with N$_{seg}$(1) connected components or sub-segments. Using the NAL, the sub-segments can be labeled using a graph traversal algorithm, e.g. depth first traversal [5]. In the result of this procedure each image point (i,j) obtains a label Lab(1,i,j) (i,j $= 0,...,N$-1). All

points (i,j) with Lab(1,i,j) = m belong to the same segment m. Now, as a feature, the
mean gray value $<g>(1,m)$ can be assigned to the sub-segment m.

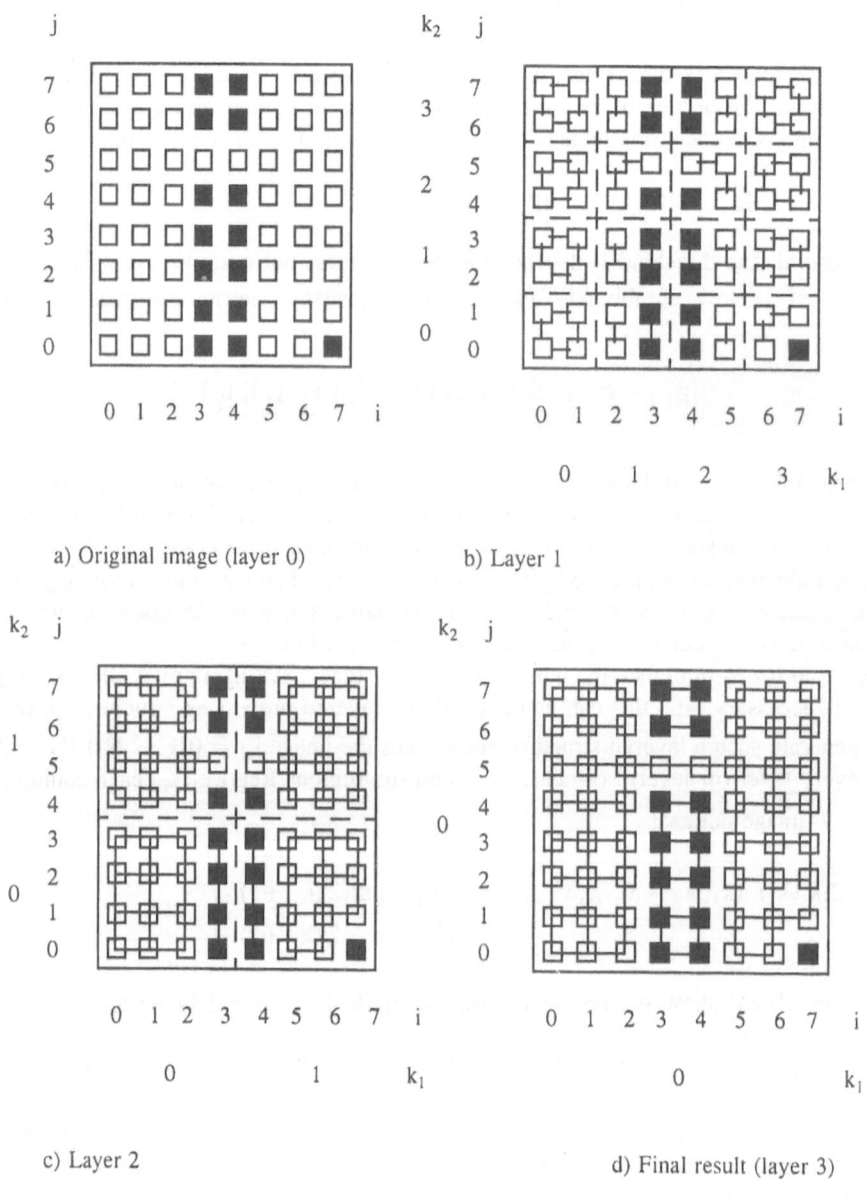

a) Original image (layer 0)

b) Layer 1

c) Layer 2

d) Final result (layer 3)

Fig. 1: Regional structure (dashed) and PAG

Now we consider network layers (levels) $l = 2,3,...$. Input elements are the sub-segments $m = 0,1,..., N_{seg}(l-1)-1$ of level $l-1$ with the features $\langle g \rangle (l-1,m)$. Sub-segments can be adjacent if they belong to the same region $Reg(l, k_1,k_2)$ and if they are '4-neighbours'. Generalizing (5), the adjacency of two segments m_1 and m_2 now is defined by

$$|\langle g \rangle (l-1, m_1) - \langle g \rangle (l-1, m_2)|$$
$$\leq MAX\{t_1(l)\sigma[\langle g \rangle (l-1, m); m \in N(m_1, m_2)], t_2(l)\} \qquad (6)$$

Here the standard deviation $\sigma[\langle g \rangle (l-1, m); m \in N(m_1, m_2)]$ of the values $\langle g \rangle (l-1,m)$ is given by

$$\sigma[\langle g \rangle (l-1, m); m \in N(m_1, m_2)]$$
$$= \frac{1}{2}[\sigma(l-1, m_1) + \sigma(l-1, m_2)]. \qquad (7)$$

$\sigma(l-1,m)$ is the standard deviation of the mean gray values $\langle g \rangle (l-1,m')$ of segments $m' \in N_8(m)$, and $N_8(m)$ is the 8-neighbourhood of segment m.

Using (6), for each sub-segment m of level $l-1$ in a region $Reg(l,k_1,k_2)$ the adjacent sub-segments which belong to the same region $Reg(l,k_1,k_2)$ can be identified and saved in a node adjacency list $NAL(l,m)$. $NAL(l,m)$ defines a new graph of level l. Again, all connected components of this special region adjacency graph can be labeled by integers $label(l,m)$. Using $Lab(l-1,i,j)$ and $label(l,m)$, the new function $Lab(l,i,j)$ can be generated by a simple updating procedure. This process can be applied recursively from layer to layer, and in layer $l=l_{max}$ the final segmentation is obtained.

Figures 1b-c display these processing steps in the three layers $l=1,2,3$ for the 8x8-image of fig.1a (letter i with noise point). Adjacent pixels are connected by lines which are equivalent to the branches connecting the nodes of the graph. The regions are marked by dashed lines. Fig.1b shows the PAG for $l=1$ with 25 segments. The PAG for $l=2$ (fig.1c) has 11 connected components, and there are 4 segments as the final result (fig.1d).

(6) is only an example for a possible adjacency criterion. Other criteria are permitted and even necessary. Experiments with various images have shown that the criterion (6) gives sometimes (if shading is substantial) bad results if the sub-segments are too large. Better results are obtained if inclined planes $f(m,i,j)=a \cdot i+b \cdot j+c$ are fitted to the gray values inside sub-segments m of level $l_{max}-1$ with more than n_{min} pixels (for smaller sub-segments we use $f(m,i,j)=\langle g \rangle (l_{max}-1,m)$). Now, sub-segments m_1, m_2 of level $l_{max}-1$ are adjacent, if there exist two 4-neighbours $(i_1,j_1) \in m_1$ and $(i_2, j_2) \in m_2$ with

$$\left| f(m_1, i_1, j_1) - f(m_2, i_2, j_2) \right| \le t_2(l_{max}) \qquad . \qquad (8)$$

(8) is applied without a partition of layer l_{max} into regions $Reg(l_{max}, k_1, k_2)$, or, with other words, $Reg(l_{max}, k_1, k_2)$ is the whole image plane. This ensures that the final segments are not confined to squared regions.

The generated PAG of level $l_{max}+1$ is the preliminary segmentation result which is presented here. Further layers of the LGN with other adjacency criteria taking into account not only gray value but also orientation, shape and spatial arrangement of sub-segments should be investigated in the future in order to segment textures and to recognize objects.

For display of the segmentation results (for $l=l_{max}+1$) it is useful to define a function $g_{mean}(i,j)$ with the constant value $<g>(l_{max}+1,m)$ in every point (i,j) of a segment m. Such a g_{mean} - image shows the segmentation of the original image $g_{i,j}$ (segments have constant gray level), and it often resembles the original image very much. Then the g_{mean} - image can be used as a (edge preserving) smoothed version of the original image $g_{i,j}$. But it must be stressed that the final result is expressed by the function $Lab(i,j)$ ($=Lab(l_{max}+1,i,j)$) which assigns the segment number to each pixel (i,j) of a segment. Therefore, a segment can be characterized by all of its pixels (i,j) with gray values $g_{i,j}$. Therefore, no information is lost and various segment features can be calculated which can be used in higher layers of the network for texture segmentation and object recognition.

3 Results

For demonstration of the ability of the method the LGN was simulated on a conventional serial computer (486 PC or SUN workstation) using the IDL language. A number of experiments with simulated and real world images was carried out in order to identify useful thresholds $t_1(l)$ and $t_2(l)$. It turned out that $t_1(l) = 0.6...0.65$ ($l = 1,...,l_{max}-1$) and $t_2(l) = 5...7$ ($l = 1,...,l_{max}$) with $l_{max} = 5$ gave best results. Sub-segments of level $l_{max}-1$ with more than $n_{min} = 32$ pixels were fitted by inclined planes $f(m,i,j)$ used in (8). The following results were obtained by using these parameter values.

A 128 x 128 part of the Lena image (figure 2a) was segmented using $t_1(l) = 0.6$, $l_{max} = 5$, and different values of $t_2(l)$. Figure 2b shows the segmentation result for $t_2(l)=0$: 2770 segments/the biggest one with 292 pixels. $t_2(l)=6$ (fig.2c) gives 719 segments/6742, and $t_2(l)=7$: 640/7582 (fig.2d). This shows that smaller values of $t_2(l)$ lead to a good quality of representation but too many segments, whereas bigger values give a coarser representation but not so much segments. In most cases, the segmentation with $t_2(l)=10$ is too coarse. Again there are many very small segments. Some of them are essential for a description of the face (e.g. the eyelashes), others are not.

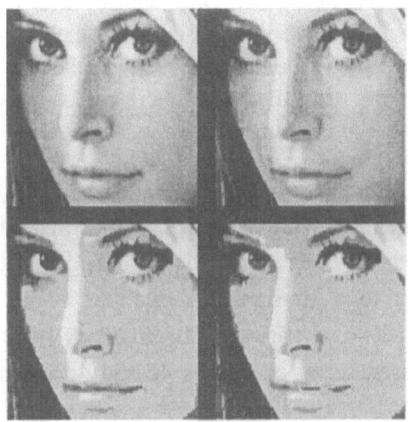

Fig.2: Lena
a) Original image (upper left)
b) Segmented image, $t_1=0.6$, $t_2=0$ (upper right)
c) Segmented image, $t_1=0.6$, $t_2=6$
d) Segmented image, $t_1=0.6$, $t_2=7$ (lower right)

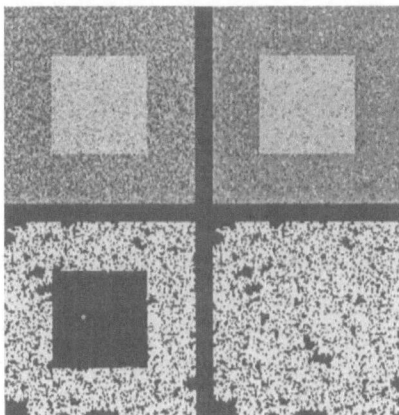

Fig.3: Background and square with noise
a) Original image (upper left)
b) Segmented image
c) The biggest segment (lower left)
d) The 2 biggest segments

A simulated image consisting of a homogeneous background and a square (gray level distance $\Delta = 20$) with additive white Gaussian noise ($\sigma = 10$) is shown in figure 3a. Figure 3b shows the segmentation result for $t_1(l) = 0.65$, $t_2(l) = 7$, and $l_{max} = 5$. There are 2989 segments, most of them very small. The biggest segment with 8232 pixels is shown in figure 3c, and the 2 biggest segments representing the background and the square are displayed in fig.3d. One can see that the background and the square are well separated and can be recognised using the two biggest segments only. The number of segments (2989) identified by the method is very big, but most of them are very small and represent randomly generated structures. In spite of this fact, a substantial amount of edge preserving smoothing took place.

Figure 4a shows a 128 x 128 cut of a Mars image obtained by a US VIKING space-craft. The image was segmented with $t_2(l)=5$, $l_{max} = 5$, and different values of $t_1(l)$. $t_1(l)=0$ (fig.4b) produced 1527 segments, the biggest one with 2386 pixels. Increa-sing values of $t_1(l)$ lead to a substantial reduction of the number of segments: $t_1(l)=0.5$: 1099/5120, $t_1(l)=0.6$ (fig.4c): 803/5125, $t_1(l)=0.7$ (fig.4d): 593/5499. Even in the coarse representations of figures 4c and 4d essential small details (e.g. small craters) are retained.

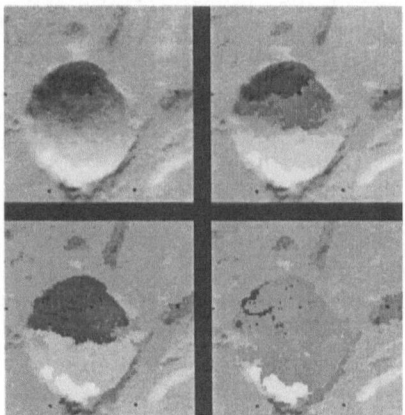

Fig. 4: Mars image from VIKING spacecraft
a) Original image
b) Segmented image, $t_1=0$, $t_2=5$
c) Segmented image, $t_1=0.6$, $t_2=5$
d) Segmented image, $t_1=0.7$, $t_2=5$

Four Brodatz textures are shown in figure 5a. The result of the segmentation (fig.5b) with $t_1(l) = 0.65$, $t_2(l)=7$, $l_{max} = 5$ and 2027 segments resembles the original image very much. Figures 5c and 5d show the 100 and 500 biggest segments, respec-tively. One can hope, that these segments (after an elimination of very small ones) can be used as texture elements in a subsequent segmentation of textures.

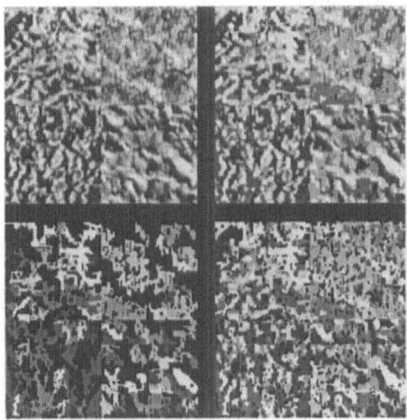

Fig.5: Brodatz textures
a) Original image (4 textures)
b) Segmented image, $t_1 = 0.65$, $t_2 = 7$
c) The 100 biggest segments
d) The 500 biggest segments

4 Conclusions

A new graph network for image segmentation basing on a hierarchical construction of the Pixel Adjacency Graph was presented. The method gives encouraging results for various types of images but some problems must be solved in the future in order to enhance the quality of the results. First, we have got a weak dependence of thresholds t_1, t_2 from the image type which has to be eliminated (probably by modifying the adjacency criterion). Secondly, because of the regular regional structure used, artefacts are sometimes generated which must be overcome too. Furthermore, it turned out that the number of generated segments is very big in most of the processed images. The overwhelming part of these segments is very small. Some of these small segments are meaningful (e.g. the eyelashes of Lena) but most of them are not and should be eliminated.

It seems that the method can be extended to the segmentation of textures using small segments as texture elements which should be decribed by features such as position, size, orientation, shape, grey value (or color) to be used in modified adjacency criteria. This must be studied in the future too.

40

References

1. Haralick, R.M., Shapiro, L.G.: Image Segmentation Techniques.
   CVGIP 29, pp. 100 -132 (1985)
2. Uhr, L.: Psychological Motivation and Underlying Concepts. In: Tanimoto,S.,
   Klinger, A. (Eds.). Structured Computer Vision. New York: Academic Press 1980
3. Jahn, H.: Image Segmentation with a Layered Graph Network. SPIE Proceedings,
   Vol. 2662, pp.217-228 (1996)
4. Levine, M.D.: Vision in Man and Machine. New York: Mc Graw-Hill 1985
5. Pavlidis, T.: Structural Pattern Recognition. Berlin: Springer-Verlag 1977
6. Jolion, J.M., Rosenfeld, A.: A Pyramid Framework for Early Vision. Dordrecht:
   Kluwer Academic Publishers 1994
7. Jahn, H.: Eine Methode zur Clusterbildung in metrischen Räumen. Bild & Ton 39,
   pp. 362 - 370 (1986)

Associative memory for images by recurrent neural subnetworks

Władysław Skarbek

1 Introduction

Pattern recognition and pattern autoassociation are related but not identical tasks attributed to intelligent systems. In pattern recognition, a system is supposed to identify a class C_i, $i = 1, \ldots, K$, where an object belongs to, giving the object's features x which were previously measured and delivered to the system. In autoassociation, an associative memory reconstructs the original pattern x when distorted or incomplete version x' is presented to the system [1, 8, 2, 3]. Usually such a system is trained to *store* many original patterns which can be considered as representatives of pattern classes.

In a sense, pattern recognition is more hard activity than autoassociation as if we can recognize an object then we can easily perform association task provided that class representatives can be obtained in the system. This paper shows that the opposite way, leading from autoassociativity to recognition, is also possible. Imagine that each class C_i has a separate autoassociative system $\mathcal{N}_i$ realizing generally a stochastic input-output operator $\mathcal{F}_i$. If the association is to be adequate then the input $x \in C_i$ should be *close* to $\mathcal{F}_i(x)$ and *far away* from $\mathcal{F}_j(x)$ for $j \neq i$ according to some proximity measure ρ. It leads to the following simplified recognition rule: decide that x is in class C_k if

$$k = \arg\min_j \rho\left(x, \mathcal{F}_j(x)\right).$$

Hence we see that the autoassociative subsystems can be used to build a recognition system. Moreover, if autoassociation is realized by neural networks then recognition is expressed in neural paradigm using a neural competition layer [9]. A simple design of an autoassociative system for a class C_i can be proposed: take any representative pattern $x_i \in C_i$ and set $\mathcal{F}_i(x) = x_i$ for all x. It can be easily observed that recognition based on such trivial autoassociative subsystems is equivalent to recognition by template matching. Though template matching is strongly criticised, its generalization to *k-NN* method is still competitive in many applications where memory space is not critical [6]. However, for face recognition, template matching approach requires huge memory space to keep sample pictures for each person in a big face data base. From this observation, we conclude that we should demand from autoassociative subsystems to be represented by much less data bits than training patterns include. Data compression paradigm gives us a constraint which leads to a different than template matching solution.

Another solution for an autoassociative system can be based on a local subspace method [10, 11]. The method takes a training subset from each class $C_i \subset R^N$, and next it applies to it the Principal Component Analysis [4]. PCA produces K-dimensional subspace of R^N with an orthonormal basis in columns of the matrix W_i. The basis is centered on the centroid c_i of the training set. Then input-output operator $\mathcal{F}_i$ for autoassociative subsystem of i-th class is defined as follows:

$$\mathcal{F}_i(\boldsymbol{x}) \doteq c_i + W_i W_i^T (\boldsymbol{x} - c_i).$$

The square of Euclidean distance used as the proximity measure of the output to the input appears to be the squared distance to the local subspace:

$$\rho(\boldsymbol{x}, \mathcal{F}_i(\boldsymbol{x})) \doteq \|\boldsymbol{x} - \mathcal{F}_i(\boldsymbol{x})\|^2 = \|Q_i(\boldsymbol{x} - c_i)\|^2,$$

where $Q_i = I - W_i W_i^T$.

The local subspace method has the memory space, required for one class, proportional to NK. Therefore its application for instance in face recognition where one person defines one face class and the number of pixels N in face image is large, is not practical.

We see from shortcomings of the local subspace method that in search for a good autoassociative subsystem we should also look for such a compression approach which has the small number of design parameters affecting computation of input-output mapping. The design of autoassociative local neural networks, described in section 2, intends to satisfy this condition.

2   Autoassociative recurrent subnetworks

Our autoassociative subsystem accepts the input image, processes pixel values, and produces the output image. Then it is natural to introduce the concept of pixel based neural network (PNN) which is defined by:

- choosing an invertible activation function a (generally nonlinear);

- specification for each pixel neural element i its input pixels $P(i)$;

- assignment of weights α_i for all links between the pixel $j \in P(i)$ and the pixel i;

- assignment for each pixel i of a bias coefficient β_i.

In this text we abbreviate the phrase *pixel neural element* by the word *pixel*. Denoting the value of i-th pixel in discrete time t by $f_i(t)$, the next value after its activation $f_i(t+1)$ is given by the formula:

$$f_i(t+1) = a\left(\beta_i + \alpha_i \sum_{j \in P(i)} f_j(t)\right) \tag{1}$$

Further, we assume that the nonlinearity a is Lipschitzian function with Lipschitz coefficient denoted by $\|a\|$. In face application the following functions a were tested: linear, clamp, and several forms of logistic function.

By PNN(d) we mean a class of PNN networks in which the input degree of element i is bounded by d, i.e. $|P(i)| \le d$.

The dynamic behaviour of PNN which is a sort of recurrent neural network can be analyzed in one of three modes: deterministic parallel, deterministic sequential, and nondeterministic sequential.

There is a simple condition for a global stability of PNN networks included in the following non trivial theorem:

Convergence Theorem If a network $\mathcal{N} \in$ PNN(d) has weights $|\alpha_i| < 1/(d\|a\|)$ then there exists a unique attracting state f^* to which the network converges (at any Minkovsky norm) in the deterministic modes and with probability one in the nondeterministic mode.

Despite severe global constraint on all weights in the network, the convergence theorem appears useful in design of autoassociative subnetworks of the recognition system.

It should be noted that in part the above network design was inspired by Jacquin's [5] fractal compression scheme. As a matter of fact our network when working in *deterministic parallel mode*, it computes in one global step a nonlinear fractal operator, i.e. the more general operator than the classical fractal operator (see Fisher [7]). In remaining modes the behaviour of our network has no counterparts in the fractal operator theory.

Using general model (1) of PNN we get more weights than pixels. In order to reduce the number of parameters we assume further, a weight sharing for pixels. An important feature of PNN network is its locality measured by the maximum distance r of a pixel to its input pixels. If r_{ij} is the distance of the pixel i to the pixel j then the *local radius* r_i is defined as $r_i \doteq \max_{j \in P(i)} r_{ij}$. Then the *global radius* $r \doteq \max_i r_i$. By PNN(d, r) we mean a subclass of PNN(d) including PNN networks with global radius not exceeding r. Though we do not define formally local pixel neural networks, intuitively we understand by this term any network from PNN(d, r) where d and r are *small*, e.g.: $d = 4, r = 10$.

Intuitively, a small distortion of object in a picture should not affect network's output significantly. We can ensure this condition requiring that pixels from $P(i)$ are mutually adjacent in the image plane. For simplicity a square $m \times m$ is chosen as $P(i)$ in the actual implementation in which m was randomly optimized in a range $[m_1, m_2]$ (typically $m_1 = 1, m_2 = 3$).

Learning of the network weights is based here on the autoassociativity condition, i.e. in the network built for the image f, the element i has its output as close as possible (in LSM sense) to pixel's value f_i:

$$\beta + \alpha \sum_{j \in P_i} f_j \simeq a^{-1}(f_i) \tag{2}$$

where a is an invertible nonlinearity function, (e.g. clamp or logistic function), i is the index of arbitrary pixel, β is the bias shared by all elements, and α is the weight shared by all elements.

Observe that invertibility condition of a can be only restricted to the range of pixel values f_i.

The replacement of typically few hundred thousands pixel values by two parameters α and β obviously cannot give satisfactory quality of the associated image. Intuitively a good idea is to consider the problem (2) restricted to small subimages $f|B_k$, $k = 1, \ldots, K$, of the original image f where disjoint pixel subsets B_k cover the whole image domain B. For instance B_k could be a block of pixels of size 8×8. Hence instead of one large LSM problem we get K small LSM problems:

$$\beta_k + \alpha_k \sum_{j \in P_i} f_j \simeq a^{-1}(f_i) \tag{3}$$

where $k = 1, \ldots, K$, i is the index of elements from B_k, β_k is the bias shared by all elements in B_k, and α_k is the weight shared by all elements in B_k.

Let $L_k = |B_k|$ be the number of pixels in the subimage B_k and $f_i' \doteq a^{-1}(f_i)$. By f_i^s we mean the total input for the i-th element:

$$f_i^s \doteq \sum_{j \in P_i} f_j.$$

Then from the normal equation of the least square problem (3) we can easily get explicit formulas for α_k and β_k, $k = 1, \ldots, K$:

$$\alpha_k = \frac{\sum_{i \in B_k} f_i^s f_i' - \frac{1}{L_k} \left(\sum_{i \in B_k} f_i^s \right) \left(\sum_{i \in B_k} f_i' \right)}{\sum_{i \in B_k} (f_i^s)^2 - \frac{1}{L_k} \left(\sum_{i \in B_k} f_i^s \right)^2} \tag{4}$$

$$\beta_k = \frac{\sum_{i \in B_k} f_i' - \alpha_k \sum_{i \in B_k} f_i^s}{L_k}$$

We should observe that the solution obtained from conditions (3) does not guarantee the convergence of the network $\mathcal{N}(f)$. Therefore in practice we fix the weight to a constant α_0 less than $1/(d\|a\|)$ what according to the convergence theorem ensures the stability of the system. Then the autoassociativity conditions have the form for $k = 1, \ldots, K$:

$$\beta_k + \alpha_0 \sum_{j \in P_i} f_j \simeq a^{-1}(f_i) \tag{5}$$

where i is the index of the element from B_k and β_k is the bias shared by all elements in B_k.

The solution of this simple least square problem (5) is given below for $k = 1, \ldots, K$:

$$\beta_k = \frac{\sum_{i \in B_k} f_i' - \alpha_0 \sum_{i \in B_k} f_i^s}{L_k} \tag{6}$$

Further by *autoassociative local neural network* we mean any local network PNN with weights learned by LSM from the conditions (3) or (5) given by formulas (4) or (6). The network obtained for the image f is denoted by $\mathcal{N}(f)$.

Grouping pixels into blocks must affect choice of their predecessors. Completely independent predecessors for neighbouring pixels would result in non continous network response to continuous changes of its input. It is rather undesirable property if the network is to be autoassociative for a class of images. In another words we must require that for close pixels from the same subimage B_k their predecessors are close in the image plane too. This is achieved by a parametrization of admissible locations of predecessing pixel blocks which are obtained relatively to the predecessor B'_k of the whole block B_k. Namely, if a pixel i has coordinates (x, y) relatively to the block B_k with the origin (b_x, b_y) then

$$P(i) \doteq \{(b_x + d_x + \gamma x' + u, b_y + d_y + \gamma y' + v) \,|\, 0 \le u, v < m\},$$

where (d_x, d_y) is the block displacement, γ is scaling factor, $(x', y') = A(x, y)$ for certain mapping A which is chosen from a fixed finite collection of mappings $\mathcal{M}$ (for instance all symmetries of square), and m^2 is the number of predecessing pixels for the pixel i. All parameters describing $P(i)$ are chosen randomly from predefined ranges.

3 Experimental results

We present here the results of associative recall of noisy and incomplete data which are relevant when discussing the features of an associative memory. However, each subnetwork in its encoded file form can be considered as compressed image form. Hence our associative memory works as an efficient image archive. Comparing its performance to the classical fractal compression, we have observed that on average the convergence speed in our approach is about two times faster and the software implementation occupies two times less of RAM storage for image data than in the case of Jacquin's scheme [5, 7].

In experiments it was chosen as the distance measure the *normalized mean square error* NMSE expressed in percents:

$$\text{NMSE}(g, g_i) = \frac{\|g - g_i\|^2}{N \cdot \sigma^2(g)} \cdot 100 \ .$$

3.1 Noisy data

In the tables with distance evaluation in the first stage of the associative recall we use abbreviations for image names: L – Lena, J – Julia, B – Baboon, M – Miyake, K – Kiuchi. The symbol I denotes the column for image names which are sorted according to the distance value. We present the results only for the first three images in this ordering.

In these experiments pixel values were normalized to the interval $[0, 1]$. Therefore for instance $\sigma = 2$ means that the standard deviation of the noise equals to double length of nominal image range.

We see from Table 1 that the distance to Lena image is the shortest for σ up to 2. The wrong recall is observed for enormous noise with $\sigma = 16$. Though the classification is correct for $\sigma < 16$ the distance differences are insignificant.

For the speckle noise we have more significant distance differences for the winner than in Gaussian noise case. However, the wrong classification occurs for smaller

Table 1: Sorted distance measures for Lena image corrupted by additive Gaussian noise with various standard deviations σ.

#	$\sigma = 0.1$		$\sigma = 0.6$		$\sigma = 1.0$		$\sigma = 2.0$		$\sigma = 16.0$	
	I	NMSE	I	NMSE	I	NMSE	I	NMSE	I	NMSE
1	L	28.6	L	96.4	L	99.2	L	99.9	M	99.99
2	B	85.9	B	102.5	J	101.4	J	100.5	L	100.00
3	J	94.5	J	102.7	B	101.5	B	100.6	J	100.00

Table 2: Sorted distance measures for Lena image corrupted by multiplicative uniform (speckle) noise for various standard deviations σ.

#	$\sigma = 0.1$		$\sigma = 0.6$		$\sigma = 1.0$		$\sigma = 2.0$		$\sigma = 8.0$	
	I	NMSE	I	NMSE	I	NMSE	I	NMSE	I	NMSE
1	L	4.6	L	59.2	L	86.0	L	102.7	J	111.0
2	B	79.1	B	95.8	J	104.6	J	108.9	B	111.8
3	J	91.2	J	100.0	B	105.3	B	109.6	L	111.9

σ (see Table 2). The similar very good performance has been obtained for uniform additive noise.

Table 3: Sorted distance measures for Lena image corrupted by spiky noise for various probabilities p.

#	$p = 0.1$		$p = 0.3$		$p = 0.5$		$p = 0.7$		$p = 0.9$	
	I	NMSE	I	NMSE	I	NMSE	I	NMSE	I	NMSE
1	L	38.2	L	73.9	L	97.5	L	158.3	B	242.6
2	B	90.4	B	104.3	B	116.9	B	165.1	L	246.7
3	J	100.8	J	115.1	J	132.6	J	215.5	J	357.3

Spiky noise can be reliably removed by the associative recall even if it occurs on up to 70% of the image area (see Table 3).

3.2 Incomplete data

Partial or incomplete data we get here by setting certain pixels to zero value (black color). This can be done in deterministic or in pseudo random way. In both cases the receiver of such incomplete image knows the location of missing pixels. Therefore it can approximate the missing value in the given location by taking the average of non missing values located in a vicinity. In computer experiments we have chosen as the the neighborhood, a pixel block growing from size 5×5 to the minimum size where non hidden pixel can be found. This approximation acts as a low pass filter on the input image. The preprocessed in such a way the incomplete image is next delivered to the associative memory to be completely recovered by an associative recall.

Table 4: Sorted distance measures for incomplete Lena image with different percentage of missing pixel area s.

#	$s = 10\%$		$s = 50\%$		$s = 90\%$		$s = 95\%$		$s = 99.7\%$	
	I	NMSE	I	NMSE	I	NMSE	I	NMSE	I	NMSE
1	L	1.4	L	1.5	L	4.1	L	11.9	M	100.2
2	B	77.7	B	76.5	B	75.9	B	78.5	L	102.7
3	J	90.5	J	90.0	J	90.1	J	91.9	K	105.3

From Table 4 we see that changing up to 95% pixels to the black color in deterministic way still results in numerically significant, correct association. The same conclusion we get from experiments with randomly chosen, partial data.

3.3 Face recognition

Main assumptions of face recognition system based on autoassociative local neural networks are listed below:

1. Each person is represented by a small number (3-5) of face pictures;

2. Each facial picture f_i from a training set is represented by its autoassociative neural network $\mathcal{N}_i \doteq \mathcal{N}(f_i)$ realizing input-output mapping $\mathcal{F}_i$ such that input-output distance $\rho(f_i, \mathcal{F}_i(f_i))$ is supposed to be small;

3. When a testing facial image g is presented, the network $\mathcal{N}_i$ with the lowest input-output distance, becomes the winner in a competition;

4. When a testing person p is presented by a small collection of face views (5-7), the person q from the data base with the majority of winning networks for those testing views, is recognized as the person p.

The experiments were performed on pictures collected in the ORL face database. It includes a set of photographs taken between April 1992 and April 1994 at the Olivietti Research Laboratory in Cambridge, UK[1]. There are 10 different images of each of 40 distinct subjects. For some subjects, the images were taken at different times, varying the lighting, facial expressions (open or closed eyes, smiling or not smiling) and facial details (glasses or no glasses). All the images

---

[1]The ORL database is free of charge, see http://www.cam-orl.co.uk/facedatabase.html

were taken against a dark homogeneous background with the subjects in an upright, frontal position (with tolerance for some side movement). The size of each original image is 92×112 pixels, with 256 grey levels per pixel. This database is maintained by Ferdinando Samaria.

Many design options for autoassociative networks were checked in experiments using the recognition rate R as a quality criterion. Lack of space enables to include only few of experimental results.

In Table 5, the left part includes results when the testing person was represented by a random single view and training persons have $t = 1, 3, 5$ views respectively. In the right part of this table the testing person is represented by several views, i.e. if for instance $t = 3$ then the number of input views is 7. In case when there is no majority of winning networks assigned to one person we get a *no decision* category.

Table 5: Results for face recognition – preselected choice of training faces; recognition rate – column R; no decision rate – column N; error rate – column E (all rates in percents); t – size of training set per person.

t	R	E	R	N	E
1	78.2	21.8	74.4	15.5	10.1
3	94.1	5.9	100.0	0.0	0.0
5	97.4	2.6	100.0	0.0	0.0

3.4 Comparison of memory capacity for Hopfield and subnetwork approach

Let N be number of pixels in one image, C_H – number of bytes occupied by weight matrix in a Hopfield approach, K_H – number of images stored in Hopfield case, C_S – number of bytes occupied by bias and offsets matrices in the subnetwork approach, and K_S – number of images stored in the subnetwork approach.

Then $C_H = N^2 \cdot 4$ and according Morita's implementation of Hopfield associative memory $K_H \approx 0.4N$. Hence

$$C_H = 10N \cdot 0.4N \approx 10 K_H N .$$

But

$$C_S = K_S \frac{N}{16} \cdot (1 + 2 + 2) = \frac{5}{16} K_S N .$$

Assuming $C_H = C_S$, we get:

$$10 K_H N \approx \frac{5}{16} K_S N .$$

Concluding:

$$\frac{K_S}{K_H} \approx 32 .$$

4 Conclusions

Complete neural solution is proposed which combines: architecture design, image storage, image compression, and image associative recall. Gray scale images are represented by recurrent neural subnetworks which together with a competition layer create an associative memory. The single recurrent subnetwork $\mathcal{N}_i$ is designed for the i-th image and it implements a stochastic nonlinear operator $\mathcal{F}_i$. It is shown that under realistic assumptions $\mathcal{F}_i$ has a unique attractor which is located in the vicinity of the original image. When at the input a noisy, incomplete or distorted image is presented, the associative recall is implemented in two stages. Firstly, a competition layer finds the most invariant subnetwork. Next, the selected recurrent subnetwork reconstructs in few iterations the original image. The degree of invariance for the subnetwork $\mathcal{N}_i$ on the input g is measured by the normalised MSE between g and $\mathcal{F}_i(g)$.

Associative memory based on recurrent subnetworks idea has the following features:

1. Each subnetwork represents one image and when it is encoded, the compression ratio between 10 to 20 is achieved;

2. There is no spurious states;

3. Each subnetwork has a unique stable point very close to the original image;

4. Convergence is achieved in 5–10 global iterations;

5. Images of different resolution can be memorized and associated;

6. Associative recall is based on invariance property;

7. Invariance property is checked on only 10% of pixels from the whole image;

8. Perfect associative recall for strong image distortions is observed, e.g.:

   (a) for Gaussian and speckle noise with $\sigma \leq 2*$ pixel range;

   (b) for spiky noise on $p \leq 70\%$ of pixel area;

   (c) random or deterministic partial data on $s \leq 95\%$ of image pixels;

9. Strong recognition properties in case of face data base are observed:

   (a) for random training poses the recognition rate is about 97.5%;

   (b) for three preselected training poses the recognition rate for Olivetti face data base is 100%;

   (c) local connections in subnetworks can be chosen randomly with small deterioration of system performance and significant acceleration of subnetwork design;

10. About 30 times more image objects can be represented in this associative memory than in the best implementation of Hopfield approach.

References

[1] Amari, S.: Learning patterns and pattern sequences by self-organizing nets of threshold elements, IEEE Transactions on Computers C-21, 1197-1206 (1972).

[2] Amari, S.: Neural theory of association and concept formation, Biological Cybernetics 26, 175-185 (1977).

[3] Hassoun, M.H. (ed.): Associative Neural Memories: Theory and Implementation. Oxford University Press 1993.

[4] Hotelling, H.: Analysis of a complex of statistical variables into principal components, Journal of Educational Psychology 24, 417-441 (1933).

[5] Jacquin, A.: Image coding based on a fractal theory of iterated contractive image transformations, IEEE Transactions on Image Processing 1, 18-30 (1992).

[6] Jain, A.K.: Fundamentals of Digital Image Processing. Prentice-Hall 1989.

[7] Fisher, Y. (ed.): Fractal Image Compression – Theory and Application. Springer Verlag 1995.

[8] Kohonen, T.:, Correlation matrix memories, IEEE Transactions on Computers C-21, 353-359 (1972).

[9] Kohonen, T.: Self-Organization and Associative Memory. Springer Verlag 1988.

[10] Oja, E.: Principal components, minor components, and linear neural networks, Neural Networks 5, 927-935 (1992).

[11] Skarbek, W., Ghuwar, M., Ignasiak, K.: Character classification by projections into KLT subspaces, Proc. of 8th Portuguese Conference on Pattern Recognition RECPAD'96, Guimaraes, 223-226 (1996).

Optimal models for visual recognition [1]

Matevž Kovačič, Bojan Kverh, and Franc Solina

1 Introduction

Over the years building models of objects from sensory data has been tackled in various ways. Following [1], model based recognition methods are divided into graph theoretic and non graph theoretic. Graph theoretic methods use graphs as a representation for objects and scenes. An object is divided into parts. Nodes of a graph that describes an object characterize the parts of the object and arcs of the graph represent spatial relations among parts of the object. Recognition of an object in the scene is performed as search for a subgraph isomorphism between the scene graph and each of the model graphs. In non graph theoretic methods, local features are used to describe the object. Grimson and Lozano-Peres [3], used a constrained tree search to efficiently coordinate values of point features and surface normals in models to those found in the scenes.

We are not interested in comparing the efficiency of the models in terms of time and space complexity, but to select the most *probable* model among the predetermined set of classes of models.

Suppose the scene consists of an object represented as a set of points in a two dimensional plane. For the sake of the argument, let us limit the set of possible models to the set of single valued functions. If there are n such points then the object can always be explained by a model of a form of a polynomial of degree up to $n - 1$. Statistical measures would prefer such a model over, say, a much simpler model such as a linear curve which, for example, misclassifies a single instance in our set of observations. Clearly, the measure of a model justification must take into account the complexity and the accuracy of a model.

In general, there is an infinite number of models which explain the data. A crucial question is which model to choose. There are four principles for model justification. William of Ockham proposed the principle known as *Occam's razor:* if there are alternative explanations for a phenomenon, then, all other things being equal, we should select the simplest one[2]. Identification of the 'simplicity of an object' with 'an object having short effective description' is the adaptation of Occam's razor principle to science. From the set of *consistent* models $\mathcal{M}$ of observations of objects E we should choose the one which is the shortest:

$$\arg \min_{M \in \mathcal{M}} I(M) \qquad M \text{ is consistent with } E,$$

where $I(x) = -\log_2 P(x)$ denote the information of event x.

[1] This work was supported by the Ministry of Science and Technology of Republic of Slovenia (Project J2-6187), European Union Copernicus Program (Grant 1068 RECCAD), and by U.S. – Slovene Joint Board (Project #95-158).

[2] According to Bertrand Russel, the actual phrase used by William of Ockham was: "It is vain to do with more that can be done with fewer."

Fisher's *maximum likelihood principle* says that for given data E the model M which maximizes the posterior probability of data given model should be selected:

$$\arg \max_{M \in \mathcal{M}} P(E|M) = \arg \min_{M \in \mathcal{M}} I(E|M) .$$

We may observe several characteristics provided by empirical data or considerations based on symmetry probabilistic laws etc., which can be used as constraints in determining the model given data. Usually, these constraints are not sufficient to determine the distribution of models. E.T. Jaynes proposed the *maximum entropy principle* which is used to select the appropriate prior distribution of models given constraints. Maximum entropy selects the prior probability of models $p_i = p_{M_i}$ which maximize the entropy function and is consistent with obtained constraints

$$\arg \max H(p_1, \ldots, p_n) = -\sum_{i=1}^{n} p_i \log_2 p_i \qquad p_i \text{ is consistent with constraints}$$

For example, consider a loaded die ($n = 6$). If we observed that the average throw gives the average a, we have two constraints

$$\sum_{i=1}^{n} i\,p_i \;=\; a$$

$$\sum_{i_1}^{n} p_i \;=\; 1,$$

which must be taken in consideration in maximizing the entropy. Observe that if we selected any prior distribution of models which would not maximize the entropy given constraints we would decrease entropy (i.e. add information) without justification.

Rissanen [12] advocates the use of information content of observations relative to a model which is called *Minimum Description Length (MDL) principle*. According to the MDL principle not only the accuracy of the model given data but also the complexity of the model should be taken in the consideration when selecting the appropriate model of the data. The MDL principle balances two factors: the encoding of a model and the encoding of data given the model. The selected model minimizes the sum of the encoding of the model and the data given model:

$$\arg \min_{M \in \mathcal{M}} \{I(M) + I(E|M)\}$$

In the process of growth (specialization) of a model the number of misclassified instances of data decreases and so does the encoding of data given refined model; on the other hand, specialization results in the increase of the model encoding, since the length of a model increases.

It can be proven (see [8], pp. 316-317) that both, the maximum likelihood principle and the maximum entropy principle are special cases of the MDL principle. The paper describes the use of MDL principle in selecting appropriate models of objects. In Sect. 2 MDL principle is briefly presented. It is shown that the ML (maximum likelihood) principle is a special case of MDL principle. Finally, in Sect 3 an approximate encoding for non graph theoretic models are presented. A greedy algorithm for model selection is presented in Sect 4. The algorithm takes the line segments obtained by the Hough transform [13] on an edge image and eliminates unnecessary edges based on the MDL principle.

2 MDL Principle–an Overview

Since there will generally be several models that explain objects we need a sound basis for grading models. From the set of all possible models $\mathcal{M}$ we shall choose the most probable model. Let $P(M)$ be the probability of model M in the set of all possible models (the definition of $P(M)$ will be discussed in Sect 3) and let $P(E)$ be the probability of object E in the given scene(s). If we assume that the above events are independent, we can express the probability of the model M *given* object E in the scene(s) using Bayes' theorem:

$$P(M|E) = \frac{P(E|M)\,P(M)}{P(E)}.$$

Since the probability $P(E)$ is constant for all $M \in \mathcal{M}$ it follows that the ordering of probability of models depends only of $P(E|M)\,P(M)$. If we express this product using information instead of probabilities it follows immediately that the most probable model given E is the one which minimizes the expression:

$$\arg \min_{M \in \mathcal{M}} \{I(E|M) + I(M)\} \ . \tag{1}$$

Equation 1 balances two factors: $I(E|M)$ the information needed to encode observations E given model M which decreases when M gets more specialized; but on the other hand this causes the increase of $I(M)$, the information needed to encode M itself, and vice versa. Using Bayes' Theorem we have

$$I(E|M) + I(M) = I(M|E) + I(E) \ . \tag{2}$$

Using (2), we can rewrite (1):

$$\arg \min_{M \in \mathcal{M}} \{I(E|M) + I(M)\} \ = \ \arg \min_{M \in \mathcal{M}} \{I(M|E) + I(E)\}$$

Since $I(E)$ is constant (the set of scenes and objects in them is fixed), we have

$$\arg \min_{M \in \mathcal{M}} \{I(E|M) + I(M)\} \ = \ \arg \min_{M \in \mathcal{M}} \{I(M|E)\}$$
$$= \ \arg \max_{M \in \mathcal{M}} \{P(M|E)\} \tag{3}$$

which states that Rissanen's MDL principle actually maximizes $P(M|E)$ over $\mathcal{M}$.

The purpose of concept formation is *information compression;* a model describes or "explains" given data. A model M *compresses* data E if

$$I(E) > I(M) + I(E|M).$$

The most compressible hypothesis is the one with minimal encoding length and with the greatest posterior probability (see Eq 3).

Since results from algorithmic information theory have shown that finding an optimal encoding of a model is equivalent to the halting problem [9], a decidable coding scheme approximation must be adopted for calculating $I(M)$. The problem of calculating $I(M)$ will be discussed in detail in Sect. 3.

3   Approximate Encoding of Models

If we want to apply the MDL principle to model selection we have to compute, according to Eq 1 the probabilities $P(E|M)$ and $P(M)$. The former is usually easy: if we have enough scenes and objects the relative frequency of the success of recognizing object E among all objects in the scene(s):

$$P(E|M) = \frac{correct(M, E)}{correct(M, E) + incorrect(M, E)}$$

is a good approximation.

The evaluation of $P(M)$ (i.e. $I(M)$) is more difficult. How to define the probability (the information) of a model? The exact formulation is beyond the scope of this paper (see [8] for the details); let us just state that the information of the model equals the length of the shortest program that produces a model. Since finding the shortest program that produces a model is undecidable (see [9]), we have to approximate $I(M)$. Therefore we need to encode a model as well as we can to obtain a good approximation of $P(M)$.

The importance of simple explanations has a long history in modeling visual data. Gestalt psychologists summarized their observations in a number of Gestalt principles, one of them being the law of Prägnanz, or the minimum principle, which states that the visual field will be organized in the *simplest* or *the most likely* possible way [4]. Recently, simplicity in terms of the MDL principle has found its applications in computer vision [10, 7, 2, 5, 11]. The MDL principle was proposed, for example, to select the appropriate scale of observing visual data [15].

In the following subsection we encode the information needed to encode a non graph theoretical model. The program that decodes the model is omitted since it is assumed to be fixed and known in advance.

3.1   Model Encoding

In the following we restrict ourselves to modeling binary edge images (the approach can be easily extended to intensity images). Following the MDL principle, we seek to compress the image by using models for description of the image. To evaluate the compression we propose a model for the encoding of intensity images and two models for binary images which enable us to determine the compression of image using a model. The MDL principle will also be used for searching for the most probable model of the image from the set of possible models.

An $m \times n$ intensity image with k levels of intensity can be encoded as a message of length $m \times n$ with k code symbols. Using coding based on stochastic complexity [6], the code length for such a message is:

$$I(E) = L(f_1, \ldots, f_k) = \sum_i f_i \ln \frac{f}{f_i} + \frac{k-1}{2} \ln \frac{f}{2} + \ln \frac{\pi^{k/2}}{\Gamma(k/2)} \tag{4}$$

where $f_i > 0$ is the frequency of symbol (intensity) i in the image, and $f = \sum f_i$. For example, the encoding of $m \times n$ binary image with p zeroes takes

$$L(p, m \times n - p).$$

Let us now consider an alternative way of encoding a $m \times n$ binary image. If we apply an edge detection algorithm the resulting line segments can serve as the model of the image. Every line segment can be encoded by the coordinates of its end points. If the image is presented by k line segments, we have to encode $2\,k$ points in the $m \times n$ image which takes (see Eq 4)

$$I(M) = L(2\,k, m \times n - 2\,k). \tag{5}$$

Every black point in the image is modeled by exactly one line segment. If there are s line segments and $f_i > 0$ points is modeled by the i-th line segment, the information needed to encode the points to segments mapping takes

$$L_{p,s} = L(f_1, \ldots, f_s). \tag{6}$$

Let $P_s = \{p_1, \ldots, p_{f_i}\}$ be the set of points which belong (i.e. are modeled by) to the segment s defined by points A and B. (see Fig. 1).

Using line segment s to model the point $p_j = (x_j, y_j)$ we only need to encode x_j since y_j can be computed using the equation of the line segment s. Note that in the case that the line segment s does not accurately model the point p_j, the error $\delta_{s,j}$ must also be encoded to determine y_j. Every point in our model is represented by its x coordinate and the error of its corresponding line segment model

$$p_j = (x_j, y_j) = (x_j, k\,x_j + \delta_j + n)$$

where line segment s is defined as $y = k\,x + n$. To encode points belonging to segment s we first need to encode the x coordinate for every point. We may choose the segment $s = (A, B) = (x(A), y(A), x(B), y(B))$ in such a way that all x coordinates of points in P_s fall within $[x(A), x(B)]$. Clearly, the x coordinate of every point in P_s can be mapped to $X'_s = [0, x(B) - x(A) + 1]$. Let $X_s = \{f_{s,x} \mid x \in X'_s \wedge f_{s,x} > 0\}$ be the non-zero part of frequency distribution

56

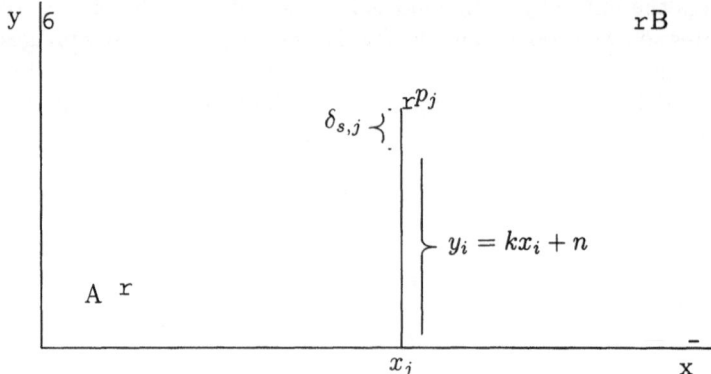

Figure 1: A set of points $p_1, \ldots, p_j, \ldots, p_{f_i}$ modeled by line segment (A, B)

of x coordinates of points in P_s mapped onto X'_s. To encode the x coordinates of points in P_s using segment s and mapping X'_s we need

$$L_{s,X_s} = L_{\{f_{s,x_i} \in X_s\}}(f_{s,x_i}) \qquad (7)$$

bits of information.

The set of corrections of a line segment model s of points in P_s is coded in a similar fashion as the coding of x coordinates of points in P_s. Let Δ_s be the non-zero part of frequency distribution of corrections of model s of P_s. To encode the corrections needed to determine P_s using line segment s as a model of points in P_s we need

$$L_{s,\Delta_s} = L_{\{f_{s,\delta_i} \in \Delta_s\}}(f_{s,\delta_i}) \qquad (8)$$

To summarize, the information needed to encode the points P_s given model s is the sum of encodings given in Eqs 7-8. The encoding of the complete model M of image of p points which consists of s line segments is the sum of the encodings of the constituent line segment models with addition of the mapping of points to line segments encoding

$$I(M) = L_{p,s} + \sum_{i=1}^{s} (L_{i,X_i} + L_{i,\Delta_i})$$

4 Algorithm

The implementation of the MDL principle to modeling of binary edge images with line segments is relatively simple. According to Eq 1 we search for minimal (i.e. most compressive) model of the image. In our case candidate models are sets of line segments. The input image is a typical result of processing an intensity image with an edge finder operator. Such edge images must be typically "cleaned" before higher level processing such as stereo matching or recognition can start. Typically such "cleaning" operations consist of: thinning of edges, filling small gaps, linking of edge elements, different kinds of filtering etc. Running the Hough transform on an "uncleaned" edge image results in a multitude of overlapping lines. Different methods, for example cluster analysis [14], are proposed to select a subset of lines obtained by the Hough transform. We propose to use the MDL principle to select from this multitude of possible line models only the necessary ones. The algorithm starts with the full model (all line segments resulting from the Hough transform) then applies a local peak detection and a treshold in Hough space. Each edge point is then assigned to the closest line segment according to Euclidian distance. Line segments that do not contain enough points (usually 15) are deleted so that the remaining ones can be handled by the algorithm. We need to reduce the number of line segments because our algorithm has time complexity of $O(n^2)$, where n is the initial number of line segments. The main algorithm gradually refines the model by removing line segments from the model. It stops when there is no refined model which would be more compressive as the current model. We are not interested in global optimization over a set of possible models since this would be intractable. Besides, the experiments show that local optimization produces satisfactory results.

The algorithm performs a greedy search in the space of possible models minimizing the sum of the encoding of the model and of the image given the model. In every iteration of the algorithm we remove the line segment which results in the most compressive model. Let $M = \{l_1, \ldots, l_n\}$ be the original model of the image E consisting of n line segments. We obtain the approximation of the most compressive model as

1. Repeat

2. $C = I(M) + I(E|M)$ { complexity of the current model }

3.   For every line segment $l_k \in M$

4. $M' = M - \{l_k\}$

5.   If $I(M') + I(E|M') < I(M) + I(E|M)$

6.   Let $M = M'$

7. Until $C > I(M) + I(E|M)$

5 Experiments

We performed several experiments on finding segment models of binary edge images. The initial model of a binary edge image was obtained by performing the Hough transform. The transform usually results in a model with many redundant line segments. When the above selection algorithm proceeds, the majority of line segments are removed. The snapshots of the process are given in Fig. 2.

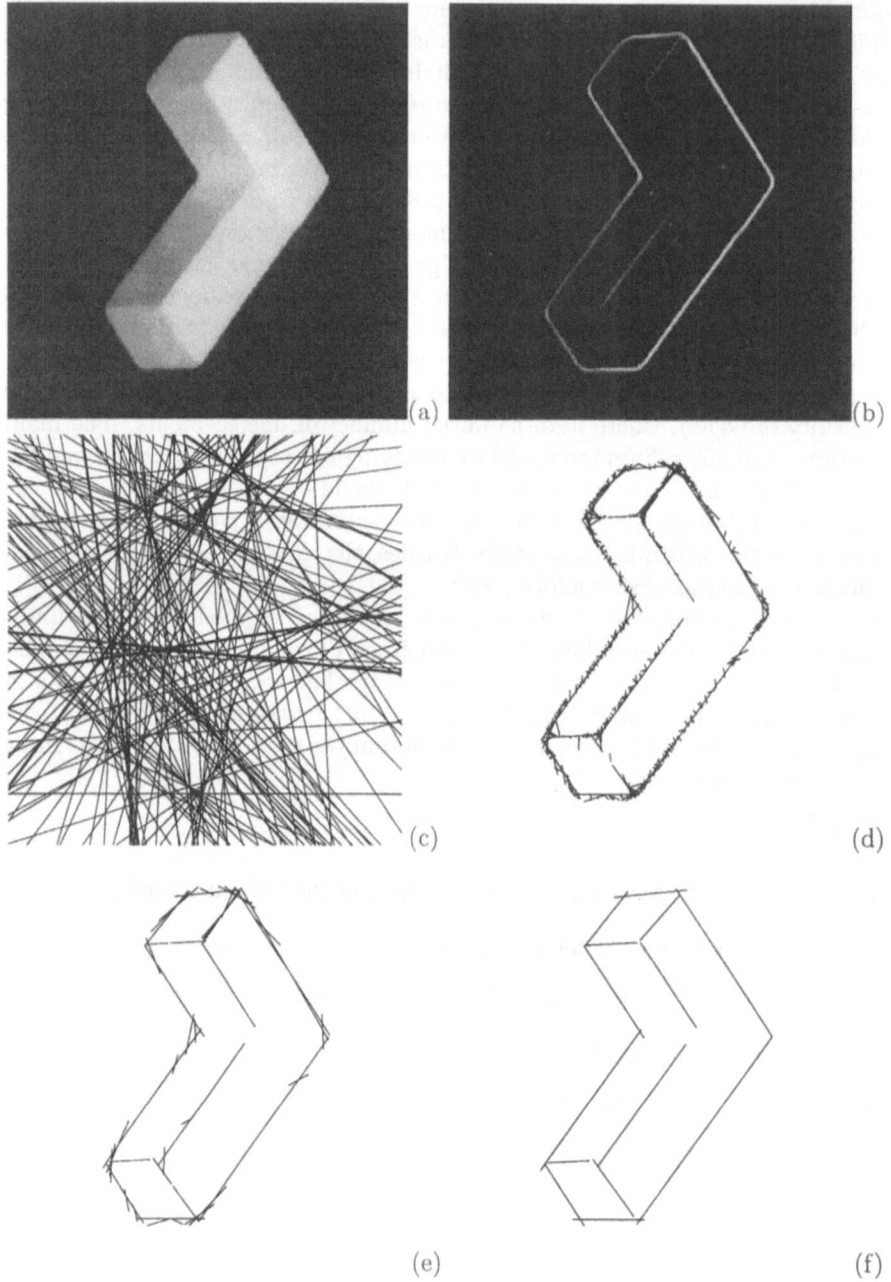

Figure 2: The algorithm performance: (a) original image (b) edges found by an edge operator (c) line segments found by the Hough transform (d) broken up line segments (e) remaining line segments after deleting those with less than 15 points (f) final model of the image

On noisy images the Hough transform produces many spurious lines. Scattered points which are far from, but on the same line as actual edges, cause the extension of the corresponding line models (see Fig. 2(c)). Therefore, we may use the above algorithm also for searching the modifications of the line segments produced by Hough transform before the actual selection of line segments.

The algorithm for breaking such line models is completely the same as described above, but instead of refining the model by eliminating line segments, we break them into more parts to obtain better models of the image. Results are shown in Fig 2(d). Fig. 2(e) shows the line segments remaining after deletion of the ones, containing less than 15 points and Fig. 2(f) the final result.

6 Conclusions

Minimum description length (MDL) principle can be used as a method for model construction from sensory data. The application of the MDL principle requires the computation of information content of the model. The paper describes the generic encoding for a non graph theoretic model. For demonstration, modeling of edges with straight line segments was performed. This example demonstrates that instead of heuristic approaches such low-level image processing tasks can be founded on sound theoretical basis.

The issue of time complexity of object reconstruction is briefly addressed. It is proposed that models with various time complexity and accuracy should be used to achieve optimal time complexity along with high reconstruction accuracy.

References

[1] R. T. Chin and C. R. Dyer. Model-based recognition in robotic vision. *ACM Computing Surveys*, 18:67–108, March 1986.

[2] P. Fua and A. J. Hanson. Objective functions for feature discrimination. In *Proceedings of the Eleventh International Joint Conference on Artificial Intelligence*, pages 1596–1602, Detroit, MI, 1989.

[3] E. Grimson and T. Lozano-Perez. Model-based recognition and localization from sparse range and tactile data. *International Journal of Robotics*, 18:67–108, March 1986.

[4] J. Hochberg. *Perceptual Organization*, chapter Levels of Perceptual Organization, pages 255–276. Lawrence Erlbaum Associates, New Jersey, 1981.

[5] K. C. Keeler. Map representations and optimal encoding for image segmentation. Technical Report CICS-TH-292, Center for Intelligent Control Systems, March 1991.

[6] R. E. Krichevsky and V. K. Trofimov. The performance of universal coding. *IEEE Transactions on Information Theory*, IT-27:199–207, 1981.

[7] Y. G. Leclerc. Constructing simple stable descriptions for image partitioning. *International Journal of Computer Vision*, 3:73–102, 1989.

[8] M. Li and P. Vitanyi. *An introduction to Kolmogorov complexity and its applications.* Springer-Verlag, New York, 1993.

[9] S. Muggleton. *Course on Inductive Logic Programming*, 1993.

[10] A. P. Pentland. Part segmentation for object recognition. *Neural Computation*, 1:82–91, 1989.

[11] M. Pilu and R.B. Fisher. Recognition of geons by parametrically deformable contour models. In R.Cipolla and B.Buxton, editors, *Fourth European Conference on Computer Vision*, volume I of *Lecture Notes in Computer Science*, Berlin, April 1996. Springer-Verlag.

[12] J. Rissanen. Universal coding, information, prediction, and estimation. *IEEE Transactions on Information Theory*, 30(4):629–636, 1984.

[13] A. Rosenfeld and A. C. Kak. *Digital Picture Processing*, volume 2. Academic Press, Orlando, FL, 1982.

[14] M. J. Silberman and J. Sklansky. Toward line detection by cluster analysis. In K. Voss, D. Chetverikov, and G. Sommer, editors, *Computer Analysis of Images and Patterns*, pages 117–122, Berlin, 1989. Akademie-Verlag.

[15] Franc Solina and Aleš Leonardis. Selective scene modeling. In *Proceedings of the 11th International Conference on Pattern Recognition*, pages A:87–90, The Hague, The Netherlands, September 1992. IAPR, IEEE Computer Society Press.

Order of points on a line segment

Atsushi Imiya

1 Introduction

The Hough transform is a method for the detection of many lines on a plane
[1,2,3,4]. This method achieves line detection by converting the line fitting problem on an imaging plane to a peak search problem in an accumulator space using
the voting procedure. Although the Hough transform provides a method for line
detection, this transform can not detect line segments. For the detection of line
segments, it is necessary to detect both endpoints of each line segment. The
detection of pairs of endpoints of line segments is mainly performed using the
point following procedure by local window operation along each line; that is,
assuming the connectivity of digitized points, the algorithm follows a series of
sample points which should lie on a line. The method is, however, equivalent to
a whole area search in the worst case, because it is necessary to investigate the
connectivity of all sample points in the region of interest, point by point.
In this paper, we define a complete order of points which lie on a line segment,
both on a plane and in a space, using the duality between points and lines on a
plane and the duality between points and planes in a space, respectively [5, 6].
This complete order is defined as the angles between normalized homogeneous
vectors of the sample points and a reference point. Furthermore, the pair of the
top and bottom elements of this complete order along a line segment corresponds
to the pair of endpoints of a line segment. Thus, the detection of line segments is
devised by sorting of the sample points according to this order after parameters
of each line segment have been determined. Moreover, segmentation of colinear
line segments is achieved by scanning the sample points along each line.

2 Duality between Points and Lines

In this section, we briefly summarize the duality between points and Grassman-
nians. We concern lines on two-dimensional Euclidean plane $\mathbf{R}^2$ and lines and
planes in three-dimensional Euclidean space $\mathbf{R}^3$. However, we deal with the problem in n-dimensional Euclidean space $\mathbf{R}^n$ if it is necessary to preserve the generality of problem in Euclidean spaces. Defining the orthogonal coordinate system
x_1-x_2-x_3-$\cdots$-x_n in $\mathbf{R}^n$, a vector in $\mathbf{R}^n$ is expressed by $\boldsymbol{x} = (x_1, x_2, \cdots, x_n)^{\top}$
where $\cdot^{\top}$ is the transpose of a vector. The inner product of vectors is defined by
$\boldsymbol{x}^{\top}\boldsymbol{y}$, and the Euclidean distance between $\boldsymbol{x}$ and $\boldsymbol{y}$ by $|\boldsymbol{x} - \boldsymbol{y}|$. The homogeneous
coordinate of $\boldsymbol{x} \in \mathbf{R}^3$ [5, 6] is defined by $\boldsymbol{\xi} = (x_0, x_1, x_2, x_3,)^{\top}$. We can set
$x_0 = 1$ for a point in $\mathbf{R}^n$.
Let S^{n-1} be the unit sphere of $\mathbf{R}^n$ consisting of all points $\boldsymbol{x}$ with distance 1
from the origin. We call S^{n-1} the n-sphere. Here, we define the n-dimensional

positive unit hemisphere S_+^{n-1}. For $n = 1$, $S^0 = [-1, 1]$. The positive half-space is defined by

$$\mathbf{R}_+^n = \{x | x_n > 0\}, \ n \geq 1. \tag{1}$$

Now, by setting

$$H_+^{n-1} = S^{n-1} \bigcap \mathbf{R}_+^n, \ n \geq 1, \tag{2}$$

the positive unit hemisphere is defined by

$$S_+^{n-1} = S_+^{n-2} \bigcup H_+^{n-1}, \ n \geq 2. \tag{3}$$

Setting a and b to be a pair of points on a line, where a and b are two-dimensional vectors and three-dimensional vectors for a planar line and a spatial line, respectively, the homogeneous coordinates of a and b are denoted by α and β, respectively. The ratio of the second order determinants of matrix L, where

$$L = \begin{pmatrix} \alpha^\top \\ \beta^\top \end{pmatrix}, \tag{4}$$

determines an oriented line uniquely[6]. Denoting $p = r(L)$ to be a transformation from a pair of vectors to a vector defined by the ratio of the second order determinants of matrix L, two vectors

$$r \begin{pmatrix} \alpha^\top \\ \beta^\top \end{pmatrix}, \ r \begin{pmatrix} \beta^\top \\ \alpha^\top \end{pmatrix} \tag{5}$$

correspond to the same line. For a planar line and a spatial line, $r(L)$ are elements of $\mathbf{R}^3$ and $\mathbf{R}^6$, respectively. Since the ratios determine a line, it is possible to normalize the length of $r(L)$ to unity.
Next, setting

$$\xi = (1, x_1, x_2, \cdots, x_n)^\top \tag{6}$$

to be the argument vector, for a point α on S_+^n,

$$\alpha^\top \xi = 0 \tag{7}$$

corresponds to a plane. Conversely, if ξ is fixed, eq. (7) defines a plane in $\mathbf{R}^{n+1}$. for $\alpha_0 \geq 0$. Therefore,

$$C = \{\alpha | \alpha^\top \xi = 0, \ \alpha \in S_+^n\} \tag{8}$$

defines a great-circle on the unit sphere.
Setting $\alpha = (a_0, a_1, a_2, a_3)^\top$ and $\beta = (b_0, b_1, b_2, b_3)^\top$, 2×2 miner determinants of L such that

$$P_{ij} = \begin{vmatrix} a_i & a_j \\ b_i & b_j \end{vmatrix}, \ 0 \leq i < j \leq 3, \tag{9}$$

determines a point

$$p = (p_{01}, p_{02}, p_{03}, p_{12}, p_{13}, p_{23})^\top, \tag{10}$$

on S_+^5 such that

$$p_{ij} = \frac{P_{ij}}{\sqrt{P_{01}^2 + P_{02}^2 + P_{03}^2 + P_{12}^2 + P_{13}^2 + P_{23}^2}}. \tag{11}$$

Conversely, from a point on S_+^5, the direction vector of a line is computed by $u = (p_{01}, p_{02}, p_{03})^\top$, and a point on a line is obtained as the solution of the equation

$$\begin{pmatrix} p_{02} & -p_{01} & 0 \\ p_{03} & 0 & -p_{01} \\ 0 & p_{03} & -p_{02} \end{pmatrix} \begin{pmatrix} a_1 \\ a_2 \\ a_3 \end{pmatrix} = \begin{pmatrix} p_{12} \\ p_{13} \\ p_{23} \end{pmatrix}. \tag{12}$$

Furthermore, setting α, β, and γ to be the homogeneous coordinates of the three-dimensional vectors a, b, and c, respectively, the equation

$$det(x, \alpha, \beta, \gamma) = 0, \tag{13}$$

where $x = (1, x_1, x_2, x_3)^\top$ is the argument vector, determines an oriented plane, which passes through a, b, and c, uniquely. Thus, setting

$$p_1 = \begin{vmatrix} \alpha_1 & \beta_1 & \gamma_1 \\ \alpha_2 & \beta_2 & \gamma_2 \\ \alpha_3 & \beta_3 & \gamma_3 \end{vmatrix}, \quad p_2 = - \begin{vmatrix} \alpha_0 & \beta_0 & \gamma_0 \\ \alpha_2 & \beta_2 & \gamma_2 \\ \alpha_3 & \beta_3 & \gamma_3 \end{vmatrix}$$

$$p_3 = \begin{vmatrix} \alpha_0 & \beta_0 & \gamma_0 \\ \alpha_1 & \beta_1 & \gamma_1 \\ \alpha_3 & \beta_3 & \gamma_3 \end{vmatrix}, \quad p_4 = - \begin{vmatrix} \alpha_0 & \beta_0 & \gamma_0 \\ \alpha_1 & \beta_1 & \gamma_1 \\ \alpha_2 & \beta_2 & \gamma_2 \end{vmatrix}, \tag{14}$$

the ration $p = (p_1 : p_2 : p_3 : p_4)$ determines an oriented plane, uniquely. Denoting $r(P)$ to be the transform from a triplet α, β, and γ to p where $P = (\alpha, \beta, \gamma)$. $r(P)$ is an element of R^4. Since the ratios determine a plane, it is possible to normalize the length of $r(M)$ to unity. Thus, $r(P)$ is an element of S_+^3. Six triplets of vectors

$$\begin{array}{ccc} P_1 = (\alpha, \beta, \gamma) & P_2 = (\gamma, \alpha, \beta) & P_3 = (\beta, \gamma, \alpha) \\ P_4 = (\alpha, \gamma, \beta) & P_5 = (\beta, \alpha, \gamma) & P_6 = (\gamma, \beta, \alpha) \end{array} \tag{15}$$

correspond to the same plane.
These geometric properties impliy the following propositions.
[Proposition 1.1] There is a one-to-one mapping between planar lines and points on S_+^2.
[Proposition 1.2] There is a one-to-one mapping between planes and points on S_+^3.
[Proposition 1.3] There is a one-to-one mapping between spatial lines and a points on S_+^5.
[Proposition 2] Equation (8) defines a one-to-one mapping from a point on the plane to a great-circle on the positive unit hemisphere.

Propositions 1.1, 1.2, and 2 determine the duality; that is, a point on the plane determines a plane on the positive unit hemisphere, and a plane on the positive unit hemisphere determines a point on the plane. This property is called the duality of lines and points, because a large circle on the positive unit hemisphere is a plane on the positive unit hemisphere.

These propositions imply that we can adopt S_+^{k-1} as the accumulator of the Hough transformation for the detection of lines and planes. Thus, we obtain the following general framework for the detection of planar lines, spatial lines, and planes.

```
 1 :  procedure  DETECT
 2 :  begin
 3 :     Set γ, T, i := 1
 4 :     while  i ≤ T  do  ;
 5 :        begin
 6 :           Select m samples from Σ
 7 :           Compute a point q = p/|p| suchthat q ∈ S_+^{k-1}
 8 :           Vote 1 to a point p
 9 :           if  the number of votings to q is larger than γ
10 :              then   output a line (or a plane) which corresponds to q
11 :           Σ := Σ \ {points on a line (or a plane) which corresponds to q}
12 :           Σ(q) := {points on a line (or a plane) which corresponds to q}
13 :           i := i + 1
14 :        end
15 :  end
```

It is possible to embed S_+^{k-1} in the positive half-cube B_+^k of R^k. Thus, it is not necessary to compute any trigonometric calculus.

The computational complexity of a $m \times m$ matrix is m^3. Since we deal with the cases in which m is 2 and 3, the computational complexity of line detection by voting procedure mainly depends on the number of iterations, T. We estimate the order of the expected number of computation time for this algorithm. Assuming the expected numbers of lines or planes and samples in each line or plane are p and q, respectively, the probability that a pair or a triplet of samples is selected from the same line or the same plane is $\binom{p \times q}{r} \times \binom{q}{r}^{-1} \times p^{-1}$, where r is the number of samples required to determine a point on S_+^{k-1}; that is, r is 2 and 3 for the line detection and the plane detection, respectively, since the total numbers of the combinations of samples and combinations of samples on a line or a plane are $\binom{p \times q}{r}$ and $p \times \binom{q}{r}$, respectively. If the threshold and the total number of iterations are γ and T, P, γ, and T should satisfy the relation $PT = \gamma$. This relation concludes that the order of T should be γp^{r-1}. Therefore, the expected time computational complexity of this algorithm is $O(\gamma p^{r-1})$. In this algorithm, a point on S_+^{k-1} is computed using the second order determinants of a $2 \times (n+1)$ matrix, where n is the number of dimensions of the space, respectively. Therefore, if we are concerned to planar line, and spatial lines and planes, r are two and three, respectively. Furthermore, because there exist p possibilities for the selection of a reference point when we detect a line from $O(p)$ samples, the order of γ is $O(p)$.

A point on S_+^{k-1} is computed using the m-th order determinants of a $m \times (n + 1)$ matrix, where m and n are the numbers of vectors which are necessary for the determination of lines and planes, and the number of dimensions of the space, respectively. For the detection of lines and planes, m are two and three, respectively. Furthermore, if we are concerned to planar line, and spatial lines and planes, n are two and three, respectively. These relations conclude that there is the relation $k = \frac{1}{2} \begin{pmatrix} m \\ n+1 \end{pmatrix}$, for the detection of lines and planes in $\mathbf{R}^2$ and $\mathbf{R}^3$.

3   Complete Order of Points on A Line Segment

Points on a line segment

$$s(ab) = \{x \mid x = sa + (1 - s)b, 0 \le s \le 1\} \tag{16}$$

define a family of great semi-circles

$$\eta^\top (s\alpha + (1 - s)\beta) = 0, \ 0 \le s \le 1, \ \eta \in S_+^{n-1}, \text{s.t. } n = 3, \text{ or } 6 \tag{17}$$

which are bounded by two great semi-circles $\eta^\top \alpha = 0$ and $\eta^\top \beta = 0$.
Setting

$$\xi = s\alpha + (1 - s)\beta, \tag{18}$$

if a point moves on $s(ab)$ from a to b, the normalized vector of a plane moves on a curve

$$c(\alpha\beta) = \left\{ \bar{\xi} \mid \bar{\xi} = \frac{\xi}{|\xi|} \right\} \tag{19}$$

from α to β. $c(\alpha\beta)$ is a part of a semi-circle $S_+^{n-1} \bigcap \mathbf{R}^n$. Conversely, if a point moves on $c(ab)$, this point defines a family of great semi-circles given by eq. (17). Furthermore, a family of eq. (17) defines a set of points defined eq. (16). These geometric properties imply the following propositions.

[Proposition 3.1] There is a one-to-one mapping between line segments in $\mathbf{R}^n$ and segments of great semi-circles on S_+^n.

[Proposition 3.2] There is a one-to-one mapping between points on a line segment in $\mathbf{R}^n$ and points on a segment of a great semi-circle on S_+^n.

Considering propositions 3.1 and 3.2, we define an order of points on line segment $s(ab)$. For a point set $\{\bar{\xi}_i\}_{i=1}^q$ on $c(\alpha\beta)$, such that $\bar{\xi}_1 = \alpha$ and $\bar{\xi}_n = \beta$, $\{\theta_i\}_{i=1}^q$,

$$\theta_i = \cos^{-1} \bar{\xi}_i^\top \bar{\xi}_1, \tag{20}$$

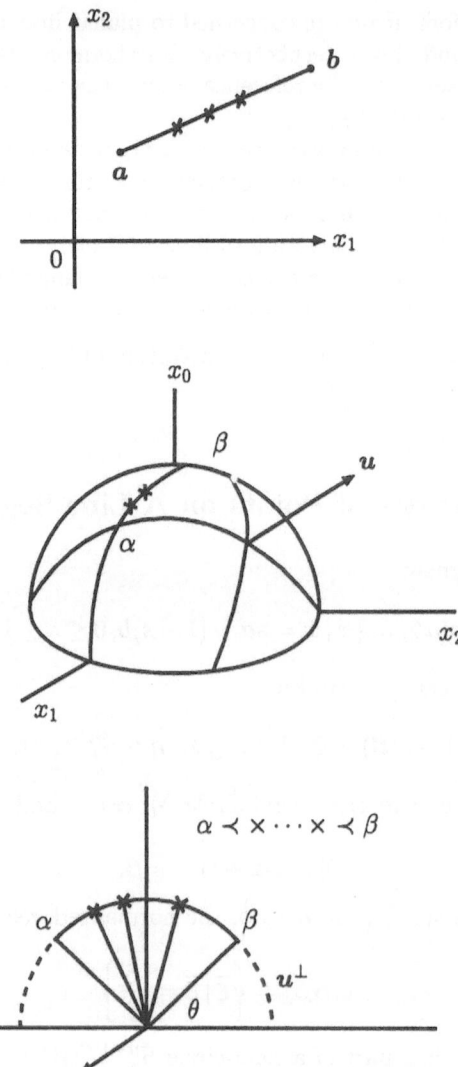

Figure 1

From top to bottom, a planar line segment, a set of great half-circles, and an order of points along a great half-circle. The half great-circle lies on plane $u^\perp$ which is perpendicular to the vector $u = \alpha \times \beta$.

are the set of angles between $\bar{\xi}_1$ and $\{\bar{\xi}_i\}_{i=1}^n$. Each θ_i satisfies the relation $0 \le \theta_i < \pi$. Since $0 \le \theta_i < \pi$, $\theta_i < \theta_j$ if and only if $\bar{\xi}_i^T \bar{\xi}_1 > \bar{\xi}_j^T \bar{\xi}_1$, we can define a complete order for points on $c(\alpha\beta)$.

[Definition 1] For points on $c(\alpha\beta)$, we set $\xi_i \prec \xi_j$ if $\theta_j > \theta_i$.

An order of $\{\bar{\xi}_i\}_{i=1}^q$ yields a complete order of a point set $\Sigma = \{x\}_{i=1}^q$, since there is a one-to-one correspondence between $(1, x_1, x_2 \cdots, x_i)^T$ and $(x_1, x_2 \cdots, x_i)^T$.

[Definition 2] For points on $s(ab)$, we set $x_i \prec x_j$ if $\xi_i \prec \xi_j$.

Figure 1 illustrates a planar line segment, a set of great semi-circles, and an order of points along a great semi-circle from top to bottom.

For the definition of this order, the homogeneous coordinate of an endpoint is used as the reference point. However, it is impossible to determine whether the first sample is an endpoint or not. Thus, we derive an algorithm for the determination of order which assumes the detection of an endpoint.

Setting p and q to be the first and second samples on a line segment, we define a vector $r = p - q$. Using vector r, it is possible to separate a set of samples Σ into three subsets

$$\Sigma_- = \{x_i \mid x_i - p = -\tau r\}, \ \Sigma_0 = \{p\}, \ \Sigma_+ = \{x_i \mid x_i - p = \tau r\} \quad (21)$$

such that $\Sigma_- \bigcap \Sigma_+ = \emptyset$ and $\Sigma_- \bigcup \Sigma_0 \bigcup \Sigma_+ = \Sigma$ for $\tau > 0$.

This decomposition implies the following property for the ordering of points on a line segment, because it is possible to assume that p is the bottom of the order for points in $\Sigma_0 \bigcup \Sigma_+$ and that p is the top of the order for points in $\Sigma_- \bigcup \Sigma_0$.

[Proposition 4] For points on $s(ab)$, $x_i \prec p$ if $\xi_i \in \Sigma_-$, and $x_i \succ p$ if $\xi_i \in \Sigma_+$.

Proposition 4 yields the following algorithm for the ordering of points on a line segment.

```
1 : procedure  ORDER
2 :   begin
3 :     Select randomly x_i and x_j from Σ
4 :     Set p := x_i, q := x_j, and r := p − q
5 :     Sort elements of Σ,
6 :     ⊥(Σ) := x_σ(1) and ⊤(Σ) := x_σ(n)
7 :   end
```

The sorting in line 5 is achieved according to the definitions 3.1 and 3.2, and proposition 4. The time complexity for the sorting in line 5 determines the total complexity of this algorithm. The random sorting achieves the procedure in line 5, because in line 3 the algorithm select a point randomly. Therefore, the time complexity of this algorithm is $O(q \log q)$ for q points, if we adopt the random sampling procedure [7].

4 Separation of Line Segments

The algorithm proposed in section 3 detects a pair of endpoints of a line segment. For the detection of colinear line segments, it is necessary to define a criterion for the separation of colinear line segments. We adopt the Euclidean distance between a pair of successive points in the order proposed in section 3 as a criterion for the separation of colinear line segments.
Setting

$$\sigma(\Sigma) = \langle x_{\sigma(1)}, x_{\sigma(2)}, \cdots, x_{\sigma(q)} \rangle \qquad (22)$$

to be the ordered list of sample points, Σ, we define the derivative of a list Σ

$$\sigma(\dot{\Sigma}) = \langle \dot{x}_{\sigma(1)}, \dot{x}_{\sigma(2)}, \cdots, \dot{x}_{\sigma(q-1)} \rangle, \qquad (23)$$

where $\dot{x}_{\sigma(i)} = x_{\sigma(i+1)} - x_{\sigma(i)}$ for $1 \leq i \leq n-1$. Furthermore, we define $|\sigma(\dot{\Sigma})|$ as

$$|\sigma(\dot{\Sigma})| = \langle d_1, d_2, \cdots, d_{q-1} \rangle, \qquad (24)$$

for $d_i = |\dot{x}_{\sigma(i)}|$.
Setting

$$d = \frac{1}{q-1} \sum_{i=1}^{q-1} d_i, \qquad (25)$$

we separate $\sigma(\Sigma)$ into a collection of partial lists which corresponds to a set of colinear line segments. This criterion divides a list to an appropriate number of lists using the Euclidean distance between a pair of points. Denoting an ordered list

$$S = \langle s(0), s(1), s(2), \cdots, s(k), s(k+1) \rangle, \qquad (26)$$

such that $d_{s(k)} > d$, $s(0) = \sigma(1)$, $s(k+1) = \sigma(n)$, and $s(m) < s(n)$, if $m < n$, we obtain a decomposition of a line segment

$$s(x_{\sigma(1)} x_{\sigma(n)}) = \bigcup_{i=0}^{n} s(i) \qquad (27)$$

where $s(i) = s(x_{s(i)} x_{s(i+1)})$. The algorithm ORDER extracts an ordered set S from $\sigma(\Sigma)$, and yields $s_i = s(x_{s(i)} x_{s(i+1)})$ for $0 \leq i \leq k$.
In line 8 the algorithm select d_i such that $d_i > d$ and determines $s(j)$. Furthermore, in line 9 the algorithm sorts S adding a new element $s(j)$ to S. Therefore lines 8 and 9 determine the total complexity of this algorithm. If we randomly select $d_i \in |\sigma(\dot{\Sigma})|$, the procedure of line 9 is achieved by representing elements of Σ as a binary search tree. Therefore, the time complexity of this algorithm is $O(n \log n)$ for n points [7, 8].
Using procedures DETECT, ORDER, and DECOMPOSE, we can obtain the following algorithm, SEGMENT for the detection of line segments. Assuming that the expected numbers of lines and samples in a line are p and q, the expected complexity of the algorithm is $O(\gamma p (q \log q)^2)$. If $\gamma \cong \left(\dfrac{q}{2} \right)^{\frac{1}{2}}$ and $p \cong \log q$, the time complexity is $O((q \log q)^3)$.

```
1 :   procedure  DECOMPOSE :
2 :    begin
3 :      S := ∅, j := 1, Λ := Σ
4 :      while  σ(Λ) ≠ ∅  do
5 :        begin
6 :          begin
7 :            Select dᵢ ∈ σ(Σ)
8 :            if  dᵢ > d,
9 :              then    set i to s(j) σ(Λ) := σ(Λ) \ {dᵢ} S := S⋃{s(j)}
10 :             Sort S, and j := j + 1
11 :          end
12 :          for   0 ≤ k ≤ max j + 1   do
13 :            begin s(k) := s(xₛ₍ₖ₎xₛ₍ₖ₊₁₎) end
14 :        end
15 :   end
```

```
1 :   procedure  SEGMENT
2 :    begin
3 :      for  Σ  do
4 :        begin DETECT end
5 :        for   Σ(p)  do
6 :          begin ORDER
7 :            for   σ(Σ(p))   do
8 :              begin DECOMPOSE end
9 :          end
10 :   end
```

The procedures ORDER and DECOMPOSE can be achieved independently for each line. Thus, we can consider a serial algorithm, which achieves ORDER and DECOMPOSE, line by line and parallel algorithm, which achieves ORDER and DECOMPOSE independently for each line.

5   Conclusions

We defined a complete order of points along a line segment on a plane and in a space. If a set of sample points along a line segment are measured, the pair of the top and bottom of this order correspond to the pair of endpoints of this line segment. The construction of binary search tree achieves the detection of the top and bottom of this order from random samples. Thus, the combination of the randomized Hough transform and this ordering algorithm yields a randomized algorithm for the detection of line segments. In this paper, we proposed basic frameworks for the detection of line segments by randomized sampling and the voting procedure. Sensitivity analysis for the numerical errors of the algorithm remains to be considered .

This research was done while the author was visiting the Department of Applied Mathematics, University of Hamburg. He expresses many thanks to Professor Dr. Ulrich Eckhardt for his hospitality. While staying in Germany the author was supported by the Program for Overseas Researchers of the Ministry of Education, Sciences, and Culture of Japan.

References

[1] Ballard, D. and Brown, Ch. M., *Computer Vision,* Prentice-Hall; New Jersey, 1982.

[2] Xu, L. and Oja, E., Randomized Hough Transform (RHT): Basic mechanism, algorithm, and computational complexities, CVGIP:Image Understanding, 57, 131-154, (1993).

[3] Levers, V.F., Which Hough transform? CVGIP:Image Understanding, 58, 250-264, (1993).

[4] Kälviäinen, H., Hirvonen, P., Xu, L., and Oja. E., Probabilistic and non-probabilistic Hough transforms: Overview and comparisons, Image and Vision Computing, 13, 239-252, (1995).

[5] Sommerville, D.M.Y., *Analytical Geometry of Three-dimensions,* Cambridge University Press; Cambridge, 1934.

[6] Cox, D., Little, J., and O'Shea, D., *Ideals, Varieties, and Algorithms: An Introduction to Computational Algebraic Geometry and Commutative Algebra,* Springer-Verlag; New York, 1992.

[7] Motwani, R. and Raghavan, P., *Randomized Algorithms,* Cambridge University Press; Cambridge, 1995.

Subjective contours detection

Souheil Ben-Yacoub

1 Introduction

Basic visual activities are related to edge detection (motion, recognition,...). We show that there are different kinds of edges. The most known and already studied are edges due to luminance variations. After a brief introduction to classical edge-detectors, we introduce another class of edges, the "subjective contours". We assume end-points as textons as proposed by B. Julesz [7] and D. Marr [11]. The first step of our algorithm consists in geometric feature (*i.e.* segments) extraction using the hierarchical Hough transform. The end-points of the detected features are then drawn on a new image. This second "feature map" (of higher level) is then processed in a second step using again the hierarchical Hough transform. The end-points acts as clues indicating the presence of "subjective contours". We show that there is a relation between the number of clues present in the "feature map" and the pop-out phenomenon of the "subjective contour".

2 Edge detection

An edge in a picture may be defined as a discontinuity of the gray level or color. These edges can occur at any orientation and at any spatial frequency.

The theoretical edge-model can be represented mathematically by a step function, however this ideal case does not occur in real scenes. The eye has to deal with edges which are related to smooth variations of luminance. In real data a wide range of gray levels are present in the image leading to the perception of texture. How should the information about edges be processed? Marr [11] considered this question and suggested that this should be done in a symbolic way rather than by using the output of edge detectors. Classical edge detectors are widely studied, a rich literature can be found on this subject (see [2]).

3 The Hierarchical Hough transform

The Hough transform was initially introduced in the area of computer vision to detect straight lines in images [2]. It was then extended to other geometric features such as circles and ellipses. It was then improved in order to detect general shapes giving rise to the Generalized Hough transform [1].

Basically, the Hough transform maps edge points from the image to the parameter space, which represents all the possible lines present in the image. Each edge point votes for the lines to which it belongs. The line with a maximum of votes defines the line present in the image.

The success of the Hough transform can be explained by its global aspect, no a priori knowledge on point distribution is needed, the voting process of each point leads to the emergence of a peak in the accumulator (space of parameters of all possible lines) and this is the consequence of the point's colinearity. This voting process gives the Hough transform robustness toward missing edge points, each point taken individually is not important but all the points will vote for a particular line. A complete study on the Hough transform (advantages and problems) is presented in [6].

The Hough transform is combined with a hierarchical structure, (*i.e.* pyramid) leading to the Hierarchical Hough transform. Introducing a hierarchical feature extraction scheme improves the efficiency and the robustness of the Hough transform [3]. We have also shown that the Hierarchical Hough transform can be seen as a tool making the transition from *perception* to *cognitive vision* [4]. It is the aim of this paper to show an example of the use of the hierarchical Hough transform as a global vision process.

4   End-points as textons

We know from texture theory [8], that segregation is discussed in terms of texture elements or place tokens. Marr [11] has suggested that short lines, small blobs, ends of long lines, and elongated blobs are examples of place tokens. Small collections of blobs and lines (and their respective end-points) are also assumed to be place tokens, thereby producing a logical transition from the local to the global patterns. It was shown (see [8]) that terminators (or end-points) of segments and elongated blobs are textons and that they are involved in pre-attentive texture discrimination (see Figure 1).

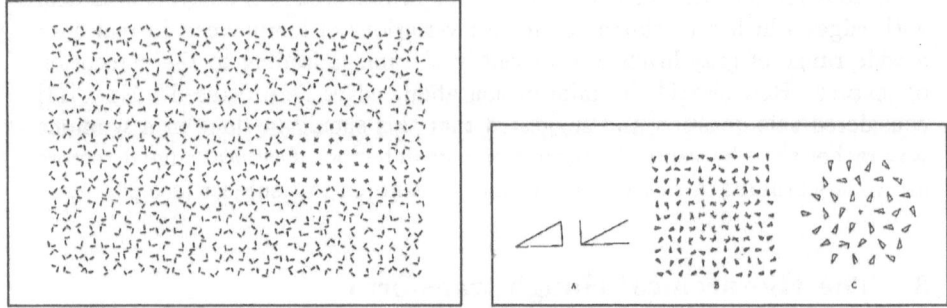

Figure 1: Texton-based discrimination (see [7])

Marr suggested that vision "goes symbolic" at any stage and that orientation for example is coded abstractly as the orientation of a "virtual line" whose ends can be marked by any kind of discontinuity or change of intensity. If that is the case, the same symbolic code may be used by the visual system to represent orientation of dot patterns and of lines. This problem was considered by A. Treisman [13], where a number of experiments were performed and showed that the obtained

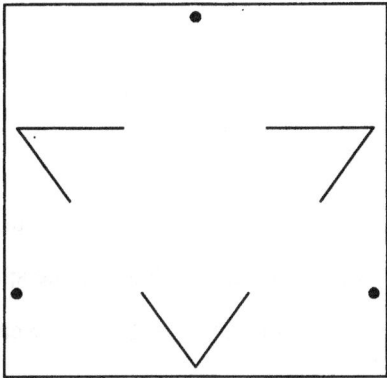

Figure 2: Kanisza triangle

results are consistent with Marr's paradigm. Hence the same representation is formed for the orientation of lines or pair of dots (*i.e.* end-points of segments).

5 Subjective contours

Subjective contours are edges which are perceived in areas where no physical change in luminance actually exists. There is a perception of a contour even if there is no stimulus for this contour. The first report on subjective contours was made by F. Schumann in 1904 [14]. These contours are also called "anomalous" or "illusory contours". Even if they are known since the beginning of the century, the explanation of the phenomenon is still not clear, there are a lot of proposed solutions. It is assumed that they are unlikely related to the functioning of low-level edge detectors. One of the best known subjective contour is the Kanisza triangle (see Figure 2). When looking at the figure a triangle appears with its edges, even if there is no luminance variation to see the triangle edges. There is no stimulus for the triangle edges (no luminance variation) but there is a perception of edges. These edges result from high-level processing in the visual task: the edges appears to be here from a global perspective but not from the point of view of local data analysis. Therefore classic edge-detectors will not be effective in detecting subjective contours.

We argue that subjective contours are perceived according to end-points property and Gestalt theory principles. There are other patterns that give rise to subjective contours: phase change, spatial frequency change, direction. Recent work tend to fill this gap and propose original approaches (see Sarkar *et al.* [12]). Subjective contours are related to Gestalt psychology principles [10, 9]. The Gestalt theory is concerned with the problem of discriminating shapes from background, a number of principle were developed to explain the perception phenomenon. The following basic rules tend to enforce the perception of shapes:

- *proximity and similarity*

- *small area*

- *closed contours*

- *symmetry*

- *smooth continuation*

Kanisza [9] suggested that perception proceeds in two stages:

- segregation of the visual field into regions having spatial regularities;

- perceptual inference of completion, i.e. find out what is absent.

6 Detection algorithm

The detection algorithm is based on the concept of end-points. The first step consists of building a "high-level" feature map by using a hierarchical Hough transform. The input image is processed in order to extract geometric features (i.e. lines). The feature map is computed by replacing each detected line by its end-points. The map represents all the end-points or place token present in the image.

The second step extracts "information" from the feature map. Here again we use a hierarchical Hough transform. The end-points of the feature map are used as inputs and may indicate the presence of a "high-level" contour. The end-points present in the map could be seen as *trigger features* [8]: this is related to the principle of *evidence accumulation*. The points present in the map vote for a particular feature, and the configuration with a maximum of votes is the "subjective contour" present in the image. The "evidence" for a particular contour is directly related to the value of the peak in the Hough accumulator. The peak can be easily computed (ρ and θ are here the parameters for line detection):

$$\mathcal{H}(\rho_{peak}, \theta_{peak}) = Max_{(\rho,\theta)}(\mathcal{H}(\rho,\theta)) = Max(\sum_i \delta(\rho - x_i cos(\theta) - y_i sin(\theta)))$$

Where δ is a Dirac function and the sum is computed over all end-points present in the map. $\mathcal{H}(\rho_{peak}, \theta_{peak})$ is the value of the peak for the line define by the parameters $(\rho_{peak}, \theta_{peak})$.

7   Results

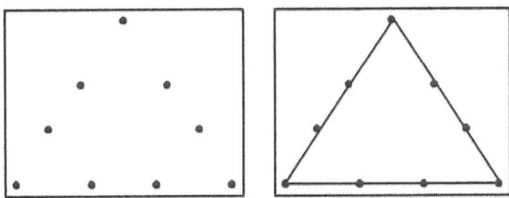

Figure 3: Endpoints of Kanisza triangle

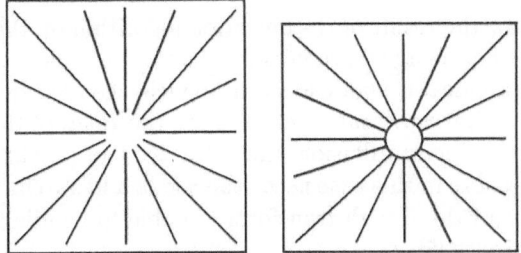

Figure 4: The sun illusion and the detected circle

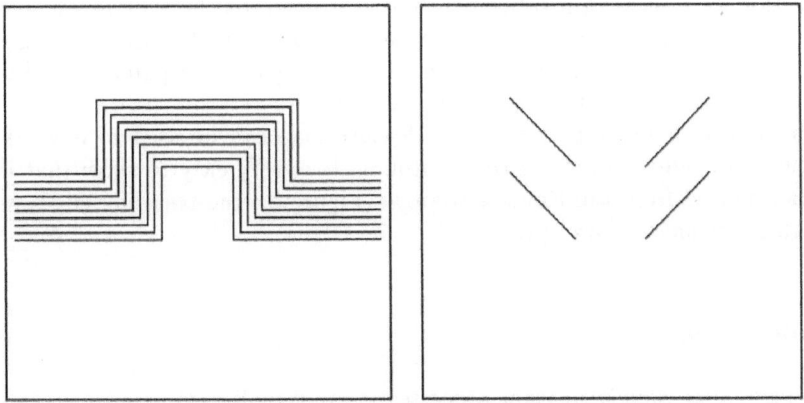

Figure 5: Detected subjective contour

Figure 6: Detected end-points

In Figure 3, we show the result of the detection algorithm on the Kanisza triangle (Figure 2). The first image represents the detected end-points which are then processed by a hierarchical Hough transform to yield the final subjective contour (i.e. the triangle). What is actually detected are the *edges* of the triangle.

In Figure 4, known as the sun illusion, the extracted end-points are shown. The processing of the feature in this case needs the use of a hierarchical Hough transform. New versions of the Hough transform are able to handle multiple models of curves such as circles [5].

In Figure 5, the subjective contour resulting from a direction change is easily detected. The textons (direction change points) are accumulated in the second step of the Hough transform: the extracted lines correspond to the illusory lines. Figure 6, this is the case of a subjective contours generated by a phase change between two patterns. We can clearly see the edge in the middle of the image, although there is no luminance variation. Extracting the end-points and findingthe subjective contour is very easy in this case.

The number of end-points present in the feature map can be used to have an idea about the evidence of subjective contours. It is very easy to show that if a point is removed from the Kanisza triangle (Figure 2), the resulting edges in the Hough space have a lower peak.

8 Conclusion

The proposed detection algorithm processes input signals into primitives and primitives to structural data yielding the detected shape. We have shown that it is possible to detect "subjective contours" by using the hierarchical Hough transform and end-points as textons. The feature map is a high-level description of the input image. The map is generated by considering only the end-points. Ongoing developments concern the creation of the feature map with other criteria like curvature.

We have also shown a relationship between the voting process in the hierarchical Hough transform and the evidence of the subjective contour.

Acknowledgement

This work was supported by a grant from the Austrian National Fonds zur Förderung der wissenschaftlichen Forschung (S7002MAT)

References

[1] D.H. Ballard: "Generalizing the Hough transform to detect arbitrary shapes". Pattern Recognition:13(2): pp 111-122 (1981).

[2] D.H. Ballard and C.M. Brown: Computer Vision, Prentice-Hall (1982).

[3] S. Ben Yacoub and J-M Jolion: "Hierarchical line extraction". Vision Image and Signal Processing:142(1), pp 7-14, 1995.

[4] S. Ben Yacoub and J-M Jolion: "Characterizing the hierarchical Hough transform through a polygonal approximation algorithm". Pattern Recognition Letters, 16(4), pp 389-398, (1995).

[5] S. Ben-Yacoub and A. Leonardis: "Making the Hough transform more robust and precise". submitted to SCIA'97.

[6] J. Illingworth and J. Jittler: "A survey on the Hough transform", CVGIP, Vol 44, pp 87-116, (1988).

[7] B. Julesz: "Textons, the elements of texture perception and their interaction". Nature:290: pp 91-96, (1981).

[8] B. Julesz: "Preconscious and conscious processes in vision". Pattern Recognition mechanisms, C. Chagas, R.Gatas, C. Grossberg (Eds), Springer-Verlag (1985).

[9] G. Kanisza: "Organisation in Vision", Praeger, New-York (1979)

[10] K. Koffka: "Principles of Gestalt Psychology", Harcourt-Brace, New-York (1935).

[11] D. Marr: "Early processing of visual information". Phil. Trans. of the Royal Society,275, pp 483-524, (1976).

[12] S. Sarkar and K.L. Boyer: " Perceptual organisation in computer vision: A review and a proposal for a classifactory structure". IEEE Trans. on Syst. Man and Cybern.,23(2), pp 382-399, (1993).

[13] A. Treisman: "Preattentive processing in vision". CVGIP, 31, pp 157-157, (1985).

[14] F. Schumann: "Einige Beobachtungen uber die Zusammenfassung von Gesichtseindrucken zu Einheiten". Psychologische Studien:1: pp 1-32, (1904)

Texture feature based interaction maps: potential and limits

Dmitry Chetverikov

1 Introduction

Motivated by the discovery of the high level texture features responsible for perceptual grouping of textures [11] and the development of the Markov-Gibbs texture model with pairwise pixel interactions [9], we have recently proposed the method of *feature based interaction maps* (FBIM) and applied this new tool to the problem of pattern orientation [4] and rotation-invariant texture classification [7]. Experimental results have demonstrated that the FBIM approach can be used to recover the basic structural properties and orientation of a wide range of patterns, including weak structures.

In [11], the fundamental, perceptually motivated high level texture features were identified as directionality (anisotropy) versus nondirectionality, periodicity versus irregularity and, probably, structural complexity. These features reflect the intrinsic symmetry properties of the process, natural or artificial, that generates the texture pattern. Figure 1 illustrates types of regularity and anisotropy originating from various components of a generating process: texel placement rules, their shape/orientation, and intensity distribution. Compound anisotropy may arise, as in figure 1d, if the directionalities of the components differ.

The above components are typical for the theory of random mosaics models for texture (e.g. [12]) which assumes that texture patterns are composed of texels. Although the applicability of such models is limited, it is nevertheless possible to use the above terminology for better understanding of the nature of regularity, anisotropy and orientation, as well as for analyzing the capabilities of different approaches to these basic texture properties. From figure 1, the following general observations can be made: (1) Texture symmetry should be defined via anisotropy (i.e. directional properties) of the pattern. (2) Regularity implies anisotropy and symmetry. (3) Anisotropy implies a dominant value in a directional property, i.e. some 'regularity' in that property. (4) Anisotropy is a lower-level description of structure than regularity. (5) Pattern orientation is often *orientation of structure* which is not a local property. (6) Component separation of a compound anisotropy may be problematic if the components 'interfere'.

The above observation concerning orientation points out an intrinsic limitation of those approaches to texture orientation that are based on orientation-sensitive local filtering. Following the original idea of Kass and Witkin [10], most of the current algorithms use local filtering that is not, and can hardly be, selective to long-range structural properties. A similar observation applies to those statistical approaches to texture regularity that are based on local operations. Intuitively, it is clear that long-range order cannot be detected at short ranges, as function

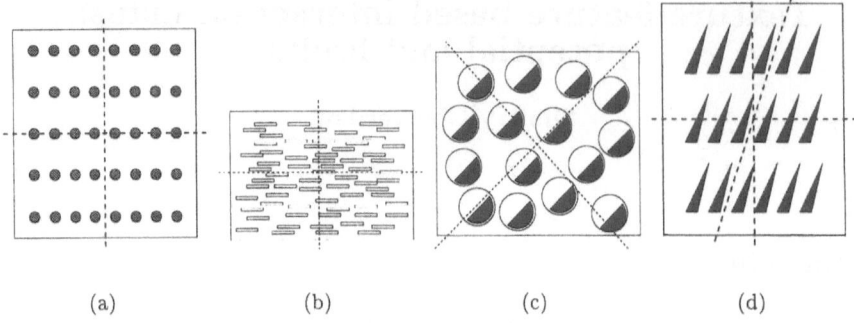

Figure 1: Different types of regularity and anisotropy: (a) texel placement rules; (b) shape/orientation; (c) intensity distribution; (d) compound (placement rules and shape/orientation). The dashed lines show the possible axes of pattern orientation.

periodicity cannot be observed in a window whose width is less than the period. (See [4, 7] for related discussions.)

Historically, one of the first studies on texture anisotropy was [1], followed by an early attempt [2] to apply anisotropy features to rotation-invariant texture classification. The term 'interaction map' has been originally introduced in the Markov-Gibbs texture model with pairwise pixel interactions [9] which will be discussed later. In our feature based approach, this term refers to the structure of the statistical pairwise pixel interactions evaluated through the spatial dependence of a gray-level difference histogram (GLDH) feature. The basic assumptions of the feature based interaction map approach can be formulated as follows: (1) The pairwise pixel interactions carry important structural information. (2) Both short- and long-range interactions are relevant; fine angular resolution is also essential. (3) Structural information can be accessed through GLDH features. This can be done more efficiently by analysis of the spatial dependence of the features than by selection of the 'optimal' features for a limited number of pre-set spacings. (4) Texture orientation can be viewed as direction of maximum statistical symmetry assessed via anisotropy.

The FBIM approach uses the EGLDH, the extended gray-level difference histogram introduced earlier in [3]. The extension was necessary in order to provide, at arbitrary spacings, the angular resolution that is needed for accurate anisotropy analysis. The EGLDH overcomes the problem of interdependence of the angle and the magnitude of the spacing vector arising in a digital image when the conventional GLDH is used. A comprehensive description of the FBIM method is given in [6]. Some of the procedures are presented in [4, 7].

The polar interaction map—the basic entity of the method—is an intensity-coded polar representation of an EGLDH feature, with the columns enumerating the magnitude, the rows the angle of the varying spacing vector. Figure 2 shows examples of Cartesian (XY) interaction maps and illustrates the superiority of the

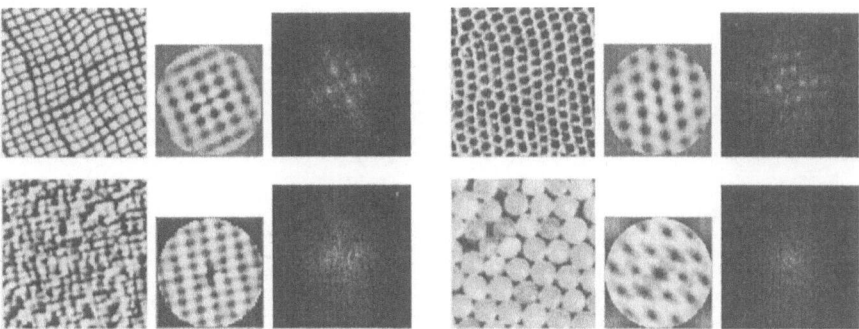

Figure 2: Comparison of interaction maps and frequency spectra. Each group of three images shows a texture, its XY interaction map and its Fourier spectrum.

FBIM over the Fourier transform in recovering texture structure. More examples of operation of the FBIM method are given in [6, 4, 7].

In section 2 we discuss in parallel the FBIM approach and a related Markov-Gibbs model based approach that provides a theoretical motivation for the FBIM method. Despite the obvious differences between the two approaches, this discussion casts light on their intrinsic conceptual similarity. Experimental results demonstrating the potential of the FBIM approach in diverse tasks and applications are presented in section 3. Finally, the advantages and limits of the proposed method are discussed in section 4.

2   Feature- and model-based interaction maps

The term 'interaction map' has been originally introduced in the framework of the Markov-Gibbs texture model with pairwise pixel interactions [9] proposed by Gimelfarb. For better understanding of the nature of the interaction maps, let us briefly compare the model- and the feature-based approaches. Figure 3 illustrates the common origin and the specifics of the two methods.

The model [9] assumes spatial homogeneity of texture and its invariance to uniform grayscale biases. This approach applies a Markov-Gibbs random field model to evaluate multiple short- and long-range pairwise pixel interactions in the raster. It gives an analytical first approximation of the Gibbs distribution parameters describing both the structure and the probabilistic strength of the pairwise interactions. The method then selects the most significant interactions (cliques) to recover the structure of texture and uses stochastic approximation to refine the interaction strength parameters. The outcome is a model based interaction map that shows the significance of each interaction. The model based approach has generative capability, i.e. is capable of synthesizing images similar to the learning sample.

The FBIM approach is supported by the model [9] in the sense that, under the model assumptions, the GLDH statistics used by both methods are sufficient

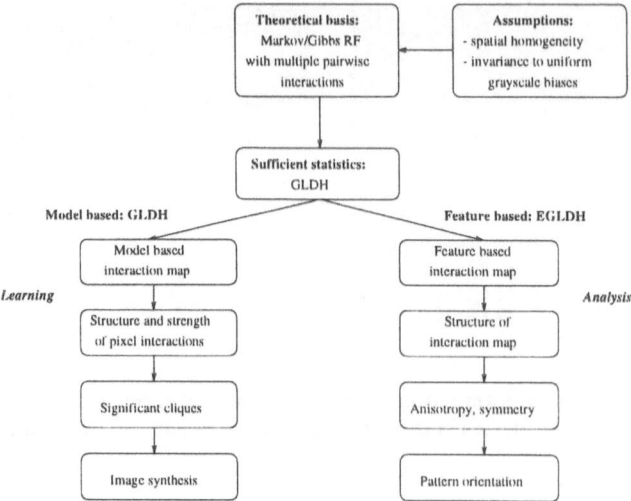

Figure 3: Relation between the model- and the feature-based interaction map methods.

statistics. In other words, the GLDH statistics form a complete description of a texture from which any other description can be derived. The FBIM method extends the GLDH statistics to arbitrary (non-integer) spacing vectors and is based on specific statistical features rather than a particular image model. It also describes short- and long-range pairwise interactions. The algorithm yields a high angular resolution feature based interaction map that indicates the significance of each interaction and is used to select the most significant interactions to recover the structure of texture. Because of its higher angular resolution, the FBIM is more stable under rotation and better suitable for precise anisotropy and orientation analysis. Further processing of the map involves evaluation of anisotropy, symmetry and pattern orientation which is defined via the axes of maximum statistical symmetry.

The analogy between the two approaches can further be illustrated by the results the two methods applied to the same texture. Figure 4 shows the most significant cliques obtained by the model based approach [9] and the corresponding feature based interaction maps. The interaction structures recovered by the two approaches are very similar.

3   Potential applications of the FBIM method

The FBIM approach has been previously shown to be useful in texture classification and structural analysis [7] as well as in determination of pattern orientation via texture symmetry [4]. In this section we will demonstrate the capabilities of the method by showing examples of its initial applications to diverse problems related to segmentation, detection and pattern orientation. Some of these results

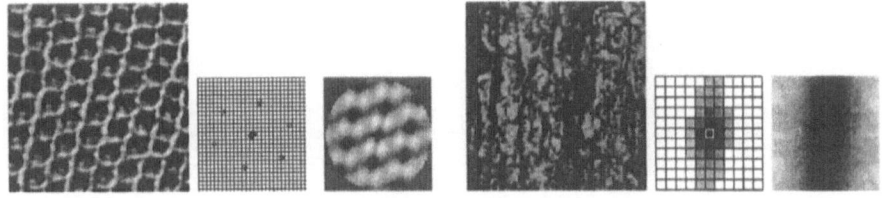

Figure 4: Examples of model- and feature-based interaction maps. The model based maps are shown as grids to emphasize their relation to image raster. For the second texture, the short-range zone is shown enlarged.

are pilot experiments while others are systematic evaluations on a large database. Figure 5 shows examples of textured object detection in a model board image. Using the fast running implementation of the FBIM [5], the maps of the windows were compared to two reference maps representing two different sample patches. A measure of matching (similarity) was computed and represented as an intensity coded picture. The textured objects specified stand out quite clearly indicating that the maps are selective enough to detect the objects. In the polar map, rotation amounts to cyclical row permutation, hence the matching procedure is easily extendable to rotation-invariant detection. This capability may be useful for object detection and query-by-image retrieval from a database, especially if the procedure is made invariant under projective transformations as well.

Another related application is illustrated in figure 6 where a hardly visible texture defect in the center of a netting pattern is detected by matching the reference map of a defect-free patch against the maps of the subimages. The defect stands out clearly as the region of low similarity. Note that this imperfection is a structural rather than intensity defect.

To demonstrate the method's selectivity to structure orientation, we have processed the image of reptile skin shown in figure 7 by the maps of two reference patches extracted from the two regions with different orientation. The regions can be discriminated as shown in figure 7d. This capability may find application in several tasks including document image processing when the image contains portions of slightly differently oriented pages, as illustrated in figure 7e. More examples of *structural filtering* with texture feature based interaction maps are given in [5].

Another typical problem of document image analysis is the text/non-text separation. In a recent study [8], we applied the FBIM approach to the problem of *zone classification* in document image processing. Document blocks were labelled as text or non-text using texture features derived from a feature based interaction map. The zone classification method proposed was tested on the comprehensive document image database UW-I created at the University of Washington in Seattle. This database comprises about 1000 digitised pages with approximately 15000 zones. Different classification procedures were considered. The performance ranged from 96 % to 98 % using 6 FBIM texture features only. The features were computed for the resolution reduced by a factor of 8 thus rendering

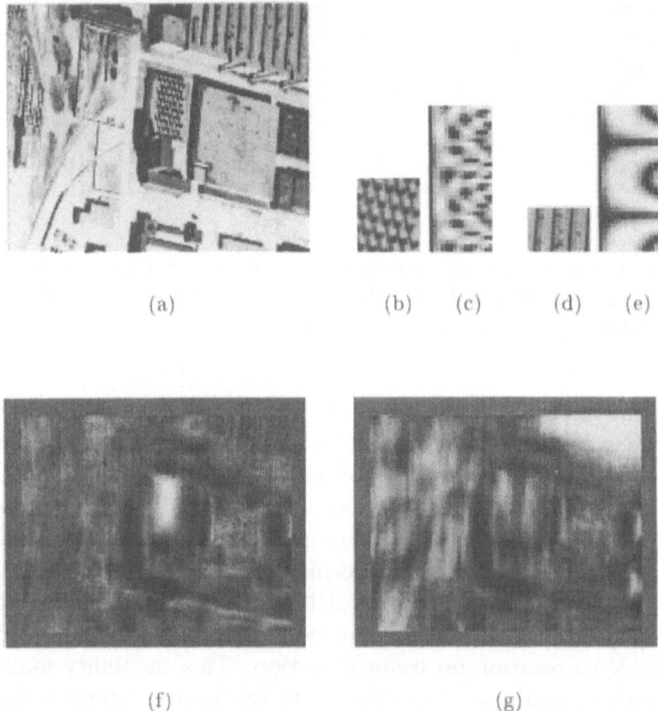

(a)   (b)   (c)   (d)   (e)

(f)   (g)

Figure 5: Detecting textured patterns in model board images: (a) model board image; (b) sample 1; (c) polar interaction map of sample 1; (d) sample 2; (e) polar interaction map of sample 2; (f) result of filtering by map 1; (g) result of filtering by map 2. The images are zoomed for better visibility.

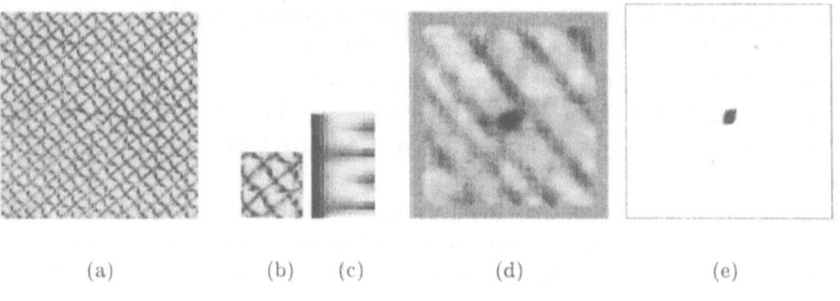

(a)   (b)   (c)   (d)   (e)

Figure 6: Detecting defect in texture: (a) texture (netting); (b) reference sample; (c) polar interaction map of reference sample; (d) enhanced result of map filtering; (e) result of blob detection in (d).

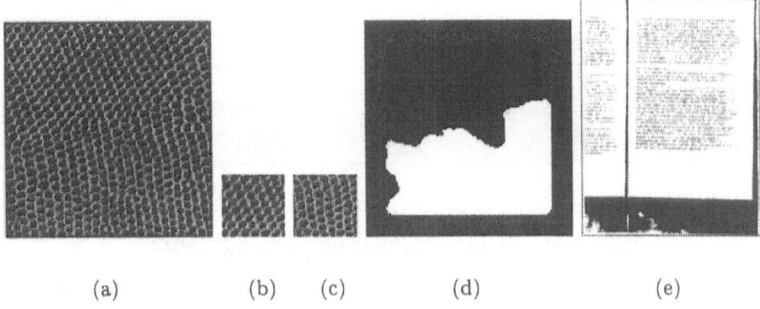

(a)   (b)   (c)   (d)   (e)

Figure 7: Texture separation by map filtering using structure orientation. (a) texture (reptile skin, enhanced); (b) reference sample 1; (c) reference sample 2; (d) enhanced result of map filtering; (e) a possible application.

the algorithm reasonably fast.

Finally, let us consider two applications related to pattern orientation. In the FBIM approach, pattern orientation is defined via the axis of maximum statistical symmetry. This feature can also be computed for non-textured patterns with reflectional symmetry, e.g. the face patterns shown in figure 8. This results in the correct pattern orientation obtained when the pairwise symmetry across the true symmetry axis is strong enough to prevail over other local symmetries in the pattern. A more realistic application is the determination of document skew for subsequent deskewing, as illustrated in figure 9. The FBIM anisotropy of the text is shown overlaid on the text image. A correct result is obtained when the orientation of the text structure is computed as opposed to the local orientation that may be biased by the different shapes of the letters.

An experimental study is in progress that is aimed at the systematic evaluation of the performance of the FBIM approach applied to skew computation. In the UW-I document image database, the skew angles range from -2 to 2 degrees. The main problems to be solved were the high angular resolution needed to obtain the accuracy required and the effects of the reduced resolution, as a horizontal structure is imposed and the rotation angles are biased towards zero. However, results obtained for the whole UW-I database indicate that these problems can be tackled and the skew accuracy of about 0.15 degrees can be achieved.

4 Conclusion

We have presented the feature based interaction map approach and have shown a range of potential applications of the method. An important advantage of the FBIM method is that it gives a rich, perceptually motivated structural description of texture that provides high angular resolution and rotation-invariance and gives a precise estimate of structure orientation. Due to the running implementation,

Figure 8: Finding orientation of face patterns.

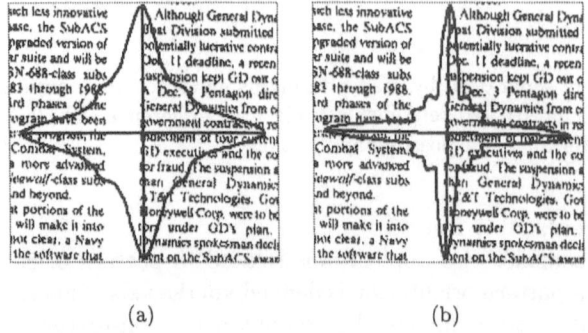

(a)   (b)

Figure 9: Finding orientation of a document: (a) biased short-range result; (b) correct long-range result (orientation of structure).

it is possible to filter image based on the orientation of structure or dominant local orientation.

There are drawbacks, limits and open issues as well. For highly symmetric structures, multiple orientations are obtained. It is questionable if a solution to this problem exists, at least in the framework of the current approach, since orientation is defined via symmetry. From perceptional point of view, it seems probable that any of the symmetry axes can serve as the axis of orientation. If a distinction should be made between the symmetry axes, this would require further structural analysis of the interaction map. Another limit of the FBIM method is that it is less efficient for patterns without distinct structure, i.e. irregular isotropic. For such patterns, only the short-range zone matters. As we experienced in the texture classification study [7], this zone may not be specific enough to reliably discriminate between such textures. A technical drawback is that the method becomes computationally demanding at fine spacing resolutions.

Let us finally dwell on an open issue which is related to a limit of probably not only the present method, but many alternative approaches as well. We have already mentioned that component separation of a compound anisotropy and regularity may be problematic if the components 'interfere'. (See figure 1 in the introduction.) Figure 10 illustrates this problem by an attempt to apply the FBIM method to the task of slant estimation of handwritten words. (Strictly speaking, this is not a task of texture analysis since a single word is a shape not a texture; however, it is still possible to use it to illustrate the problem in question.) There are three components to anisotropy involved: the slant, the connecting elements, and the horizontal component. In the current FBIM approach there is no straightforward way to separate these components which are 'mixed' in the same symmetry map. This may result in erroneous slant estimates as shown in figure 10c. A possible remedy could be using *skewed symmetry* which better matches the symmetry of the slanted words.

The separation of the components of anisotropy and regularity is a topic of future research. Our further research plans include structural analysis of interaction maps, reliable automatic texture classification into basic classes: regular, linear, isotropic; analysis of transformation properties of maps and design of fast algorithms for comparison of maps for image segmentation. It is also planned to apply the FBIM approach in such tasks as rotation/zoom/tilt invariant detection of textured objects, invariant query-by-texture retrieval from image database and defect detection in textures.

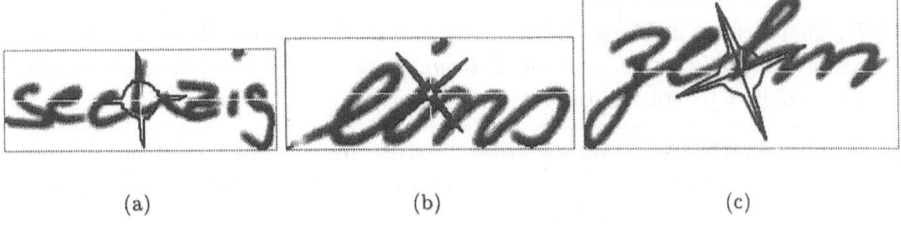

(a)   (b)   (c)

Figure 10: Finding slant of handwritten words: (a) a correct result; (b) a result slightly biased by the connecting elements; (c) a result strongly biased due to the interference of anisotropies.

5   Acknowledgment

This work was supported in part by the grants OTKA T14520 and EU COPERNICUS CT94 0153.

References

[1] D. Chetverikov. Textural anisotropy features for texture analysis. In *Proc. IEEE Conf. on Patt. Rec. and Image Processing*, pages 583–588, 1981.

[2] D. Chetverikov. Experiments in the rotation-invariant texture discrimination using anisotropy features. In *Proc. International Conf. on Pattern Recognition*, pages 1071–1073, 1982.

[3] D. Chetverikov. GLDH based analysis of texture anisotropy and symmetry: an experimental study. In *Proc. International Conf. on Pattern Recognition*, pages 444–448. Vol.I, 1994.

[4] D. Chetverikov. Pattern orientation and texture symmetry. In *Computer Analysis of Images and Patterns*, pages 222–229. Springer Lecture Notes in Computer Science vol.970, 1995.

[5] D. Chetverikov. Structural filtering with texture feature based interaction maps: Fast algorithm and applications. In *Proc. International Conf. on Pattern Recognition*, pages 795–799. Vol.II, 1996.

[6] D. Chetverikov. Texture feature based interaction maps and structural filtering. In *Proc. 20th Workshop of the Austrian Pattern Recognition Group*, pages 143–157. Oldenbourg Verlag, 1996.

[7] D. Chetverikov and R.M. Haralick. Texture anisotropy, symmetry, regularity: Recovering structure from interaction maps. In *Proc. British Machine Vision Conference*, pages 57–66, 1995.

[8] D. Chetverikov, J. Liang, J. Kőműves, and R.M. Haralick. Zone classification using texture features. In *Proc. International Conf. on Pattern Recognition*, pages 676–680. Vol.III, 1996.

[9] G. Gimel'farb. Non-Markov Gibbs texture models with multiple pairwise pixel interactions. In *Proc. International Conf. on Pattern Recognition*, pages 591–595. Vol.II, 1996.

[10] M. Kass and A. Witkin. Analyzing oriented patterns. *Computer Vision, Graphics and Image Processing*, 37:362–385, 1987.

[11] A.R. Rao and G.L. Lohse. Identifying high level features of texture perception. *CVGIP: Image Processing*, 55:218–233, 1993.

[12] B.J. Schachter, A. Rosenfeld, and L.S. Davis. Random mosaics models for textures. *IEEE Trans. Systems, Man, and Cybernetics*, 8:694–702, 1979.

Non-Markov Gibbs image model with almost local pairwise pixel interactions

Georgy L. Gimel'farb

1 Introduction

Markov/Gibbs models represent digital images as samples of Markov random fields (MRF) on finite 2D lattices with Gibbs probability distributions (GPD). Most of the known models take account of only pairwise pixel interactions. These models, studied in general form by Dobrushin [11], Averintsev [1], and Besag [3], were first applied to the images by Cross and Jain [9], Hassner and Sklansky [23], Lebedev et al. [25], Derin et al. [10], Geman and Geman [15]. Later, they were studied in numerous works (see, for instance, surveys [24, 13, 7, 28]). The models have features useful for describing and analysing image textures.

Markov/Gibbs image models The GPD specifies the MRF by an explicit geometric structure of the pixel interactions described by a system of *cliques*, or complete subgraphs, of a *neighborhood graph*. The graph is defined on the lattice by joining interacting pixel pairs, called the neighbors. If each possible signal configuration on the lattice has non-zero probability (the positivity condition) then the MRF has an equivalent GPD factorized over a particular subset of the cliques (the well-known Hammersley - Clifford theorem [3]).
The interaction strength is given by (Gibbs) *potentials* depending on signal values in the clique. Spatially uniform MRFs are described by translation - invariant clique families. The cliques of the family have the same relative arrangement of the pixels and possess the same potential function.
The GPD for a given training sample is strictly log-concave with respect to model parameters if can be defined as or reduced to an exponential family distribution [2, 16]. This feature ensures an identifiability of the parameters.
The joint and conditional GPDs are mutually compatible so that image samples under the given GPD can be simulated by a pixelwise *stochastic relaxation* of a moderate computational complexity [26, 15]. This allows to verify the model both by quantitative and visual comparisons of simulated and training samples.

Drawbacks of most popular models In most cases, so-called automodels [3], in particular, *auto-binomial* and *auto-normal* (Gauss-Markov) models, are used. These models, introduced first in physics, for many years attract widespread attention as a promising tool for modeling image textures ([4, 8, 21, 14], to name but a few).
But, the pixel interactions differ from the physical ones and reflect only frequencies of signal configurations in the cliques: the higher the frequency, the stronger the interaction, that is, the greater the potential value. Thus, the models borrowed from physics have evident drawbacks as regards to the images due to mostly pre-defined interaction structures and inadequate potentials.

Multiple pairwise pixel interactions The Markov/Gibbs model with multiple pairwise pixel interactions [17] overcomes in part these drawbacks by learning both the interaction structure and the potentials from a given training sample. The model admits arbitrary shifts of the image gray ranges. To avoid the non-Markov case, the interaction strength is considered to be invariant with respect to these shifts so that the potential values depend only on the gray level differences. The model has a subset of gray level difference histograms (GLDH) as a *sufficient statistic* for estimating the potentials and, therefore, supports well-known approaches to describe the textures by diverse statistical features of the GLDHs [22, 6].

Experiments show good potentialities of this model for simulating and retrieving some types of real or artificial noisy and textured images [17, 20] yet reveal its limitations. Different image sensors represent the same natural texture by a set of images with varying gray ranges and even these simple gray range stretches involve non-local and, therefore, non-Markov interactions.

To take account of the admissible gray range stretches, a non-Markov Gibbs model that preserves most attractive features of the initial Markov/Gibbs one was introduced [18]. Generally, non-Markov random fields are too complex for applications. But, the proposed model causes only a rather moderate increase in a computational complexity of parameter estimation and image simulation.

Contents of the paper The paper is organized as follows. In Section 2 we discuss the non-Markov Gibbs image model that allows for the linear gray range stretches. Section 3 outlines essential features of this model which are the same as or almost similar to the features of the initial Markov/Gibbs model and shows specific differences between both the models. Some experiments in modeling the uniform textures and conclusions are presented in Section 4.

2   Non-Markov model of grayscale images

2.1   Basic notation and assumptions

Let $\mathbf{R} = \{(m,n) : m = 0,\ldots,M-1; n = 0,\ldots,N-1\}$ denote a finite arithmetic 2D lattice, or raster, with $M \cdot N$ sites, or pixels. For brevity, we will use a shorthand symbol $i \equiv (m,n)$ for the pixels. Let $\mathbf{g} = \{g(i) : i \in \mathbf{R}\}$ be a digital grayscale image. Gray levels $g(i)$ have a finite set of integer values $\mathbf{G} = \{0,\ldots,q_{max}\}$. Minimum $q_{low}(\mathbf{g}) = \min_{i \in \mathbf{R}}\{g(i)\}$ and maximum $q_{upp}(\mathbf{g}) = \max_{i \in \mathbf{R}}\{g(i)\}$ gray values for the image $\mathbf{g}$ specify its gray range $\mathbf{S}(\mathbf{g}) = [q_{low}(\mathbf{g}), q_{upp}(\mathbf{g})]$.

We assume that the uniform textures are the samples of a *spatially uniform*, except for the lattice borders, Gibbs random field so that the pairwise pixel interactions are independent on the absolute pixel positions. The structure of the interactions is specified by several families of pixel pairs $\{\mathbf{C}_a : a \in \mathbf{A}\}$ where $\mathbf{A}$ denotes a set of indices. Each family is defined by the shift (μ_a, ν_a) between the pixels in the pair:

$$\mathbf{C}_a = \{(i = (m, n), \; j = (m + \mu_a, n + \nu_a) : \; (m, n), \; (m + \mu_a, n + \nu_a) \in \mathbf{R}\}.$$

In the Markov/Gibbs case it is the second-order clique family. In the non-Markov case the pixel pairs are not the cliques but represent still the stable and most significant pairwise part of the resulting "lattice-wide" interactions. For brevity, we preserve for them the same terms "cliques" and "clique families".

We assume that all the images that differ by the gray range stretches are equivalent to the same reference image obtained by normalising the gray ranges. The normalisation $Norm_{\mathbf{g}} : \mathbf{S}(\mathbf{g}) \to \mathbf{S}^{\mathrm{rf}}$ maps the gray ranges $\mathbf{S}(\mathbf{g})$ of the different images $\mathbf{g}$ on a reference range $\mathbf{S}^{\mathrm{rf}} = [0, q_{\max}]$, for instance, $[0, 255]$ or $[0, 15]$. After the normalisation each pixel depends on all pixels in the lattice.

2.2 Image model with almost-local interactions

To admit the gray range stretches, the Gibbs model in [18] embeds the gray range normalisation into potentials of the Markov/Gibbs model introduced in [17]. Also, the family of the pixels themselves is added to describe the marginal probabilities of the gray levels in the normalized image. We simplify this model by an additional assumption that the potentials for the pairwise cliques have the same value for all the signal pairs q, q' with the same difference $d = q - q'$; $(q, q') \in \mathbf{G}^2$; $d \in \mathbf{D}$. In this case, the following non-Markov model is obtained:

$$\Pr(\mathbf{g}|\mathbf{V}) = \frac{1}{Z_{\mathbf{V}}} \cdot \exp\left(\sum_{i \in \mathbf{R}} V(q_i^{\mathrm{rf}}) + \sum_{a \in \mathbf{A}} \sum_{(i,j) \in \mathbf{C}_a} V_a(d_{i,j}^{\mathrm{rf}} = q_i^{\mathrm{rf}} - q_j^{\mathrm{rf}}) \right) \quad (1)$$

where $q_i^{\mathrm{rf}} = Norm_{\mathbf{g}}(g(i))$. It has the following equivalent form of an exponential family distribution:

$$\Pr(\mathbf{g}|\mathbf{V}) = \frac{1}{Z_{\mathbf{V}}} \cdot \exp\left(\sum_{q \in \mathbf{G}} V(q) \cdot H(q|\mathbf{g}^{\mathrm{rf}}) + \sum_{a \in \mathbf{A}} \sum_{d \in \mathbf{D}} V_a(d) \cdot H_a(d|\mathbf{g}^{\mathrm{rf}}) \right). \quad (2)$$

where $\mathbf{g}^{\mathrm{rf}}$ denotes the normalised image $\mathbf{g}$ and $H(q|\mathbf{g}^{\mathrm{rf}})$ and $H_a(d|\mathbf{g}^{\mathrm{rf}})$ are components of the gray level histogram (GLH) and of the GLDHs for the normalised image. These histograms form the *sufficient statistic* for the model.

In fact, the pixel interactions in Eq. (1) are almost-local because their non-locality manifests itself only for a pixel with the maximal $q_{\mathrm{upp}}(\mathbf{g})$ or minimal $q_{\mathrm{low}}(\mathbf{g})$ gray level which is a solitary one in the lattice. In other cases, the interactions are indistinguishable from the really local pixelwise or pairwise interactions.

3 Features of the non-Markov Gibbs model

The basic features of the model in Eqs. (1) and (2) are similar to or can be obtained by a minor modification from the features of the Markov/Gibbs model in [17]. Below we will briefly outline their common and distinct sides.

3.1 Unique specification of the model

For the unique specification of the GPD in Eqs. (1) and (2), a big variety of possible ways exists based on a concept of a relative Hamiltonian (see [12] for the details). Here, we dwell on a centering of the potentials for each clique family to zeroth mean values proposed in [17]:

$$\sum_{q\in G} V(q) = 0; \quad \sum_{d\in D} V_a(d) = 0; \ \forall a \in \mathbf{A}. \tag{3}$$

The centering is more convenient than alternate variants (introduced, for instance, in [1, 3]) because treats uniformly all the gray level or gray level difference values. This facilitates the subsequent parameter estimation, as shown below in Sections 3.3 and 3.4 and, more fully, in [17].

3.2 Identifiability of the potentials

The log-likelihood function $LF(\mathbf{v}|\mathbf{g}^\circ) \equiv \dfrac{\ln \Pr(\mathbf{g}^\circ|\mathbf{V})}{|\mathbf{R}|}$ for the GPD in Eqs. (1) and (2) is strictly concave for any given normalised sample $\mathbf{g}^\circ$ with respect to the potential values $\mathbf{V}$. The strict log-concavity of the GPD in Eqs. (1) and (2) follows from general features of the exponential families of distributions [2, 16].

Let $F(q|\mathbf{g}^\circ) = \dfrac{H(q|\mathbf{g}^\circ)}{|\mathbf{R}|}$ and $F_a(d|\mathbf{g}^\circ) = \dfrac{H_a(d|\mathbf{g}^\circ)}{|\mathbf{C}_a|}$ be, respectively, marginal sample frequencies of the gray levels and gray level differences for the given normalized training sample $\mathbf{g}^\circ$. Also, let $MP(q|\mathbf{V}^*)$ and $MP(d|\mathbf{V}^*)$ denote corresponding marginal probabilities under the given GPD with the potentials $\mathbf{V}^*$:

$$MP(q|\mathbf{V}^*) = \sum_{\mathbf{g}\in\mathcal{G}} F(q|\mathbf{g}) \cdot \Pr(\mathbf{g}|\mathbf{V}^*); \quad MP_a(d|\mathbf{V}^*) = \sum_{\mathbf{g}\in\mathcal{G}} F_a(d|\mathbf{g}) \cdot \Pr(\mathbf{g}|\mathbf{V}^*).$$

and $\rho_a = \dfrac{|\mathbf{C}_a|}{|\mathbf{R}|}$ be the scaling factors.

The components of the gradient of the function $LF(\mathbf{v}|\mathbf{g}^\circ)$ in the point $\mathbf{V} = \mathbf{V}^*$ are as follows:

$$\begin{aligned} \left.\frac{\partial LF(\mathbf{V}|\mathbf{g}^\circ}{\partial V(q)}\right|_{\mathbf{V}=\mathbf{V}^*} &= F(q|\mathbf{g}^\circ) - MP(q|\mathbf{V}^*); \ q \in G; \\ \left.\frac{\partial LF(\mathbf{V}|\mathbf{g}^\circ}{\partial V_a(d)}\right|_{\mathbf{V}=\mathbf{V}^*} &= \rho_a \cdot (F_a(d|\mathbf{g}^\circ) - MP_a(d|\mathbf{V}^*)); \ d \in D; \ a \in \mathbf{A} \end{aligned} \tag{4}$$

so that in the maximum point case $\mathbf{V} = \mathbf{V}^*$, the following system of equations holds:

$$\begin{aligned} F(q|\mathbf{g}^\circ) &= MP(q|\mathbf{V}^*); \ \forall q \in G; \\ F_a(d|\mathbf{g}^\circ) &= MP_a(d|\mathbf{V}^*); \ \forall d \in D; \ a \in \mathbf{A}. \end{aligned} \tag{5}$$

This system has a solution (or, what is the same, the finite MLE of the potentials $\mathbf{V}^* = \arg\max_{\mathbf{V}}\{LF(\mathbf{V}|\mathbf{g}^\circ)\}$ exists) if all the above marginal frequencies have non-zeroth and non-unity values: $0 < F(\ldots), F_{...}(\ldots) < 1$.

Markov chains of the images having the given GPD in an equilibrium state can be generated by pixelwise stochastic relaxation techniques, in particular, by the Metropolis or Gibbs sampler algorithms [26, 15]. Therefore, the system in Eq. (5) can be solved by stochastic approximation [29, 30]. The like parameter estimation technique was first applied to the Markov/Gibbs image model with multiple pairwise interactions in [21].

3.3   Initial approximation of the MLEs

The stochastic approximation solves the system in Eq. (5) starting from certain initial potential values and updating them, at each step of the image generation, according to the GLH and GLDHs for the current generated sample. The initial approximations $V_{[0]}$ are computed analytically from the GLH and GLDHs for the learning sample just as was derived in [17]:

$$
\begin{aligned}
V_{[0]}(q) &= \lambda_{[0]}\left(F(q|g^\circ) - MP_{\text{irf}}(q)\right); \quad q \in G; \\
V_{a,[0]}(d) &= \lambda_{[0]}\rho_a\left(F_a(d|g^\circ) - MP_{\text{dif}}(d)\right); \quad d \in D; \quad a \in A.
\end{aligned}
\tag{6}
$$

Here, $MP_{\text{irf}}(q)$ and $MP_{\text{dif}}(d)$ denote marginal probabilities of the gray levels q or gray level differences d for the independent random field (IRF). The IRF corresponds to the zero-valued potentials $V = 0$ in Eqs. (1) or (2). The marginal probabilities of the signals for the IRF and their variances, denoted below by $\text{Var}(q)$ and $\text{Var}_{\text{dif}}(d)$, are well-known:

$$
MP_{\text{irf}}(q) = \frac{1}{q_{\max} + 1}; \quad MP_{\text{dif}}(d) = \frac{q_{\max} + 1 - |d|}{(q_{\max} + 1)^2},
\tag{7}
$$

$$
\text{Var}(q) = MP_{\text{irf}}(q)\cdot(1 - MP_{\text{irf}}(q)); \quad \text{Var}_{\text{dif}}(d) = MP_{\text{dif}}(d)\cdot(1 - MP_{\text{dif}}(d)).
\tag{8}
$$

The common scaling factor $\lambda_{[0]}$ in Eq. (6) is obtained also from the same sample histograms in a following form:

$$
\lambda_{[0]} = \frac{\sum_{q \in G}(\Delta(q|g^\circ))^2 + \sum_{a \in A}\rho_a^2\sum_{d \in D}(\Delta_a(d|g^\circ))^2}{\sum_{q \in G}\text{Var}(q)\cdot(\Delta(q|g^\circ))^2 + \sum_{a \in A}\rho_a^3\sum_{d \in D}\text{Var}_{\text{dif}}(d)\cdot(\Delta_a(d|g^\circ))^2}
\tag{9}
$$

where $\Delta(q|g^\circ) = F(q|g^\circ) - MP_{\text{irf}}(q)$ and $\Delta_a(d|g^\circ) = F_a(d|g^\circ) - MP_{\text{dif}}(d)$. Relative to [17], the estimates in Eqs. (6) and (9) differ in essence only by the training sample to collect the histograms: the original image for the Markov/Gibbs model and the normalized image for the non-Markov one.

3.4   Stochastic approximation refinement of the MLEs

At each step t of the stochastic approximation, the current image $g^{[t]}$ is generated from a previous one $g^{[t-1]}$ under the current GPD $\Pr(g|V_{[t-1]})$. The generation is performed by a particular stochastic relaxation technique (for experiments we use mostly the Metropolis algorithm [26]). Potential estimates $\mathbf{V}_{[t]}$ are updated using the GLH and GLDHs for the current generated image and a contracting step along the current approximated gradient of the log-likelihood function:

$$
\begin{aligned}
V_{[t]}(q) &= V_{[t-1]}(q) + \lambda_{[t]} \left(F(q|\mathbf{g}^\circ) - F(q|\mathbf{g}^{[t]}) \right) ; \; q \in \mathbf{G}; \\
V_{a,[t]}(d) &= V_{a,[t-1]}(d) + \lambda_{[t]} \rho_a \left(F_a(d|\mathbf{g}^\circ) - F_a(d|\mathbf{g}^{[t]}) \right) ; \; d \in \mathbf{D}; \; a \in \mathbf{A}.
\end{aligned}
\tag{10}
$$

For the step contraction, the scaling factor $\lambda_{[t]}$ decreases from the starting value $\lambda_{[0]}$ in Eq. (9) as $\dfrac{c_0 + 1}{c_1 + c_2 \cdot t}$. The control parameters c_0, c_1, c_2 can be chosen theoretically but these values yield too slow convergence to the desired estimates [30]. Thus, in practice we set them empirically as $c_0 = 0$; $c_1 = 1$; $c_2 = 0.001$.

The potential refinement in Eq. (10) is based on a standard stochastic approximation technique of solving the system in Eq. (5). The main distinction from the like solutions used in [21, 17] lies in the stochasic relaxation itself.

In the Markov/Gibbs model, each step of the pixelwise relaxation involves the summation of the potentials only over the local neighborhood of the current pixel. This neighborhood is formed by a "star-like" union of all the cliques containing this pixel.

The non-Markov model with almost-local pixel interactions preserves the like computations for all the pixels in the normalized image, except for the case when the pixel has the maximum or minimum gray level and is a solitary one in the whole image. Only in this latter and mostly very rare case the actual neighborhood of the pixel used in the relaxation coincide with the total lattice and potentials are summed up over the lattice. As a result, the computational complexity of the relaxation does not increase substantially.

3.5 Learning the interaction structure

The initial potential estimates in Eqs. (6) and (9) are used to recover the characteristic interaction structure, that is, the clique families that describe best the training sample. As shown in Eq. (6), the closer the initial potential estimates to the zeroth point, the weaker the interaction. So, the families with a sufficiently weak interaction can be excluded from the model or, what is the same, the potential values for them can be set to zero. The procedure to recover most characteristic clique families for the non-Markov model in Eqs. (1) and (2) is quite similar to the same procedure in [17] and based on a thresholding of an *interaction map*. The map represents relative contributions of different clique families to the total Gibbs energy (that is, to the exponent of the GPD) for the training sample (see [17, 20] for more details).

The given texture type is approximated by a reduced model with the zero-valued potentials for the families with the weak interaction strengths. Generally, all the models have the same interaction structure formed by all the possible cliqie families and differ only in the potentials: non-zeroth values for the characteristic families and zeroth values for all the other families. This feature simplifies comparisons of the different textures (for instance, for the image retrieval [20]) and allows to expand the model onto piecewise-homogeneous textures [19].

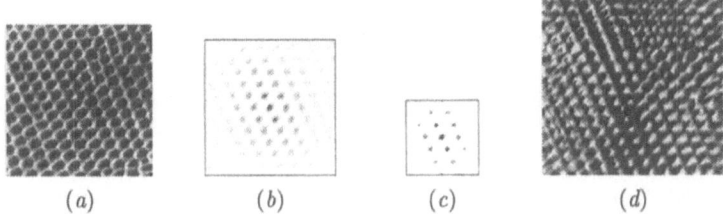

(a)   (b)   (c)   (d)

Figure 1: Training sample a, interaction map (b, 5100 clique families), learnt structure (c, 62 families), and simulated sample (d) of the texture D3 (Reptile skin)

Figure 1 shows the interaction map for the training texture sample D3 (Reptile skin) [5] and the interaction structure recovered by thresholding the map. Also, the texture sample simulated using the learnt structure and potentials is presented. Here, the learnt structure (and, therefore, the generated sample) reflects the basic hexagonal pattern of this texture which is perceived visually.

This technique for recovering the interaction structure holds much promise in texture simulating and retrieving [18, 19, 20, 17]. On a basis of this technique, the feature-based interaction maps, derived from the extended GLDHs, are introduced recently [6] to analyze such structural features of the image textures as symmetry, anisotropy, and regularity.

Of course, this technique cannot reveal structural features perceived easily by human vision if the local signal configurations are not sufficiently uniform over the image. In such a case, due to averaging of different non-uniform interactions in the GLDHs, the resulting interaction maps and learnt interaction structures do not reflect the essential local features of these textures. Also, a proper choice of the thresholds to reveal the characteristic interaction structures of different textures is not obvious and needs further theoretical justification.

4   Experimental results and conclusions

Several results in simulating natural textures from [5, 27] using the proposed model are shown in Figure 2. In these cases, $q_{max} = 15$ so that the model contains $|D| = 31$ potential values per a pairwise clique family to be estimated. The textures were generated by a "controllable simulated annealing" technique of the stochastic relaxation [17]. It changes, at each relaxation step, all the potentials as to approach most closely the GLDHs for the normalized training sample by the sample frequencies for the generated images. The potentials are changing in a stochastic approximation mode (see Section 3.4). This technique is similar to the original simulated annealing [15] but involves another quantitative measure of proximity between the current generated image and the training one (in terms of the chosen subset of the GLDHs). The like parallels between the simulated annealing and stochastic approximation of the Gibbs model parameters have been studied in [30].

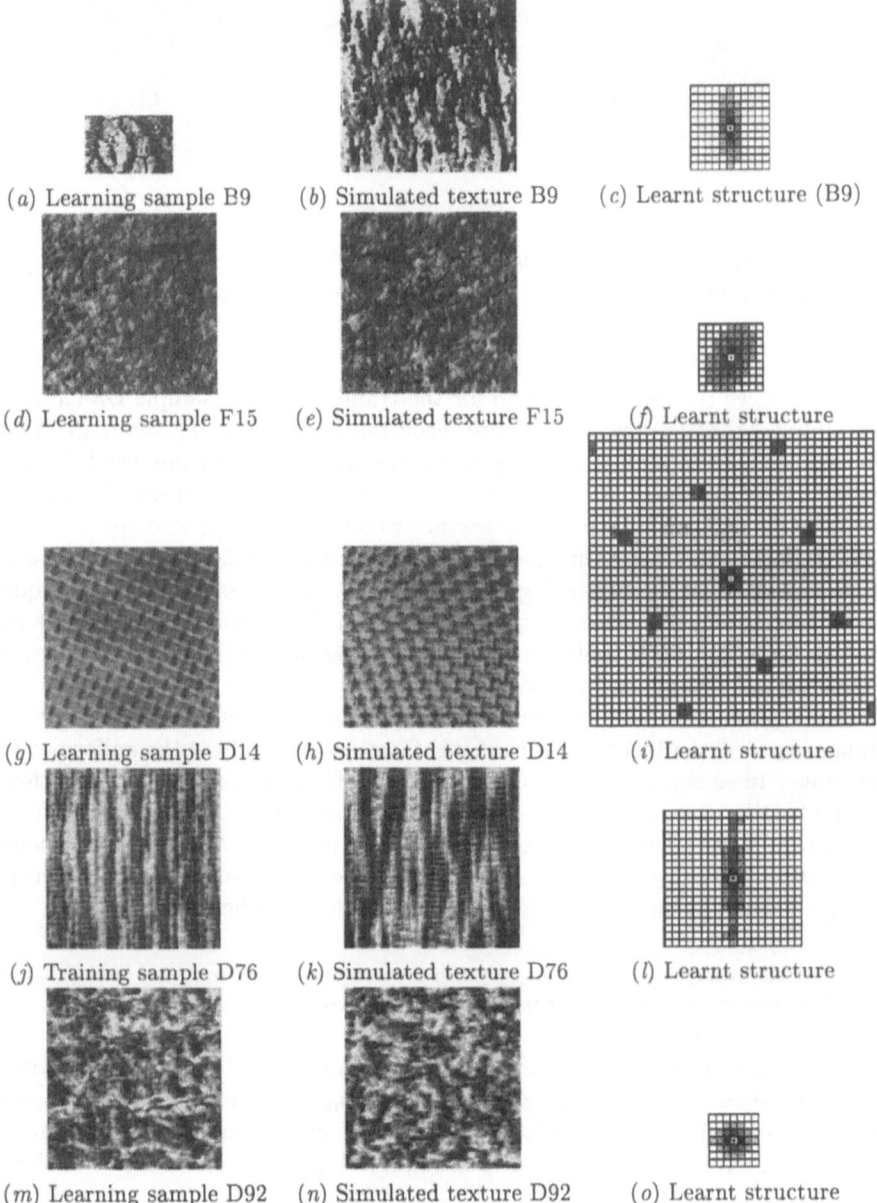

(a) Learning sample B9   (b) Simulated texture B9   (c) Learnt structure (B9)

(d) Learning sample F15   (e) Simulated texture F15   (f) Learnt structure

(g) Learning sample D14   (h) Simulated texture D14   (i) Learnt structure

(j) Training sample D76   (k) Simulated texture D76   (l) Learnt structure

(m) Learning sample D92   (n) Simulated texture D92   (o) Learnt structure

Figure 2: Simulation of the natural textures B9 (Bark0009), F15 (Fabric0015), D14 (Aluminum woven wire), D76 (Grass fiber cloth), and D92 (Pigskin)

These and other similar experiments show that the described non-Markov Gibbs image model is promising in simulating different natural uniform textures. The model involves moderate volumes of computations for implementing the stochastic relaxation (for instance, about 75 μs per single relaxation step and one clique family on the HP 9000 Model 715/50 workstation). But, these computations are parallel in essence, and this feature can facilitate the practical use of this model.

References

[1] Averintsev, M.B.: Description of Markov random fields by Gibbs conditional probabilities. Probability Theory and Its Applications, 17, 21-35 (1972). *In Russian.*

[2] Barndorff-Nielsen, O.: Information and Exponential Families in Statistical Theory. Chichester: Wiley 1978.

[3] Besag, J.E.: Spatial interaction and the statistical analysis of lattice systems. J. Royal Stat. Soc. London, B36, 192-236 (1974).

[4] Besag, J.E.: On the statistical analysis of dirty pictures. J. Royal Stat. Soc. London, B48, 259-302 (1986).

[5] Brodatz, P.: Textures. New York: Dover Publications 1966.

[6] Chetverikov, D., Haralick, R.M.: Texture anisotropy, symmetry, regularity: Recovering structure and orientation from interaction maps. In: Proc. of the 6th British Machine Vision Conf., Sept. 11-14, 1995, Birmingham. Sheffield: Univ. of Sheffield 1995, 57-66.

[7] Chellappa, R., Kashyap, R.L., Manjunath, B.S.: Model-based texture segmentation and classification, In: Chen C.H., Pau L.F., Weng P.S.P. (eds.): Handbook of pattern recognition and computer vision. Singapore: World Publishing 1993, pp. 277-310.

[8] Cohen, F.S., Patel, M.A.S.: Modeling and synthesis of images of 3D textured surfaces. CVGIP: Graphical Models and Image Processing, 53, 501-510 (1991).

[9] Cross, G.R., Jain, A.K.: Markov random field texture models. IEEE Trans. Pattern Anal. Machine Intell., 5, 25-39 (1983).

[10] Derin, H., Elliot, H., Cristi, R., Geman, D.: Bayes smoothing algorithm for segmentation of images modelled by Markov random fields. IEEE Trans. Pattern Anal. Machine Intell., 6, 707-720 (1984).

[11] Dobrushin, R.L.: Gibbs random fields for lattice systems with pairwise interaction. Functional Analysis and Its Applications, 2, 31-43 (1968). [*In Russian*].

[12] Dobrushin, R.L., Pigorov, S.A.: Theory of random fields. In: Proc. 1975 IEEE-USSR Joint Workshop on Information Theory, December 1995, Moscow, USSR. New York: IEEE 1976, pp. 39-49.

[13] Dubes, R.C., Jain, A.K.: Random field models in image analysis. J. of Applied Statistics, 16, 131-164 (1989).

[14] Elfadel, I.M., Pikard, R.W.: Gibbs random fields, cooccurrences, and texture modelling. IEEE Trans. Pattern Anal. Machine Intell., 16, 24-37 (1994).

[15] Geman, S., Geman, D.: Stochastic relaxation, Gibbs distributions, and the Bayesian restoration of images. IEEE Trans. Pattern Anal. Machine Intell., 6, 721-741 (1984).

[16] Gidas, B.: Parameter estimation for Gibbs distributions from fully observed data. In: Chellappa R., Jain A. (eds.): Markov random fields: theory and applications. Boston: Academic Press 1993, pp. 471-483.

[17] Gimel'farb, G.L.: Texture modelling by multiple pairwise pixel interactions. IEEE Trans. Pattern Anal. Machine Intell., 18, 1110-1114 (1996).

[18] Gimel'farb, G.L.: Non-Markov Gibbs texture model with multiple pairwise pixel interactions. In: Proc. 13th Int. IAPR Conf. on Pattern Recognition, August 25-29, 1996, Vienna, Austria. Vieanna: TU Wien, 1996, pp. 760-764.

[19] Gimel'farb, G.L.: Gibbs models for Bayesian simulation and segmentation of piecewise-unifirm textures. *Ibid.*, pp. 591-595.

[20] Gimel'farb, G.L., Jain, A.K.: On retrieving textured images from an image database. Pattern Recognition, 29, 1461-1483 (1996).

[21] Gimel'farb, G.L., Zalesny, A,V.: Low-level Bayesian segmentation of piecewise-homogeneous noisy and textured images. Int. J. of Imaging Systems and Technology, 3, 227-243 (1991).

[22] Haralick, R.M.: Statistical and structural approaches to textures. Proc. IEEE, 67, 786-804 (1979).

[23] Hassner, M., Sklansky, J.: The use of Markov random fields as models of textures. Computer Graphics and Image Processing, 12, 357-370 (1980).

[24] Kashyap, R.L.: Image models. In: Young, T. Y., Fu, K.-S. (eds.): Handbook on pattern recognition and image processing. Orlando: Academic Press 1986, pp. 247-279.

[25] Lebedev D.S., Bezruk A.A., Novikov V.M.: Markov Probabilistic Model of Image and Picture. Moscow: VINITI 1983 (Preprint: Inst. of Information Transmission Problems, Acad. of Sci. of the USSR). [*In Russian*].

[26] Metropolis N., Rosenbluth A.W., Rosenbluth M. N., Teller A. H., Teller E.: Equations of state calculations by fast computing machines. J. of Chemical Physics 21, 1087-1091 (1953).

[27] Pickard R., Graszyk C., Mann S., Wachman J., Pickard L., Campbell L.: VisTex Database. Cambridge: MIT Media Lab. 1995.

[28] Tuceryan M., Jain A.K.: Texture analysis. In: Chen C.H., Pau L.F., Weng P.S.P. (eds.): Handbook of pattern recognition and computer vision. Singapore: World Publishing 1993, pp. 235-276.

[29] Wazan,M.: Stochastic Approximation. Cambridge: University Press, 1969.

[30] Younes, L.: Estimation and annealing for Gibbsian fields. Annales de l'Institut Henri Poincare, 24, 269-294 (1988).

Equivalent contraction kernels to build dual irregular pyramids*

Walter G. Kropatsch

1 Introduction

A raw digital image consists of a 2D spatial arragement of pixels each of which results from measuring the light at a specific location of the image plane. Currently most of the artificial sensors (e.g. CCD cameras) have the rigid structure of an orthogonal grid, whereas most natural vision systems are based on non-regular arrangements of sensors [1]. Although arrays are certainly easier to manage technically, topological relations seem to play an even more important role for vision tasks in natural systems than precise geometrical positions.

A second aspect concerns the projection from the real (3D-) world into the 2D image. Surfaces of 3D-objects reflect the light in a very specific way that somehow 'codes' the structure of the object: reflectivity within homogeneous regions does not vary much, it changes abruptly between different surfaces or from the object to its background [9]. The topological structure on a visible surface patch is preserved in the image while its geometry may be severly distorted.. But also the arrangement of different objects in the 3D-world will be mapped to the regions in the image, be it regularly or irregularly sampled. Hence the idea pursuit in this paper to start with arbitrarily but densely sampled measurements of which only the topology is known and to successively shrink the number of descriptive elements until the structure of the imaged scene becomes evident.

The third aspect addresses computer vision models. They have in general a parametric and a structural component. While parameter optimization models quantitative image properties well, the qualitative image and scene properties rely more on the structural component.

The presented approach addresses a representation of pure structure, a hierarchy of plane graphs, with a clear interface, the decimation parameters, to control generation and modification of the structure. Dual graph contraction is the basic process [5] that builds an irregular 'graph' pyramid by successively contracting a dual image graph of one level into the smaller dual image graph of the next level. Dual image graphs are typically defined by the neighborhood relations of image pixels or by the adjacency relations of the region adjacency graph. The above concept has been used for finding the structure of connected components [8]. It also embeds Meer's stochastic pyramid [11], the adaptive pyramid [4], and a further variant of Meer's approach, Mathieu's optimal stochastic pyramid [10] which produced excellent segmentation results by decimating a minimal spanning tree instead of the original graph.

---

*This work was supported by the Austrian Science Foundation under grant S 7002-MAT

The paper is organized as follows. We first summarize dual graph contraction in Section 2. The observation that the parameters that control the process form forests is then generalized by the concept of contraction kernels. They are necessary if repeated dual contractions are to be replaced by a single dual contraction using equivalent contraction kernels (ECKs, section 2.2). ECKs are able to compute any level of an irregular pyramid directly from the base. Decimation parameters can be designed now at the base without the need to first generate the lower pyramid levels. The ECK of the apex becomes especially important in section 3. If labels are attached to the vertices and edges of this spanning tree all the individual decimation parameters can be recovered from this representation which is embedded in the base graph. As a consequence the labeled spanning tree (LST) determines the structure of the dual irregular pyramid completely.

2 Dual graph contraction

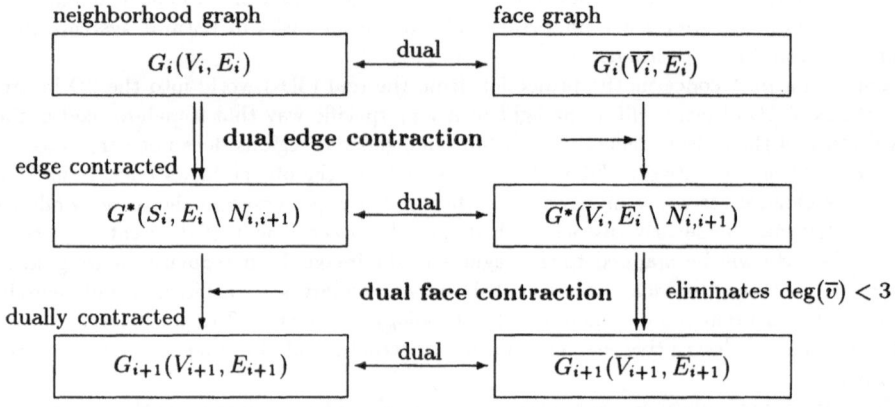

Figure 1: Dual Graph Contraction: $(G_{i+1}, \overline{G_{i+1}}) = C[(G_i, \overline{G_i}), (S_i, N_{i,i+1})]$

Dual graph contraction proceeds in two basic steps (Fig. 1): dual edge contraction and dual face contraction. The base of the pyramid consists of the pair of dual image graphs $(G_0, \overline{G_0})$. Following *decimation parameters* $(S_i, N_{i,i+1})$ determine the structure of an irregular pyramid [5][Def.5]: a subset of *surviving vertices* $S_i = V_{i+1} \subset V_i$, and a subset of *primary non-surviving edges*[1] $N_{i,i+1} \subset E_i$. Every non-surviving vertex, $v \in V_i \setminus S_i$, must be connected to one surviving vertex in a unique way. The relation between the two pairs of dual graphs, $(G_i, \overline{G_i})$ and $(G_{i+1}, \overline{G_{i+1}})$, as established by dual graph contraction with decimation parameters $(S_i, N_{i,i+1})$ is expressed by function $C[.,.]$:

$$(G_{i+1}, \overline{G_{i+1}}) = C[(G_i, \overline{G_i}), (S_i, N_{i,i+1})] \tag{1}$$

The contraction of a primary non-surviving edge consists in the identification of its endpoints and in the removal of both the contracted edge and its dual edge (Fig. 2f).

---

[1] Secondary non-surviving edges are removed during dual face contraction.

Dual face contraction simplifies most of the multiple edges and self-loops, but not those inclosing any surviving parts of the graph (see [5]). Two steps of dual graph contraction shows the example of Fig. 2. They can be formally written as $(G_1, \overline{G_1}) = C[(G_0, \overline{G_0}), (S_0, N_{0,1})]$, and $(G_2, \overline{G_2}) = C[(G_1, \overline{G_1}), (S_1, N_{1,2})]$. Note that graph G_2 in this example contains both a self-loop and a double edge. [5] compares three different types of graph contractions.

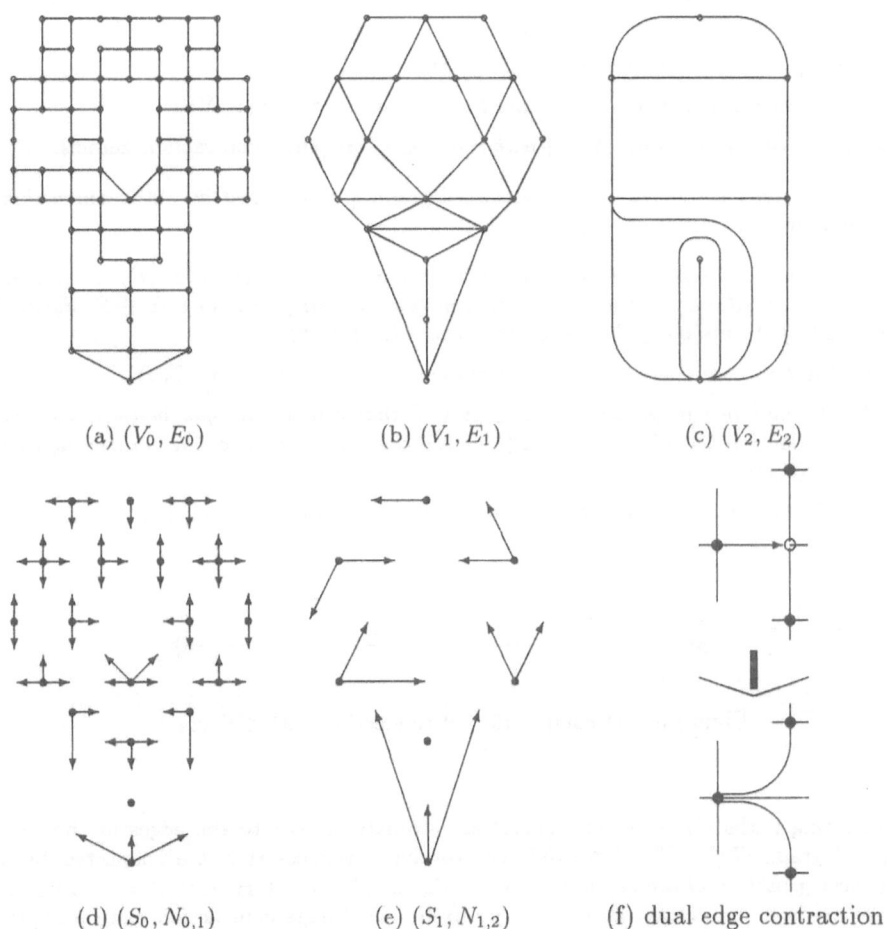

(a) (V_0, E_0) (b) (V_1, E_1) (c) (V_2, E_2)

(d) $(S_0, N_{0,1})$ (e) $(S_1, N_{1,2})$ (f) dual edge contraction

Figure 2: Example of a dual irregular pyramid and decimation parameters

2.1 Contraction kernels

To define the parameters that control the process of dual graph contraction we observe that the subgraphs in our example graph (Fig. 2d and e) form small tree structures $T(s)$ that collaps into surviving vertex s of the contracted graph. $T(s)$ is a *spanning tree* of the connected component of the surviving root vertex, or equivalently, (V, N) is a spanning forest of graph $G(V, E)$.

Definition 1 *A decimation of a graph $G(V, E)$ is specified by a selection of surviving vertices $S \subset V$ and a selection of primary non-surviving edges $N \subset E$ such that following two conditions are fulfilled:*

1. *Graph (V, N) is a spanning forest of graph $G(V, E)$.*

2. *The surviving vertices $S \subset V$ are the roots of the forest (V, N).*

The trees $T(v)$ of the forest (V, N) with root $v \in V$ are called contraction kernels.

The connectivity structure of the contracted graph is established by paths connecting two surviving vertices:

Definition 2 *Let $G(V,E)$ be a graph with decimation parameters (S, N). A path in $G(V, E)$ is called a* connecting path *between two surviving vertices $v, w \in S$, denoted $CP(v, w)$, if it consists of three subsets of edges E (Fig. 3):*

1. *The first part is a possibly empty branch of contraction kernel $T(v)$.*

2. *The middle part is an edge $e \in E \setminus N$ that bridges the gap between the two contraction kernels $T(v)$ and $T(w)$. We call e the* bridge *of the connecting path $CP(v, w)$.*

3. *The third part is a possibly empty branch of contraction kernel $T(w)$.*

Connecting paths $CP(v, w)$ in $G(V, E)$ are strongly related to the edges in the contracted graph $G'(V', E')$: Two different surviving vertices that are connected by a connecting path in G are connected by an edge in E'. For every edge $e' = (v, w) \in E'$ there exists a connecting path $CP(v, w)$ in G. Dual edge contraction can be implemented by (1) simply renaming all the non-surviving vertices to their surviving parent vertex, (2) deleting all non-surviving edges N and (3) their duals $\overline{N}$.

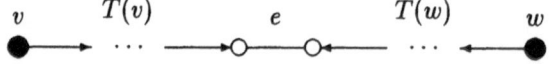

Figure 3: Decomposition of connecting path $CP(v, w)$

2.2 Equivalent contraction kernels

Burt [3] compared iterated reduction with direct computation of higher levels of a Gaussian pyramid by means of the 'equivalent weighting function'. Similarly we combine two (and more) dual graph contractions (see Fig. 4) of graph G_{k-2}, $k > 2$ with decimation

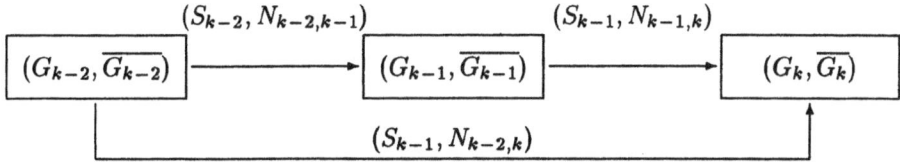

Figure 4: Equivalent contraction kernel

parameters $(S_{k-2}, N_{k-2,k-1})$ and $(S_{k-1}, N_{k-1,k})$ into a single *equivalent contraction kernel* (ECK) $N_{k-2,k} = N_{k-2,k-1} \circ N_{k-1,k}$ (for simplicity G_i stands for $(G_i, \overline{G_i})$):

$$C[C[G_{k-2}, (S_{k-2}, N_{k-2,k-1})], (S_{k-1}, N_{k-1,k})] \;=\; C[G_{k-2}, (S_{k-1}, N_{k-2,k})] \quad (2)$$

Equivalent contraction kernels are constructed in the following way: Assume that the dual irregular pyramid $((G_0, \overline{G_0}), (G_1, \overline{G_1}), \ldots, (G_k, \overline{G_k}))$, $k > 1$, is the result of k dual graph contractions. The structure of G_k is fully determined by the structure of G_{k-1} and the decimation parameters $(S_{k-1}, N_{k-1,k})$. Furthermore, the structure of G_{k-1} is determined by G_{k-2} and the decimation parameters $(S_{k-2}, N_{k-2,k-1})$. $S_{k-2} := V_k$ are the vertices surviving from G_{k-2} to G_k. The searched contraction kernels must be formed by edges $N_{k-2,k} \subset E_{k-2}$. This is true for $N_{k-2,k-1}$ but not for $N_{k-1,k} \subset E_{k-1}$ if we would simply overlay the two sets of decimation parameters. An edge $e_{k-1} = (v_{k-1}, w_{k-1}) \in N_{k-1,k}$ corresponds to a connecting path[2] $CP(v_{k-1}, w_{k-1})$ in G_{k-2}. By definition 2, $CP(v_{k-1}, w_{k-1})$ consists of one branch of $T_{k-2}(v_{k-1})$, one branch of $T_{k-2}(w_{k-1})$, and one surviving edge $e_{k-2} \in E_{k-2}$ connecting the two contraction kernels $T_{k-2}(v_{k-1}), T_{k-2}(w_{k-1})$.

Definition 3 *Function* bridge: $E_{k-1} \mapsto E_{k-2}$ *assigns to each edge* $e_{k-1} = (v_{k-1}, w_{k-1}) \in E_{k-1}$ *one of the bridges* $e_{k-2} \in E_{k-2}$ *of the connecting paths* $CP(v_{k-1}, w_{k-1})$:

$$\text{bridge}(e_{k-1}) := e_{k-2}. \quad (3)$$

Two disjoint tree structures connected by a single edge become a new tree structure. The result of connecting all contraction kernels T_{k-2} by bridges fulfills the requirements of a contraction kernel:

$$N_{k-2,k} := N_{k-2,k-1} \;\cup\; \bigcup_{e_{k-1} \in N_{k-1,k}} \text{bridge}(e_{k-1}) \quad (4)$$

The contraction kernels $(V_2, N_{0,2})$ in Fig. 5a are equivalent to the successive contraction with kernels of Fig. 2d and e. The above process can be repeated on the remaining contraction kernels until the base level 0 contracts in one step into the apex $V_n = \{v_n\}$. The edges of the corresponding spanning tree are contained in $N_{0,n}$. Fig. 5(b) shows spanning tree $N_{0,4}$ overlaid with the base graph G_0. The apex, $v_4 \in V_4$, is marked by a filled circle and the edges of the spanning tree $N_{0,4}$ are differentiated from edges E_0 by triple lines.

---

[2] If there are more than one connecting paths, one must be selected.

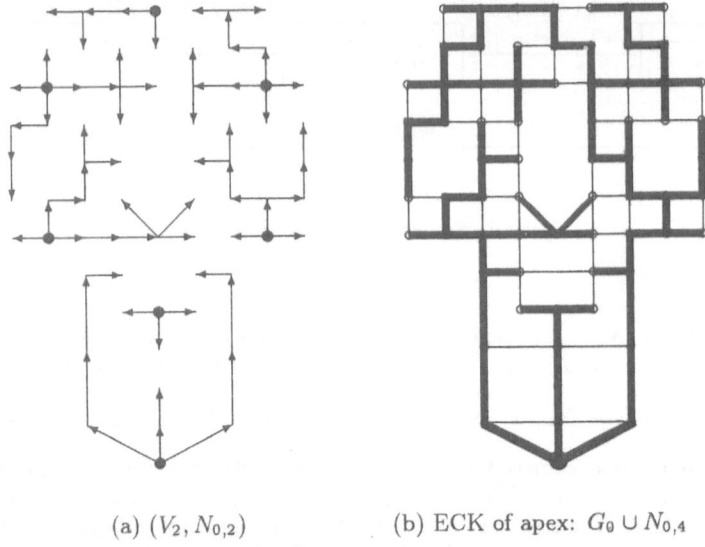

(a) $(V_2, N_{0,2})$ (b) ECK of apex: $G_0 \cup N_{0,4}$

Figure 5: Equivalent contraction kernels

3 Labeled spanning trees

Bottom-up construction of a dual irregular pyramid $((G_0, \overline{G_0}), (G_1, \overline{G_1}), \ldots, (G_n, \overline{G_n}))$ is formally described by dual contraction:

$$(G_{i+1}, \overline{G_{i+1}}) = C[(G_i, \overline{G_i}), (V_{i+1}, N_{i,i+1})] \qquad i = 0, 1, \ldots, n-1 \qquad (5)$$

$N_{i,i+1}$ denotes the subset of primary non-surviving edges at level i, e.g. $N_{i,i+1} \subset E_i$, that disappear during contraction of level i. Using the concept of equivalent contraction kernel,

$$N_{i,i+k} = N_{i,i+1} \circ N_{i+1,i+2} \circ \ldots \circ N_{i+k-1,i+k} \qquad \forall 0 \le i, 0 \le k, i+k \le n \qquad (6)$$

can be constructed such that any arbitrary level i can be directly derived from level 0:

$$(G_i, \overline{G_i}) = C[(G_0, \overline{G_0}), (S_{i-1}, N_{0,i})] \qquad i = 1, \ldots, n \qquad (7)$$

Following Table (8) summarizes all ECKs based on graph G_0. The left-side graph G_i can be dually contracted using contraction kernel $(V_k, N_{i,k})$ in the same row into graph G_k as shown in the last row. To produce higher pyramid levels with less vertices, obviously more edges need to be contracted as expressed by $N_{i,k} \subset N_{i,k+1}$.

G_0	$N_{0,1} \subset$	$N_{0,2} \subset$	$N_{0,3} \subset$	$\ldots \subset$	$N_{0,n}$
G_1		$N_{1,2} \subset$	$N_{1,3} \subset$	$\ldots \subset$	$N_{1,n}$
G_2			$N_{2,3} \subset$	$\ldots \subset$	$N_{2,n}$
$\vdots$				$\ddots$	$\vdots$
G_{n-1}					$N_{n-1,n}$
	G_1	G_2	G_3	$\ldots$	G_n

$$(8)$$

3.1 Labels indicate pyramid levels

Surviving vertices are ordered by set-inclusion, e.g. $V_0 \supset V_1 \supset \ldots \supset V_n$, as well as are
the ECKs $N_{0,i}, i = 1, \ldots n$, in Table (8). Hence the vertex set V_0 and the edge set $N_{0,n}$
contain all decimation parameters needed to dually contract the base graph G_0 into
any other pyramid level. We use labels to attach the whole construction history to the
spanning tree $(V_0, N_{0,n})$ of the base graph G_0.
The vertices receive as a label the highest level to which they survive:

$$l(v) := k \Longleftrightarrow v \in V_k \setminus V_{k+1} \qquad \forall v \in V_0, 0 \le k < n. \tag{9}$$

Edges receive the highest level as label to which they survive:

$$l(e) := k \Longleftrightarrow e \in N_{0,k+1} \setminus N_{0,k} \qquad \forall e \in N_{0,n}, 0 \le k < n. \tag{10}$$

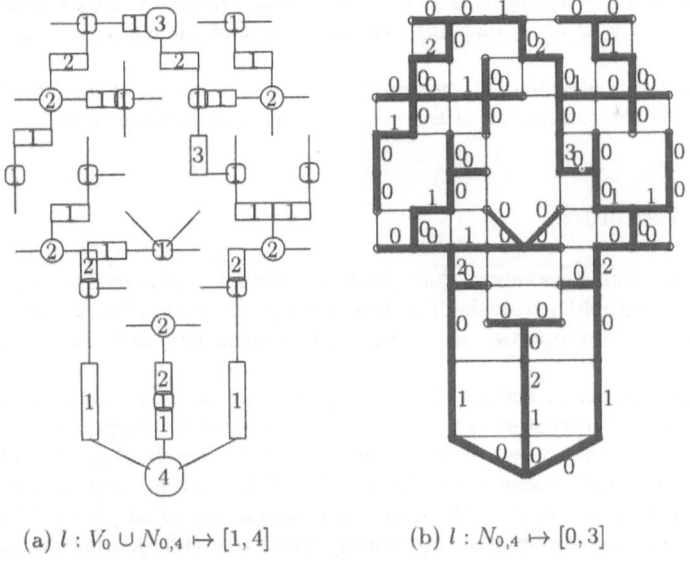

(a) $l : V_0 \cup N_{0,4} \mapsto [1,4]$ (b) $l : N_{0,4} \mapsto [0,3]$

Figure 6: Labels of the spanning tree

Figure 6(a) and (b), show such a labeling for the levels 0, 1, 2, 3, and 4 in our example
pyramid. The labels of the vertices in Fig. 6a are shown inside the circles identifying
them. The bridges of $N_{0,4}$ are displayed as elongated rectangles surrounding the label.
The edges of level 0 are indicated by straight lines and the vertices of level 0 are omitted.
The above labeling assigns labels to the tree $T = (V_0, N_{0,n})$ spanning the base graph
$G_0 = (V_0, E_0)$.

3.2 Reconstruction of decimation parameters

The hierarchy of surviving vertices can be reconstructed from V_0 by thresholding the
vertex labels $l : V_0 \mapsto \{0, 1, \ldots, n\}$:

$$V_i = \{v \in V_0 | l(v) \le i\} \qquad i = 1, \ldots, n \tag{11}$$

The ECKs for the base level, $N_{0,i}$, result similarly by thresholding the edge labels $l : N_{0,n} \mapsto \{0, 1, \ldots, n-1\}$:

$$N_{0,i} = \{e \in N_{0,n} | l(e) < i\} \qquad i = 1, \ldots, n-1 \qquad (12)$$

The ECKs of the higher levels $j > 0$ can be derived by contracting lower level ECKs $k < j$:

$$(V_j, N_{j,i}) = C[(V_k, N_{k,i}), (V_j, N_{k,j})] \qquad \forall 0 \le k < j < i \le n \qquad (13)$$

The two conditions that (13) is a valid decimation are quickly verified: (1) $(V_k, N_{k,j})$ is a forest spanning $(V_k, N_{k,i})$ since $N_{k,j} \subset N_{k,i}$ for $j < i$, and (2) V_j are the roots of $(V_k, N_{k,j})$ by construction. To see that the dual contraction $C[G_j, (V_i, N_{j,i})]$ with the reconstructed primary non-surviving edges from (13) reproduces the same G_i, we recall the inclusions $N_{k,j} \subset N_{k,i} \subset E_k$. We can assume that $N_{k,j}$ and $N_{k,i}$ are equivalent contraction kernels allowing to contract graph G_k into G_j and G_i respectively, e.g. $C[G_k, (V_j, N_{k,j})] = G_j$ and $C[G_k, (V_i, N_{k,i})] = G_i$. The result follows from considering connecting paths in G_k connecting vertices of G_i and the effects of contracting them with $N_{k,j}$.

Note that the contraction of the forest in (13) does not need dual face contraction because only the contraction of a cycle can generate redundant faces.

4   Conclusion

Decimation parameters control dual graph contraction, a process that iteratively builds an irregular (graph) pyramid. The new concept of contraction kernel preserves the graph's structural properties, its connectivity, its planarity, and the face degrees of its dual graph.

Equivalent contraction kernels (ECKs) allow to skip the construction of intermediate pyramid levels. The contents of aggregations of cells can be computed efficiently and in parallel through the tree structure of the contraction kernels. The ECK of the apex is a spanning tree of the base graph. By attaching labels to the vertices and to the edges of this spanning tree we pack the decimation parameters of all pyramid levels into one single equivalent structure, the labeled spanning tree (LST), which is additionally a substructure of the base graph. The decimation parameters can be computed without dually contracting the graphs step by step. Instead we can first generate a spanning tree and then determine the labels. The new concept of contraction kernels has been effectively used to prove that all possible segmentations (as defined in [12]) can be represented at one pyramid level [7]. This is not possible with regular pyramids [2].

Primitive modifications of the LST correspond to modifications of dual irregular pyramid that can be done to optimize global properties after the pyramid is built ([6]) without the need of complete bottom-up reconstruction. This opens the possibilities to optimize the pyramidal structure in the pyramid domain and to dynamically adapt the structure to a changing input.

References

[1] Peter K. Ahnelt and Dietmar Pum. The foveal photoreceptors. a model for the comparison of physiologic and algorithmic image compressions. In Peter Mandl, editor,

Modelling and New Methods in Image Processing and in Geographical Information Systems, OCG-Schriftenreihe, Österr. Arbeitsgemeinschaft für Mustererkennung, pages 223–232. Oldenbourg, 1991. Band 61.

[2] M. Bister, J. Cornelis, and Azriel Rosenfeld. A critical view of pyramid segmentation algorithms. *Pattern Recognition Letters*, Vol. 11(No. 9):pp. 605–617, September 1990.

[3] P. J. Burt and E. H. Adelson. The Laplacian pyramid as a compact image code. *IEEE Transactions on Communications*, Vol. COM-31(No.4):pp.532–540, April 1983.

[4] Jean-Michel Jolion and Annick Montanvert. The adaptive pyramid, a framework for 2D image analysis. *Computer Vision, Graphics, and Image Processing: Image Understanding*, 55(3):pp.339–348, May 1992.

[5] Walter G. Kropatsch. Building Irregular Pyramids by Dual Graph Contraction. *IEE-Proc. Vision, Image and Signal Processing*, Vol. 142(No. 6):pp. 366–374, December 1995.

[6] Walter G. Kropatsch. Equivalent Contraction Kernels and The Domain of Dual Irregular Pyramids. Technical Report PRIP-TR-42, Institute f. Automation 183/2, Dept. for Pattern Recognition and Image Processing, TU Wien, Austria, 1995. Also available through http://www.prip.tuwien.ac.at/ftp/pub/publications/trs/tr42.ps.gz.

[7] Walter G. Kropatsch and Souheil BenYacoub. A revision of pyramid segmentation. In Walter G. Kropatsch, editor, *13th International Conference on Pattern Recognition*, volume II, pages 477–481. IEEE Comp.Soc., 1996.

[8] Herwig Macho and Walter G. Kropatsch. Finding Connected Components with Dual Irregular Pyramids. In Franc Solina and Walter G. Kropatsch, editors, *Visual Modules, Proc. of 19th ÖAGM and 1st SDVR Workshop*, pages 313–321. OCG-Schriftenreihe, Österr. Arbeitsgemeinschaft für Mustererkennung, R. Oldenburg, 1995. Band 81.

[9] David Marr. Visual information processing: The structure and creation of visual representations. *Philosophical Transactions of the Royal Society London*, Ser. B(290):pp.199–218, 1980.

[10] Christophe Mathieu, Isabelle E. Magnin, and C. Baldy-Porcher. Optimal stochastic pyramid: segmentation of MRI data. *Proc. Med. Imaging VI: Image Processing*, SPIE Vol.1652:pp.14–22, Feb. 1992.

[11] Peter Meer. Stochastic image pyramids. *Computer Vision, Graphics, and Image Processing*, Vol. 45(No. 3):pp.269–294, March 1989.

[12] Theo Pavlidis. *Structural Pattern Recognition*. Springer, New York, 1977.

Towards a generalized primal sketch

Christophe Duperthuy and Jean-Michel Jolion

1 Introduction

Seeing is probably the leading goal of Computer Vision. Yet, what to see may be more difficult to analyze as it is mainly application-dependent. Hence, if we commonly accept to represent a scene by means of a set of pixels (picture elements), independently of the acquisition process, or the pixels topology, treatments applied on such elements differ greatly according to the approaches. Similarly, biological vision is in agreement with the "sampling" principle of the scene; yet, subsequent treatments are not clearly defined but "global" functions leading to cortical specializations.

This way, most of the applications consist in transformations from the raw representation to more symbolic ones, accounting for different features. Our goal here is to define basic primitives for raw picture representation : this is the primal sketch, as defined by Marr [1]. In a first part, we define the primal sketch notion and our surrounding framework. Then we expose a "feature" classification and its results. The third part deals with a directional approach and its adaptation to a texture discrimination process.

2 Framework

2.1 The primal sketch

Definition Since 1978, David Marr defined the primal sketch as being the first stage within a visual system : it consists in the extraction of 2D visual data from pictures. This process is followed by subsequent "abstraction" levels, from visual data to object recognition, in order to reach the goal of the system... Hence, the primal sketch is not an end per se !

Now, one may ask what are visual data at all ? If the more common one is the shape (shape detection for pattern recognition), we can also encounters for color and motion (for Computer Vision in general) : color is not essential for most tasks, but it can be of help *e.g.* in differencing pomelos from oranges (is this really an application ?); and motion may be of importance for "dynamic" visual systems, as seeing is not a single passive state... Finally, another attribute, texture, may be added to visual data set, though its notion is not clearly defined. To sum up, we can say that seeing is an "abstraction" phenomenon that enables a virtual world reconstruction, from a sampled world acquisition. In such a way, the primal sketch just follows the sampling process : its aim is to extract local relationships on pixels' neighbourhood, in order to enhance what is to be seen.

Main approaches Marr and Hildreth [1] were the instigators of the primal sketch. They based their approach on light discontinuities, searching then for edges by means of $\nabla^2 G$ (where G is Gaussian) kernels of various sizes. This way, they obtain the raw primal sketch *i.e.* a set of "edge" maps. Yet, we have to face here expensive convolutions (they could be solved with the Laplacian Pyramid of Burt and Adelson [2]), and more problematic is the "reductive" aspect of an edge based approach : all problems do not reduce to edge detection...

Lindeberg suggested in 1993 [3] a "blob" (region) approach to the primal sketch, within the scale-space framework, so called the scale-space primal sketch. Here, blob could be seen as dual with edges : they consist in a seed (a local extrema) and an iterated growth around the seed according to a predicate (region growing). Hence a blob corresponds to a hill or a basin, and combinations through scale-space improve their confidence level, leading to the definition of scale-space blobs. Thus, this approach rises a more "volumic" description of a scene and edges can be found on blob's boundary (poor localization). It is also time consuming, and the complexity depends on the scene because of the data-driven process.

Expectations From previous approaches, the expectations of a more general primal sketch follows : first, the compromise between robustness and calculation delays holds (the representation should be obtained fastly, though significant). Then, a retinotopic representation (matrix) is also kept for simplicity. Third, a data-driven process could be of interest in order to treat each picture according to its content... And finally, fine features representation could be a plus.

2.2 Binary pictures

The Contrasts Pyramid In [4], Jolion defines the Contrasts Pyramid and uses it to simplify pictures from grey level to binary information : the Contrasts Pyramid principle follows that of the Laplacian Pyramid of Burt [2]; the only change is that, in place of computing the difference between a level and its "approximation" from the upper level, we compute their ratio. Thus, we obtain a comparison of each pixel, from its background, which somewhat corresponds to contrast.

We can then enhance each contrast, *e.g.* with a power function applied on them. Moreover, a top-down process ensures that we take into account all background sizes (within pyramidal architecture at least !), as opposed to fixed width models. Iterating this enhancement process leads to a quasi-binary picture : in about five iterations (10 seconds for the 512×512 picture of the mandrill, Figure 1), we obtain more than 90% of black-and-white pixels. A thresholding ends the binarization.

If we consider the results of this binarization processi, we can state that : though simplifying pictures, global information remains; homogeneous areas results in "textured" areas, with various transition densities, *e.g.* left-and-right against central parts of the nose; finally, the algorithm 's parallel complexity is quite low, $O(\#iterations \log Image\_Size)$.

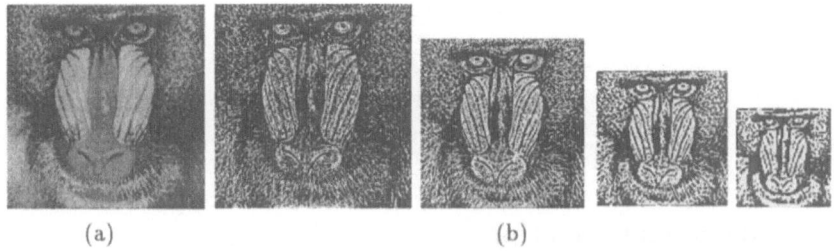

(a)   (b)

Figure 1: (a) original grey level picture of the mandrill, size 512 × 512 (b) Contrasts Pyramid for levels 0 to 3

Why using binary pictures ?　Our choice of binary pictures may seem strange. Indeed, current technology permits grey-level and even color picture acquisition at low costs. Yet, if we consider the primal sketch as a simplification process, binarization follows this principle : the amount of data is reduced to basic information, *e.g.* if there is a significant contrast between two pixels, there will be a black-white transition in the Contrasts Pyramid.

But the binarization does not limit to the Contrasts Pyramid : Computer Vision uses many binary representation such as edge maps, labelized objects (reduced to many binary maps), thresholded gradients... Moreover, the "atomic" nature of binary information could be compared to the activation of neurons, within the brain. And finally, we shall mention the interest of binary information for its manipulation, storage and even, hardware implementation.

3×3 **binary masks**　Obtaining binary pictures is a step towards picture simplification : yet, if we reduce the range of possible values, for each pixel, we still not have extracted visual data at all. As exposed above, we shall extract now local relationship between pixels. For that, we suggest to use fixed neighbourhoods and realize then classifications of them.

The choice of 3×3 binary masks is inspired from the study of Canning *et al.* in [5]. Indeed, 3×3 masks represent only 512 centered patterns, which provides a small set of patterns, but large enough to consider direct neighbours. Keeping in mind the idea of centered masks, larger widths would result in millions masks to classify (*e.g.* over 33 millions for 5×5 patterns). Another point to be mentioned is that in case of a parallel computation, and even a hardware implementation, local short links to 8-neighbours are to be preferred against larger neighbourhoods.

We suggest now to split 3×3 binary patterns on four overlapping 2×2 submasks (see Figure 2) in order to study them at a finer scale on next sections. The central pixel which should respond for the whole mask, is still present on all sub-pattern.

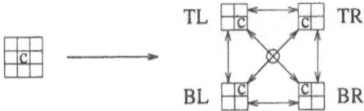

Figure 2: Splitting the 3 × 3 pattern on four overlapping 2 × 2 sub-patterns.

3   A feature classification

3.1   Principles

Classification   By "feature" classification we mean the study of transitions according to their continuity. For example, Figure 3 represents the transitions types for 2 × 2 sub-masks : we consider as "line" the double transitions; steps are the single transitions; and plateaus have no transition.

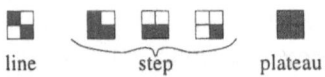

Figure 3: Features on 2 × 2 masks

Coming back to 3×3 patterns, we choose to classify only half of them, considering the white-center masks as duals with black-center ones... Moreover, studying feature width, we consider that a rotation of $\frac{n\Pi}{4}$ (n being an integer) of a mask does not change its nature.

Thus, we define "impulse noise" as a central pixel different from all of its neighbours (Figure 4). Edges consist in at least one plateau and one step-or-line, contrary to lines that contain a step or a line on each sub-mask. And finally, blobs (homogeneous masks) are made of four plateaus. This way, we classify all the 3 × 3 masks, upon 8 classes that are black or white noise, black or white line, black or white edge and black or white blob.

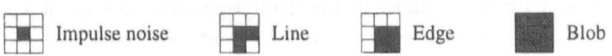

Figure 4: Examples of features on 3 × 3 masks

Extraction of features   In principle, each pixel of a binary picture (borders excepted) can "compute" its mask and then consults a look-up table of features, in parallel, to respond in the appropriate map. But here, the extraction process follows the successive refinements principle.

Indeed, if we consider noises, they are by definition not significant (robust-less at least). Suppose now that we suppress them; extracting edges or lines after this suppression will prevent abusive responses on noises' neighbours. This holds for textures (lines) too : we mentioned that fine features appear on "globally" homogeneous areas; suppressing thus those fine features will increase "homogeneity" of a surrounding blob.

Hence, the successive refinements enables a "more robust" extraction of features : though 3 × 3 binary masks consider only direct 8-neighbours, assumptions on a 5 × 5 neighbourhood are made.

3.2 Results

Noises For simplicity, black and white noises are gathered on a single map : they are scattered over pictures and thus do not seem to contain information (so we do not show the pictures). An auto and inter correlation (between levels) study confirms this statement.

Textures Black lines are called "Black textures", because of the textured aspect of fine features. Thus we can see on Figure 5a the distribution of black textures : they're less numerous on edges' neighbourhood-s, due to the binarization process (textures could be seen as low contrasts, against edges that are high contrasts). The correlation study shows for black textures, a short continuity within each level (auto correlation), and no significant continuity from a level to the upper one : this confirms the "robust-less" nature of textures (or low contrasts) within a picture. Yet, texture distribution may appear differently from a part to the other *e.g.* the nose against the coat. We will not show the white texture results : they are quite similar with black textures (considering their behaviour through resolutions), though less numerous.

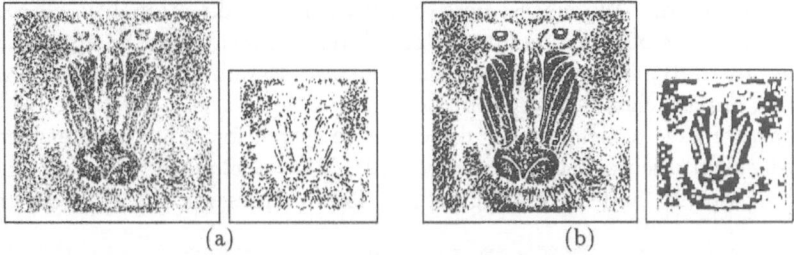

(a)   (b)

Figure 5: (a) black textures (b) white blobs for the mandrill (level 0 and 2)

Blobs The white blobs effectively correspond to homogeneous areas (Figure 5b). They have a great continuity within each level, and a significant one from a level to the upper one : homogeneity is quite robust upon resolutions. Black blob maps are similar for continuity, and they appear as duals with white blobs.

Edges Figure 6a shows black edges for the mandrill : their continuity (within a level, *i.e.* auto correlation) is greater than that of textures, and we also find a continuity from a level to the upper one (inter correlation). That means that, according to their definition, edges are robust through resolutions.
A comparison with the Canny-Deriche operator (6b), at alpha equal to 1, shows that our edge points are more continuous within and through resolutions (correlation study). Yet, we obtain raw responses, and we don't have any criterion

114

preventing two responses of the same edge point. Nevertheless, our calculation delays (binarization include) are about twice-and-half that of Canny-Deriche, for outputs increased sevenfold in terms of maps. A final remark here is that the mandrill picture doesn't seem well suited to edge detection : due to coat-texture, too many edges are detected...

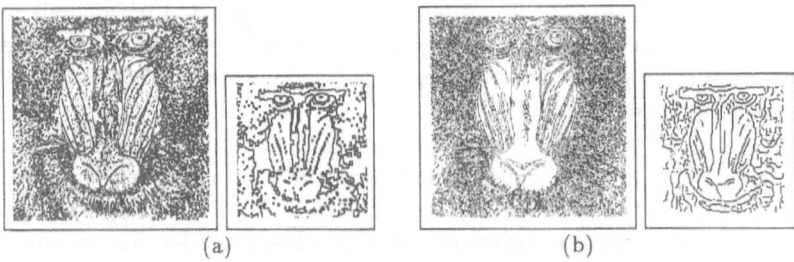

(a)   (b)

Figure 6: (a) black edges for the mandrill with the binary masks approach (b) Canny-Deriche edges (at $\alpha = 1$) on the Gaussian Pyramid (level 0 and 2)

4   A directional approach

4.1   Principle

Basic directions   We suggest here to study features' directionality. Of course, usual approaches of directionality on grey-level pictures, could be applied here. But because of the binary nature of the Contrasts Pyramid, we suggest to adopt here too, a mask classification approach.

For that, we have to define basic directions to search for. Thus we consider the following eight orientations : $0° = arctan(0)$, $27° = arctan(\frac{1}{2})$, $45° = arctan(1)$, $63° = arctan(2)$, and so on (Figure 7). These represents the only directions

0°   27°   45°   63°   90°   117°   135°   153°

Figure 7: Basic orientations on 3×3 binary masks

given a 3×3 pattern (according to Bresenheim algorithm of one pixel wide lines, passing through central pixel).

Here we make some assumptions for masks classification : some masks (noises or blobs for example) have no direction; a mask may have many directions (junctions...); and finally, a mask and its dual have the same orientation(s).

2×2 **sub-mask orientation**   Using the splitting principle of Figure 2, we suggest to study our eight basic orientations at a finer scale. Thus basic directions upon 2×2 patterns are less numerous (4 directions); moreover, they depends on the position of the central pixel c. See Figure 8 for an example on the Top-Left sub-mask.

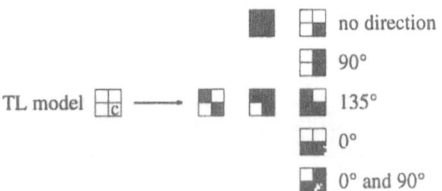

Figure 8: Top-Left sub-mask orientations

A grammatical approach Now the sub-masks being classified, we can set the identification rules for usual directions. We thus obtain :

0° :	(TL=0° and TR=0°) or (BL=0° and BR=0°)
27° :	(TR=45° and (TL or BL)=0°) or (BL=45° and (BR or TR)=0°)
45° :	(TR=45° and BL=45°)
63° :	(TR=45° and (BR or BL)=90°) or (BL=45° and (TL or TR)=90°)
90° :	(TL=90° and BL=90°) or (TR=90° and BR=90°)
117° :	(TL=135° and (BR or BL)=90°) or (BR=135° and (TL or TR)=90°)
135° :	(TL=135° and BR=135°)
153° :	(TL=135° and (BR or TR)=0°) or (BR=135° and (TL or BL)=0°)

A ninth class has to be considered, containing other non-oriented masks : it consists mainly in terminations, corners, blobs, noises and noise-like masks. Indeed, corners and terminations are considered unoriented, due to their lack of directional continuity.

4.2 Results

Test pictures Masks directional classification has then been tested on four first levels of the Contrasts Pyramid of "ploop" picture : this picture consists in *cosine* and *sine* functions in grey level (size 512 × 512) and results in concentric black-and-white circles that deteriorate rapidly through resolutions, due to "moiré" effects and aliasing.
The results of those tests pictures are not shown here : directions are extracted in accordance with their model. They are continuous within and upon resolutions though their quality decreases rapidly from level two upwards (see [6]).

Quadratic maps Inspired from a model of pre-attentive texture discrimination (the model of Bergen and Landy [7]), we suggest to compute quadrature maps : the advantage is that we can reduce the amount of maps twofold, and we enhance also maps' sense. Indeed, opposite directional responses contrasts on the same map.
So we adapt Bergen and Landy's algorithm to our binary maps : we subtract to each map within $[0, \frac{\Pi}{2}]$ its orthogonal map within $[\frac{\Pi}{2}, \Pi]$. We realign results from [-255,255] to [0,255], apply a 5 × 5 Gaussian kernel blur, and subsample the picture (half-size horizontally and vertically). The sub-sampling reduces the amount of data, while the Gaussian kernel enables a reinforcement or inhibition of neighbours' responses. A final normalization for each pixel is applied. We

obtain then four quadratures : $0°vs90°$, $27°vs117°$, $45°vs135°$ and $63°vs153°$ (Figure 9).

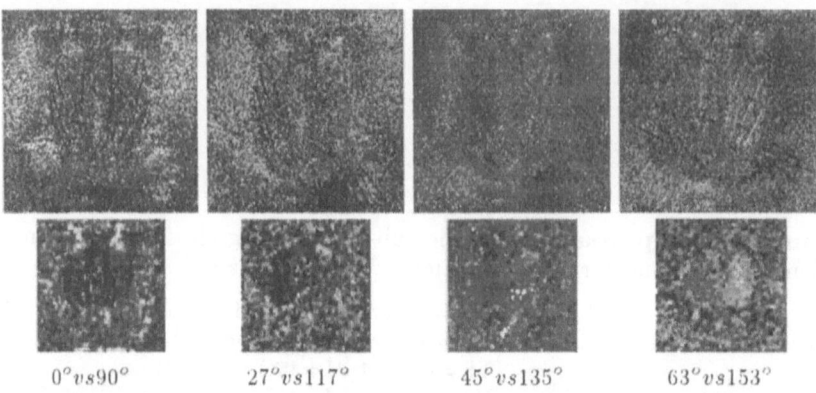

$0°vs90°$ $\quad\quad$ $27°vs117°$ $\quad\quad$ $45°vs135°$ $\quad\quad$ $63°vs153°$

Figure 9: directional quadratures for the mandrill (level 0 and 2)

Finally, an edge detection algorithm is applied on those pictures, in order to extract "quadratic textures" boundary : here we choose Canny-Deriche operator at α equal respectively to $0.1, 0.2, 0.4$ for levels 0, 1 and 2. Upper levels are not considered. They seem non significant because of the nature of binary maps and the sub-sampling. Concerning the α parameter, we choose it quite low in order to be robust (quadratures are "noisy") : thus, we loose in localization, which may not be a problem for "pre-attentive" discrimination.

Boundaries A test picture of orthogonal bars (Figure 10, ones in a central square oriented to $45°$ and the others in a surrounding square, oriented to $135°$, is first studied.

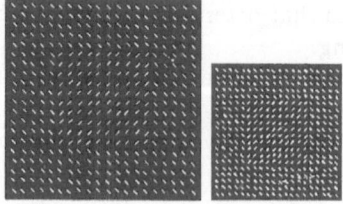

Figure 10: test image for directional quadrature boundary detection (level 0 and 2)

Obtained boundaries are shown in Figure 11. Though spurious responses, the quadrature $45°vs135°$ responds correctly from level 0 upwards, contrary to quadrature $0°vs90°$ which remains silent. Quadratures $27°vs117°$ and $63°vs153°$ respond also for level 1 and 2, with almost noisy edges. Thus, directional quadrature boundary detection enables discrimination of simple oriented and orthogonal patterns.

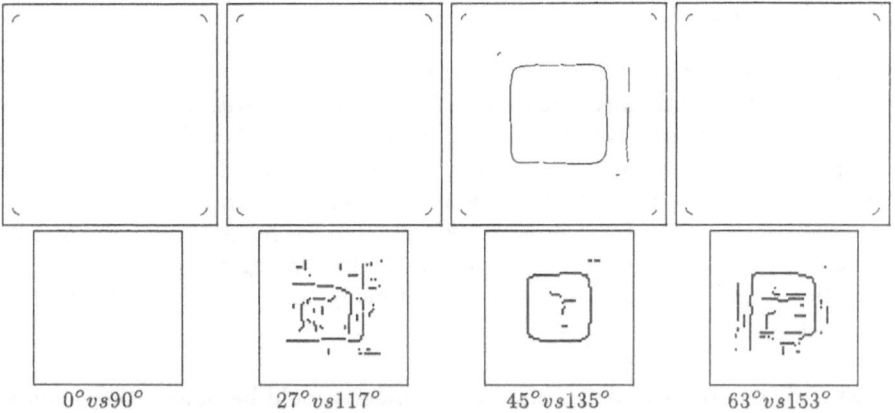

$0°vs90°$ $27°vs117°$ $45°vs135°$ $63°vs153°$

Figure 11: directional quadrature boundaries for quadratic bars (level 0 and 2)

We suggest finally to apply this boundary detection on the mandrill quadratic maps of Figure 9. We obtain then boundaries of Figure 12 : here, we do not have perfect quadratic patterns, so results are more difficult to analyze. If we look at level 2 of quadrature $0°vs90°$, we have a quite closed contour in its center : this corresponds to the vertically oriented aspect of the noise, against the rest of the head. For quadrature $27°vs117°$, we find the left part of the noise (oriented according to $117°$) on levels 1 and 2, whereas the right part is found in quadrature $63°vs153°$ on same levels. Quadratures $45°vs135°$ do not seem significant here (no closed contour).

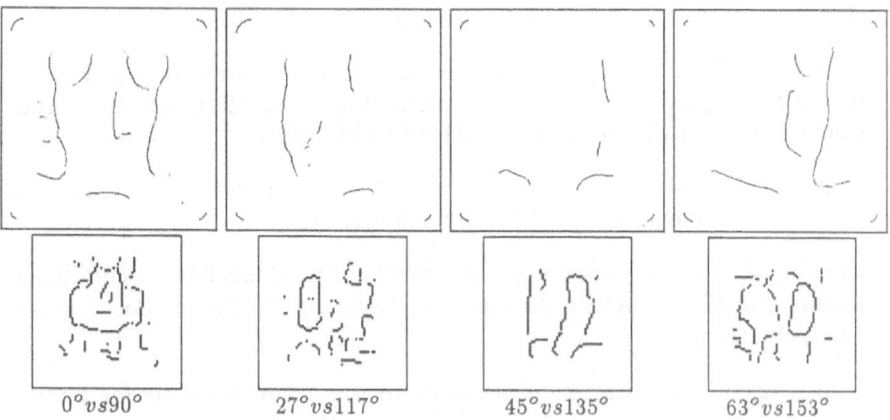

$0°vs90°$ $27°vs117°$ $45°vs135°$ $63°vs153°$

Figure 12: directional quadrature boundaries for the mandrill (level 0 and 2)

118

5 Conclusion

Discussion We show in this paper a new approach of primal sketch : we obtain efficient algorithms ($O(\log Image\_Size)$ complexity within pyramidal framework) and we obtain several maps (for many resolutions), well suited to combinations. The data-driven aspect of our approach, arises from the binarization process that is "auto-adaptive" to pictures content, though we have a parameter for the convergence of the process. Finally, our representations exhibit edges (coarse features), textures (fines features), blobs (homogeneity), noises and orientations. Thus, we consider our approach being "generalized" (or trying to be at least !).

Extension At this point, some improvements could be done : the boundary detection applied on quadratic maps has to be robust. A region growing approach on those maps may reduce important blurring of edge operators, and then, improve localization. An extension of orientation detection could also be "curvature information" from those orientations. This could be used for key points extraction. Finally, motion have not yet been studied : should we treat time dimension at the binarization stage, or after ?

References

[1] Marr, D., Hildreth, E.: Theory of edge detection. Proceeding of the Royal Society London B 207, 187-217 (1980).

[2] Burt, P.J., Adelson, E.H.: The Laplacian pyramid as a compact image code. IEEE Transactions on Communications 31, 532-540 (1983).

[3] Lindeberg, T.: Detecting salient blob-like image structures and their scales with a scale-space primal sketch: A method for focus-of-attention. International Journal of Computer Vision 11, 283-318 (1993).

[4] Jolion, J.-M.: Multi-resolution analysis of contrast in digital images (in french). Traitement du Signal 11, 245-255 (1994).

[5] Canning, J., Kim, J.J., Rosenfeld, A.: Symbolic pixel labeling for curvilinear feature detection. DARPA Image Understanding Workshop, Los Angeles, 242-256 (1987).

[6] Duperthuy, C.: A directional approach to 3 × 3 binary masks for texture discrimination (*in french*). Research Report RR-9601, Laboratoire Reconnaissance de Formes et Vision (1996).

[7] Bergen, J.R., Landy, M.S.: Computational Modeling of Visual Texture Segregation. In: Landy M.S., Movshon J.A. (eds.): Computational Models of Visual Processing. Bradford Book, MIT Press, 1991 (pp. 253-271).

Categorization through temporal analysis of patterns

Jean-Michel Jolion

1. About a methodology

Fifteen years ago, in *Vision* [1], David Marr proposed a "computational investigation into the human representation and processing of visual information". This book is considered by many in the field of computer vision as the main work of these last fifteen years. Indeed, Marr was the first to propose a complete methodology for computer vision which became known as the Marr paradigm. Considering vision as an information-processing system and a system as a mapping from one representation to another, Marr defined more precisely vision as a process that produces, from images of the external world, a description that is useful to the viewer and not cluttered with irrelevant information. Marr's hypothesis was "if we are able to create, using vision, an accurate representation of the three-dimensional world and its properties, then using this information we can perform any visual task" [2]. Visually perceiving the external world and using these information were clearly separated.

Let us grant this thesis. The goal of our information process is thus clearly defined. The next question is : how do we achieve this goal? This is where Marr makes his main contribution, his proposed, methodology, which formulates the different levels at which an information processing device must be understood before one can say to have understood it completely. This is the so-called three levels : computational theory (what is the goal of the computation, why is it appropriate, and what is the logic of the strategy by which it can be carried out ?), representation and algorithm (how can this computational theory be implemented ? in particular, what is the representation for the input and output, and what is the algorithm for the transformation ?) and hardware implementation (how can the representation and algorithm be realized physically ?).

This methodology can be viewed as an ordered list of questions whose answers should be obtained from information, *e.g.*, constraints, we can get about vision process. However, where are these constraints coming from? For instance, the first question of Marr's methodology is "what is the goal of the computation?" Marr and his colleagues argued that the underlying purpose of vision was to describe scenes. This resulted in attempts of describing the geometry of the visible surfaces, since the information encoded in images, for example by stereopsis, shading, texture, contours, or visual motion, is due to shape's local surface properties. However, an image does not contain enough information for a complete and unambiguous reconstruction of a three-dimensional scene. This often results in ill-posed problems. The main approach is thus the regularization theory [3].

Of course there exist other sources of information like the constraints related to the observer, *e.g.*, the sensor and the computer. On this particular aspect Marr said : "In the early stages of the analysis of an image, the representations used depend more on what it is possible to compute from an image than on what is ultimately desirable, but later representations can be more sensitive to the specific needs of recognition."

However, there is no explicit use of the last kind of constraints, and *possible to compute* has to be understood as *what is actually present in the scene*. The constraints related to the goal to achieve are limited to high levels of image interpretation. On the contrary, active perception [4] and other related concepts such as active vision [5] and purposive vision try to understand how does the fact that an observer is active affect the levels (in the Marr sense) of a visual system? The underlying goal of the observer thus becomes a source of information as important as the scene. Reconciling the scene-based and the observer's goal-based approaches seems to be very promising and may be the ultimate approach (even if a recent debate on these approaches shows that we still are a long way from this compromise [6]).

But observer-based constraints are still not taken into account. In that sense Poggio [7] argued that the information processed in a machine is only loosely constrained by the physical properties of the machine. As a minimal constraint, Marr argued that the implementation details don't matter so much from this perspective provided that they do the right thing. On the contrary we consider that the third level of the Marr's paradigm is not only concerned with the implementation and that we must try to understand which kind of information should be extracted from the fact that any hardware implementation has its own properties. Note that human vision is just a particular (of course quite complex) class of hardware implementation of a vision process. Neurophysiologists attempt to understand how sensory and neural mechanism of biological systems function. They thus are going up in the Marr's paradigm, *e.g.* starting with a particular implementation.

As another example, consider the Content based Retrieval problem in video databases. Classic products make use of characteristics coming from theoretical studies on image motion. Then one try to manage them with implementation constraint, *e.g.* MPEG format. Another approach is to consider MPEG as a constraint at the very beginning of the study and to build new characteristics which take into account MPEG's particularities. However this is often considered as too domain dependent, like is industrial vision.

2. The dataflow pyramid model

We report in this paper some experiments we have done to show how one can take advantage of a particular implementation. Suppose we choose a pyramid architecture for our computer vision system [8]. An image pyramid is a stack of representations of a digital image at successively reduced resolutions. The basic pyramid architecture is presented in Figure 1. Successive levels of the pyramid decrease two-fold in size. The basic idea of pyramid-based approach is that to compute information about block, *i.e.* sub-image of size $2^k \times 2^k$, the algorithms consists of k computational stages, each of which involves only a bounded amount of computation. In this sense, we can say that the total amount of computation, *i.e.* the computational complexity, is proportional to the logarithm of the block size. So, these algorithms are often called O(log n) algorithm (if n is the size of the image). This approach is also known as divide-and-conquer when using a more general hierarchy. This architecture has been shown to be an efficient framework for early vision.

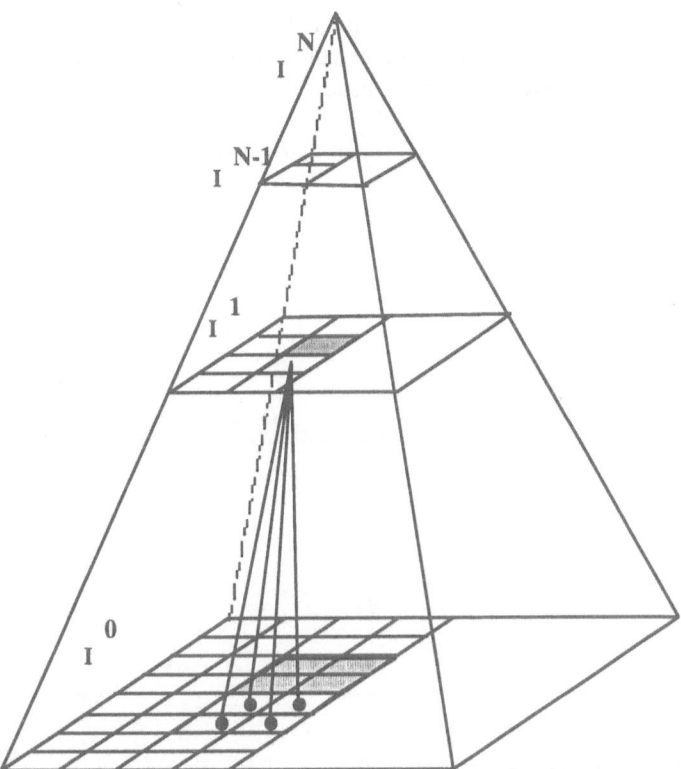

Figure 1 : The basic pyramid architecture. A processor on level k received information from its four children on level k-1. This architecture is used both for multiresolution representation of images and implementation of local_to_global evidence accumulation strategies. The lower level is the base, the higher the apex of the pyramid. Any information spatially distributed on the base is extracted by the pyramid computer in O(log image_size) computational steps.

We considered a basic function of vision systems: the extraction of connected components in binary images. Figure 3a is an example of a binary image containing 37 connected components of various sizes. Many algorithms exist for sequential or parallel computers [9]. Note that this function is of interest because the result is unique whatever algorithm you use. On a pyramid computer, the algorithm is as follows: each processor on a given level of the pyramid gets from any of its children a list of the connected components contained in the receptive field of this child. It then builds a new list by merging the elements coming from the same connected component (see Figure 2) and send the new list to its parent. The process is iterated from the base (which is directly related to the image) to the apex.

Let us now consider a real implementation without a global synchronization of the processors. So, any processor performs its task as soon as the information coming

122

from the children are available, yielding a data flow behavior of the pyramid computer. It is also easy to allow any processor to start merging connected component elements without having received all the lists.

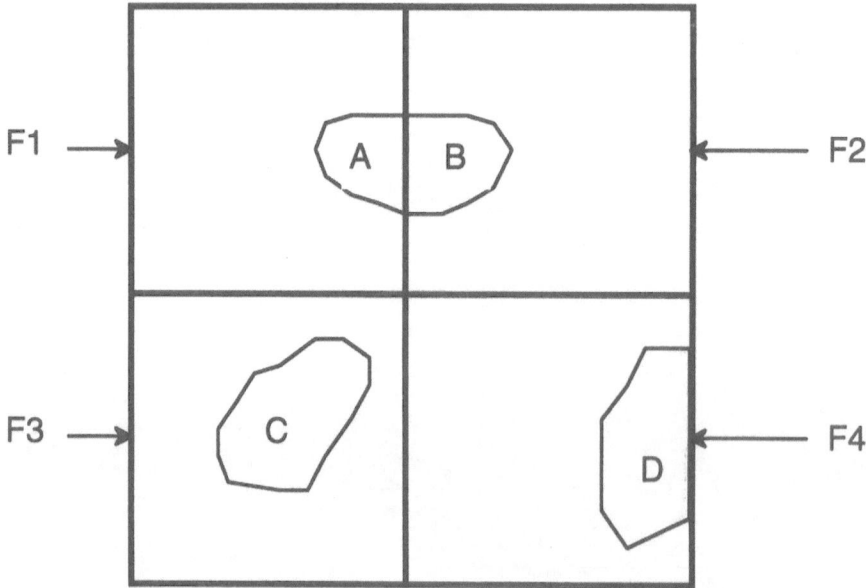

Figure 2 : Connected component extraction. Processor F see the four components A, B, C and D. When sent by child F_3, connected component C is already known to be complete as it has no intersection with the border of the receptive field of F_3. So, it has only to be transferred, without any processing, up the pyramid. On the other hand, A and B are incomplete for their respective processors F_1 and F_2. When processed, these components result in only one which is also a complete component. D is incomplete for child F_4. However, when processed, processor F knows that it cannot be completed by other connected components coming from the other children. So, D is transferred as incomplete. Imagine a connected component made of four sub-components coming from the four children of the processor. When arriving, the three first parts are known to be incomplete. The processing step results in a bigger and bigger connected component, still incomplete but "completable". When the fourth part has been processed, the connected component becomes complete and can then be transferred up the pyramid. Thus different configurations yield different running times.

Indeed, as shown in Figure 2, a connected component being complete for a processor, is complete for any of its parents in the upper levels. So, this connected component can come out the pyramid without waiting at each upper level that the parent merges non complete connected components. With this implementation, we get exactly the same connected components as with other algorithms (recall that the result is unique).

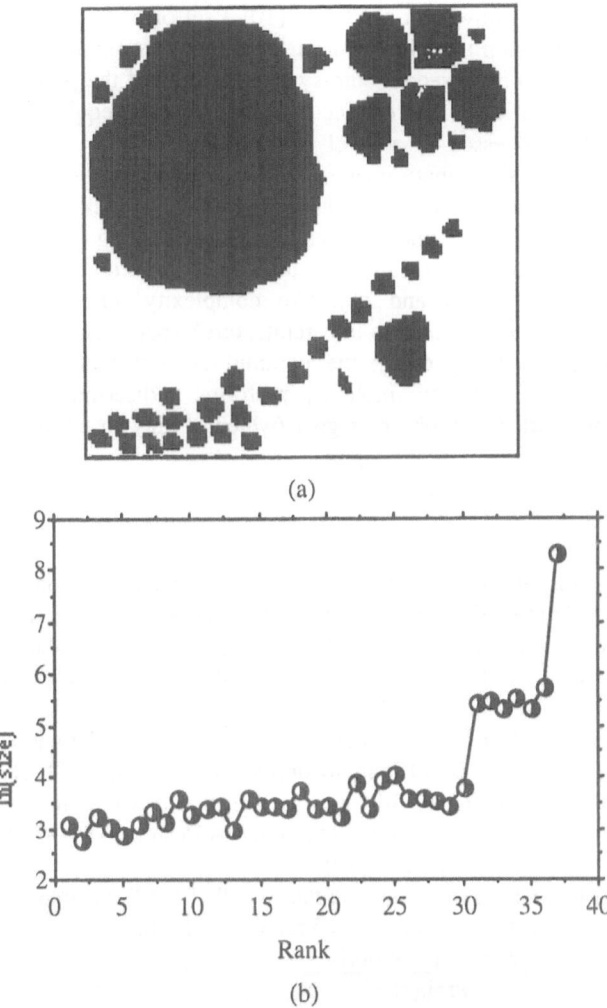

(a)

(b)

Figure 3 : A binary image containing 37 connected components (a). The graph (b) shows the sizes of the connected components as a function of their extracted ranks when extracted by the apex of the pyramid. It clearly shows that small connected components are extracted faster. However, the extraction rank is not only related to the size of the connected component (the curve (b) is not strictly increasing); it also takes into account its neighborhood. Indeed, it has been shown [10] that for a given size, the extraction time is faster when the connected component is different from its background (*e.g.* of different size and shape).

However, we now have a new information: the order in which the connected components are coming out of the apex. The connected component set only depends on the scene. But, the connected component ordered list depends on the **observed scene**. This supplementary information is neither contained in the scene nor in the classic hiearchical connected component extraction algorithm. Figure 3 is an example of such a process.

Recently, S. Bataouche showed in her thesis [10] a set of particular behaviors of the pyramid architecture when used for connected components extraction in a data flow mode. For instance, we observed an auto-synchronization of the processors when the spatial and size distributions of the connected components are equivalent to the spatial distribution of the processor in a level (for instance a classic pyramid structure analyzing a chessboard like binary image). By auto-synchronization, we mean that all the processors in a given level are doing the same elementary task at the same time. As there is no longer delay, the connected components are coming out the apex linearly. We have also shown that the result, *e.g.*, the order, is a function of the size, the complexity (not an *a priori* and objective complexity, but rather an observer dependent complexity, *e.g.*, related to the architecture's spatial characteristics) and the spatial distribution. In many cases, the pyramid computer not only extracts the connected components but also implicitly performs a discrimination/classification even if this is not part of the observer-goal (which is only to extract the connected components).

3. A Bayesian formulation

Of course, this is just an example and we need a more general approach. We will now present some trends towards a more complex framework which can take into account all the components of an artificial visual system. What we are looking for is to start from a given scene and to extract some useful information about it, *e.g.* an interpretation.

Let **s** be the scene and **i** its interpretation. It is quite natural to look for the best interpretation. However, it is difficult to define the concept of "best" without any reference model. One way to do this is to assume that this best interpretation is the most probable one. Thus we can use the Maximum A Posteriori (MAP) framework :

$$i \, ? \, \text{Prob} \, (i \mid s) = \text{Max}_j \, \text{Prob}(j \mid s) \tag{1}$$

Using the Bayes theorem, we end up with the so-called MAP formulation :

$$\text{Prob}(i,s) = \text{Prob} \, (i \mid s) \, . \, \text{Prob}(s) = \text{Prob} \, (s \mid i) \, . \, \text{Prob}(i)$$

$$\text{Prob} \, (i \mid s) = \frac{\text{Prob} \, (s \mid i) \, . \, \text{Prob}(i)}{\text{Prob}(s)} \tag{2}$$

Looking for the most probable interpretation is then equivalent to looking for the interpretation maximizing

$$i \, ? \, \text{Max}_i \, \text{Prob} \, (s \mid i) \, . \, \text{Prob}(i) \tag{3}$$

This product is made of two terms :

Prob (s | i) : Given an interpretation, what is the probability of the scene, *e.g.*, what is the adequation of the scene refering to the interpretation. This is mainly a distance evaluation (like the least-square approach when interpreting noisy data).

Prob(i) : Are all the interpretation equivalent ? In this approach, the only source of information is the scene (this is classic Marr's approach). However, we cannot find an interpretation only based on the scene as there is no way to evaluate the second probability. Thus, what we need is to use some contextual information which can help us finding the best interpretation.

Let **C** be the context. It is made of all the knowledge about the underlying application. For instance, it includes the goal of the artificial visual system. The new formulation is still to identify the scene and thus to find the most probable interpretation but not only considering the scene but the couple scene + context (s.C).

$$i ? \text{Prob}(i \mid s,C) = \text{Max}_j \text{ Prob}(j \mid s,C) \tag{4}$$

Using again the Bayes theorem leads us to

$$\text{Prob}(i,s,C) = \text{Prob}(i \mid s,C) . \text{Prob}(s,C) = \text{Prob}(i \mid s,C) . \text{Prob}(s \mid C) . \text{Prob}(C)$$
$$\text{Prob}(i,s,C) = \text{Prob}(s \mid i,C) . \text{Prob}(i,C) = \text{Prob}(s \mid i,C) . \text{Prob}(i \mid C) . \text{Prob}(C)$$
$$\text{Prob}(i \mid s,C) = \frac{\text{Prob}(s \mid i,C) . \text{Prob}(i \mid C)}{\text{Prob}(s \mid C)} \tag{5}$$

Maximizing for the interpretation results in:

$$i ? \text{Max}_i \{ \text{Prob}(s \mid i,C) . \text{Prob}(i \mid C) \} \tag{6}$$

Let us first assume that the scene and the context are independents. The first probability reduces to Prob(s | i) so again an *a posteriori* validation. In this new approach, Prob(i | C) stands for the biais or *a priori* probability on our interpretation. So the best interpretation will be the best one compromizing *a priori* and *a posteriori*. This kind of framework has already been applied to noisy data interpretation [11].

In order to go further, we will now focus on our scene-context independence hypothesis. More precisely, it means the independence between the scene and the observer. Under this assumption, how do we evaluate Prob(s | i) ? Practically speaking, we do not *a posteriori* validate a scene regarding a given interpretation but an internal representation of this scene, **R(s)**, where R stands for the acquisition process. We thus have a dependence between R(s) and C. However, our assumption can be maintained if we consider that R do not influence the interpretation choice. This is the passive vision paradigm's hypothesis as it assumes that the observer does not act towards the scene. On the contrary, the active vision paradigm considers that we do not see but look at the scene which means that we only get what we are looking for.

We argue here that R(s) and C are dependents because our interpretation does not characterize the scene but the observed scene. This kind of reasoning is quite novel in artificial vision community but is not in general science and more particularly in theoretical physic. Indeed, when looking for new particules, the scientist has to consider its influence on the scene [12].

Let us point out that this is a way to explicit why the expert knowledge approach has not been so successful in computer vision. Indeed, with this technique, one try to build a context model including the knowledge of a given human expert. However, whatever is the quality of the context model, it cannot help us if we do not apply it on the same data as the expert does, *e.g.* R(s) of the expert is not the same as R(s) of the artificial system. In other words, whatever is your camera, it is still a camera and not an artificial eye!

These remarks lead us to the definition of what we call the **perceptive model** as opposed to the cognitive model used in expert system. The perceptive model will be the main tool for the evaluation of Prob(R(s)|i,C) in the same way the cognitive model helps us to evaluate Prob(i|C).

This approach has many potential applications. For instance, this results in new compression techniques by means of taking into account the human perceptive model if the underlying application is mainly visualization. Another example is the process of documents and analysis of handwritting where the perceptive model takes into account the kinetic of the ocular shifting on a document [13].

Note that this framework has been presented for a given scene which may result in image

sequence. We now try to figure out how to make explicit this temporal information.

4. Discussion

Let us come back to our pyramid example. We argue that these cases are not only a border effect of a particular implementation. Indeed, Tsotsos has shown that the complexity of the vision process induces that any implementation must be made of highly parallel and distributed processes and uses multiresolution mechanism [14]. So, any observer must be viewed as a dynamic system which internal behavior, *e.g.* communications between elementary components, is of importance, maybe as important as its input / output relationships: "How" we process information may be more important than "what" we actually process.

Note that neurophysiologists have already investigated a temporal effects in the human visual system. For instance, Bullier *et al.* shown that although neurons in V2 depend upon V1 for their activation, there are many neurons in V2 that are active earlier than some of V1 neurons; therefore, these 'early' V2 neurons are in a position to drive some of the 'later' V1 neurons [15]. Moreover, the results of latency studies provide evidence that the M pathway (mainly concerns with high temporal frequency and low contrast) is characterized by early activation and fast information transfer. This suggests that not only feedforward but also feedback connections may play a role in establishing some receptive field properties and, ultimately, in perception, as suggested by recent theoretical studies [16].

Another related work is known as the temporal tagging hypothesis [17]. However, in these examples, the auto-synchronization or implicit-classification behavior has been detected by an external agent. Is the observer aware of its own internal behavior ? As pointed by Tsotsos for the temporal tagging hypothesis [18], the path lengths required for communication between the elementary processors and an external gating control seems to be wasteful. However, a multi-pyramid architecture is likely to be an economic solution to efficiently implement this inside mechanism. In such an architecture, a pyramid, such as the one presented in Figure 1, starts from any level of the main pyramid, so the apex of each of these pyramids gets information from a particular level, yielding an inside observer. Thus this architecture process more information about what it is currently doing than information directly related to the external stimulus.

Following the active vision paradigm, we must now try to understand how does the fact that an observer has a particular internal behavior, affect the levels of a visual system ? In other words, how can we take advantage of these particularities when designing a computer vision system ? For instance, can this implicit-classification effect be tuned so as to exhibit an external behavior similar to the famous popout phenomenon ? It is indeed well-known that humans are able to recognize objects in unexpected, complex images "at a glance". For example, a human can "immediately" detect a long straight line in the visual field without being disturbed by noise (generally small straight line segments). Does that mean that the human vision system uses robust extractors or that the pattern pops out because being processed faster than other patterns in the visual field or that messages arising from elementary processors, *e.g.* neurons, seeing the line, are better temporally synchronized ? Other kind of architecture (any multiprocessor based architecture) can be studied that way. Connexionism and related neural networks are also of interest in such a study (especially as it has been shown that pyramid architectures and neural networks are highly related [19], similar behaviors can be investigated).

In our current research, we try to extend the bayesian model to the "how" side of the visual process *versus* the classic "what" side. First attempts toward such a methodology have already been reported [20].

References

[1] Marr, D. :Vision , Freeman, San Francisco, 1982.
[2] Aloimonos, Y., Rosenfeld, A.: Computer Vision, Science, 253, 1249-1254 (1991).
[3] Poggio, T., Torre, V., Koch, C.: Computational vision and regularization theory, Nature, 317, 314-319 (1985).
[4] Bajcsy, R.: Active Perception , Proceedings of the IEEE, Special issue on computer vision, 76(8), 996-1005 (1988).
[5] Aloimonos, Y.: Active Perception, L. Erlbaum eds., Hillsdale, 1993.
[6] Tarr, M.J. et al.: Dialogue on "A Computational and Evolutionary Perspective on the Role of Representation in Vision", CVGIP: Image Understanding, 60 (1), 65-118 (1994).
[7] Poggio, T.: Marr's computational approach to vision,Trends Neurosci, 4, 258-262 (1981).
[8] Jolion, J.M., Rosenfeld, A.: A Pyramid Framework for Early Vision, Kluwer, Dordrecht, 1993.
[9] Rosenfedl, A., Kak, A.C.: Digital Picture Processing, 2nd edition, Academic Press, New York, 1982.
[10] Bataouche, S.: Ph.D. thesis (in french), Université Lyon I, France, 1993.
[11] Rosenfeld, A.: Explaining noisy data: a qualitative bayesian approach, CS-TR-2022, University of Maryland, 1988.
[12] Trinh Xuan Thuan: La Mélodie Secrète (in french), Fayard, Le Temps des Sciences, 1988.
[13] Eglin, V., Emptoz, H.: Space and Time-Variant Representation of the Retinal Image for the Simulation of Scan-Path and Attentional Mechanisms on a Document, Laboratoire Reconnaissance de Formes et Vision, Research Report, RR-96.08, 1996.
[14] Tsotsos, J.K.: How Does Human Vision Beat the Computational Complexity of Visual Perception ? , Computational Processes in Human Vision : An

Interdisciplinary Perspective, Z.W. Pylyshyn eds., Ablex Publishing Corporation, 286-338 (1990).

[15] Bullier, J., Nowak, L.G.: Parallel versus serial processing: new vistas on the distributed organization of the visual system, Current Opinion in Neurobiology, 5, 497-503 (1995).

[16] Ulman, S.: Sequence seeking and counter streams: a computational model for bidirectional information flow in the visual cortex. Cereb. Cortex, 5, 782-792 (1995).

[17] Niebur, E., Koch, C., Rosin, C.: An Oscillation-Based Model for the Neuronal Basis of Attention, Vision Research, 33-18, 2789-2802 (1993).

[18] Tsotsos, J.K.: Towards a Computational Model of Visual Attention, in Linking Psychophysics, Neurophysiology, and Computational Vision, MIT Press, Bradford Books, 1994.

[19] Bischof, H.: Ph.D. thesis , Technische Universität Wien, Austria, 1994.

[20] Jolion, J.M.: Computer Vision Methodologies, CVGIP: Image Understanding, 59, 53-71 (1994).

Detection of regions of interest via the Pyramid Discrete Symmetry Transform

Vito Di Gesú and Cesare Valenti

1. Introduction

Pyramid computation has been introduced to design efficient vision algorithms [1], [2] based on both *top-down* and *bottom-up* strategies. It has been also suggested by biological arguments that show a correspondence between pyramids architecture and the mammalian visual pathway, starting from the retina and ending in the deepest layers of the visual cortex.

This paradigm of computation can also be related to the work made by Pomerantz and Sager [3] in their study on visual perception; the authors describe the visual perception as a transition in which the attention goes from global to local features, (*olystic* phase), and from local to global features, (*analytic* phase). In [4] Navon synthesises in a phrase this mechanism of perception: *Are we seeing the forest before trees or trees before the forest?* the author supports the precedence of global features in visual perception (see figure 1.1).

Pyramid computation has suggested both new data structures (quad-trees, multi-resolution), and new machine vision architectures (**PAPIA**) [5]. The concept of irregular pyramid has been introduced in [6] to handle connectivity problems that can arise when spatial data are mapped through the pyramid layers.

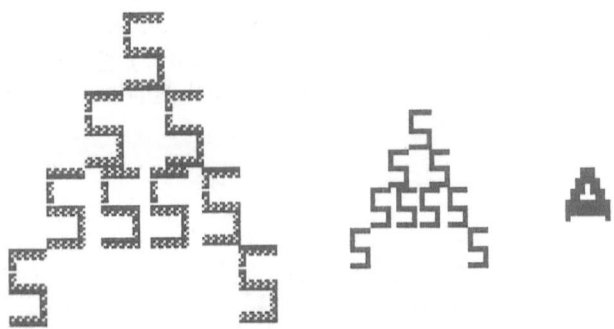

Fig. 1.1. Multiresolution and level of perception.

The implementation of local operators in a pyramid structure allows to detect image feature at different level of *details*. Aim of this paper is to study the capability of symmetry operators to detect regions of interest in a pyramid environment.

Symmetry plays a remarkable role in perception problems. For example, peaks of brain activity are measured in correspondence with visual patterns showing *symmetries*. Relevance of symmetry in vision was already noted by psychologists [7]. Symmetry operators have been included in vision systems to perform different visual tasks. For example, a set of annular operators can be used to identify enclosed symmetry points, and then a grouping algorithm is applied to represent and to describe object-parts [8]; axial symmetry properties have been applied to perform image segmentation [9].

Here an algorithm, that computes the pyramid Discrete Symmetry Transform ($PDST$) of a digital scene, is presented. It has been implemented on the *regular pyramid*, and applied to a multiresolution scene representation. The hierarchy of symmetries is stored by starting from the first level on which *significant* local symmetries are detected. The choice of the top layer is based on a theoretic result, discussed in the paper, which sets a criterion to maintain *interesting* image features.

Several experiments on real complex scenes have been performed to show the performance of the proposed approach.

In Section 2 general concepts and definitions of pyramid computation are given; Section 3 describes a new symmetry operator; Section 4 shows the pyramid algorithm; experimental results are shown in Section 5; conclusion are given in Section 6.

2. Pyramid computation

Let D be a digital image, of dimension $n \times n$, defined on the set of gray values G. The pyramid representation of D, is a triple $< PD, F, V >$, where:

a) PD is an ordered sequence of images $(D_0, D_1, ..., D_r, D_{L-1})$, of decreasing sizes. The rule of decimation is determined by the spatial mapping defined in b).

b) $F : D_r^k \longrightarrow D_{r+1}$ is the spatial mapping between two consecutive layers, with $0 \le r < L - 1$. The inverse mapping allows to map an element of D_{r+1} with a subset of elements of D_r: $F^{-1} : D_{r+1} \longrightarrow D_r^k$, with $0 < r \le L - 1$. In the case of a 2×2 pyramid the function F generates the usual *quadtree*, and the dimension of D_r is $2^{L-r-1} \times 2^{L-r-1}$, for $r = 0, 1, ..., L - 1$.

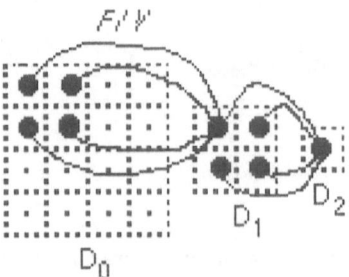

Fig. 2.1. The regular pyramid.

Spatial mapping characterises the hierarchy and the topology of a pyramid. Figure 2.1 shows the case of the 2×2 pyramid also named *regular* pyramid.

However, regular pyramid performs a partition of the digital space that may cause edge and connectivity problems. Other pyramid topologies have been proposed in order to minimize such effects. For example, figure 2.2 shows the spatial mapping for the 3×3 and the DUAL pyramids.

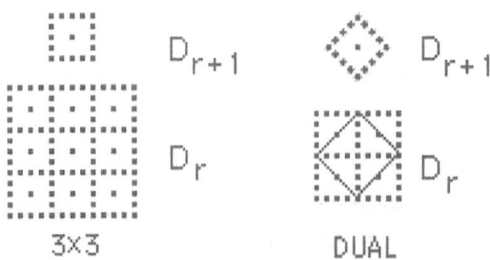

$$3 \times 3 \qquad \text{DUAL}$$

Fig. 2.2. Examples of F-functions.

c) $V : D_r^k \longrightarrow D_{r+1}$, with $0 \leq r < L - 1$, is the gray level mapping, such that if $F^{-1}(x) = (x_1, x_2, ..., x_k)$ is the spatial mapping for a pixel $x \in D_{r+1}$ then its gray level $g_{r+1}(x) = V(g_r(x_1), g_r(x_2), ..., g_r(x_k))$. $V^{-1} : D_{r+1} \longrightarrow D_r^k$ is the inverse function, such that if $F(y) = x$ then $g_r(y) = V^{-1}(g_{r+1}(x))$. Examples of gray level mapping functions are: max, min, $\vee$, &, xor, $average$.

For $D \equiv D_0$ the pyramid PD is computed by the recursive application of F and V. In the following, the whole transition from D_r to D_{r+1} is indicated by $D_{r+1} = \wp(D_r)$ then $PD = \wp^{L-1}(D_0)$.

3. Symmetry

An object is said to exhibit symmetry if the application of certain isometrics, called symmetry operators, leaves it unchanged while parts are permuted. The letter A, for instance, remains unchanged under reflection, the letter Z under half-turn, and the letter H under both reflection and half-turn, the circle has circular symmetry around its centre. Moreover, an object in a $2D$ space exhibits a symmetry with respect to an axis x, if x divides the object in two mirror-like components.

In [10] a new symmetry transform, named the Discrete Symmetry Transform (DST), has been introduced. The DST algorithm has been applied to guide the *attention* of a robot visual system in real scenes. A comparison with other techniques, currently used to compute local symmetry [Reisfeld95], has given coherent results and faster computation.

The DST of a digital image D is computed as the product of two local operators: $DST(D) = S(D) \times E(D)$.

The first operator is function of the axial moments computed in a circle, C_R, of radius R and centred in each pixel $x \equiv (i, j)$ of D:

$$T_k(i, j) = \sum_{r=-R}^{+R} \sum_{s=-R}^{+R} |r \times sin(\tfrac{k\pi}{N}) - s \times cos(\tfrac{k\pi}{N})| \times g_{i,j}$$

with $k = 0, 1, 2, ..., N-1$. In the discrete retina N is function of R. The definition of S depends on the kind of symmetry to be detected. For example, in case of circular symmetry:

$$S_{i,j} = 1 - \sqrt{\frac{\sum_k (T_k(i,j)^2}{n} - \left(\frac{\sum_k (T_k(i,j))}{n}\right)^2}$$

The second operator, E, weights S according to the local smoothness of the image, and it is defined as:

$$E_{i,j} = \sum_{(l,m)\in C_R, (r,s)\in C_{R+1}} |g_{l,m} - g_{r,s}|$$

where C_R and C_{R+1} are centred in (i,j). Moreover, the condition $(l-p)^2 + (m-q)^2 = 1$ $(4-connectivity)$ must be satisfied.

It is easy to see that $E_{i,j} = 0$ iff the image is locally flat.

The DST is invariant for image size and rotation. The choice of the kernel radius depends on the *area* of the objects in D.

Note that, for a given a kernel size, the computation returns zero values only on uniform zones. The computation of the DST, for increasing values of R, is related to skew local symmetry operators based on the Medial Axis Transform. The evaluation of significant zones depends on the probability distribution of the intensity levels in the transformed image, and it can be performed by using conventional tests of normality.

4. Pyramid symmetry

In this section the pyramid DST, $PDST$, algorithm is described. The $PDST$ can be performed following two paradigms of computation:

Direct computation In this case the computation is done directly on the pyramid $\wp^{L-1}(D_0)$, by using pyramid symmetry kernels: $PS \equiv \{S_0, S_1, ..., S_{L-1}\}$ and $PE \equiv \{E_0, E_1, ..., E_{L-1}\}$:
$$PDST(PD) = PS(PD) \otimes PE(PD)$$
the operator $\otimes$ indicates: $DST(D_r) = S(D_r) \times E(D_r)$ for $r = 0, 1, ..., L-1$.

Indirect computation In this case the pyramid of the $DST(D_0)$ is built:
$$PDST(PD) = \wp^{L-1}(DST(D_0))$$

The first approach requires to set the layer where to stop the computation, in order to obtain meaningful results. On the contrary, the second one requires to set the layer where to start the computation.

It must be noted that in general $\wp(DST(D_r)) \neq DST(\wp(D_r))$. In the following, a condition of *approximate* commutativity between *direct* and *indirect* computation is given. This result allows to choose the *best* layer, k, where to start the computation with the indirect $PDST$-algorithm. The time complexity is usually reduced. For example, in the case of a regular pyramid the heavy computation is performed only at the layer k, size of which is 2^{L-k-1}, followed by the propagation of the result to the layer 0 which is of the order $\mathbf{O}(2^L)$). Therefore the whole complexity becomes $O(4^{L-2k} \times R^2)$ instead of $O(4^L \times R^2)$.

Theorem 1. Let $DFT(D_0)$ be the *Discrete Fourier Transform* of image D_0, and $\nu_{max}^{(0)} = \nu_{max} = max\{\nu_x, \nu_y\}$ its highest signal frequency, then the $DFT(D_k)$, maintain ν_{max} *iff* the sampling size, d, at layer 0 satisfies the following relation: $d \le \frac{1}{4^k \nu_{max}}$.

Proof. The proof derives from Shannon's sampling theorem. In fact, in case of a 2×2 pyramid the layer $r+1$ is a sub sampling of layer r (see figure 4.1). Therefore the size of d must satisfy the inequality: $d \le \frac{1}{4\nu_{max}^{(r)}}$, where $\nu_{max}^{(r)}$ is the maximum frequency value at the layer r. The application of this relation, starting from layer 0, k-times brings to the relation: $d \le \frac{1}{4^k \nu_{max}}$.

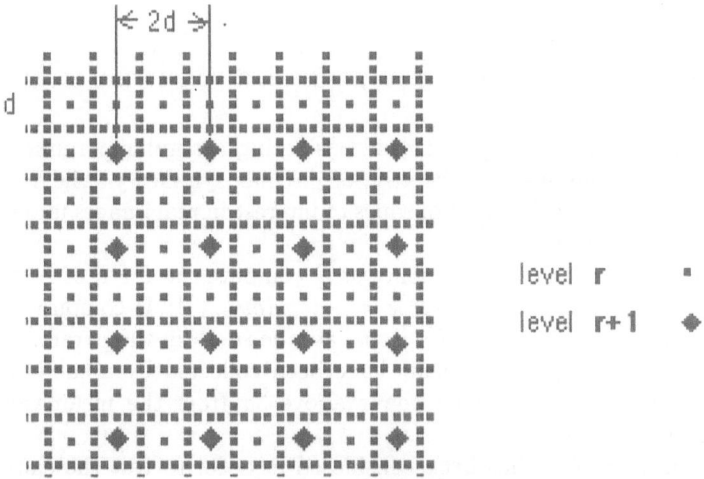

Fig. 4.1. Sampling rule in a 2×2 pyramid.

This property indicates the layer $k = -\lfloor log_4(d\nu_{max}) \rfloor$ *from* which to start or *where* to stop the computation. In practical cases d can become too small (over sampling) and a good compromise can be found by taking the maximum of the most significant frequencies in the $DFT(D_0)$.

Theorem 2. If the sampling condition of **Theorem 1** holds, and the gray level mapping is the mean value then:

$$\wp^{k-1}(S_0(D_0)) = PS(\wp^{k-1}(D_0))$$

Proof. First of all let us show that: $\wp(S_r(D_r)) = S_{r+1}(\wp(D_r))$. In fact if $D_r(i, j) = \frac{1}{4} \sum_{p=0}^{+1} \sum_{q=0}^{+1} D_{r-1}(2i + p, 2j + q)$ it follows that:

Direct Computation:
$$S_{r+1}(i,j) = \tfrac{1}{4} \sum_{p,q=0}^{+1} \sum_{l,m,-R}^{+R} S_{l,m} D_r(2i + 2l + p, 2j + 2m + q)$$
Indirect Computation:
$$S_r(i,j) = \sum_{l,m=-R}^{+R} S_{l,m} D_r(2i + l, 2j + m)$$
$$S_{r+1}(i,j) = \tfrac{1}{4} \sum_{p,q=0}^{+1} S_r(2i + p, 2j + q) =$$
$$\tfrac{1}{4} \sum_{p,q=0}^{+1} \sum_{l,m=-R}^{+R} S_{l,m} D_r(2i + l + p, 2j + m + q)$$

But $\sum_{l,m=-R}^{+R} S_{l,m} D_{r-1}(2i + 2l + p, 2j + 2m + q)$ is the sampled version of $\sum_{l,m=-R}^{+R} S_{l,m} D_{r-1}(2i + l + p, 2j + m + q)$. Therefore, for a given k, satisfying the condition of **Theorem 1**, it can be stated that: $\wp^{k-1}(S_0(D_0)) = PS(\wp^{k-1}(D_0))$.

Unfortunately, because of the $4 - connectivity$ condition, the operator PE do not satisfy fully the commutativity property, therefore direct and indirect pyramid computations of the $PDST$ are *approximately* commutative: $\wp^{k-1}(DST(D_0)) \approx PDST(\wp^{k-1}(D_0))$

5. Experimental results

The experiments have been performed considering a regular pyramid, and the $PDST$ has been computed in the case of circular symmetry. The $PDST$ has been applied to the identification of zones of interest in real images under natural conditions of illumination.

The algorithm can be sketched as follows: 1) compute the DFT of D; 2) choose the frequency ν_{max}; 3) set the level $k = -\lfloor log_4(d\nu_{max}) \rfloor$; 4) compute DST_k; 5) select areas of interest at level k; 6) propagate the result in the pyramid base D_0. The images used in the experiments have been collected by a camera or by a scanner. Signal frequencies, with power above 3σ from the mean value, have been considered.

The image in figure 6.1a has been considered in order to test the capability of the method to detect heads in a crouwd. In this case: $d\nu_{max} = 0.027$, and $k = 2$. Figure 6.1a,b show the input image D_0 and the layer D_2. Figure 6.1c,d show, the $DST(D_0)$ and the $\wp^2(DST(D_2))$ respectively. Figure 6.1e,f show the areas of interest as detected by the direct and the indirect computations respectively. The results of a second experiment are shown in figure 6.2a,b. In this case: $d\nu_{max} = 0.03$, and $k = 2$. The selected zones are centered on the people and the books in the room.

Both experiments show that a good agreement exists between the areas of interest found by the direct computation of the DST and its indirect computatation via the $PDST$.

The CPU time on a 486-100MHz for an image of size **256** was of about $3.5sec$ for the direct computation of the DST and $0.21sec$ for the computation via the $PDST$.

Fig. 6.1. a) The input image D_0; b) the $DST(D_0)$; c) the image D_2; d) the $\wp^{-2}DST(D_0$; e) zones of interest obtained via direct computation; f) zones of interest obtained via indirect computation.

Fig. 6.2. a) Zones of interest obtained via direct computation; b) zones of interest obtained via indirect computation.

6. Conclusion

The pyramid version of the Discrete Symmetry Transform has been described; theoretic conditions, based on Shannon's sampling theorem, let us set the approximated equivalence between the *direct* and *indirect* computation of the *PDST*. This allows to determine the condition under which to use the indirect version of the *PDST*. Experimental results, performed on complex scenes, confirm the validity of the theoretic prevision. Further work will be done in order to compare the implementation of the proposed method on different kind of pyramid topologies.

References

1. L.Uhr, L.: Layered Recognition Cone Networks that Preprocess, Classify and Describe. *IEEE Trans.Comput.*, C-21, 1972.
2. Pavlidis T.A., Tanimoto S.L.: A Hierarchical Data Structure for Picture Processing. *Comp.Graphycs & Image Processing*, Vol.4, 1975.
3. Pomeranzt J.R. and Sager L.C.: Asymmetric integrality with dimensions of visual pattern. *Perception & Psycophysics*, Vol.18, 460-466, 1975.
4. Navon D.: Forest befor trees: the precedence of global features in visual perception. *Cognitive Psychology* , Vol.9, 353-385, 1977.
5. Cantoni V., Di Gesú V., Ferretti M., Levialdi S., Negrini R., Stefanelli R.: The Papia System. *Journal of VLSI Signal Processing*, Vol.2, 195-217, 1991.
6. Kropatsch W.G., Building Irregular Pyramids by Dual Graph Contraction. *Technical Report PRIP-TR-35*, Institute f. Automation 183/2, Dept.for Pattern Recognition and Image Processing, TU Wien, Austria, 1995.
7. Khöler W. and Wallach H.: Figural after-effects:an investigation of visual processes. *Proc. Amer. Phil. Soc.*, Vol.88, 269-357, 1944.
8. Kelly M.F. and Levine M.D.: From symmetry to representation. *Technical Report*, TR-CIM-94-12, Center for Intelligent Machines. McGill University, Montreal, Canada, 1994.
9. Gauch J.M. and Pizer S.M.: The intensity axis of symmetry application to image segmentation. *IEEE Trans. PAMI*, Vol.15, N.8, 753-770, 1993.
[Reisfeld95] Reisfeld D., Wolfson H., Yeshurun Y, Context Free Attentional Operators, the Generalized Symmetry Transform. *Int. Journal of Computer Vision*, Vol.14, 119-130, 1995.
10. Di Gesú V. and Valenti C., Symmetry Operators in Computer Vision. *Vistas in Astronomy*, Elsevier Science, in press.

Dense depth maps by active color illumination and image pyramids

Andreas Koschan and Volker Rodehorst

1 Introduction

Only few problems in computer vision have been investigated more vigorously than stereo vision. The key problem in stereo is how to find the corresponding points in the left and in the right image, referred to as the correspondence problem. Whenever the corresponding points are determined, the depth can be computed by triangulation. Although, more than 300 papers have been published dealing with stereo vision this technique still suffers from a lack in accuracy and/or long computation time needed to match stereo images. Therefore, there is still a need for more precise and faster algorithms.

Stereo techniques can be distinguished by either matching edges and producing sparse depth maps or matching all pixels in the images and producing dense depth maps. The objective of the application always effects the decision whether the preference is given to dense stereo correspondence or to edge-based correspondence. For a successful reconstruction of complex surfaces it is essential to compute dense disparity maps defined for every pixel in the entire image. Unfortunately, most of the existing dense stereo techniques are very time consuming (see, e.g., [1, 2]). In an earlier investigation [3], we found the Block Matching technique using color information to be very suitable for dense stereo. The precision of the matching results always improved by 20 to 25 % when using color information instead of gray value information. We present a hierarchical algorithm using an image pyramid for obtaining dense depth maps from color stereo images. We show that matching results of higher quality are obtained when using the hierarchical algorithm instead of the non-hierarchical algorithm we developed earlier. Additionally, the algorithm becomes faster than the standard one at the same time. Furthermore, we present some studies on parallel implementations of both types of algorithms.

Most stereo matching algorithms can not compute correct dense depth maps in homogenous image regions. From other experiments we realize that the discriminability of objects can be enhanced by controlling the illumination color [4]. Therefore, finding the optimal illumination color for recognizing objects in structured environments [5] is a promising but rather difficult task. Fortunately, we do not have to find an optimal illumination color to improve stereo matching results. Kanade and his colleagues [6] projected a sinusoidal varying intensity onto the scene. They found an improvement in the results but still got some false matches due to the limited dynamic range of their camera, particularly with dark surfaces. In this paper, we propose to project a color code onto the scene. This color code represents a rainbow like spectrum. The quality of the matching results always improves, especially in homogenous regions, when this active color illumination is used. We present an investigation for synthetic and for real images.

2 Stereo analysis using chromatic Block Matching

Block Matching is based on a similarity check between two equal sized blocks ($n \times m$-matrices) in the left and the right image (area-based stereo). The mean square error MSE between the pixel values inside the respective blocks defines a measure for the similarity of two blocks. We propose to employ an approximation of the Euclidean distance to measure color differences. The left color image F_L and the right color image F_R may be represented in the RGB color space as $F_L(i, j) = (R_L(i, j), G_L(i, j), B_L(i, j))$ and $F_R(i, j) = (R_R(i, j), G_R(i, j), B_R(i, j))$. The MSE is defined with $n = m = 2k + 1$ as

$$MSE_{color}(x, y, \Delta) = \frac{1}{n \cdot m} \sum_{i=-k}^{k} \sum_{j=-k}^{k} (\, | R_R(x + i, y + j) - R_L(x + i + \Delta, y + j) |^2$$

$$+ | G_R(x + i, y + j) - G_L(x + i + \Delta, y + j) |^2 \qquad (1)$$

$$+ | B_R(x + i, y + j) - B_L(x + i + \Delta, y + j) |^2 \,),$$

where Δ is an offset describing the difference $(x_L - x_R)$ between the column positions in the left and in the right image. The block (of size $n \times m$) is shifted pixel by pixel inside the search area. Using standard stereo geometry the epipolar lines match the image lines. The disparity D of two blocks in both images is defined by the horizontal distance, showing the minimum mean square error. Furthermore, the search area in the right image is limited by a predefined maximum disparity d_{max}.

$$D = \min_{|\Delta| \le d_{max}} \{ MSE_{color}(x, y, \Delta) \}. \qquad (2)$$

Block disparities are median filtered to avoid outliers. A dense disparity map is generated when applying a pixel selection technique to every pixel in the image. Afterwards, median filtering is applied to pixel disparities (see [3] for further details). We applied the proposed algorithm to a stereo image pair named "ANDREAS" (see Fig. 1). It can be easily seen that the left eye in the left image is falsely matched to the right eye in the right image. This error occurs due to the repetitive pattern in the scene because the chromatic Block Matching method matches all single blocks independently to each other. As stated above the search area for corresponding blocks is only constrained by the maximum disparity d_{max}.

Reducing the search space for the disparities could be a solution to the problem. This could be obtained by a very restrictive use of the continuity constraint proposed in [7]. It produces a smoothed depth map where fine structures can not be represented. Discontinuities in depth that are typical for object edges get smoothed. Thus, any segmentation may fail. This disadvantage can be solved using a pyramid model.

2.1 Hierarchical Block Matching using image pyramids

The idea of using pyramid models in image analysis was introduced by Tanimoto and Pavlidis [8] as a solution to edge detection. One important property of the pyramid model is that it is computationally extremely efficient [9]. We enhanced the chromatic Block Matching algorithm by using a quad pyramid. Each level is obtained by a

Figure 1: Gray value reproduction of the color stereo image "ANDREAS" and the depth map (right) obtained when applying standard Block Matching to the images.

reduction of factor 4 in resolution from the next lower level. The values for the pixels are obtained by calculating the mean value in each color channel.

The disparities $D(s+1)$ at level $(s+1)$ can be derived from the disparities $D(s)$ of the preceding level (s) by applying a modified block matching algorithm to the image of level $(s+1)$. The search space for the disparity of each block at level $(s+1)$ is derived from the disparity of the corresponding block at level (s) by a tolerance factor D_T. This parameter defines the width D_Δ of the reduced search space $[D_{MIN}, D_{Max}]$ and controls the smoothness of the disparity map.

$$D_\Delta(s) = 2^{(s-1)} \cdot D_T \ ,$$

$$D_{MIN}(s) = \begin{cases} D(0) - D_\Delta(s) & \text{for} \quad s = 1 \\ D_{MIN}(s-1) - D_\Delta(s-1) & \text{for} \quad s > 1 \end{cases}$$

$$D_{MAX}(s) = \begin{cases} D(0) - D_\Delta(s) & \text{for} \quad s = 1 \\ D_{MAX}(s-1) - D_\Delta(s-1) & \text{for} \quad s > 1 \end{cases} \qquad (3)$$

When choosing a small value for the tolerance factor D_T, the difference between the final disparities and the average disparity found at level 0 will be very small. This is equivalent to a small variation of disparities over the whole image. A larger tolerance factor will cause a bigger search space and the influence of the computed disparities in the preceding levels will decline. Then the artifacts described above may occur.

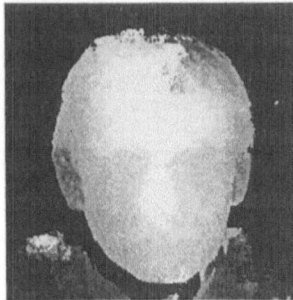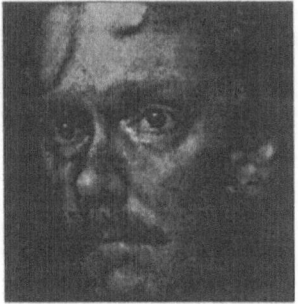

Figure 2: Enhanced depth map using hierarchical Block Matching and the 3-d reconstruction with texture mapping.

Nevertheless, this hierarchical method is more robust than the non-hierarchical one. Furthermore, the hierarchical Block Matching algorithm shows better results (see Fig. 2) than the non-hierarchical standard algorithm (cp. Fig. 1). Not only the artifact with the eyes can be prevented, even the depth of small structures as the ears are estimated more correctly. Additionally, matching the blocks at one level is still possible in parallel, because the blocks within one level are matched independently.

2.2 Parallel implementation of hierarchical and non-hierarchical chromatic Block Matching

Within one row of an image consisting of m blocks each containing $n \times n$ pixels, there are (theoretically)

$$n \cdot \left(1 + 2 + 3 + \ldots + (m-1)\right) + m = n \cdot \frac{m \cdot (m-1)}{2} + m \tag{4}$$

chances to match the blocks. Taking the maximum disparity d_{max} into account yields

$$n \cdot \left(\sum_{i=1}^{d_{max}-1} i + \sum_{d_{max}}^{m-1} (d_{max} - 1) \right) + m = n \cdot \frac{d_{max} \cdot (d_{max} - 1)}{2} + n \cdot (m - d_{max}) \cdot (d_{max} - 1) + m \tag{5}$$

matching possibilities. Assuming a maximum disparity d_{max} of half of the image size and using an image of 512×512 pixels and a block size of 8×8 pixels, the number of possible matches that have to be examined for every image row is 11968.
When using the hierarchical approach this estimation is true for level (0). At the finer levels with $m(s)$ blocks in one row only

$$\left(2 \cdot D_\Delta(s) + 1\right) \cdot m(s) = \left(D_{MAX} - D_{MIN} + 1\right) \cdot m(s) \tag{6}$$

matching possibilities remain in the worst case. When using five levels and a tolerance factor of $D_T = 3.0$ the widths of the search spaces are 7, 13, 25, and 49 pixels, respectively (see Fig. 3). Thus, the number of possible matches that have to be

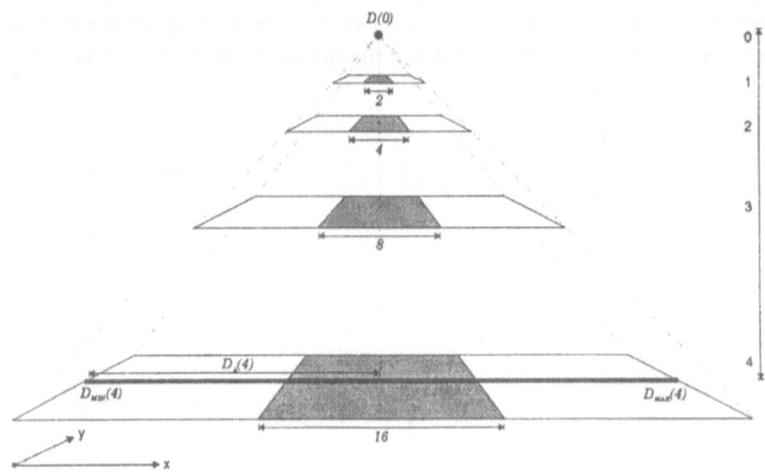

Figure 3: Definition of the search space with a tolerance factor $\cdot D_T = 3.0$.

Image size	Non-hierarchical Block Matching		Hierarchical Block Matching	
in pixel	1 PU	10 PUs	1 PU	10 PUs
256 x 256	0.96 sec.	0.13 sec.	0.25 sec.	0.03 sec.
768 x 566	10.14 sec.	1.07 sec.	3.51 sec.	0.64 sec.

Table 1: Comparison between non-hierarchical and hierarchical Block Matching (without post-processing) as sequential and parallel implementation.

examined for every image row is reduced to $48 + 56 + 208 + 800 + 3136 = 4248$. Compared to the 11968 chances that have to be checked by the non-hierarchical algorithm the hierarchical algorithm reduces the number of checks by about 65%.

A further acceleration of the algorithm is achieved when employing a parallel implementation. Several ways exist to develop parallel algorithms for Block Matching. He and Liou [10] give a summary of Block Matching algorithms that are already designed in VLSI. Unfortunately, none of these algorithms are developed for color images. Furthermore, they are designed for motion estimation and not for stereo matching. Thus, the algorithms can be simplified taking into consideration the epipolar geometry. We found [11] that best results can be obtained by dividing the image into several segments and computing *MSE*s inside every segment in parallel. In principle, both images can be divided into many segments (e.g., 70 segments for PAL resolution). Utilizing an individual processing unit (PU) for every segment will speed up the matching process.

We compared the performances of the non-hierarchical algorithm and the enhanced hierarchical Block Matching algorithm. Tab. 1 illustrates the time gain for matching the blocks without post-processing. The computational cost of both approaches does not depend linearly on the image size. Therefore, we applied both approaches to several images of different sizes. By way of example we present some results obtained on a SGI Power Challenge with twelve R8000 processors (75 MHz). The results encourage an implementation on a highly parallel architecture.

3   Active color illumination for enhancing stereo matching

Most stereo matching algorithms can not compute correct dense depth maps for homogenous image regions. This is due to the ambiguity of image values inside these regions. The ambiguity can be eliminated by adding a synthetic texture to the scene. The results improve when intensity coded light is projected onto the scene [6]. Nevertheless, several false matches occur with this technique, particularly with dark surfaces.

These effects can be considerably reduced when projecting a color code onto the objects instead of an intensity code since color provides much more distinguishable information than intensity [12, 13]. Since the projected colored light mixes with the unknown object colors, blended colors are reflected onto the image planes of the two cameras. Thus, identifying the projected colors in the image would cause some major problems and the resulting color of the object in the image cannot be predicted.

142

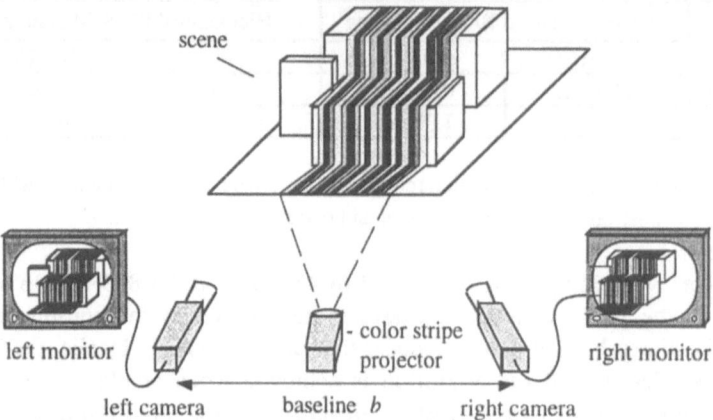

scene

left monitor

color stripe projector

right monitor

left camera   baseline *b*   right camera

Figure 4: Principle of the stereo system using active color illumination.

Fortunately, we must not determine either object colors or projected colors, when using stereo vision [14, 15]. The colors obtained by superimposing object colors with the color coded illumination are identical in both images. Therefore, the pixels in the images can be matched without any additional knowledge about the object colors or the light colors, respectively. The principle of the stereo arrangement using active color illumination is outlined in Fig. 4.

We projected a rainbow like color spectrum onto the scene. Every row of length n in the color spectrum S_{RGB} was generated using the equations

$$S_R = \sin\left(\frac{i}{n}\cdot\pi\right)\cdot\left(\frac{G_{max}}{2}-1\right)+\frac{G_{max}}{2} ,$$

$$S_G = \sin\left(\left(\frac{2}{3}+\frac{i}{n}\right)\cdot\pi\right)\cdot\left(\frac{G_{max}}{2}-1\right)+\frac{G_{max}}{2} , \quad \text{for } i = \{0,...,n\}, \qquad (7)$$

$$S_B = \sin\left(\left(\frac{4}{3}+\frac{i}{n}\right)\cdot\pi\right)\cdot\left(\frac{G_{max}}{2}-1\right)+\frac{G_{max}}{2} ,$$

where i denotes the column position in the spectrum image and G_{max} denotes the maximum intensity value in every color channel.

The color spectrum was synthetically generated using the equations mentioned above. Afterwards, a slide representing this synthetic color stripe code was exposed by using a scanner for color reversal films. This slide is projected onto the objects using a standard slide projector. The two stereo images are acquired with color CCD-cameras.

Using the standard geometry the epipolar lines match the image line. Therefore, the matching process can be simplified as corresponding pixels can only be found in the same row in both images. To take advantage of the structured illumination we chose the chromatic Block Matching algorithm for stereo matching, because it considers the color coding best.

3.1 Experimental results with synthetic images

The quality of a stereo algorithm can hardly be evaluated if exclusively real images and the computed disparity maps are investigated. Often there does not exist enough information to predict the correct disparity values, particularly in dense disparity maps. Opposed to this, the correct depth map and an integer map representing the disparity values can be generated when using synthetic images and a stereo simulator. Thus, the quality of a matching algorithm can be easily checked by comparing the computed disparity map with the ideal one.

Now we present some results using a synthetic image pair, we name "CUBE", of size 512×512 pixels. The imaging geometry was determined placing the 90 cm high cube in a distance of 3 m to the virtual camera with focal length $f = 50$ mm. The direction of the light source was determined as $L_{XYZ} = (2, 3, -4)$. The right stereo image was generated with a horizontal camera displacement of 50 cm (see Fig. 5).

The matching of surface patches with uniform shading and without texture is ambiguous. Fig. 5 shows the computed disparity map obtained when applying the Block Matching algorithm to the original images. Several mismatches occurred due the ambiguity of the intensity values of the cube.

As stated above the ambiguities can also be solved by adding a synthetic texture to the scene. We superimposed the synthetic images with the color spectrum introduced in the previous section. The resulting disparity map is shown in Fig. 6.

Additionally, we compared both disparity maps to the ideal disparity map generated by the stereo simulator. The computed results improved significantly when using structured light (see Fig. 6 and Tab. 2). The image "CUBE" was chosen to clarify the effect of colored light to the matching problem. Of course the results can not be used to predict similar improvements for real scenes.

We generated a more complex synthetic stereo image called "BEETHOVEN" of size 512×512 pixels. The selected 3-d object represents a bust of Beethoven and consists of 4500 polygons. The imaging geometry was determined placing the 35 cm high bust in a distance of 75 cm to the virtual camera with focal length $f = 50$ mm. The surface was shaded due to perfect Lambertian reflection and the intensities were interpolated along the edges of the polygons with Gouraud shading. The direction of the light source was determined as $L_{XYZ} = (-1, 2, -4)$. The right stereo image was generated with a horizontal camera displacement of 10 cm (see Fig. 7).

Figure 5: The synthetic gray value stereo images "CUBE" and the reconstructed disparity map.

144

Difference (in pixel)	Intensity images (%)	Color images (%)
0	7.9	62.2
1	12.2	25.8
≥2	79.8	12.0

Table 2: Distribution of the matching errors (in percentage) for the gray value images and for the images superimposed with the color spectrum.

Figure 6: Disparity map computed for the stereo image superimposed with the color spectrum.

We computed the differences between the ideal disparity map and the disparity maps computed when applying the Block Matching algorithm to the gray value images and to the images superimposed with the color spectrum. Results are shown in Tab. 3.

Furthermore, we carried out some experiments to investigate the robustness of the new technique concerning noise, variation in contrast, and variation in intensity between the left and the right stereo image. The results of these experiments will give a closer prediction of what can be expected from real images.

The first experiment investigates the sensitivity of the matching results regarding noise in one of the images. Therefore, Gaussian noise of $\sigma = 10.0$ was added to the intensity function of the right image (before projecting the color code). The Block Matching algorithm was applied to the intensity images and to the images superimposed with the color spectrum. The differences between the ideal disparity map and the computed disparity maps were determined. Results are shown in Tab. 4.

Second we investigated the sensitivity of the matching results regarding variation in contrast between both images. Therefore, the intensity I_R of the right image was transformed to I'_R (before projecting the color code) using the equation

$$I'_R = \frac{3}{4} \cdot I_R + \frac{1}{8} \cdot G_{\max}, \tag{8}$$

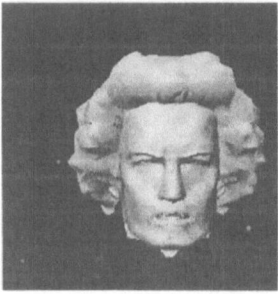

Figure 7: Left and right intensity stereo image representing a bust of "BEETHOVEN".

Difference (in pixel)	Intensity images (%)	Color images (%)
0	59.6	63.3
1	34.0	31.8
≥ 2	6.3	4.8

Table 3: Distribution of the matching errors (in percentage) for the gray value images and for the images superimposed with the color spectrum.

Difference (in pixel)	Intensity images (%)	Color images (%)
0	39.8	44.3
1	42.5	43.5
≥ 2	17.7	12.2

Table 4: Distribution of the matching errors (in percentage) when one the images is disturbed with Gaussian noise of $\sigma = 10.0$.

where G_{max} denotes the maximum intensity. The Block Matching algorithm was applied to the intensity images and to the images superimposed with the color spectrum. The differences between the ideal disparity map and the computed disparity maps were determined. Results are shown in Tab. 5.

The third experiment was carried out to investigate the sensitivity of the matching results regarding differences in intensities between both images. Therefore, the intensity I_R of the right image was transformed to I'_R (before projecting the color code) using a gamma correction of

$$I'_R = \left(\frac{I_R}{G_{max}}\right)^{\frac{1}{\chi}} \cdot G_{max} ,\tag{9}$$

where G_{max} denotes the maximum intensity and $\chi = 1.5$.

The Block Matching algorithm was applied to the intensity images and to the images superimposed with the color spectrum. The differences between the ideal disparity map and the computed disparity maps were determined. Results are shown in Tab. 6.

Several additional investigations were carried out for synthetic images. Unfortunately, we can not present further details due to limited space. In summary, we found that the matching results always improved when a color spectrum is projected onto the scene. Furthermore, the results are rather robust concerning noise, contrast variations, and intensity variations.

Difference (in pixel)	Intensity images (%)	Color images (%)
0	14.7	37.7
1	20.9	42.6
≥ 2	64.4	19.7

Table 5: Distribution of the matching errors for images with different contrast (in percentage).

Difference (in pixel)	Intensity images (%)	Color images (%)
0	9.6	28.6
1	18.4	36.7
≥ 2	72.0	34.7

Table 6: Distribution of the matching errors for images with different intensities (in percentage).

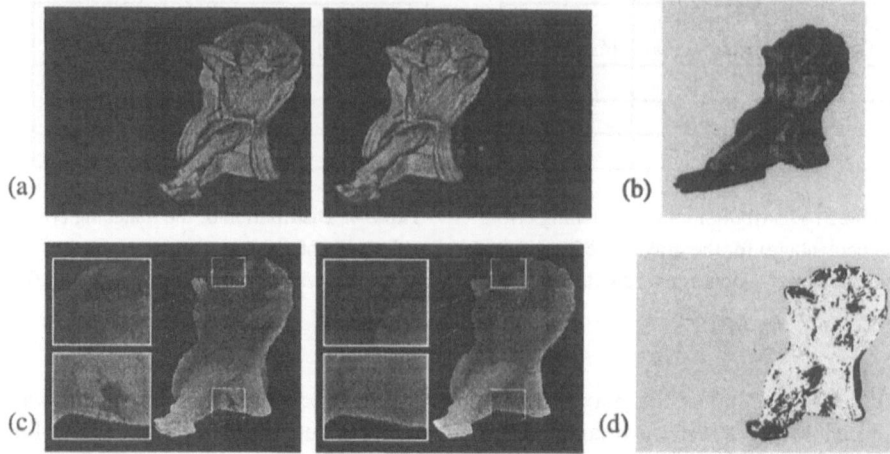

Figure 8: (a) Gray value representation of the real color stereo image "RELAXING JACK", (b) a shaded representation of the reconstructed scene, (c) the computed depth maps without (left) and with active illumination (right), (d) the difference (scaled) between both depth maps.

3.2   Experimental results for real images

Since the projection of color codes onto the scene considerably improves the quality of the matching results for synthetic images we applied the same technique to real images. We applied the Block Matching algorithm to a color stereo image named "RELAXING JACK" (see Fig. 8 (a)). The computed depth map, that was obtained by triangulation from the disparity map, shows a defect beneath the head (magnified section). An other artifact occurs at the bottom part of the arm-chair, although this uniform shaded section is quite small (see Fig. 8 (c)). In another experiment the color spectrum was projected onto the same scene. The artifacts that occurred when using the original color images, do not show up (see magnified sections in Fig. 8 (c) right). Visualizing the difference of the two depth maps (see Fig. 8 (d)) points out more distinctions. Additionally, Fig. 8 (b) shows the reconstructed scene mapped with the texture of the right image.

The experiments mentioned above show a considerable improvement in the matching results for synthetic and for real images when active color illumination is utilized. Regarding other investigations with structured illumination the main advantage of this method is, that it deals with only one pair of images. Thus, the method can also be applied to moving or non-rigid objects.

4   Conclusion

A combination of two approaches for dense stereo matching has been presented. The first approach uses an image pyramid model and a hierarchical implementation of Block Matching for color stereo images. It has been shown that the quality of the matching results can be improved with this hierarchical approach. The computing time is reduced by a factor of two at the same time. Furthermore, the hierarchical approach can be implemented very efficiently in parallel to achieve high speed execution.

The second approach we presented uses active color illumination for stereo matching. We showed the benefit of the approach for synthetic and for real images. The quality of the matching results always considerably improved when employing active colored illumination, particularly in homogenous regions. This holds for every dense stereo technique. We used the combination of the hierarchical approach with active color illumination to produce high quality results. Additional tests and investigations are necessary for a more detailed investigation of the technique. Currently, this is under investigation and further results will be presented soon.

In summary, we should like to emphasize that active colored illumination always serves to improve stereo matching results. Therefore, we believe that more precise results can be efficiently obtained in dense stereo matching when combining hierarchical chromatic Block Matching with the active color illumination approach.

Acknowledgment

This work was funded by the Deutsche Forschungsgemeinschaft (DFG). Furthermore, we thank K. Spiller for helpful assistance to the tests and to the implementations.

References

[1] Jordan III, J.R., Bovik, A.C.: Using chromatic information in dense stereo correspondence. Pattern Recognition 25, 367-383 (1992).

[2] Okutomi, M., Yoshizaki, O., Tomita, G.: Color stereo matching and its application to 3-d measurement of optic nerve head. Proc. 11th IAPR Int. Conf. on Pattern Recognition ICPR´93, the Hague, the Netherlands, vol. I, pp. 509-513, 1992.

[3] Koschan, A.: Dense stereo correspondence using polychromatic block matching. Proc. of the 5th Int. Conf. on Computer Analysis of Images and Patterns CAIP'93, D. Chetverikov, W. Kropatsch (eds.), Budapest, Hungary, pp. 538-542, 1993.

[4] Vriesenga, M., Healey, G., Peleg, K., Sklansky, J.: Controlling illumination color to enhance object discriminability. Proc. Int. Conf. on Computer Vision and Pattern Recognition CVPR´92, Champaign, Illinois, pp. 710-712, 1992.

[5] Murase, H., Nayar, S.K.: Illumination planning for object recognition in structured environments. Proc. Int. Conf. on Computer Vision and Pattern Recognition CVPR´94, Seattle, Wa., pp. 31-38, 1994.

[6] Kang, S.B., Webb, J.A., Zitnick, C.L., Kanade, T.: A multibaseline stereo system with active illumination and real-time image acqisition. Proc. 5th Int. Conf. on Computer Vision CVPR´95, Cambridge, Ma., pp. 88-93, 1995.

148

[7] Marr, D.: Vision - A Computational Investigation Into the Human Representation and Processing of Visual Information. New York: Freeman & Co 1982.

[8] Tanimoto, S., Pavlidis, T.: A hierarchical data structure for picture processing. Computer Graphics and Image Processing 4, 104-119 (1975).

[9] Kropatsch, W.G.: Properties of pyramidal representations. Computing Suppl. 11, 99-111 (1996).

[10] He, Z.L., Liou, M.L.: Design trade-offs for real-time block-matching motion estimation algorithms. Proc. 2nd Asian Conf. on Computer Vision ACCV´95, Singapore, vol. I, pp. 305-309, 1995.

[11] Koschan, A., Rodehorst, V.: Towards real-time stereo employing parallel algorithms for edge-based and dense stereo matching. Proc. of the IEEE Workshop on Computer Architectures for Machine Perception CAMP´95, Como, Italy, pp. 234-241, 1995.

[12] Sasse, R.: Bestimmung von Entfernungsbildern durch aktive stereoskopische Verfahren. Braunschweig, Wiesbaden: Vieweg 1994.

[13] Knoll, A., Sasse R.: An active stereometric triangulation technique using a continuous colour pattern. In: W. Straßer, F. Wahl (eds.): Graphics and Robotics. Berlin: Springer 1995, pp. 191-206.

[14] Koschan, A., Rodehorst, V., Spiller, K.: Color stereo vision using hierarchical block matching and active color illumination. Proc. 13th Int. Conf. on Pattern Recognition ICPR´96, Vienna, Austria, vol. I, pp. 835-839, 1996.

[15] Klette, R., Koschan, A., Schlüns, K.: Computer Vision - Räumliche Information aus digitalen Bildern. Braunschweig, Wiesbaden: Vieweg 1996.

Local and global integration of discrete vector fields

Karsten Schlüns and Reinhard Klette

1   Introduction

Several methods in the field of shape reconstruction [6, 8, 11] (most shading based methods) lead to gradient data that still have to be transformed into (scaled) height or depth maps, or into surface data for many applications. Thus the reconstruction accuracy also depends upon the performance of such a transformation module. Surprisingly, not much work was done so far in this area. This paper starts with a review of the state of the art and discusses two approaches in detail. Several experimental evaluations of both methods for transforming gradient data into height data are reported. The studied (synthetic and real) object classes are curved and polyhedral objects. General qualitative evaluations of the compared transformation procedures are possible in relation to these object classes and in relation to different types of noise simulated for synthetic objects.

The outline of the paper is as follows: Section 2 contains a description of different methods for height from gradients. Methodologies for comparing selected algorithms are discussed in Section 3. A concluding discussion of evaluation results is given in Section 4. We consider the reconstruction of a surface function $Z(x, y)$, defined in Cartesian xyz-space $\Re^3$, where only gradient field information $\mathbf{K}(\mathbf{p}): \Re^2 \to \Re^2$,

$$\mathbf{K}(\mathbf{p}) = grad(Z(x,y)) = \left(p(x, y), q(x, y)\right) = \left(\frac{\partial Z(x, y)}{\partial x}, \ \frac{\partial Z(x, y)}{\partial y}\right) \qquad (1)$$

about this surface function is available as input data. The function Z is the *potential* of the vector field $\mathbf{K}$ in terms of vector analysis [2]. The gradient field information is given at discrete points $\mathbf{p} = (x, y)$ in computer vision. The task consists in inverting differentiation, i.e., a certain anti-derivative has to be calculated by (discrete) integration up to a certain additive constant. A vector field $\mathbf{K}$ that has a potential, i.e., that is integrable, is called *conservative*.

2   Surface Integration

Essentially there are two types of known approaches in literature, local integration along paths [3, 5, 10, 12] or global techniques [1, 4, 6, 7].

2.1   Classification of integration techniques

Path integration techniques are directed on local calculations of height increments by curve integrals. Specific curves, i.e., scan lines are suggested by such techniques as

150

well as special procedures for local approximations of height increments. These techniques are easy to implement and very efficient in computing speed. However, the locality of calculations causes a high dependency on data accuracy, and the propagation of height increments along paths means also propagation of errors. The known local integration techniques are not based on any assumption about the integrability condition.

Surface integration is treated as an optimization problem in global techniques. Surface integration can be considered to be a variational problem where a certain functional has to be minimized [6, 7]. In general this does not lead to a global analytical solution because local iterative schemes are used for calculating discrete height data. Also a certain representation of the unknown surface, e.g., the Fourier base functions, and the integrability condition can be used to constrain the global optimization process [4]. This method defines global analytical functions as final solution. It can be expected that both global techniques should be more robust against noise in comparison with local path integration because the surface gradient data have global impact on the solution process.

2.2 Survey of integration techniques

Local techniques are based on curve integrals and differ in specifying an integration path and a local neighborhood. Coleman and Jain [3] start in the middle of the gradient field and their initial path forms a cross in the array. Then the integration is performed in all four quadrants in column direction. For two points in sequence the averaged surface normal is calculated defining a surface tangent from the previous point to the next location. Their technique is known as *two-point method* in the computer vision literature. Healey and Jain [5] have extended this to an *eight-point method*. Wu and Li [12] also suggested paths parallel to the x-axis or the y-axis, but averaging gradient values for obtaining increments in height. Rodehorst [10] was using four different scans through the gradient field starting at the four corners. Averaging the results of all four scans for obtaining the final height data is based on the assumption that the same initial height value is adequate in all four corners of the gradient data array. In each scan the local calculation of increments is based on a 2×2 neighborhood. This multiple-scan method was selected to represent local techniques in comparison with global techniques. Details are given in [9, 10].

Two different global techniques are known in the computer vision literature. The method suggested by Horn and Brooks [7] is directed on minimizing the error functional

$$\mathbf{F}(\tilde{p}, \tilde{q}) = \iint |p(x, y) - \tilde{p}(x, y)|^2 + |q(x, y) - \tilde{q}(x, y)|^2 \, dx \, dy \tag{2}$$

where p, q denote the given gradient field components and

$$\tilde{p}(x, y) = \tilde{Z}_x(x, y) = \frac{\partial \tilde{Z}(x, y)}{\partial x}, \quad \tilde{q}(x, y) = \tilde{Z}_y(x, y) = \frac{\partial \tilde{Z}(x, y)}{\partial y} \tag{3}$$

denote the unknown (ideal) gradient field components that have to be reconstructed. A surface is calculated by minimization of **F** what ensures a maximum consistency of the reconstructed surface with the given data array. The difficulty with this method consists in selecting proper initial values at the boundary of the integration process. Horn [6] was suggesting some boundary conditions.

Frankot and Chellappa [4] assume that the unknown surface function Z satisfies the integrability condition. Furthermore they were assuming a Fourier coefficient representation

$$Z(x, y) = \tfrac{1}{2\pi} \int\limits_{-\infty}^{+\infty}\int\limits_{-\infty}^{+\infty} Z^{(F)}(u, v) \cdot e^{-j(u \cdot x + v \cdot y)} du \, dv \qquad (4)$$

of this function, where

$$Z^{(F)}(u, v) = \tfrac{1}{2\pi} \int\limits_{-\infty}^{+\infty}\int\limits_{-\infty}^{+\infty} Z(x, y) \cdot e^{j(u \cdot x + v \cdot y)} dx \, dy \qquad (5)$$

denote the Fourier coefficients of Z. Based on these assumptions they could prove a theorem allowing the reconstruction of function Z in the Fourier space. Then an inverse Fourier transform leads to the desired surface data. This method was selected to represent global techniques in comparison with local techniques.

3 Evaluation

Several experiments were performed to evaluate the quality of surface integration applying the local four-path integration algorithm (**fpi**) and the global Fourier expansion algorithm (**FE**).

Errors in surface integration arise from various sources. From the mathematical point of view, surface integration is only possible if a conservative vector field is given. Image acquisition causes a certain distortion, since we are dealing with discrete images (and hence with discrete gradient fields) in computer vision. Furthermore, most surface integration algorithms require a discrete formulation of the differentiation. The input data of the integration procedure is also determined by using a numerical differentiation model, in general.

Moreover, the shape and orientation of the surface have an effect on the surface reconstruction process. This can be regarded as a special type of gradient field distortion. In particular, the following three surface characteristics can lead to heavy problems: occluding boundaries, surface edges, and especially occluding edges. Occluding boundaries can cause distortions because of undefined gradients and different height values. The latter is also valid for edges at the surface boundary. We carried out experiments with various types of local and global surface shapes. Five typical objects which possesses one or more of the mentioned surface characteristics were examined. The gradient fields of these objects have different levels of deviation from an ideal gradient field. One of these polyhedra was available as synthetic and as real data. In addition to distortions produced through discretization and surface properties, the integration process is affected by different kinds of noise. We consider additive Gaussian noise with different standard deviations as well as spike noise.

In the following subsection we specify the evaluation procedure according to the types of distortions described in the previous paragraph in more detail.

3.1   Evaluation methodology

A local technique [10] and a global technique [4] were selected for this paper as representatives for both classes of approaches. These two techniques were chosen based on theoretical comparisons and on the availability of complete documentation for implementation.

Discrete 256×256 gradient fields resulting from shading based surface analysis of real objects as well as synthetic 256×256 gradient fields are used as input data for surface integration. If a gradient value is not defined then value zero is assumed. Height maps are initialized with a constant at all 256×256 positions.

Curved and polyhedral object surfaces are studied. A synthetic sphere, a synthetic Mozart statue, and a plaster statue ("man in chair") were selected as curved objects. The sphere is very useful because visible orientations cover a Gaussian hemisphere, and because it allows evaluations of reconstructions based on noisy gradient data. The Mozart statue is of "medium shape complexity", and the plaster statue is of "high shape complexity".

A synthetic as well as a real K-shaped polyhedron was selected as polyhedral objects. Ideal polyhedrons do not satisfy surface conditions for integration at certain surface locations due to existing surface edges or occluding edges. However, these objects are especially of interest for industrial shape reconstruction. Gradient fields of synthetic objects are generated either by analytic differentiation (sphere) or by approximate numerical differentiation if the surface data are given as height values on a discrete array (Mozart, K-polyhedron). In the latter case three different methodologies were applied: backward difference quotient, central difference quotient, and a regularized numerical differentiation by convolution with the derivatives of a Gaussian kernel with standard deviation $\sigma = \sqrt{2}$. The gradient fields of real objects (plaster statue, K-shaped object) were obtained using photometric stereo analysis [8, 11].

Different types of noise can be simulated for synthetic objects for studying the robustness of the implemented techniques. Gaussian noise with different standard deviations is used for modeling image acquisition errors. Outliers in gradient fields are modeled by spike noise.

Quantitative and qualitative evaluations are used for comparing the two selected integration techniques. The absolute differences in height between synthetic model (ground truth) and reconstructed surface define quantitative errors. These height differences are statistically characterized by histograms, maximum differences, averaged differences, and standard deviations. Synthetic objects (i.e., given ground truth) allow the measurement of height differences. For obtaining discrete histogram data a certain interval width ΔZ is assumed for counting real height data Z. Percentages are calculated with respect to the total height of the object (i.e., maximum height minus minimum height).

Integration techniques lead to relative height values. The differences between maximum and minimum height could be used for adjusting model and reconstructed data into the same range of height values. However, this approach would be very sensitive to noise. Therefore least-square optimization was used for shifting (not scaling!) of height values of calculated height maps into the proper range of height values.

3.2 Experiments with smooth objects

A synthetic Mozart statue was given as a discrete array of height data, see Fig. 1. Three different numerical methods (see Section 3.1) were used to calculate the input data arrays for surface integration; the evaluation for analytic differentiation is given in [9]. Then both algorithms used these generated gradient fields as input. The reconstructed height values are shifted in the range of the original surface using LSE optimization. The resulting errors, i.e., the absolute differences in height, are shown in Tab. 1 (maximum error, averaged error, and standard deviation). Positions with long gradients (length greater than 4) were excluded from this statistical analysis of resulting height values.

Table 1: Different discrete differentiation schemes were used to generate the input gradient fields. The upper rows (bold numbers) denote the resulting errors using **fpi**, and the lower rows correspond to **FE**.

gradient method	maximum error	averaged error	σ_z
backward difference quotient	**18.9** 14.3	**2.6** 2.9	**2.3** 2.0
central difference quotient	**33.0** 13.2	**2.9** 3.0	**2.3** 2.0
Gaussian kernels $\sigma = \sqrt{2}$	**12.4** 14.7	**4.0** 2.7	**2.5** 1.9

The regularization through Gaussian kernels leads to the worst results for **fpi** (see averaged error and standard deviation). The simple differentiation schemes correspond to the simple local integration techniques. The reconstructed **FE** height data are more robust, see maximum errors and standard deviations in Tab. 1. The **FE** values were essentially improving against the **fpi** values if the regularized differential scheme was used. However, an explicit numerical differentiation is not contained in the **FE** algorithm. Therefore the regularized differential scheme was used for further comparisons.
The quality of the results of the simple **fpi** algorithm as shown in Tab. 1 is quite surprising in comparison with the **FE** results. The competitive behavior of the **fpi** algorithm is also illustrated by the error histogram in Fig. 1. The percentage is calculated with respect to the maximum height of the statue. The width of the 15 classes in this histogram is about 1.54%. About 80% of the **fpi** results have errors $\leq 7.7\%$, and about 80% of the **FE** results have errors $\leq 4.6\%$. If all gradient data, i.e., gradient vectors of any length are used as input to the **FE** algorithm then the reconstructed surface is heavily distorted. This problem does not appear with the

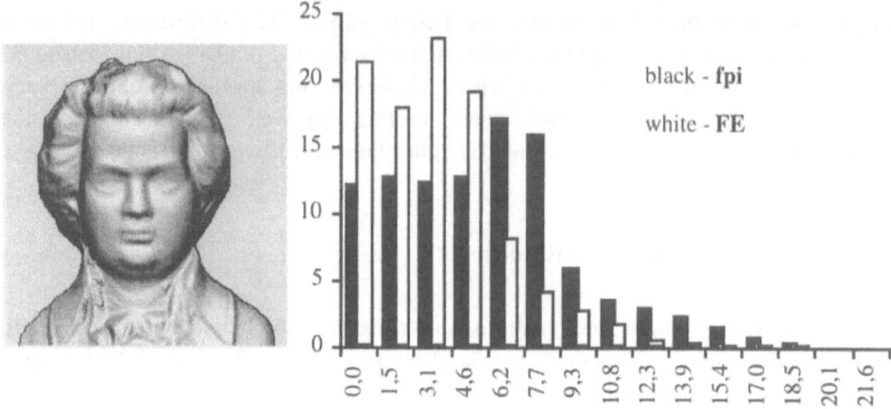

Figure 1: Mozart statue (shaded representation) and histograms of height differences.

fpi algorithm. Error distributions over the surface range are also very descriptive besides global error statistics, they can be found in [9].

A large number of real smooth objects was used to compare the behavior of both integration techniques. The gradient maps were generated using photometric stereo analysis [8, 11]. Here we illustrate two typical examples. Fig. 2 shows three input images for photometric stereo analysis of the "man in chair". This plaster statue is of "very complex shape".

A serious difficulty is that the object border has different height values. The reconstruction results are illustrated in Fig. 3.

Both methods produce reasonable results for such curved objects in general. The **fpi** algorithm generated erroneous height values in the head region and in the knee region for this specific object.

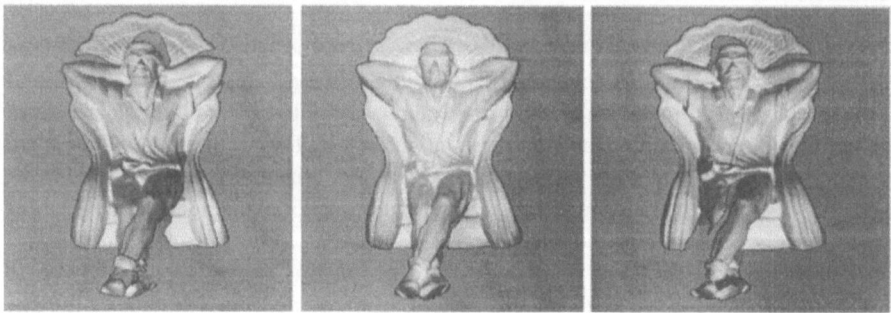

Figure 2: Input images for a three-source photometric stereo analysis (plaster statue "man in chair"). The estimated light source directions are (-0.388, 0.060, -1.0), (0.032, 0.557, -1.0), and (0.389, 0.105, -1.0), respectively. The ratios of the light source strengths are 1.0:0.563:0.526.

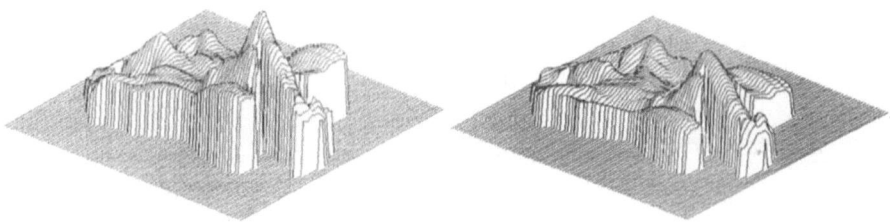

Figure 3: Reconstructed "man in chair" (**fpi** is on the left).

3.3 Experiments with polyhedral objects

A synthetic polyhedral K-shaped object was given as a discrete 256×256 array of height data, see Fig. 4 (on the left). The height extent is 162.43 grid units. This object turned out to be a very complicated one for height data integration based on gradient information. There are locations for this surface function where integration is not possible. At surface edges there is no C^1-continuity, and at occluding edges there is even no C^0-continuity. Some faces of the polyhedron are not visible that would be needed to reconstruct the polyhedron which is diagonally placed into the view space. A further difficulty arises from the fact that the object border has very different height values. The concavity of the object also renders more difficulties.

The gradient field was generated using the backward difference quotient method. This method possesses the advantage of less smoothing at object edges in comparison with the numerical approximation (Gaussian kernel). The property of edge preserving should be used to evaluate integration techniques.

Fig. 4 (middle) illustrates the results using local path integration. The visual comparison shows roughness for originally planar faces. The four-path method assumes the same height values at the four array corners. This was about adequate for the sphere and the Mozart statue but not for this K-shaped polyhedron. These objects had about the same height value at the object border. The K-shaped polyhedron takes its minimum and its maximum height value at certain border points! The initialization of the height map with a uniform constant is extremely disadvantageous for this polyhedron as for polyhedra in general.

Fig. 4 (on the right) illustrates the results using the global **FE** integration technique. Also this global technique was not able to cope with the large height differences. However, the reconstructed surface is much closer to the originally planar surfaces than in case of the **fpi** results. The statistical analysis shows similar results for both techniques **fpi / FE**: maximum errors 90.94 / 77.15, averaged error 23.03 / 21.71, and standard deviation 18.25 / 18.82. From the error histograms it follows that both techniques reconstruct 73% of height values with errors $\leq 15\%$. In case of not defined or long gradients (length at least equal to 4) it was assumed that the value 0 (i.e., no impact on height changes) was used instead. This was reasonable for the sphere and the Mozart statue but not for the polyhedron.

Figure 4: A K-shaped synthetic polyhedron with a maximum height of 162.43 grid units: height map (shown on the left), the maximum height error of the reconstructed **fpi** surface (middle) is equal to 90.94 grid units, and 77.15 grid units for the reconstructed **FE** surface (right).

Altogether, both techniques are not adequate to reconstruct this polyhedron as well as polyhedrons in general within reasonable quality limits. However, it can be suggested that a locally adaptive path integration technique should be sensitive to local patterns in the gradient map to obtain adequate reconstruction results. The use of the edge map of the given irradiance image could also support the proper choice of the integration path, and of the locally adaptive integration procedure.

The reconstruction results for polyhedral real world objects had the same essential distortions as demonstrated for the synthetic K-shaped object. Fig. 5 shows the reconstruction results of a real K-shaped object which is similar to the synthetic one shown in Fig. 4. Especially remarkable are the strong **fpi** distortions of planar faces (wave-like distortion pattern - as for the Mozart statue). Errors in the generated gradient map (especially at locations of very low albedo) result in reconstruction errors for both integration techniques. This also points out that further improvements of shading based gradient calculations are required to ensure applications in 3-D object modeling. More results for polyhedrons and polyhedron-like objects are shown in [9].

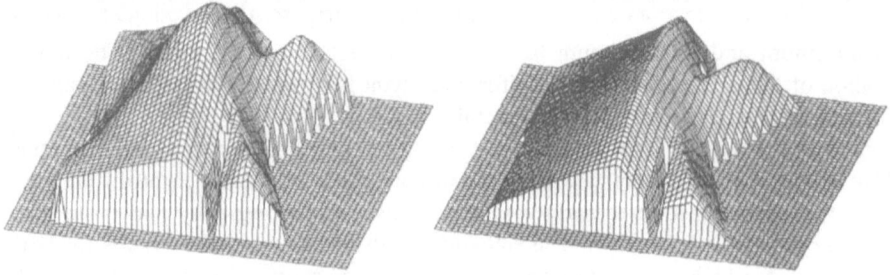

Figure 5: Grid representations of the reconstructed real K-shaped object for both methods. The result of the **fpi** based method is shown on the left.

3.4 Experiments with introduced noise

For a synthetic sphere with the projected sphere centroid at point $\mathbf{p} = (0, 0)$ and a radius of 100 grid units, a single point noise is simulated by modifying slant $30°$ at point $\mathbf{p} = (50, 0)$ into $arctan(4) \approx 76°$. The same slant value is assigned to three neighbors of point $\mathbf{p} = (50, 0)$ - on the left, below, below on the left. All the remaining gradient values remain unchanged including all the tilt values. The four-path integration generates an adequate error pattern (propagation into the direction of the four array corners). The **FE** maximum error is higher than the **fpi** maximum error, but the **FE** error function is faster decreasing than the **fpi** error function. In both cases the spike noise resulted into a spike distortion of the reconstructed shape.

Besides spike noise we introduced additive Gaussian distributed noise to synthetic images to compare the influence of image acquisition errors on the surface integration process. We used an ideal planar surface patch of size 200×200 with constant gradients $(p, q) = (0, 0)$.

We measured the quality of the integration by calculating the difference ΔZ_{max} between the lowest and the highest height value. Further, we calculated the average $\Delta \bar{Z}$ and the standard deviations σ_Z of absolute height differences. The data for different Gaussian standard deviations σ_D are given in Tab. 2.

4   Conclusions

The advantages of the Fourier expansion in comparison with **fpi** are a better robustness with respect to Gaussian noise as well as spike noise, and better qualitative evaluations for real scenes, especially for curved objects. The advantage of the four-path integration in comparison with **FE** is robustness with respect to high gradient values (however, this seems to be of low importance in real scenes). The most difficult reconstruction situation is defined by polyhedral objects as the synthetic or the real K-shaped polyhedron. The computing time of the **FE** algorithm was about 1.6 times the computing time of the **fpi** algorithm for 256×256 maps.

More generally speaking, the reconstruction results depend upon the object shape. Polyhedral objects (e.g., especially relevant to industrial applications) are the most critical shapes for the studied local and global methods.

Table 2: Different standard deviations were used to simulate additive Gaussian noise in the input gradient fields. The upper rows (bold numbers) denote the resulting errors using fpi, and the lower rows correspond to **FE**.

σ_D	ΔZ_{max}	$\Delta \bar{Z}$	σ_Z
2	**0.195**	**0.059**	**0.052**
	0.176	0.053	0.045
4	**0.449**	**0.144**	**0.122**
	0.381	0.116	0.097
8	**1.045**	**0.298**	**0.253**
	0.790	0.214	0.183

The proposed error measures should be discussed in relation to applications of shape reconstruction techniques. In the ideal case, certain "data sheets" about transformation modules should support the decision which one can be chosen for a specific application context.

There is a remarkable deficiency of literature about integration techniques for discrete vector fields, at least in computer vision. Further research could be directed on refinement of methods (esp. for serving polyhedral objects). The global technique seems to be slightly in favor in relation to the local technique so far. However, it can be expected that the local techniques will have restrictions to deal with complex shapes. The development of locally adaptive methods (e.g. relaxation) could be appropriate. There is also a need in developing quantitative evaluation measures characterizing the qualitative appearance.

References

[1]   Bichsel, M.: Fast Photometric Stereo: Regularization vs. Wiener Filtering. IAPRS, Vol. 30, Part 5W1, ISPRS Intercommission Workshop "From Pixels to Sequences", Zurich, Mar. 22-24, 1995, 245-252.

[2]   Bourne, D.E., Kendall, P.C.: Vektoranalysis. Stuttgart: Teubner 1988.

[3]   Coleman, N.E., Jr., Jain, R.: Obtaining 3-dimensional shape of textured and specular surfaces using four-source photometry. CGIP 18, 309-328 (1982).

[4]   Frankot, R.T., Chellappa, R.: A method for enforcing integrability in shape from shading algorithms. IEEE Trans. on PAMI 10, 439-451 (1988).

[5]   Healey, G., Jain, R.: Depth recovery from surface normals. ICPR´84, Montreal, Canada, Jul. 30-Aug. 2, 1984, 894-896.

[6]   Horn, B.K.P.: Height and gradient from shading. Int. J. of CV 5, 37-75 (1990).

[7]   Horn, B.K.P., Brooks, M.J.: The variational approach to shape from shading. CVGIP 33, 174-208 (1986).

[8]   Klette, R., Koschan, A., Schlüns, K.: Computer Vision - Räumliche Information aus digitalen Bildern. Braunschweig: Vieweg 1996.

[9]   Klette, R., Schlüns, K.: Height data from gradient fields, Proc. Machine Vision Applications, Architectures, and Systems Integration V, SPIE 2908, Boston, Massachusetts, Nov. 18-19, 1996, 204-215.

[10] Rodehorst, V.: Vertiefende Analyse eines Gestalts-Constraints von Aloimonos und Shulman". Technischer Bericht, CV-Bericht 8, Institut für Technische Informatik, TU Berlin, 1993.

[11] Woodham, R.J.: Photometric method for determining surface orientations from multiple images. Optical Engineering 19, 139-144 (1980).

[12] Wu, Z., Li, L.: A line-integration based method for depth recovery from surface normals. CVGIP 43, 53-66 (1988).

A new approach to shape from shading

Vladimir A. Kovalevsky

1   Introduction

Most of the works on Shape from Shading [e.g. 1, 2] consider the problem as the restoration of the spatial shape of a smooth continuous surface when a continuous function representing the brightness at each point of a plane projection of the surface is given. In order to solve the problem, properties of nonlinear partial differential equations are investigated. The ultimate solution is then performed by some numerical methods. As seen e.g. from the recent review [3], this approach has not led to a practically usable solution. The author sees the reason of the lack of success in the discrepancy between continuous models and the theory of differential equations on the one hand and the digital nature of the images as well as the use of numerical methods on the other hand. Thinking first about continuous functions and differential equations, and then coming back to a finite numerical representation and a numerical solution, is irrational.

The author suggests therefore an essentially digital approach: the surface to be reconstructed is considered as a polyhedron. The image contains then a finite number of plane polygonal regions each having a constant grey value. The problem consists in finding the heights of the vertices of the polyhedron. The heights must satisfy a system of quadratic equations.

In the present paper the conditions for the existence and the uniqueness of the solution of the system of equations are investigated. It turns out that the system is strongly overdetermined. Therefore the solution must be performed by minimizing the sum of the squared discrepancies. An improved nonlinear least-squares method of solution is suggested and some results of computer experiments are reported.

2   Problem statement

2.1   The simplest version

Given is a digitized grey value image in a rectangular region of the plane. We consider it as the result of viewing a polyhedron surface being illuminated by a single infinitely distant light source, e.g. the sun. In the simplest case we suppose that the surface obeys the Lambertian law of reflection and has a constant albedo (reflectance ability). We also suppose (in the simplest case) the direction of a vector pointing to the sun to be known. Thus each face of the polyhedron must have a constant grey value. Correspondingly, we subdivide the given image into regions with constant grey values and approximate the boundaries of the regions by polygonal lines. In this way we get the X- and Y-coordinates of their vertices. The problem consists in finding such values of the Z-coordinates of the vertices that the grey values calculated on the basis of these Z-coordinates be equal (or approximately equal) to the given grey values. The formal problem statement looks as follows:

Given a subdivision of a (rectangular) region of the plane into polygons, a grey value of each polygon and a vector pointing to the infinitely distant light source (the sun)

Find the height (i.e. the Z-coordinate) of each vertex of the given polygons such that the grey value of each polygon, calculated from the heights, be equal to the given grey value of the corresponding polygon.

2.2 More complicated versions

More complicated versions of the problem statement include also finding an unknown sun vector, or two vectors of two light sources, and/or the albedo of certain parts of the surface. It is also possible to look for the best matching of the grey values rather then for an exact one.

3 The solution

3.1 Existence of the solution

Consider first the simplest case when all given polygons are triangles. In the general case it is possible to subdivide polygons into triangles. Consider the dependence of the grey value of the surface of a triangle in the 3D space from the heights of their vertices. It is well known that according to the Lambertian law the grey value GV (or the brightness) of a surface is proportional to the cosine of the angle between the sun vector and the normal to the surface. A value proportional to the cosine may be calculated as the scalar product of that vectors divided by the norm of the normal. Division by the norm of the sun vector is not necessary since (in the case of an infinitely distant light source) this vector does not depend on the heights of vertices while we are only interested in this dependence.

Let us denote the coordinates of the vertex $P0$ by:

$$P0.X, \; P0.Y \text{ and } P0.Z,$$

and similarly for other vertices and vectors. Then the components of the normal N to the surface of the triangle $(P0, P1, P2)$ are:

$$N.X = (P1.Y{-}P0.Y){\cdot}(P2.Z{-}P0.Z) - (P1.Z{-}P0.Z){\cdot}(P2.Y{-}P0.Y);$$

$$N.Y = (P1.Z{-}P0.Z){\cdot}(P2.X{-}P0.X) - (P1.X{-}P0.X){\cdot}(P2.Z{-}P0.Z); \qquad (1)$$

$$N.Z = (P1.X{-}P0.X){\cdot}(P2.Y{-}P0.Y) - (P1.Y{-}P0.Y){\cdot}(P2.X{-}P0.X).$$

We are seeking for the Z-coordinates of all three vertices.

The calculated grey value *GV* is then equal to

$$GV=(N.X\times S.X+N.Y\times S.Y+N.Z\times S.Z)/\sqrt{(N.X^2+N.Y^2+N.Z^2)}, \qquad (2)$$

where *S.X*, *S.Y* and *S.Z* are the components of the vector *S* pointing to the sun. The calculated value *GV* must be equal to the given grey value *GG*. Thus we arrive at the equation:

$$(N.X\times S.X+N.Y\times S.Y+N.Z\times S.Z)/\sqrt{(N.X^2+N.Y^2+N.Z^2)}=GG.$$

After having squared both sides of it we arrive at the quadratic equation in the components of *N*:

$$(N.X\times S.X+N.Y\times S.Y+N.Z\times S.Z)^2-GG^2\times(N.X^2+N.Y^2+N.Z^2) = 0. \qquad (3)$$

If the heights of the vertices *P0* and *P1* are supposed to be known, then it is a quadratic equation in *P2.Z*, since the only terms in (3) depending on *P2.Z* are *N.X* and *N.Y*, and they depend linearly on *P2.Z*.

Note that (3) contains the square of *GG*. Thus a solution of (3) may correspond to a negative value of *GG* which is inadmissible: such a solution corresponds to a surface, not visible from above. The sign of a solution may be checked by means of (2). As we see, equation (3) may have none, or one, or two admissible solutions.

Consider the case when the given image is subdivided into *NT* triangles. The height of one of the points may be always chosen arbitrarily, since according to (1) and (2) the grey values depend only on the *differences* of the heights. Thus we have a *system of NT equations in NP−1 unknowns*, *NP* being the number of points (i.e. vertices of the triangles). Let us look for the relation between these two numbers. According to the Euler's formula for a closed polyhedron surface (of genus 0):

$$NF-NE+NP=2,$$

where *NF* is the number of the faces, *NE* is the number of the edges (triangle sides) and *NP* is the number of vertices. Our triangle system is however not closed. Nevertheless we can apply Euler's formula if we consider the system as being placed onto a sphere. Then the outside of the system must be considered as one more face of the corresponding polyhedron surface. Thus we have for our triangle system: *NF=NT+1* and hence:

$$NT+1-NE+NP=2. \qquad (4)$$

Now let us establish a relation between *NT* and *NE*. Denote NE_e the number of the *exterior* triangle sides which separate a triangle from the outside of our system. The rest of $NT-NE_e$ sides are the *interior* ones each of which is incident with exactly two triangles. Let us introduce the notion of a "half-side": we split each interior side *S* into two half-sides and assign each half-side to one of the two adjacent triangles incident with the original side *S*. The exterior sides are not split: each exterior side corresponds to exactly one half-side. It is assigned to their incident triangle. Now every triangle has three half-sides assigned to it and the number NH of the half-sides is equal to $3NT$. On the other hand:

$$NH = NE_e + 2(NE-NE_e),$$

and hence:

$$NH = NE_e + 2(NE-NE_e) = 3NT.$$

After having combined this equation with (4) one obtains:

$$NT = 2NP-NE_e-2. \tag{5}$$

For example, if we have a square image raster of $N{\times}N$ pixels and we subdivide each pixel (being considered as a small square) into two triangles, then we have $NP=(N+1)^2$ points, $NE_e=4N$ exterior sides and we obtain $NT=2N^2$ triangles which number is in accordance with (5). Equation (5) is true for any triangulation of a connected plane region.

This knowledge may be useful to consider, to which extent our system of equations is overdetermined. Important is the difference between the number NT of the equations and the number $NP-1$ (see above) of the unknowns. Let us denote the difference OVR. Then we have:

$$OVR = NT-NP + 1.$$

After having substituted (5) into this equation one obtains:

$$OVR = NP-NE_e -1.$$

For example, for the raster of $N{\times}N$ pixels:

$$OVR = (N+1)^2-4N-1 = (N-1)^2-1.$$

Thus we see that, except of some trivial cases of very small images, the system of equations is *strongly overdetermined*. An exact solution is only possible if the equations are mutually dependent and exactly $NP-1$ equations among them are independent. In practice this is impossible because of inexact measuring of the grey values. Thus one of the possible ways of solution is the *least-squares method*, in which case we must look for the minimum of the sum of squared differences between the measured and the calculated grey values. This problem will be discussed in Section 4.

3.2   Uniqueness

It is well known (see e.g. [1]) that in the particular case of a vertical sun vector (the sun stays in zenith) for any solution of the Shape from Shading problem there exists another twinned solution. It contains the same absolute values of the height differences but with opposite signs. This can easily be seen from equations (1) and (2): if we change the sign of all Z-differences, the value of GV will not change, since the terms containing $N.X$ and $N.Y$ in the numerator of (2) disappear, $N.Z$ does not depend on the heights, and the denominator contains only squares of the differences.

In the case of other sun vectors the problem of uniqueness becomes more complicated: we have a system of quadratic equations each of which may have up to two solutions. However, the number of the solutions of the whole system remains open. The author has tried to investigate this question experimentally.

Consider a triangulation of the given image, each triangle having a constant grey value, and a subset U of the triangles having all a common vertex. Each triangle of U must have exactly two adjacent triangles of U. We shall call such a subset of triangles „umbrella". We use umbrellas since the solution for an umbrella is easier than the general solution, and there is a hope to dissolve the general solution into solutions for single umbrellas.

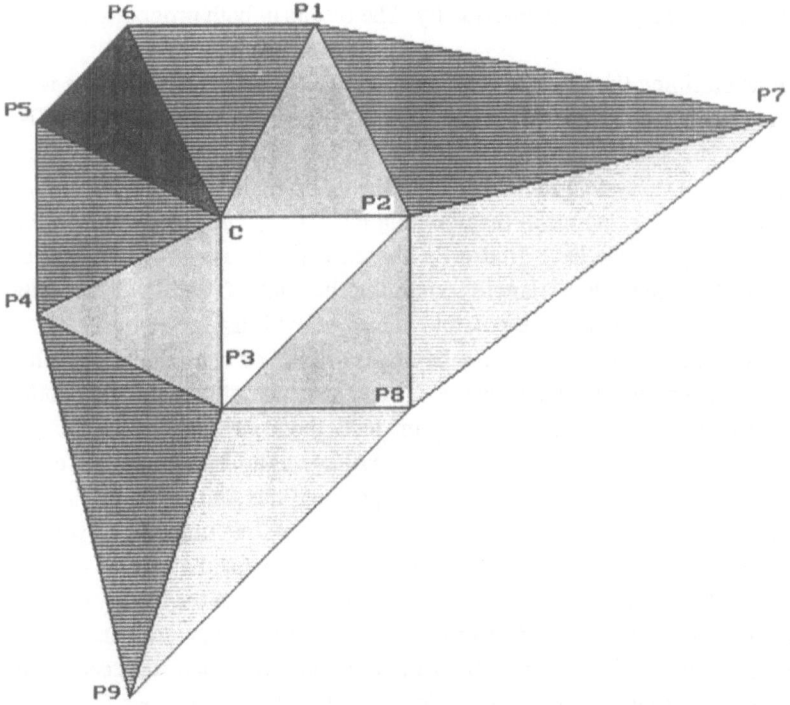

Fig. 1. Illustration to the calculation of the heights discrepancy in an umbrella

As already mentioned, the height of one of the points may be chosen arbitrarily. Let it be the centre point C of the umbrella containing the points $P1$ to $P6$ (Fig. 1). Consider now one of the boundary points P of the umbrella. Since the grey values of the triangles are given, it is possible to define the range of the admissible heights of P. The idea is as follows.

Consider a triangle T of U containing P. The angle between the normal N of T and the sun vector is uniquely defined by the grey value of T. Let us rotate N around the sun vector while preserving the angle. Consider a plane E through C perpendicular to N. It rotates together with N. Consider now the vertical line through P and the intersection of this line with E. At any rotation of E a unique value Z of the Z-coordinate of the intersection point is defined. When having rotated the normal N through a full circle, we obtain the full set of the possible values of Z. Some of them correspond to negative values of $N.Z$. They must be dropped, since a negative $N.Z$ corresponds to a turned over position of the triangle's surface in which case it is invisible. Also a zero value of $N.Z$ has no sense: it corresponds to a vertical plane which is only possible under an infinite value of $P.Z$. The author has developed two computer programs: one simulating the rotation of the plane and another one calculating the range of $P.Z$ analytically. The results of both programs coincide.

When determining the range of $P.Z$ from the two triangles of U incident with P, the common range (being the intersection of both ranges) may become smaller. Now it is possible to check each admissible value of $P.Z$, whether it may belong to the solution of the equation subsystem for all points of the umbrella U. This test works as follows. Denote the boundary points of the umbrella $P1, P2, ..., Pn$. The point $P1$ is our point P, whose height Z_s we have arbitrarily chosen from the range of admissible values. The point $P2$ belongs to a triangle containing the points C and $P1$. Their heights are known. Now we can find the possible values of $P2.Z$ using the quadratic equation (3). As explained above, there may be none, or one, or two admissible solutions. If there is no solution, the chosen value Z_s of $P1.Z$ is not admissible and another value must be chosen. Otherwise the program tests the next boundary point $P3$ for all values found for $P2.Z$ etc. The point $P2$ may have up to 2 solutions, $P3$ up to 4 etc., the point $P(n+1)$ up to 2^n. The process stops when the starting point $P1$ is reached. The program compares all the 2^n solutions (n is the number of points in the umbrella) with the chosen starting value Z_s and looks for the nearest one which we denote Z_n. The discrepancy $DZ(Z_s)=Z_n-Z_s$ is the measure of the quality of the value Z_s for $P1.Z$. The values of $P1.Z$ leading to a zero discrepancy are candidates for the global solution for the umbrella U. If there is more than one such candidate, all of them must be tested by means of repeating the test described above for all umbrellas having the boundary points of U as their centre points. A true solution must lead to all discrepancies equal to zero.

The author has made hundreds of experiments with different triangulations and different values of the sun vector. The results are as follows.

The above introduced function $DZ(Z_s)$ turned out to be discontinuous at some values of its argument. A discontinuity may even happen at a value of Z_s belonging to the true solution (the latter is always known in our experiments since the program generates the image from a given polyhedron by calculating the grey values of the triangles according to equation (2)). The discontinuity of $DZ(Z_s)$ makes the use of the well-known bisection method (or a similar one) for finding the roots of $DZ(Z_s)$ impossible. However, the program finds the true solution nevertheless because, if a value of a height of a point was a discontinuity point of $DZ(Z_s)$ of one umbrella, it always was a „good" point in another umbrella. Up to now the program has always found a single solution. Thus we can hazard the conjecture, that under nonvertical sun vectors the solution is unique, if it exists.

As mentioned above, the system of equations is in all practically important cases strongly overdetermined. This means, the unique solution exists only if the given grey values are exactly specified. In our experiments they were double precision floats. In all practical cases, when the given grey values come from a scanner or a similar device, they have a relatively low precision. Only a subset of as many equations as the number of points minus one may have a solution. This is the reason for using an entirely different technique to solve the problem.

4   The Levenberg-Marquardt method

The well-known version of the least-squares method solves the following problem:

Find the set $\{a_1, a_2, ..., a_m\}$ of unknown parameters which minimizes the merit function:

$$F = \sum_{i=1}^{N} [y_i - y(x_i; a_1, a_2, ..., a_m)]^2.$$

In the simplest case the function $y(.)$ is linear in the desired parameters $\{a_1, a_2, ..., a_m\}$ and the solution of the problem can be reduced to solving the well-known normal equations by Gauss. Our problem may be also regarded as a least-squares problem, however our functions are nonlinear. In this case the Newton method may be implemented. This is an iterative method of finding roots of nonlinear functions. The method may be generalized for systems of equations and for multidimensional minimization. In the latter case the equations arise from differentiating the merit function with respect to the desired parameters and demanding that the partial derivatives be zero. The merit function is in our case the sum of squared differences GV_i-GG_i, i being the index of a triangle, GG_i its given grey value and GV_i its calculated grey value. The derivatives may be linearized by representing them by Taylor series containing only terms with the first derivatives of y(.). Thus one obtains a system of normal equations, however not in the desired parameters $\{a_1, a_2, ..., a_m\}$ but rather in their increments. The coefficients of the equations are calculated for some initial set of the parameters accepted as the initial approximation. The increments obtained as the solution of the normal equations are then added to the current approximation which gives the next approximation etc.

Unfortunately this method does not ensure a monotone convergence to the minimum. Sometimes it does not converge at all, depending upon the choice of the initial approximation.

An improvement of the Newton method is the Levenberg-Marquardt method [4]. This method represents a combination of the Newton method and the steepest descent method. According to the Levenberg-Marquardt method, the diagonal elements of the matrix of the normal equations are artificially increased by multiplying each diagonal element by $1+\lambda$ while λ is a small positive control parameter. The matrix gets more *diagonally dominant*. The increments of the parameters obtain in this way an additional value proportional to the components of the gradient of the merit function and the process tends to that of steepest descent. This is appropriate if the merit function *increases* during the current iteration instead of decreasing, what it is supposed to do. In the case when the merit function really decreases, the control parameter λ must be also decreased. The process tends then to that of Newton. This is more appropriate in the vicinity of the desired minimum.

5   Computer experiments

The author has performed hundreds of computer experiments both with solving systems of quadratic equations and with minimizing the merit function. The latter was performed both with the Newton and the Levenberg-Marquardt method. Artificial images computed from reliefs represented in the computer (Fig. 2) have been processed. The best results have been obtained with the Levenberg-Marquardt method.

Fig. 2. Example of an artificial relief used in computer experiments

Experiments with true photographs are now in preparation. For this purpose photographs are scanned, contrasted, smoothed with an edge preserving filter and subdivided into regions with constant grey values. A special new method of encoding grey level images by means of the so-called cell lists is used. A cell list is a data structure proposed by the author [5, 6]. It contains descriptions of regions, boundary curves (approximated by polygons) and branch points. The cell list contains explicit and complete topological and geometrical information about the image: the image may be reconstructed from the list. On the other hand, the topological information as for example about bounding relations between curves and regions, branch points and curves etc., is directly accessible from the list. Geometrical information is also explicitly represented in the form of coordinates of the branch points and polygon vertices. The image may be subject to geometrical transformations without changing the basic contents of the list: only the coordinates must be changed, and this can be done by means of the well-known matrix multiplication method.

Having obtained the cell list of an image, one may subdivide the regions into triangles and then apply the above described method of calculating the heights of the vertices. In this way the problem of Shape from Shading may be solved not only for artificial images but also for true photographs, e.g. that of human faces. Because of the fact that the equations are strongly overdetermined there is the possibility to calculate the direction to the light source and eventually also the directions to more than one light source. We also consider the possibility of calculating the albedo (i.e. reflectance) of some parts of human faces, of course with some aid of a human operator who must help the computer to identify regions in the face where the albedo may differ from that of other parts of the face.

References

[1] Horn, B.K.P.: Obtaining shape from shading information. In: Horn, B.K.P. and Brooks, M.J. (eds.): Shape from shading. Cambridge, Massachusetts, The MIT Press 1989.

[2] Brooks, M.J. and Choinacki, W.: Direct computation of shape from shading. Rapport de recherche $n°$ 2176, INRIA, France, January 1994.

[3] Hildebrand, A.: Von der Photographie zum 3D-Modell. Berlin, Springer 1996.

[4] William H. Press et. all, Numerical recipes in C, Cambridge, Massachusetts, Cambridge University Press 1988.

[5] Kovalevsky, V.A.: Finite topology as applied to image processing, CVGIP 46, 141-161, 1989.

[6] Kovalevsky, V.A.: Finite topology and image analysis. In: Hawkes, P. (ed.): Image mathematics and image processing. Boston San Diego New York London Sydney Tokyo Toronto Academic Press 1992 (Advances in Electronics and Electron Physics, vol. 84, pp. 197-259).

Recent uniqueness results in shape from shading

Ryszard Kozera

1 Introduction

The main purpose of this paper is to discuss briefly two topics. The first one is to show that Sneddon's claim ([9, Section 7 pp. 61]) about representability of any solution to a given first-order partial differential equation in terms of either *a complete* or *a general* or *a singular integral* is erroneous. The literature on complete integrals is a bewildering collection of incomplete and false statements (see *e.g.* Dou [6] or [9]). Recent results by Chojnacki [3] and Kozera [8] shed new light on this topic and fill a gap in the literature. The second goal of this paper is to critically inspect uniqueness results (see Brooks [1, 2]) concerning the images of a Lambertian hemisphere and a Lambertian plane, which resort to Sneddon's erroneous assertion and as such are invalid. Finally, we adopt a different approach so that the results claimed in [1, 2], subject to minor reformulations, become valid. For a more detailed analysis an interested reader is also referred to [3] or [8].

2 Some remarks on representing solutions of first-order P.D.E. in terms of complete integral and envelopes

In this section we shall refer to the erroneous assertion of Sneddon about representability of solutions to a first-order partial differential equation in terms of a *complete integral* and *envelopes* (see [9, Section 7]).

2.1 Preliminaries

We first recall the notion of a *complete integral* (see also [3] and [6]). For a given first-order partial differential equation

$$F(x, y, u, u_x, u_y) = 0, \tag{1}$$

defined over an open region $\Omega \subset \mathbb{R}^2$, a function $G(x, y, P_1, P_2)$ of class C^2 over $\Omega \times V$ (where V is an open region of $\mathbb{R}^2$) is called a *complete integral* of (1) if

(Ci) for each $(P_1, P_2) \in V$, the function G is a C^2 solution to (1) on Ω,

(Cii) for each $(x, y) \in \Omega$ and for each $(P_1, P_2) \in V$, the rank of the matrix

$$\begin{pmatrix} G_{P_1} & G_{x_1 P_1} & G_{x_2 P_1} \\ G_{P_2} & G_{x_1 P_2} & G_{x_2 P_2} \end{pmatrix} (x, y, P_1, P_2) \tag{2}$$

equals two.

Condition (2) assures that parameters P_1 and P_2 are independent (see [6, Section 6]). Any graph of $G(x, y, P_1^0, P_2^0)$ with both P_1^0 and P_2^0 fixed, is called *zero-parameter envelope* of G. Moreover, for a given C^1 (C^2) function ϕ : $\mathbb{R} \rightarrow \mathbb{R}$, we can form a one-parameter subfamily of functions $u_\phi(x, y; P_1) = G(x, y, P_1, \phi(P_1))$, and then can generate, either locally or globally (if possible), its *general integral* (which graph is called *a one-parameter envelope of G*), i.e. a function

$$u(x, y) = G(x, y, P_1(x, y), \phi(P_1(x, y))), \tag{3}$$

by eliminating parameter P_1 from the system of the form

$$u(x, y) = G(x, y, P_1, \phi(P_1)) \quad \text{and} \quad (G(x, y, P_1, \phi(P_1)))_{P_1} = 0. \tag{4}$$

It can be then shown that under certain conditions (see [3] and [6]), formulae (3) and (4) define a new C^1 (C^2) solution to (1). By choosing different functions ϕ we can thus obtain (still under certain conditions) many distinct general integrals of G and hence distinct solutions to (1). Furthermore, given a complete integral G, we can form, either locally or globally (if possible), its *singular integral* (which graph is called *a two-parameter envelope of G*), i.e. a function

$$u(x, y) = G(x, y, P_1(x, y), P_2(x, y)), \tag{5}$$

by eliminating parameters P_1 and P_2 from the following system

$$u(x, y) = G(x, y, P_1, P_2), \quad G_{P_1}(x, y, P_1, P_2) = 0, \quad \text{and} \quad G_{P_2}(x, y, P_1, P_2) = 0. \tag{6}$$

As previously, one can also show that under certain conditions (see [3] and [6]), formulae (5) and (6) define a C^1 (C^2) solution to (1).

So far, we have revisited a method of generating new solutions to (1) based on complete integrals. In other words, given an equation (1) with complete integral G we may generate locally (or globally) C^1 (C^2) solutions to (1) which turn out to be general (singular) integrals of G (if they exist). We shall now address a *converse problem*. Given a complete integral G and a solution u of a class C^1 (C^2) to (1), the problem is to represent u in terms of a general (singular) integral of a complete integral G. There are many results in the literature addressing this issue, some of them being in fact false. One such result reads (see [9, Section 7 pp. 61]):

(CII) *"When, however, one complete integral has been obtained, every other solution, including every other complete integral, appears among the solution of type (3) and (5) corresponding to the complete integral we have found."*

2.2 Counterexample to Sneddon's claim

In this subsection we shall show that the above assertion is *invalid*. The example to follow indicates fundamental difficulties that arise when CII claim is treated as a true statement.

EXAMPLE 1. Consider the following *image irradiance equation* (corresponding to the image of a Lambertian plane $u(x,y) = ax + by + c$, with $a^2 + b^2 = 1$, illuminated by an overhead distant point light-source direction)

$$\frac{1}{\sqrt{1 + u_x^2(x,y) + u_y^2(x,y)}} = \frac{1}{\sqrt{2}} \tag{7}$$

defined over some region $\Omega \subset U_1$, where $U_1 = \{(x,y) \in \mathbb{R}^2 : x^2 + y^2 < 1\}$. This equation can be rewritten in the equivalent *eikonal form*

$$u_x^2(x,y) + u_y^2(x,y) = 1. \tag{8}$$

Consider now a two-parameter C^2 family of cones

$$G(x,y,a,b) = \sqrt{(x-a)^2 + (y-b)^2} \tag{9}$$

defined over $\Omega \times V$, where $V \subset (\mathbb{R}^2 \setminus \bar{U}_1)$. It is easy to observe that, for any fixed $(a^*, b^*) \in V$, a function $G(x,y,a^*,b^*)$ is a C^2 solution to (8). Morover, a simple verification shows that the rank of the matrix (2) equals two. Thus, formula (9) defines a complete integral for the eikonal equation (8).

We shall show now that the function $v(x,y) = x + 2$, being a C^2 solution to (8), cannot be represented as a general integral of (9) expressed in the form $v(x,y) = G(x,y,a(x,y),b(a(x,y)))$. Suppose the contrary. Then, for some $a \to b(a)$, and for some $(x,y) \to a(x,y)$, we have

$$(x-a)^2 + (y-b(a))^2 = (x+2)^2, \tag{10}$$

$$(x-a) + (y-b(a))b'(a) = 0. \tag{11}$$

Differentiating (10) with respect to y, we get

$$[(x-a) + (y-b(a))b'(a)]\frac{\partial a}{\partial y} + b(a) - y = 0.$$

Hence, in view of (11), $y = b(a)$ and further, still by (11), $x = a$. Finally, $y = b(x)$, which is absurd. On the other hand, note that the graph of the function v is a one-parameter C^2 envelope of $G(x,y,a(b),b)$ with $a(b) \equiv -2$; that is, the envelope of surfaces $\mathcal{T} = \{(x,y,G(x,y,a,b)) : G(x,y,-2,b) = \sqrt{(x+2)^2 + (y-b)^2}\}$, where $(a(b),b) \in (\mathbb{R}^2 \setminus \bar{U}_1)$. Upon analyzing the above case we come to the following critical conclusion:

if Sneddon's assertion CII is to be correct, then the definition of a general integral, specified by (3) and (4), needs to be treated at least in a symmetric manner.

Analogously, the function $v_1(x,y) = x$ (being a solution to (8)) cannot be represented as the general integral of any subfamily of (9) expressed in the form $G(x,y,a,b(a))$. On the other hand, if v_1 happens to be a general integral of $G(x,y,a(b),b)$, we obtain

$$(x-a(b))^2 + (y-b)^2 = x^2, \tag{12}$$

$$(x-a(b))a'(b) + (y-b) = 0. \tag{13}$$

By differentiating (12) with respect to y, we get

$$[(x - a(b))a'(b) + (y - b)]\frac{\partial b}{\partial y} + b - y = 0.$$

Hence, in view of (13), $b(x, y) = y$, and further, by (12), we have $(x - a(b))^2 = x^2$. The latter is only possible for $a(b) = 0$ or $a(b) = 2x$. The first case is impossible as $(a(b), b) \notin (\mathbb{R}^2 \setminus \bar{U}_1)$. So is the second, as then $2x = a(y)$, which is absurd. A straightforward verification of conditions (6) shows that v_1 cannot be either represented as a singular integral of (9).

Thus we arrive at the conclusion that the assertion CII cannot be universally true. $\square$

The last example shows that some of the solutions may also be represented in terms of a symmetric uniform parametrisation $G(x, y, a(b(x, y)), b(x, y))$, whereas the others can be expressed in none of the representations $G(x, y, a(b(x, y)), b(x, y))$ or $G(x, y, a(x, y), b(a(x, y)))$. For a more extensive analysis including correction of Sneddon's assertion CII an interested reader is referred to [3] and [8].

3   Erroneous application of complete integrals in computer vision

In this section, we revisit the proofs of the uniqueness results, contained in [1, 2] which concern the images of *a Lambertian unit hemisphere* centered at the origin and of *a Lambertian plane*, both illuminated by an overhead, distant point-light source. As the above Brooks' both proofs resort to an incomplete Sneddon's assertion we show that a clear contradiction results from the above mentioned uniqueness claims. We begin by quoting the precise statements of the uniqueness results presented in [1, 2].

(BI) *Consider an image of the Lambertian unit hemisphere centered at the origin and illuminated from an overhead distant point light-source direction. Then the functions $u(x, y) = \pm\sqrt{1 - x^2 - y^2} + C$ are the only solutions to the corresponding image irradiance equation (14) defined over $\Omega_{(x,y)} = \{(x, y) \in \mathbb{R}^2 : x^2 + y^2 < 1\}$.*

(BII) *Consider an image of the Lambertian plane $u(x, y) = ax + by + C$ illuminated from an overhead distant point light-source direction. Then any solution to the corresponding image irradiance equation (21) is a ruled surface (see Klingenberg [7, Definition 3.7.4]).*

3.1   Revisiting uniqueness proof for an image of a Lambertian hemisphere

We shall first briefly revisit the proof of claim BI which takes Sneddon's assertion CII for granted and involves the following pattern:

(a) first, to generate a complete integral to (14),

(b) next, to generate all of its general and singular integrals (introduced by (4) and (6)) and to show that they are not smooth over $\Omega_{(x,y)} = \{(x,y) \in \mathbb{R}^2 : x^2 + y^2 < 1\}$,

(c) finally, by using (b) combined with assertion CII, to claim a uniqueness result for (14) over $\Omega_{(x,y)}$.

Suppose that a Lambertian northern unit hemisphere S centered at the origin (represented by the graph of the function $u_+(x,y) = \sqrt{1 - x^2 - y^2} + C$, where C is an arbitrary constant) is illuminated by a distant, overhead point light-source. We have the following image irradiance equation

$$\frac{1}{\sqrt{z_x^2(x,y) + z_y^2(x,y) + 1}} = \sqrt{1 - x^2 - y^2}, \tag{14}$$

defined over a unit disc $\Omega_{(x,y)}$. This can be rewritten into an equivalent eikonal form $z_x^2(x,y) + z_y^2(x,y) = (x^2 + y^2)(1 - x^2 - y^2)^{-1}$. Note that the function $u_-(x,y) = -\sqrt{1 - x^2 - y^2} + C$ constitutes another solution to equation (14). The last equation rewritten in polar coordinates takes the form

$$z_r^2(r,\theta) + \frac{1}{r^2} z_\theta^2(r,\theta) = \frac{r^2}{1 - r^2}, \tag{15}$$

over $\Omega_{(r,\theta)} = \{(r,\theta) \in \mathbb{R}^2 : 0 < r < 1, \ 0 \le \theta < 2\pi\}$. Consider now the following two-parameter system of solutions $z(r, \theta; k, M) = k\theta + g(r,k) + M$ to (15), where the function $g(r,k)$ satisfies

$$\left(\frac{\partial g}{\partial r}(r,\theta)\right)^2 + \frac{k^2}{r^2} = \frac{r^2}{1 - r^2},$$

that is, g is up to a constant, given by $g(r,k) = \pm \int_{r_0}^{r}((s^2/(1-s^2)) - (k^2/s^2))^{1/2} ds$. According to Brooks' claims, we hence obtain the complete integral

$$z(r, \theta; k, M) = k\theta \pm \int_{r_0}^{r} \sqrt{\frac{s^2}{1 - s^2} - \frac{k^2}{s^2}} ds + M \tag{16}$$

having, among others, the following properties:

(i) $z(r, \theta; 0, M) = \pm \int_{r_0}^{r} \sqrt{\frac{s^2}{1-s^2}} ds + M = \pm\sqrt{1 - r^2} + C$, which corresponds to our hemisphere solutions u_- and u_+,

(ii) $g(r,k)$ is only defined for $(r^2/(1 - r^2)) \ge (k^2/r^2)$. Thus we require that

$$r_k = \sqrt{\frac{|k|\sqrt{k^2 + 4} - k^2}{2}} \le r < 1, \qquad r_k < r_0 < 1,$$

and so when $k \ne 0$, $z(r, \theta; k, M)$ is defined only over the annulus $\Omega_{(r,\theta)}^{r_k} = \{(r,\theta) \in \mathbb{R}^2 : r_k < r < 1, \ 0 \le \theta < 2\pi\}$.

Note, however, that in order to be able to claim that formula (16) defines a complete integral we need to be more rigorous with what we understand by a complete integral. First, it is easy to check that any member of the two-paramenter family of functions $z(r, \theta; k, M)$ is a C^2 function over $(\Omega_{(r,\theta)}^{r_k} \setminus ([0, 1) \times \{0\})) \times \mathbb{R}^2$ which, for any fixed (k^*, M^*), satisfies (15). Note, moreover, that as $rank(A) = 2$, the parameters k and M are clearly independent. The fulfillment of conditions Ci and Cii is still not sufficient to claim that (16) defines a complete integral to (15). Observe first that, for any fixed (k^*, M^*), we should obtain a uniquely defined function $z(r, \theta; k^*, M^*)$ that is a solution to (15). This is not the case for the family of functions defined by (16). Clearly, for any fixed (x, y, k^*, M^*), formula (16) yields two values. In order to eliminate this ambiguity (which will turn out to be a decisive factor in reaching a contradiction), we need to determine which sign should be chosen. For the sake of convenience, we choose the plus sign and hence obtain

$$z(r, \theta; k, M) = k\theta + \int_{r_0}^{r} \sqrt{\frac{s^2}{1 - s^2} - \frac{k^2}{s^2}} ds + M \qquad (17)$$

(the opposite case can be treated analogously). Consequently, we see here that, part of the condition (i) is not satisfied as u_- cannot be now represented by (17), for some (k, M). This "lost solution", however, should easily be obtained from either a general or a singular integral of (17) (provided Sneddon's claim is correct). As the assertion CII is not true (see Example 1), we may hope that u_- cannot be retrieved from the complete integral (17) as either a general or a singular integral. This will stand in obvious contradiction with CII. In order to claim that (17) defines a complete integral of (15), still, one more aspect has to be taken into account. Note that any properly defined complete integral needs to be a two-parameter family of functions defined over the same subregion $U_{r\theta} \subset \Omega_{(r,\theta)} \setminus ([0, 1) \times \{0\})$. As a result, we need to determine an open set $V_{kM} \subset \mathbb{R}^2$ such that for any $(k, M) \in V_{kM}$ each function $z(r, \theta; k, M)$ is defined over the same open subset $U_{r\theta} \subset \mathbb{R}^2$. As was claimed in (ii), the function $g(r, k) = \int_{r_0}^{r}((s^2/(1-s^2)) - (k^2/s^2))^{1/2}ds$, is only defined over the annulus $\Omega_{(r,\theta)}^{r_k}$. It may readily be seen that, for any $(k, M) \in \mathbb{R}^2$, $0 < r_k < 1$, $lim_{k\to\pm\infty}r_k = 1$, and $lim_{k\to 0}r_k = 0$. Hence, as the annulus $\Omega_{(r,\theta)}^{r_k}$ depends on the choice of k (its internal radius changes with k running over $\mathbb{R}$), we need to find an open subset $V_{kM} \subset \mathbb{R}^2$ such that $g(r, k)$ is defined over the same $U_{r\theta}$. Let ε be a positive number. A simple inspection yields that, given $0 < \varepsilon < 4$, we have

$$-\sqrt{\frac{\varepsilon}{4 - 2\sqrt{\varepsilon}}} < k < \sqrt{\frac{\varepsilon}{4 - 2\sqrt{\varepsilon}}} \quad \text{if and only if} \quad r_k = \sqrt{\frac{|k|\sqrt{k^2 + 4} - k^2}{2}} < \sqrt{\frac{\sqrt{\varepsilon}}{2}}.$$

Now we are ready to claim that z defined by (17) over a region $(\Omega_{(r,\theta)}^{\delta(\varepsilon)} \setminus ([0, 1) \times \{0\})) \times V_{kM}^{\sigma(\varepsilon)} \subset \mathbb{R}^4$, where $\delta(\varepsilon) = \sqrt{\frac{\sqrt{\varepsilon}}{2}}$, $\sigma(\varepsilon) = \sqrt{\frac{\varepsilon}{4 - 2\sqrt{\varepsilon}}}$, and $V_{kM}^{\sigma(\varepsilon)} = \{(k, M) \in \mathbb{R}^2 : -\sigma(\varepsilon) < k < -\sigma(\varepsilon)\}$ defines a complete integral to (15) (note that r_0 is any fixed number such that $\delta(\varepsilon) < r_0 < 1$). Following Sneddon's representation claim CII we can now obtain a general integral of (17) by eliminating k from the system of the equations:

$$f(r, \theta, z, k) = k\theta + g(r, k) + M(k) - z = 0, \qquad (18)$$

$$\frac{\partial f}{\partial k}(r, \theta, z, k) = 0. \qquad (19)$$

Assume temporarily that such a general integral exists (if it does not exist then u_- cannot be expressed as a general integral). In view of (4), we obtain $h(r, \theta) = f(r, \theta, z(r, \theta), k(r, \theta)) = 0$ for some smooth real function $M(k)$. The chain rule applied to the last equation yields

$$0 = \frac{\partial h}{\partial \theta}(r, \theta) = \frac{\partial f}{\partial \theta}(\kappa) + \frac{\partial f}{\partial r}(\kappa)\frac{\partial r}{\partial \theta}(r, \theta) + \frac{\partial f}{\partial z}(\kappa)\frac{\partial z}{\partial \theta}(r, \theta) + \frac{\partial f}{\partial k}(\kappa)\frac{\partial k}{\partial \theta}(r, \theta),$$

where $\kappa = (r, \theta, z, k)$. By (18) and (19), we have $f_z \equiv -1$, $f_\theta = k$, and $f_k \equiv 0$. Accordingly,

$$\frac{\partial z}{\partial \theta}(r, \theta) = k(r, \theta). \qquad (20)$$

Thus, the angular rate of change of depth of any general integral of (17) at $(r, \theta) \in \Omega^{\delta(\varepsilon)}_{(r,\theta)} \setminus ([0, 1) \times \{0\})$ is equal to the value of k at point (r, θ).

From now on we shall drop a further course of Brooks' uniqueness proof, which in conclusion claims that all general integrals of the type (4) fail to be smooth functions over $\Omega^{\delta(\varepsilon)}_{(r,\theta)}$ (as not being periodic functions) and thus, by applying assertion CII, infers uniqueness. We shall now show that (similarly to Example 1) a complete integral (17) and any of its general and singular integrals of type (4) and (6), respectively, cannot generate all possible solutions to the equation (15).

Note that, for uniqueness consideration a specific class of functions has to be *a priori* specified (we implicitly assume that the chosen class is that of C^2 function.

To reach a contradiction, note first that the third case of Sneddon's claim CII, referring to the singular integral, does not need to be considered here. Analyzing the existence of singular integrals, one can, however, easily verify that the system (6) is never satisfied as $(\partial z/\partial M) \equiv 1$ (parameters (k, M) are treated here as independent). Thus, we can infer that there is no singular integral to (15). Recall that the "complete integral" (16) had to be re-shaped so as to become a meaningful function as introduced in (17) (the latter does not contain u_-). If Sneddon's statement were to be correct, we should be able to represent (at least locally) the function u_- as a general integral of some subfamily $z(r, \theta; k, M(k))$ (there is no singular integral here). This, however, never happens as (20) combined with $u_{-\theta}(r, \theta) = 0$ yields

$$\frac{\partial u_-}{\partial \theta}(r, \theta) = k(r, \theta) = 0.$$

Furthermore, in order to obtain the function u_- either locally or globally, a parameter k has to vanish everywhere in which case we find that $z(r, \theta; 0, M(0)) =$

$u_+(r, \theta) + C$, which is obviously different than u_-, a contradiction. Note, moreover, that $k(r, \theta) \equiv 0$ cannot define a differentiable function $M = M(k)$ in some neighbourhood of $k_0 = 0$. This fact is another source of contradiction. In a final effort to save this uniqueness proof for the image of a Lambertian hemisphere, we might try to treat Sneddon's statement CII in a broader sense. Namely, we could include symmetric case of general integral of the family $G(x, y, \phi(P_2), P_2)$ (see aslo Example 1). An easy verification shows, however, that then we also have $k(M) \equiv 0$. Hence, we cannot represent (even locally) the graph of u_- as an envelope of

$$z(r, \theta; k(M), M) = \theta k(M) + \int_{r_0}^{r} \sqrt{\frac{s^2}{1 - s^2} - \frac{k(M)^2}{s^2}} \, ds + M$$

and thus we obtain the same type of contradiction as before. Consequently, it is clear that complete integral (17) together with its general and singular integrals do not generate (either locally or globally) all solutions to the equation (15) corresponding to the image of the Lambertian hemisphere. □

Interestingly, assertion (c) was proved correctly for the set of C^2 functions by Deift and Sylvester [5].

3.2 Revisiting uniqueness proof for an image of a Lambertian plane

In this closing subsection we shall briefly refer to the uniqueness assertion BII appearing in [1, 2] that concerns the image of a Lambertian plane illuminated from an overhead, distant point light-source direction. In this case the corresponding image irradiance equation

$$\frac{1}{\sqrt{u_x^2(x, y) + u_y^2(x, y) + 1}} = \frac{1}{\sqrt{a^2 + b^2 + 1}}$$

can be transformed into the equivalent eikonal equation

$$u_x^2(x, y) + u_y^2(x, y) = c, \tag{21}$$

where $a^2 + b^2 = c$. One can easily show that the family of planes

$$u(x, y) = ax + by + C \tag{22}$$

together with the family of cones $v(x, y, a_1, b_1) = \sqrt{c}\sqrt{(x - a_1)^2 + (y - b_1)^2} + C$ constitute C^2 solutions to (21) over any open $U \subset \mathbb{R}^2$, where C is an arbitrary constant and $(a_1, b_1) \notin U$. In order to obtain all other solutions to (21) a similar approach to that applied for the image of a Lambertian hemisphere is adopted in [1, 2]. Namely, by initially choosing a particular complete integral of (21) (of the type (22)) and by using assertion CII the following final conclusion is reached:

all solutions to (21) are ruled surfaces (see [7, Definition 3.7.4]).

As in the previous case, given the invalidity of Sneddon's claim, we cannot assume the validity the proof for the above stated uniqueness result. It should be noted, however, that, for C^2 surfaces, the above assertion, subject to minor reformulations, can be proved without any recourse to the theory of complete integrals and envelopes (see Section 4, Proposition 1).

4 Uniqueness for images of Lambertian hemisphere and plane

A natural question arises as to whether incomplete uniqueness assertions from [1, 2] are true. Uniqueness for equation (14) has been demonstrated by Deift and Sylvester [5], who showed that $\pm(1 - x^2 - y^2)^{1/2} + k$ are the only C^2 solutions to this equation over the unit disc $D(1) = \{(x, y) \in \mathbb{R}^2 : x^2 + y^2 < 1\}$. Interestingly, Deift and Sylvester also showed that this result fails in class of C^1 solutions (there exist infinitely many C^1 functions over $D(1)$ satisfying (14)). As for the image of the Lambertian plane, one can prove the following:

PROPOSITION 1. *The graph of any C^2 solution to the eikonal equation (21) defined over some region $\Omega \subset \mathbb{R}^2$, with $c \geq 0$, is a developable surface (and so its Gaussian curvature vanishes).*

Proof. The validity of the proposition is obviously true for c vanishing (the only solution to (21) is a constant function).

Assume now that $c > 0$. Suppose that u is a solution of class C^2 to (21) over some region U. For each $s \in (-s_0, s_0)$, let

$$t \to (\tilde{x}(t, s), \tilde{y}(t, s), \tilde{u}(t, s), \tilde{p}(t, s), \tilde{q}(t, s))$$

be the solution of the characteristic system of equations associated with (21)

$$(i) \quad \frac{d\tilde{x}}{dt}(t, s) = 2\tilde{p}(t, s),$$

$$(ii) \quad \frac{d\tilde{y}}{dt}(t, s) = 2\tilde{q}(t, s),$$

$$(iii) \quad \frac{d\tilde{u}}{dt}(t, s) = 2c, \tag{23}$$

$$(iv) \quad \frac{d\tilde{p}}{dt}(t, s) = 0,$$

$$(v) \quad \frac{d\tilde{q}}{dt}(t, s) = 0,$$

that satisfies the initial conditions

$$(i) \quad \tilde{x}(0, s) = x_0(s),$$
$$(ii) \quad \tilde{y}(0, s) = y_0(s),$$
$$(iii) \quad \tilde{u}(0, s) = u_0(s), \tag{24}$$
$$(iv) \quad \tilde{p}(0, s) = p_0(s),$$
$$(v) \quad \tilde{q}(0, s) = q_0(s),$$

where $u_0(s) = u(x_0(s), y_0(s))$, $p_0(s) = u_x(x_0(s), y_0(s))$, $q_0(s) = u_y(x_0(s), y_0(s))$, and is defined on a maximal interval. It is readily verified that (23)(i,ii) combined first with (23)(iv,v), (24)(iv,v), and then with (24)(i,ii) yield

$$\tilde{x}(t, s) = 2tq_0(s) + x_0(s) \qquad \tilde{y}(t, s) = 2tp_0(s) + y_0(s). \tag{25}$$

Clearly, (23) *(iii)* with (24) *(iii)* imply

$$\widetilde{u}(t, s) = 2ct + u_0(s). \tag{26}$$

By the fundamental property of solutions to characteristic system (see *e.g.* Courant and Hilbert [4, Chapter 2, Paragraph 3] we have $\widetilde{u}(t, s) = u(x(t, s), y(t, s))$. Thus, by (25) and (26), a C^2 surface S_u, being a graph of u, can be represented in the following parametric form

$$\begin{pmatrix} \widetilde{x}(t, s) \\ \widetilde{y}(t, s) \\ \widetilde{u}(t, s) \end{pmatrix} = \begin{pmatrix} x_0(s) \\ y_0(s) \\ u_0(s) \end{pmatrix} + t \begin{pmatrix} 2p_0(s) \\ 2q_0(s) \\ 2c \end{pmatrix}.$$

Thus S_u is a ruled surface. Observe now that by differentiating both sides of (21) with respect to x and then with respect to y, we obtain the following system of equations

$$-u_y u_{xy} = u_x u_{xx}, \qquad u_x u_{yx} = -u_y u_{yy}. \tag{27}$$

Multiplying the first equation by the second one and taking into account that u is a C^2 function we deduce that u satisfies the following equation

$$u_x u_y (u_{xx} u_{yy} - u_{xy}^2) = 0. \tag{28}$$

Let (x', y') be an arbitrary point in Ω. We now show that equation (28) implies that the Gaussian curvature of the graph S_u of u at point $(x', y', u(x', y'))$ expressed as

$$K_u(x', y') = \frac{u_{xx}(x', y') u_{yy}(x', y') - u_{xy}^2(x', y')}{(1 + u_x^2(x', y') + u_y^2(x', y'))^2}$$

vanishes. To this, assume that $u_x(x', y') u_y(x', y') \neq 0$. Then clearly (28) yields that $K_u(x', y') = 0$. If, on the other hand, $u_x(x', y') u_y(x', y') = 0$, then as $c > 0$ only one derivative can vanish (say $u_x(x', y') = 0$). Hence by simple inspection of (27) we deduce that $u_{xy}(x', y') = u_{yy}(x', y') = 0$, and thus we also have $K_u(x', y') = 0$. As surface S_u is ruled and its Gaussian curvature everywhere vanishes [7, Proposition 3.7.5] assures that S_u is developable. $\square$

5 Acknowledgments

This research was conducted under Alexander von Humboldt Research Fellowship during author's stay at Technical University of Berlin and at Warsaw University.

References

[1] Brooks, M.J.: Two results concerning ambiguity in shape from shading. In: Proceedings of the National Conference on Artificial Intelligence, American Association for Artificial Intelligence. Washington D.C.: 1983 (pp. 26-39).

[2] Brooks, M.J.: Shape from shading discretely, PhD. Thesis, Essex University, Essex, 1983.

[3] Chojnacki, W.: A note on complete integrals. Proceedings of the American Mathematical Society (2) 123, 393-401 (1995).

[4] Courant, R. and Hilbert, D.: Methods of Mathematical Physics. New York, London: vol. 2, Interscience Publishers 1962.

[5] Deift, P. and Sylvester, J.: Some remarks on the shape-from-shading problem in computer vision. Journal of Mathematical Analysis and Applications (1) 84, 235-248 (1981).

[6] Dou, A.: Lectures on Partial Differential Equations of First Order. Notre Dame, Indiana: University of Notre Dame Press 1972.

[7] Klingenberg, W.: A Course in Differential Geometry. New York, Heidelberg, Berlin: Springer-Verlag 1978.

[8] Kozera, R.: On complete integrals and uniqueness in shape from shading. Applied Mathematics and Computation (1) 74, 1-37 (1995).

[9] Sneddon, I.: Elements of Partial Differential Equations. New York: Mc-Graw-Hill 1957.

Computation of time-varying motion and structure parameters from real image sequences

John L. Barron and Roy Eagleson

1 Introduction

We address the problem of robust estimation of motion and structure parameters, which describe an observer's translation, rotation, and environmental layout
(i.e. the relative depth of visible 3-d points) from noisy time-varying optical flow.
Allowable observer motions include a moving vehicle and a broad class of robot
arm motions. We assume the observer is a camera rigidly attached to the moving
vehicle or robot arm, which moves along a smooth trajectory in a stationary environment. As the camera moves it acquires images at some reasonable sampling
rate (say 30 images per second). Given a sequence of such images we analyze
them to recover the camera's motion and depth information for various surfaces
in the environment. As the camera moves, with respect to some 3-d environmental point, the relative 3-d velocity that occurs is mapped (under perspective
projection) onto the camera's image plane as 2-d **image motion**. **Optical flow**
or **image velocity** is an infinitesimal approximation to this image motion. Since
the camera moves relative to a scene we can compute image velocity fields at each
time. Given the observer's translation, $\vec{U}$, and rotation, $\vec{\omega}$, and the coordinates
of a 3-d point, $\vec{P}$, a non-linear equation that relates these parameters to the 2-d
image velocity, $\vec{v}$, at image point $\vec{Y}$, where $\vec{Y}$ is the perspective projection of $\vec{P}$,
is as follows [10]:

$$\vec{v}(\vec{Y},t) = \vec{v}_T(\vec{Y},t) + \vec{v}_R(\vec{Y},t), \qquad (1)$$

where $\vec{v}_T$ and $\vec{v}_R$ are the translational and rotational components of image velocity:

$$\vec{v}_T(\vec{Y},t) = A_1(\vec{Y})\vec{u}(\vec{Y},t)||\vec{Y}||_2 \quad \text{and} \quad \vec{v}_R(\vec{Y},t) = A_2(\vec{Y})\vec{\omega}(t) \qquad (2)$$

and

$$A_1 = \begin{pmatrix} -1 & 0 & y_1 \\ 0 & -1 & y_2 \end{pmatrix} \quad \text{and} \quad A_2 = \begin{pmatrix} y_1 y_2 & -(1+y_1^2) & y_2 \\ (1+y_2^2) & -y_1 y_2 & -y_1 \end{pmatrix}. \qquad (3)$$

Given a number of image velocities we can solve a system of equations based
on the image velocity equation to recover the camera's motion and the scene's
relative depth parameters. This type of calculation is usually called a **structure
from motion** calculation. It is a two-step process: first, compute image velocity
information from a sequence of images and second, invert the projection process
to recover motion and structure from the image velocity data.

Since we are dealing with a single moving (monocular) camera, we cannot recover the camera's absolute translation, $\vec{U}$, or the actual 3-d coordinates, $\vec{P}$, of

environmental points at any instant, but rather the ratio of the two. We define the depth-scaled observer translation as

$$\vec{u}(\vec{Y}, t) = \frac{\vec{U}(t)}{||\vec{P}(t)||_2} = \hat{u}\mu(\vec{Y}, t), \tag{4}$$

where $\hat{u} = \hat{U} = (u_1, u_2, u_3)$ is the normalized direction of translation and $\mu(\vec{Y}, t) = \frac{||\vec{U}||_2}{||\vec{P}||_2} = \frac{||\vec{U}||_2}{X_3||\vec{Y}||_2}$ is the depth-scaled observer speed at $\vec{Y}$ at time t. We also refer to μ as the **relative** depth or the scene structure.

2 Overview

A complete literature survey can be found in [4]. From this survey we see that most motion and structure algorithms require solving systems of equations that involve some type of non-linearity. In general, it is difficult to handle such non-linearities; the solution techniques require iterations from some initial guess with no guarantee of convergence and the non-linearity also means the possibility of multiple solutions arises [5, 7]. The algorithm we present here address the non-linearity as follows: Our algorithm takes advantage of the fact that the rotational component of the image velocity depends only on the observer rotation and the image location. Thus the difference in the image velocity at the same image location at two different times is entirely due to the observer's translation (we assume the observer's rotational acceleration remains constant over time – a valid assumption for a large class of motions, for example, when a camera is mounted on a moving vehicle or fixed to a joint-based robot).

We can integrate our computed parameters over time by using nested Kalman filters [9]. The result is increased parameter accuracy over time. We demonstrate the robustness of our solution technique on real image data. A complete description of the algorithm, including synthetic data results as well, is available in [4]. An outline of a binocular solution that requires camera rotation and allows the recovery of absolute translation and depth is also available [3].

3 The least squares solution

Modelling uniform rotational acceleration as

$$\vec{\omega}(t + \delta t) = \vec{\omega}(t) + \delta\vec{\omega}\,\delta t, \tag{5}$$

we can write

$$\frac{r_1}{r_2} = \frac{v_1(\vec{Y}, t_1) + v_1(\vec{Y}, t_{-1}) - 2v_1(\vec{Y}, t_0)}{v_2(\vec{Y}, t_1) + v_2(\vec{Y}, t_{-1}) - 2v_2(\vec{Y}, t_0)} \tag{6}$$

which is a linear equation in terms of velocity differences and the components of $\hat{u}$. Note we have assumed that $\delta t = |t_{i+1} - t_i| = |t_i - t_{i-1}|$, where t_i is the central frame, i.e. the flow is sampled at every δt. Note that Longuet-Higgins and Prazdny [10] and others have used a similar idea to cancel rotational image velocity at two close image points at the same time that have different depths. The ratios of the two components of $\vec{r}$ give us 1 linear equation in (u_1, u_2, u_3):

$$\frac{r_1}{r_2} = \frac{-u_1 + y_1 u_3}{-u_2 + y_2 u_3}. \tag{7}$$

Since only 2 components of $\hat{u}$ are independent, then if u_3 is not zero, we can write

$$r_2 \frac{u_1}{u_3} - r_1 \frac{u_2}{u_3} = r_2 y_1 - r_1 y_2. \tag{8}$$

This is 1 linear equation in 2 unknowns, $\left(\frac{u_1}{u_3}, \frac{u_2}{u_3}\right)$. Given m image velocities we obtain m equations of the form in (8) which we can write as

$$W M_2 \left(\frac{u_1}{u_3}, \frac{u_2}{u_3}\right) = W B_2, \tag{9}$$

where M_2 is a $m \times 2$ matrix, B_2 is a $m \times 1$ matrix. W is an $m \times m$ diagonal weight matrix that is based on confidence measures of the computed optical flow for the real data (see section 5.1 below). To continue, we can solve this system of equations in the least squares sense as

$$\left(\frac{u_1}{u_3}, \frac{u_2}{u_3}\right) = (M_2^T W^2 M_2)^{-1} M_2^T W^2 B_2, \tag{10}$$

which involves solving a simple 2×2 system of linear equations to obtain the direction of translation $(u_1/u_3, u_2/u_3, 1)$, which when normalized yields $\hat{u}$. In the event u_3 is zero (or near-zero) we can in principle solve for $(1, u_2/u_1, u_3/u_1)$ or $(u_1/u_2, 1, u_3/u_2)$ by appropriate manipulation of equation (8). Again, systems of equations of the form (10) can be set up for these cases. We compute $\hat{u}$ using all three methods and then choose the $\hat{u}$ from the system of equations having the smallest condition number, κ[1]. If there is no observer translation, all three systems of equations for $\left(\frac{u_1}{u_3}, \frac{u_2}{u_3}\right)$, $\left(\frac{u_1}{u_2}, \frac{u_3}{u_2}\right)$ and $\left(\frac{u_2}{u_1}, \frac{u_3}{u_1}\right)$ will be singular. We can detect this situation by choosing the result with the smallest condition number. If this κ is large enough (indicating singularity as $\hat{u} \approx (0,0,0)$) then only $\vec{\omega}$ can be recovered by solving a linear system of equations comprised of equations of the form

$$\vec{v}(\vec{Y}, t) = A_2(\vec{Y}) \vec{\omega}(t). \tag{11}$$

Results in [2] indicate this system of equations is quite robust in the face of noisy data. Given $\hat{u}$ computed using this strategy we can then compute $\vec{\omega}$ and then the μ's. Note that in order to compute $\hat{u}$ we have assumed we can measure image velocities at the same image locations at all three times. Since poor velocity measurements should have small confidence measures, an image location with

---

[1] κ is computed as the ratio of the largest and smallest diagonal elements of the Singular Value Decomposition of the matrix.

one or more poor velocity measurements at any time should have little or no effect on to the computation of $\hat{u}$.

Given $\hat{u}$, we follow the solution technique by Heeger and Jepson [6, 8] to compute $\vec{\omega}$. We first compute the normalized direction of $\vec{v}_T$ as

$$\hat{d} = \frac{(A_1(\vec{Y})\hat{u})}{||A_1(\vec{Y})\hat{u}||_2}. \tag{12}$$

Given $\hat{d} = (d_1, d_2)$ we can compute $\hat{d}^\perp$ as $(d_2, -d_1)$. Hence we obtain one linear equation in the 3 components of $\vec{\omega}(t)$

$$\hat{d}^\perp \cdot \vec{v} = \hat{d}^\perp \cdot (A_2(\vec{Y})\vec{\omega}(t)). \tag{13}$$

Given m image velocities we obtain m equations of the form in (13) which we can write as

$$W M_3 \vec{\omega} = W B_3, \tag{14}$$

where M_3 is a $m \times 3$ matrix, B_3 is a $m \times 1$ matrix and W is the same $m \times m$ diagonal matrix whose diagonal elements are based on the confidence measures of the corresponding velocity measurements. We can solve (14) as

$$\vec{\omega} = (M_3^T W^2 M_3)^{-1} M_3^T W^2 B_3, \tag{15}$$

which involves solving a simple 3×3 linear system of equations. If $\hat{d}$ and $A_2(\vec{Y})\vec{\omega}$ are parallel, then $\vec{\omega}$ cannot be recovered. Now rotational acceleration can be found at frame i as

$$\delta\vec{\omega}(t_i) = \frac{\vec{\omega}(t_{i+1}) - \vec{\omega}(t_{i-1})}{2}. \tag{16}$$

Finally, given $\hat{u}$ and $\vec{\omega}(t)$, each image velocity, $\vec{v}(\vec{Y}, t)$ yields two equations for $\mu(\vec{Y}_i, t)$

$$\vec{r} = \vec{v} - A_2(\vec{Y}_i)\vec{\omega}(t) = A_1(\vec{Y})\hat{u}\mu(\vec{Y}_i, t)||\vec{Y}_i||_2 = \vec{s}\mu(\vec{Y}_i, t), \tag{17}$$

which we solve for each image velocity measurement as:

$$\mu(\vec{Y}_i) = \frac{r_1}{s_1} = \frac{r_2}{s_2}. \tag{18}$$

If $\vec{v}$ is purely horizontal or vertical at some image location then one of s_1 or s_2 will be zero, but the other can still allow μ to be recovered. If both s_1 and s_2 are non-zero we average the two computed μ values:

$$\mu(\vec{Y}_i) = \frac{1}{2}\left(\frac{r_1 s_2 + r_2 s_1}{s_1 s_2}\right). \tag{19}$$

If both s_1 and s_2 are zero we have a singularity and μ cannot be recovered. Typically, these singularities arise at the focus of expansion (FOE) where the velocity is zero. Note that while we have assumed the direction of translation in the observer's coordinate system is constant, there can be acceleration in the translational speed. Changing translational speed cannot be separated from changing depth values and the combined effect of both are reflected in changing μ values.

3.1 Robustness through summing

Assuming mean zero random error in the image velocities, we can sum (6) for regions of the image, obtaining more accurate velocity differences as the random velocity error will on average cancel out. Given 2 or more summed equations of this form (from 2 or more regions) we can solve for $\left(\frac{u_1}{u_3}, \frac{u_2}{u_3}\right)$ in the same manner as specified in (10). We can obtain similar equations if we hypothesize $u_1 \neq 0$ or $u_2 \neq 0$. We choose the regions R of the velocity fields to be 8×8 squares. We have observed that in the case of diverging flows, velocities at the focus of expansion or along horizontal/vertical lines passing through it will have relatively large errors computed for their zero (or very small) velocity components. Thus the velocity difference errors at such points can be quite large. In the implementation presented here, we removed all equations with any velocity sum having a magnitude < 10.0 from the weighted least squares calculation.

4 Kalman filtering

We have outlined how to recover $\hat{u}$, $\vec{\omega}$, $\delta\vec{\omega}$ and μ in batch mode given three images in a sequence. These are essentially batch computations involving the construction and solution of 2×2 and 3×3 systems of equations. We refer to the solutions found from these computations as the motion and structure "measurements," for that particular frame, and subscript them with M. We compute the variances in these measurements as the difference between computed and measured data, i.e. the residuals squared:

$$\sigma_{M\hat{u}}^2 = ||WM_2\hat{u}_M - WB_2||_2^2 \quad \text{and} \quad \sigma_{M\vec{\omega}}^2 = ||WM_3\vec{\omega}_M - WB_3||_2^2. \quad (20)$$

Since $\hat{u}$ has only two independent components we can express them as two angles, θ and ϕ, in a right hand system with respect to the $(0,0,1)$ axis (details in [4]). We use a Kalman filter to update the θ and ϕ angles rather than updating the $\hat{u}$ vectors directly to avoid adding normalized vectors together in the Kalman equations. Updating θ and ϕ can be viewed simply as moving a point on the unit sphere, since $\hat{u}$ is a unit 3D vector.

We use a series of nested Kalman filters [9] to integrate these measurements over time. Below we outline the steps in our filter computation for $n + 2$ images, numbered 0 to $n + 1$, and show how we continually update the solutions for frames 1 to n. We subscript items by M if they are measured quantities, by C if they are computed quantities and by P if they are predicted quantities.

[1] Initialize predicted parameters:

$$\hat{u}_P = \vec{0}, \quad \sigma_{P\hat{u}}^2 = \infty$$
$$\vec{\omega}_{P\vec{\omega}_0} = \vec{\omega}_{P\vec{\omega}_1} = \vec{\omega}_{P\vec{\omega}_2} = \vec{0}$$
$$\sigma_{P\vec{\omega}_0}^2 = \sigma_{P\vec{\omega}_1}^2 = \sigma_{P\vec{\omega}_2}^2 = \infty$$
$$\sigma_{P\delta\vec{\omega}}^2 = \infty \quad \delta\vec{\omega} = \vec{0}$$
$$i = 1$$

186

[2] Compute $\hat{u}_{Mi}$ from (9) and σ^2_{ui} from (20). These are considered the measured quantities. Compute θ_{Mi} and ϕ_{Mi} from $\hat{u}_{Mi}$ and θ_{Pi} and ϕ_{Pi} from $\hat{u}_{Pi}$. Then:

$$
\begin{aligned}
K_{\hat{u}i} &= \frac{\sigma^2_{P\hat{u}i}}{\sigma^2_{P\hat{u}i}+\sigma^2_{M\hat{u}i}} \\
\theta_{Ci} &= \theta_{Pi} + K_{\hat{u}i}(\theta_{Mi} - \theta_{Pi}) \\
\phi_{Ci} &= \phi_{Pi} + K_{\hat{u}i}(\phi_{Mi} - \phi_{Pi}) \\
\sigma^2_{C\hat{u}i} &= K_{\hat{u}i}\sigma^2_{M\hat{u}i}
\end{aligned}
$$

$K_{\hat{u}i}$ is the Kalman filter gain for $\hat{u}_{Ci}$ at time i. From θ_{Ci} and ϕ_{Ci} we can compute $\hat{u}_{Ci}$.

[2a] Given $\hat{u}_{Ci}$ compute $\vec{\omega}_{Mj}$ and $\sigma^2_{M\vec{\omega}_j}$, for $j = i-1, i, i+1$. Then:

$$
\begin{aligned}
K_{\vec{\omega}j} &= \frac{\sigma^2_{P\vec{\omega}_j}}{\sigma^2_{M\vec{\omega}_j}+\sigma^2_{\vec{\omega}_j}} \\
\vec{\omega}_{Cj} &= \vec{\omega}_{Pj} + K_{\vec{\omega}j}(\vec{\omega}_{Mj} - \vec{\omega}_{Pj}) \\
\sigma^2_{C\vec{\omega}_j} &= \frac{\sigma^2_{P\vec{\omega}_j}}{\sigma^2_{P\vec{\omega}_j}+\sigma^2_{M\vec{\omega}_j}}
\end{aligned}
$$

[2b] Compute $\delta\vec{\omega}_{Mi}$ from $\vec{\omega}_{Ci-1}$, and $\vec{\omega}_{Ci+1}$ as per (16). Compute $\sigma^2_{M\delta\vec{\omega}_j}$ as $\sigma^2_{C\vec{\omega}_{i-1}} + \sigma^2_{C\vec{\omega}_{i+1}}$. This sum indicates we place less weight on $\delta\vec{\omega}$ than we do in $\vec{\omega}_{i-1}$ and $\vec{\omega}_{i+1}$. Then:

$$
\begin{aligned}
K_{\delta\vec{\omega}_i} &= \frac{\sigma^2_{P\delta\vec{\omega}}}{\sigma^2_{P\delta\vec{\omega}}+\sigma^2_{M\delta\vec{\omega}_i}} \\
\delta\vec{\omega}_C &= \delta\vec{\omega}_P + K_{\delta\vec{\omega}}(\delta\vec{\omega}_{Mi} - \delta\vec{\omega}_P) \\
\sigma^2_{C\delta\vec{\omega}} &= \frac{\sigma^2_{P\delta\vec{\omega}}}{\sigma^2_{P\delta\vec{\omega}}+\sigma^2_{M\delta\vec{\omega}_i}}
\end{aligned}
$$

[3] Update predicted quantities:

$$
\begin{aligned}
\hat{u}_P &= \hat{u}_{Ci} \\
\sigma^2_{P\hat{u}} &= \sigma^2_{M\hat{u}i}K_{\hat{u}i} \\
\vec{\omega}_{Pj} &= \vec{\omega}_{Cj} + \delta\vec{\omega}_C, \quad j = 1, ..., 3 \\
\sigma^2_{P\vec{\omega}_j} &= \sigma^2_{C\vec{\omega}_j}K_{\vec{\omega}j} \\
\delta\vec{\omega}_P &= \delta\vec{\omega}_C \\
\sigma^2_{P\delta\vec{\omega}} &= \sigma^2_{\delta\vec{\omega}}K_{\delta\vec{\omega}}
\end{aligned}
$$

[4] $i = i+1$, goto step [2].

Since μ values are unrelated over time (the μ values at the same image location at different times correspond to different 3-d environmental points) they are simply computed in batch mode at each time using (18) and the current best estimates for $\hat{u}$ and $\vec{\omega}$.

5 Experimental results

We tested our algorithm with real image sequences. We can measure the actual error in the motion and structure parameters for our experiments because the correct answer is known. Subscripting variables with k for known quantities and with m for measured quantities then $\theta_{\hat{u}} = \cos^{-1}(\hat{u}_m \cdot \hat{u}_k)$ serves as an angle error measurement for direction of translation. If either $\|\vec{\omega}_m\|_2$ and $\|\vec{\omega}_k\|_2$ are zero we compute absolute error as $\theta_{\vec{\omega}} = \|\vec{\omega}_m - \vec{\omega}_k\|_2$, otherwise we compute relative error as $\theta_{\vec{\omega}} = \frac{\|\vec{\omega}_m - \vec{\omega}_k\|_2}{\|\vec{\omega}_k\|_2} \times 100\%$. We use the same error metrics to measure error in $\delta\vec{\omega}$. Since computed depth maps were poor we did not compute error for them.

5.1 Real image experimental results

We have applied our algorithm to two long sequences of images [2]. Both sequences are generated by a camera moving on a motorized rail table setup relative to a stationary scene comprised by several boxes and cylinders covered with newspaper. The newspaper provides textured surface and facilitates the measurement of optical flow vectors over the entire image. Both sequences consist of 36 images with (1) the camera translating directly towards the scene ($\hat{u} = (0,0,1)$, $\vec{\omega} = (0,0,0)$ and $\delta\vec{\omega} = (0,0,0)$) or (2) the camera motion comprised of simple line-of-sight translation and angular rotation about the camera's vertical axis ($\hat{u} = (0,0,1)$, $\vec{\omega} = (0, 0.00145, 0)$, i.e. $\frac{1}{12}^{\circ}$ per frame, and $\delta\vec{\omega} = (0,0,0)$). Optical flow was measured using Lucas and Kanade's method as described in [1]. The prefiltering and differentiation requirements of the method meant that only 22 flow fields can be computed for the 36 input images. Confidence measures based on the smallest eigenvalues of a least squares normal velocity integration matrix, λ_1, were used to weight "good" image velocities. Those velocities for which $\lambda_1 < 1.0$ were rejected outright (assigned a confidence measure of 0.0). The confidence measures of the surviving image velocities were used as the weights in the W matrix; since our algorithm requires tuples of image velocities at the same image location at three consecutive times, each weight, a diagonal element of W, is computed as $\min(\lambda_1(t_{k-1}), \lambda_1(t_k), \lambda_1(t_{k+1}))$ for each set of velocities at the same location at times t_{k-1}, t_k and t_{k+1}. Figures 1 and 2 show the 19th image, its flow field and its eigenvalue image for both sequences. In these latter grayvalue images, white indicates high eigenvalues ("good" velocities") while black indicates low eigenvalues ("poor" velocities). Since our algorithm assumes a focal length of 1, we convert velocity positions from pixels to f units and image velocities from pixels/frame to f units/frame by the appropriate scaling [4].

Figure 3 shows the experimental results for the purely translational sequence. Each graph has 3 plots, the original measured parameter error (**solid** lines) computed from the flow fields for each consecutive overlapping set of 3 adjacent images and 2 plots of the Kalman-filtered parameter error. One of the 'Kalman' plots shows parameter error when the variances were computed as the actual error squared (**dashed** lines) [3] while the other Kalman plot shows parameter error when the residual squared is used as the variance (**dotted** lines).

We can see that Kalman filtering significantly reduced error in all parameter calculations and that actual and residual Kalman filtered error are similar; the residual is a good estimate of the actual variance.

---

[2] Thanks to Professors R. Woodham and J. Little for allowing use of their equipment at the UBC vision lab in 1993.

[3] This is a "perfect" variance measurement

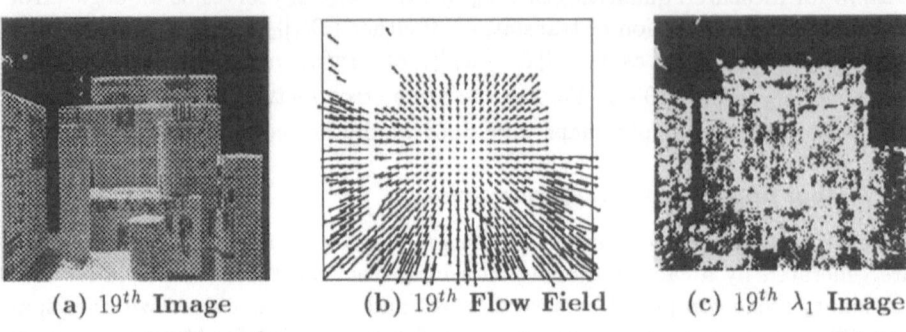

(a) 19th **Image**   (b) 19th **Flow Field**   (c) 19th λ_1 **Image**

Figure 1: (a) The 19th image of the translational newspaper sequence, (b) its flow field thresholded using $\lambda_1 \geq 1.0$ (subsampled and scaled by 15) and (c) an image of the confidence values (λ_1) for the flow field.

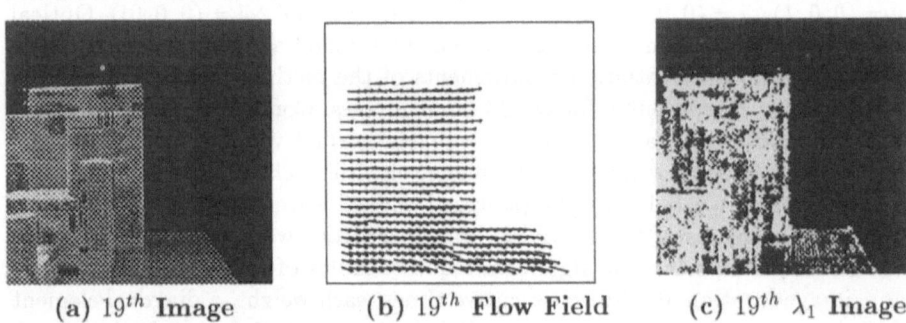

(a) 19th **Image**   (b) 19th **Flow Field**   (c) 19th λ_1 **Image**

Figure 2: (a) The 19th image of the general newspaper sequence, (b) its flow field thresholded using $\lambda_1 \geq 1.0$ (subsampled by 15 and scaled by 25) and (c) an image of the confidence values (λ_1) for the flow field.

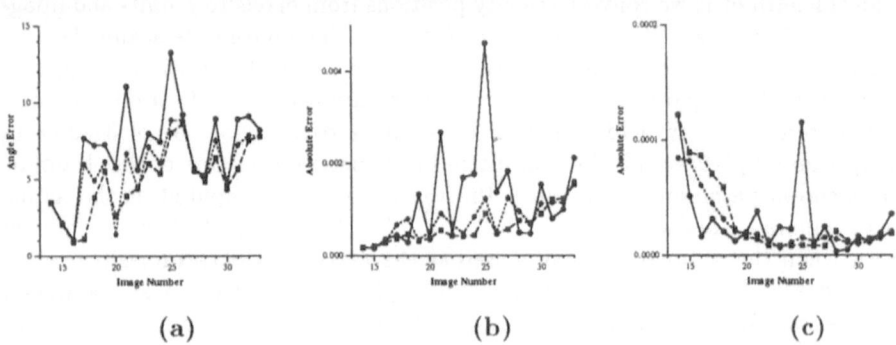

(a)   (b)   (c)

Figure 3: Measured (solid lines) and actual and residual Kalman filtered error (dashed and dotted lines) for (a) $\hat{u}$, (b) $\bar{\omega}$ and (c) $\delta\bar{\omega}$ for for the (line-of-sight) translational newspaper sequence.

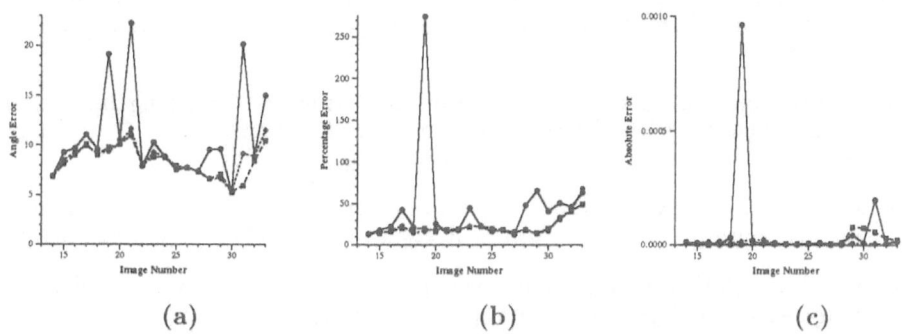

(a)   (b)   (c)

Figure 4: Measured (solid lines) and actual and residual Kalman filtered error (dashed and dotted lines) for (a) $\hat{u}$, (b) $\bar{\omega}$ and (c) $\delta\bar{\omega}$ for the general motion (line-of-sight translation and vertical rotation) newspaper image sequence.

Experimental results for the second sequence are given in Figure 4. A velocity sum threshold of 60.0 was used in the computation of $\bar{\omega}$. Lowering this threshold to 10.0 increased the inaccuracy towards 50% error. This was due to the inclusion of image velocities on the table in the calculation, which were interpretated as vertical rotation.

We also computed depth values for both cases of real image motion. We observed that the depth error depends on the accuracy of individual recovered image velocities and only slightly on the accuracy of the recovered motion parameters. It was difficult to recover accurate depth because of the presence of a FOE in the first sequence or because of the rotational flow dominated the translational flow in the second sequence.

6   Conclusions

We have presented a linear "motion and structure" algorithm that only requires the solution of 2×2 or 3×3 linear systems of equations. A Kalman filter framework was used to integrate these calculations (the "measurements") over time, resulting in a real-time frame-by-frame best estimate of each unknown parameter. Currently, accurate depth maps cannot be recovered.

Acknowledgements: Both authors gratefully acknowledge support from NSERC (the National Science and Engineering Research Council of Canada).

References

[1] J. L. Barron, D. J. Fleet, and S. S. Beauchemin. Performance of optical flow techniques. *IJCV*, 12(1):43–77, 1994.

[2] J. L. Barron, A. D. Jepson, and J. K. Tsotsos. The feasibility of motion and structure from noisy time-varying image velocity information. *IJCV*, 5(3):239–269, 1990.

[3] J.L. Barron and R. Eagleson. Motion and structure from long binocular image sequences with observer rotation. In *IEEE International Conference on Image Processing (ICIP'95)*, volume 2, pages 193–196, Oct 1995.

[4] J.L. Barron and R. Eagleson. Recursive estimation of time-varying motion and structure parameters. *Pattern Recognition*, 29(5):797–818, May 1996.

[5] J.C. Hay. Optical motions and space perception: An extension of gibson's analysis. *Psychological Review*, 73(6):550–565, 1966.

[6] D.J. Heeger and A.D. Jepson. A simple method for computing 3d motion and depth. In *ICCV*, pages 96–100, 1990.

[7] B. K. P. Horn. Motion fields are hardly ever ambiguous. *IJCV*, 1:259–274, 1987.

[8] A.D. Jepson and D.J. Heeger. Subspace methods for recovering rigid motion 2: Algorithm and implementation. Technical Report RBCV-TR-90-35, Dept. of Computer Science, University of Toronto, Nov. 1990.

[9] R. Kalman, P. Falb, and M. Arbib. *Topics in Mathematical System Theory*. McGraw-Hill, 1969.

[10] H. C. Longuet-Higgins and K. Prazdny. The interpretation of a moving retinal image. *Proc. R. Soc. Lond.*, B 208:385–397, 1980.

A theory of occlusion in the context of optical flow

Steven S. Beauchemin and John L. Barron

1 Introduction

Traditionally, image motion and its approximation known as optical flow have been treated as continuous functions of the image domain [9]. However, in realistic imagery, one finds cases verifying this hypothesis exceedingly rarely. Many phenomena may cause discontinuities in the optical flow function of imagery [16]. Among them, occlusion and translucency are frequent causes of discontinuities in realistic imagery. In addition, their information content is useful to later stages of processing [8] such as motion segmentation [1] and 3-d surface reconstruction [17].

Occlusion boundaries are described as the partial occlusion of a surface by another, while translucency is defined as occlusion of a surface by translucent material. In realistic imagery, one finds occlusion to be the most frequent cause of discontinuous motion.

Recently, a number of algorithms have been designed to handle multiple motions [2]. Among these, we find constraint-line clustering algorithms [15], which use a form of cluster analysis applied to sets of constraint lines to determine the dominant motion of a given image region. Similarly, robust estimators are used to recover dominant motion [6]. However, approaches focusing on the determination of dominant motion do not explicitly form a multiple motion model in the sense that they only provide one velocity measurement in regions where many motions may prevail. Alternatively, a number of authors have studied inhibitory smoothness constraints [13] which relax smoothness requirements at image regions of high grayvalue gradients. Nonetheless, intensity discontinuities may not necessarily represent motion discontinuities. Other approaches consist of refining the boundaries of closed curves delimiting regions exhibiting coherent motion [14]. Again, such schemes are limited by an explicit single motion model.

Schemes for estimating optical flow at regions of partial translucency have also appeared in the recent literature [5]. In the case of spatiotemporal frequency models [8], translucency could be easily handled, given an appropriate constraint-integration algorithm. In addition, schemes capable of handling both occlusion and translucency have been devised. For instance, sequential tracking and registration algorithms which independently compute the velocity of objects from a scene exhibiting different motions, while handling both occlusion and translucency, have been used [10]. Multilayer and superposition models also provide paradigms for the estimation of multiple velocities. These approaches consider the optical flow function of the image as a superposition of motion layers, each one described by a unique set of parameters, thus allowing discontinuous and multiple-valued optical flow functions [7, 11, 16].

These approaches, while constituting valuable contributions, do not provide descriptive models of phenomena such as occlusion and translucency. Further, it is often difficult if not impossible to determine the nature of the image events giving rise to multiple motions. In these schemes, occlusion may not be differentiated from translucency and the explicit identification of the motions associated with both the occluding and occluded signals remains an open problem. In this contribution we demonstrate, under a minimal set of assumptions, that such distinctions can be made through a Fourier analysis of these image events. We also show that translucency may be handled as a special case of occlusion.

2   Multiple motions

Given an arbitrary environment and a moving visual sensor, the motion field generated onto the imaging plane by a 3-d scene within the visual field is represented as a function of the motion parameters of the visual sensor, usually expressed as instantaneous translation $\mathbf{T}^T = (T_x, T_y, T_z)$ and rotation $\Omega^T = (\Omega_x, \Omega_y, \Omega_z)$:

$$\mathbf{v} = \begin{pmatrix} Z(\mathbf{x})^{-1}(xT_z - T_x) + xy\Omega_x - (1+x^2)\Omega_y + y\Omega_z \\ Z(\mathbf{x})^{-1}(yT_z - T_y) + (1+y^2)\Omega_x - xy\Omega_y - x\Omega_z \end{pmatrix}, \tag{1}$$

where $\mathbf{x}^T = (x, y)$ is the perspective projection of a point $\mathbf{P}^T = (X, Y, Z)$ in the visual field. Assuming that the motion of the visual sensor is continuous (that is to say: Ω and $\mathbf{T}$ are differentiable with respect to time), discontinuities in image motion are then introduced in (1) whenever the depth function $Z(\mathbf{x})$ is other than single-valued and differentiable. The occurrence of occlusion causes the depth function to exhibit a discontinuity, whereas translucency leads to a multiple-valued depth function.

Our motivation for conducting this study is to use occlusion phenomena as a source of information rather than an obstacle in conflict with too simple hypotheses concerning the structure of optical flow fields, such as the single surface assumption. Crucial information, such as the identification of image events leading to multiple motions, the determination of these motions and, under occlusion, their identification as velocities of occluding and occluded surfaces, can be obtained through a Fourier analysis of occlusion and transparency phenomena. Throughout this contribution, we consider velocities as locally constant quantities and image signals as satisfying Dirichlet conditions.

2.1   Occlusion in the frequency domain

The Fourier transform of the optical flow constraint equation is obtained with the differentiation property as:

$$\mathcal{F}\left[\nabla \mathbf{I}(\mathbf{x}, t)^T \mathbf{v} + \mathbf{I}_t\right] = i\hat{\mathbf{I}}(\mathbf{k}, \omega)\delta(\mathbf{k}^T \mathbf{v} + \omega), \tag{2}$$

where i is the imaginary number, $\hat{\mathbf{I}}(k, \omega)$ is the Fourier transform of $\mathbf{I}(x, t)$ and $\delta(\mathbf{k}^T \mathbf{v} + \omega)$ is a line-mass Dirac delta function. Expression (2) yields $\mathbf{k}^T \mathbf{v} + \omega = 0$

as a constraint on velocity. Similarly, the Fourier transform of a translating intensity profile $\mathbf{I}(\mathbf{x}, t)$ is obtained with the shift property as:

$$\hat{\mathbf{I}}(\mathbf{k}, \omega) = \int \int \mathbf{I}(\mathbf{x} - \mathbf{v}t) e^{-i(\mathbf{k}^T \mathbf{x} + \omega t)} d\mathbf{x} dt$$

$$= \hat{\mathbf{I}}(\mathbf{k}) \delta(\mathbf{k}^T \mathbf{v} + \omega), \tag{3}$$

which also yields the constraint $\mathbf{k}^T \mathbf{v} + \omega = 0$. Hence, (2) and (3) demonstrate that the frequency analysis of image motion is in accordance with the motion constraint equation [8]. It is also observed that $\mathbf{k}^T \mathbf{v} + \omega = 0$ represents, in the frequency domain, an oriented plane passing through the origin, with normal vector $\mathbf{v}$ representing full velocity, onto which the Fourier spectrum of $\mathbf{I}(\mathbf{x})$ lies[1]. The discontinuities in optical flow arising from occlusion may be written by considering two translating intensity profiles, one partially occluding the other. Let $\mathbf{I}_1(\mathbf{x})$ and $\mathbf{I}_2(\mathbf{x})$ be the intensity profiles of an object and a background scene. An object indicator function such as

$$\mathbf{U}(\mathbf{x}) = \begin{cases} 1 & \text{if } \mathbf{I}_1(\mathbf{x}) \neq 0 \\ 0 & \text{otherwise} \end{cases}$$

may be defined to specify the actual location of the object on the image plane. The resulting intensity pattern is then written as a function of the intensity profiles of the object, the background and the object indicator:

$$\mathbf{I}(\mathbf{x}, t) = \mathbf{I}_1(\mathbf{x} - \mathbf{v}_1 t) + [1 - \mathbf{U}(\mathbf{x} - \mathbf{v}_1 t)] \mathbf{I}_2(\mathbf{x} - \mathbf{v}_2 t). \tag{4}$$

By using the shift property of Fourier transforms, (4) is rewritten in spatiotemporal frequency space as:

$$\begin{aligned} \hat{\mathbf{I}}(\mathbf{k}, \omega) &= \hat{\mathbf{I}}_1(\mathbf{k}) \delta(\omega + \mathbf{v}_1^T \mathbf{k}) + \hat{\mathbf{I}}_2(\mathbf{k}) \delta(\omega + \mathbf{v}_2^T \mathbf{k}) \\ &- \left[\hat{\mathbf{U}}(\mathbf{k}) \delta(\omega + \mathbf{v}_1^T \mathbf{k}) \right] * \left[\hat{\mathbf{I}}_2(\mathbf{k}) \delta(\omega + \mathbf{v}_2^T \mathbf{k}) \right]. \end{aligned} \tag{5}$$

The first two terms of (5) are the signals associated with the object and the background. The frequency spectra of $\mathbf{I}_1$ and $\mathbf{I}_2$ are located on the planes defined by the equations $\mathbf{k}^T \mathbf{v}_1 + \omega = 0$ and $\mathbf{k}^T \mathbf{v}_2 + \omega = 0$ respectively. In addition, the respective orientations of these planes fully determine $\mathbf{v}_1$ and $\mathbf{v}_2$. The last term of (5) describes the distortion created by the occlusion boundary. In the following sections, this form of distortion is analized and its usefulness in determining image events giving rise to multiple motions is shown.

---

[1] The aperture problem arises when the Fourier spectrum of $\mathbf{I}(\mathbf{x})$ is concentrated on a line rather than on a plane [8, 12]. Spatiotemporally, this depicts the situation in which $\mathbf{I}(\mathbf{x})$ exhibits a single orientation. In this case, one may only obtain the speed and direction of motion normal to the orientation, noted as $\mathbf{v}_\perp$. If many normal velocities are found in a single neighbourhood, their respective lines fit the plane $\mathbf{k}^T \mathbf{v} + \omega = 0$ from which full velocity may be obtained.

3   Frequency analysis of occlusion

The analysis begins with the consideration of a simple case consisting of two 1-d sinusoidal intensity profiles. The results are then generalized to arbitrary 1-d and 2-d intensity profiles.

3.1   One-dimensional sinusoidal signals

The case in which two 1-d sinusoidals play the role of the object and the background is first considered. Let $I(x,t)$ be a 1-d intensity function $I_1(x)$ translating with velocity v_1: $I(x,t) = I_1(x - v_1 t)$. Its Fourier transform is $\hat{I}(k,\omega) = \hat{I}_1(k)\delta(kv_1 + \omega)$. Let $I_1(x)$ be occluding another 1-d intensity pattern $I_2(x)$ moving with velocity v_2. The resulting intensity profile can then be expressed as:

$$I(x,t) = u(x - v_1 t)I_1(x - v_1 t) + (1 - u(x - v_1 t))I_2(x - v_2 t) \tag{6}$$

where $u(x)$ is Heaviside's function representing the occluding point:

$$u(x) = \begin{cases} 1 & \text{if } x \geq 0 \\ 0 & \text{otherwise.} \end{cases}$$

The Fourier transform of the intensity profile (6) is:

$$\begin{aligned} \hat{I}(k,\omega) &= [\hat{u}(k)\delta(kv_1 + \omega)] * [\hat{I}_1(k)\delta(kv_1 + \omega)] \\ &- [\hat{u}(k)\delta(kv_1 + \omega)] * [\hat{I}_2(k)\delta(kv_2 + \omega)] \\ &+ \hat{I}_2(k)\delta(kv_2 + \omega), \end{aligned} \tag{7}$$

where $\hat{u}(k)$ is the Fourier transform of Heaviside's function $u(x)$ written as $\hat{u}(k) = \pi\delta(k) + (ik)^{-1}$.

Proposition 1 *Let $I_1(x)$ and $I_2(x)$ be cosine functions with respective angular frequencies $k_1 = 2\pi f_1 > 0$ and $k_2 = 2\pi f_2 > 0$ and let $I_1(x - v_1 t) = c_1 \cos(k_1 x - v_1 t)$ and $I_2(x - v_2 t) = c_2 \cos(k_2 x - v_2 t)$. Then the frequency spectrum of the occlusion obtained by substituting $I_1(x)$ and $I_2(x)$ into (6) is:*

$$\begin{aligned} \hat{I}(k,\omega) &= \frac{\pi}{2}c_1\delta(k \pm k_1, \omega \mp k_1 v_1) \\ &+ \frac{(1-\pi)}{2}c_2\delta(k \pm k_2, \omega \mp k_2 v_2) \\ &+ \frac{i}{2}\left(\frac{c_2\delta(kv_1 + \omega \pm k_2\Delta v)}{(k \pm k_2)} - \frac{c_1\delta(kv_1 + \omega)}{(k \pm k_1)}\right) \end{aligned} \tag{8}$$

A number of conclusions can be drawn from proposition 1: Since the signals are cosines, all their power content is real. In addition, the power content of the distortion term is entirely imaginary, and form lines of decreasing power about the frequencies of both the occluding and occluded signals. Their orientation is inversely proportional to the velocity of the occluding signal, as $-v_1$ is the slope of the constraint lines.

3.2 One-dimensional arbitrary signals

In general, the occluding and occluded signals cannot be represented as simple sinusoidal functions. To gain generality, $I_1(x)$ and $I_2(x)$ may be expanded as a series of complex exponentials, assuming that functions $I_1(x)$ and $I_2(x)$ satisfy Dirichlet conditions.

Proposition 2 *Let $I_1(x)$ and $I_2(x)$ be functions satisfying Dirichlet conditions such that they may be expressed as complex exponential series expansions:*

$$I_1(x) = \sum_{n=-\infty}^{\infty} c_{1n} e^{ink_1 x} \quad I_2(x) = \sum_{n=-\infty}^{\infty} c_{2n} e^{ink_2 x}, \tag{9}$$

where n is integer, c_{1n} and c_{2n} are complex coefficients and k_1 and k_2 are the fundamental frequencies of both signals. Then the frequency spectrum of the occlusion obtained by substituting the frequency spectra of (9) into (6) is:

$$\hat{I}(k,\omega) = \pi \sum_{n=\infty}^{\infty} c_{1n} \delta(k - nk_1, \omega + nk_1 v_1)$$

$$+ (1 - \pi) \sum_{n=-\infty}^{\infty} c_{2n} \delta(k - nk_2, \omega + nk_2 v_2)$$

$$+ i \sum_{n=-\infty}^{\infty} \left(\frac{c_{2n} \delta(kv_1 + \omega - nk_2 \Delta v)}{(k - nk_2)} - \frac{c_{1n} \delta(kv_1 + \omega)}{(k - nk_1)} \right). \tag{10}$$

Proposition 2 is an important generalization of the first one: Any signal which represents a physical quantity satisfies Dirichlet conditions and therefore may be expressed as an expansion of complex exponentials. Since c_{1n} and c_{2n} are complex coefficients, the power contents of the signals are both real and imaginary.

3.3 Two-dimensional arbitrary signals

Imagery is the result of the projection of light reflected by environmental features onto the imaging plane of the visual sensor. Hence, such signals are inherently two dimensional. Towards a generalization of (10), (9) is expanded as series of 2-d complex exponentials.

Proposition 3 *Let $I_1(\mathbf{x})$ and $I_2(\mathbf{x})$ be 2-d functions satisfying Dirichlet conditions such that they may be expressed as complex exponential series expansions:*

$$I_1(\mathbf{x}) = \sum_{\mathbf{n}=-(\infty,\infty)}^{(\infty,\infty)} c_{1\mathbf{n}} e^{i\mathbf{x}^T N \mathbf{k}_1} \quad I_2(\mathbf{x}) = \sum_{\mathbf{n}=-(\infty,\infty)}^{(\infty,\infty)} c_{2\mathbf{n}} e^{i\mathbf{x}^T N \mathbf{k}_2}, \tag{11}$$

where $\mathbf{n}^T = (n_x, n_y)$ are integers, $N = \mathbf{n}^T I$, $\mathbf{x}^T = (x, y)$ are spatial coordinates, $\mathbf{k}_1 = (k_{x1}, k_{y1})$ and $\mathbf{k}_2 = (k_{x2}, k_{y2})$ are spatial frequencies and $c_{1\mathbf{n}}$ and $c_{2\mathbf{n}}$ are complex coefficients. Also let the occluding boundary be locally represented by:

$$U(\mathbf{x}) = \begin{cases} 1 & \text{if } \mathbf{x}^T \vec{\eta} \geq 0 \\ 0 & \text{otherwise}, \end{cases} \tag{12}$$

where $\vec{\eta}$ is a vector normal to the instantaneous slope of the occluding boundary at $\mathbf{x}$. Then the frequency spectrum of the occlusion obtained by substituting the frequency spectra of (11) and (12) into a 2-d version of (6) is:

$$\hat{\mathbf{I}}(\mathbf{k},\omega) \ = \ \pi \sum_{\mathbf{n}=-(\infty,\infty)}^{(\infty,\infty)} c_{1\mathbf{n}}\delta(\mathbf{k} - N\mathbf{k}_1, \omega + \mathbf{v}_1^T N\mathbf{k}_1)$$

$$+ \ (1-\pi) \sum_{\mathbf{n}=-(\infty,\infty)}^{(\infty,\infty)} c_{2\mathbf{n}}\delta(\mathbf{k} - N\mathbf{k}_2, \omega + \mathbf{v}_2^T N\mathbf{k}_2)$$

$$+ \ i \sum_{\mathbf{n}=-(\infty,\infty)}^{(\infty,\infty)} \left(\frac{c_{2\mathbf{n}}\delta(\mathbf{k}^T\mathbf{v}_1 + \omega - \Delta\mathbf{v}^T N\mathbf{k}_2)}{(\mathbf{k} - N\mathbf{k}_2)^T\vec{\eta}} - \frac{c_{1\mathbf{n}}\delta(\mathbf{k}^T\mathbf{v}_1 + \omega)}{(\mathbf{k} - N\mathbf{k}_1)^T\vec{\eta}} \right),$$

$$(13)$$

where $\mathbf{v}_1^T = (u_1, v_1)$, $\mathbf{v}_2^T = (u_2, v_2)$ and $\Delta\mathbf{v} = \mathbf{v}_1 - \mathbf{v}_2$.

Proposition 3 is a direct extension of proposition 2 in two spatial dimensions. For this general case, the constraint lines of propositions 1 and 2 generated by both the occluding and occluded signals and the distortion terms become constraint planes. The frequency structures of individual signals are preserved to within scaling factors.

3.4   Relation to translucency

Transmission of light through translucent material may cause multiple motions to arise in the same image region. Generally, this effect is depicted on the image plane as

$$\mathbf{I}(\mathbf{x}, t) = f(\rho_1)(\mathbf{x} - \mathbf{v}_1 t)\mathbf{I}_2(\mathbf{x} - \mathbf{v}_2 t), \tag{14}$$

where $f(\rho_1)$ is a function of the density of the translucent material [8]. Under the local assumption of spatially constant $f(\rho_1)$, with translucency factor φ, (14) is reformulated as a weighted superposition of intensity profiles:

$$\mathbf{I}(\mathbf{x}, t) = \varphi\mathbf{I}_1(\mathbf{x} - \mathbf{v}_1 t) + (1 - \varphi)\mathbf{I}_2(\mathbf{x} - \mathbf{v}_2 t), \tag{15}$$

where $\mathbf{I}_1(\mathbf{x}, t)$ is the intensity profile of the translucent material and $\mathbf{I}_2(\mathbf{x}, t)$ is the intensity profile of the background. With $\mathbf{I}_1(\mathbf{x})$ and $\mathbf{I}_2(\mathbf{x})$ satisfying Dirichlet conditions, the frequency spectrum of (15) is written as:

$$\hat{\mathbf{I}}(\mathbf{k},\omega) \ = \ \varphi \sum_{\mathbf{n}=-(\infty,\infty)}^{(\infty,\infty)} c_{1\mathbf{n}}\delta(\mathbf{k} - N\mathbf{k}_1, \omega + \mathbf{v}_1^T N\mathbf{k}_1)$$

$$+ \ (1-\varphi) \sum_{\mathbf{n}=-(\infty,\infty)}^{(\infty,\infty)} c_{2\mathbf{n}}\delta(\mathbf{k} - N\mathbf{k}_2, \omega + \mathbf{v}_2^T N\mathbf{k}_2). \tag{16}$$

With the exception of the distortion term, and to within scaling factors, (16) is identical to (13). Hence, with respect to its frequency structure, translucency may be reduced to a special case of occlusion for which the distortion terms vanish.

3.5 Geometric interpretation

In the simplest case involving sinusoidal signals, Proposition 1 shows that the frequency spectra of both signals are preserved to within scaling factors. In addition, the imaginary terms represent the frequency spectrum of the occlusion boundary. Figure 2 shows one case of occlusion with a 1-d, Gaussian-windowed sinusoidal signal. The velocity of the occluding signal is $v_1 = 1.0$. The velocity of the occluded signal is $v_2 = -1.0$. The spatial frequency of the occluding and occluded signals are $k_1 = \frac{2\pi}{16}$ and $k_2 = \frac{2\pi}{8}$ respectively. The vertical axis represents temporal frequency ω while the horizontal axis is spatial frequency k. The spectral peaks located at $\pm(k_1, -k_1 v_1)$ and $\pm(k_2, -k_2 v_2)$ depict the spatiotemporal frequencies of both signals and fit the constraint lines $k v_1 + \omega = 0$ and $k v_2 + \omega = 0$. The oblique spectra intesecting the peaks represent the spectrum generated by the occlusion boundary and fit the constraint lines $k_1 v_1 + \omega \pm k_2 v_2 = 0$ and $k_1 v_1 + \omega = 0$. These lines are parallel to the constraint line of the occluding signal. It also is interesting to observe From Proposition 2 that every non-zero frequency of an occluded signal shows such a parallel line due to occlusion.

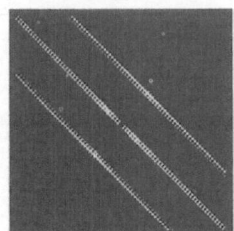 

Figure 1: **a) (left):** Gaussian-smoothed frequency spectrum produced with (8). The occluding and occluded signals have frequencies $k_1 = \frac{2\pi}{16}$ and $k_2 = \frac{2\pi}{8}$ and velocities $v_1 = 1$ and $v_2 = -1$ respectively. **b) (right):** Gaussian-smoothed frequency spectrum produced with (10). The occluding signal has frequency $k_1 = \frac{2\pi}{16}$ and velocity $v_1 = 1$ while the occluded signal is composed of frequencies $n k_2 = 2\pi \left(\frac{n}{8}\right), n = 1, 2, 3$ and velocity $v_2 = -1$.

Proposition 3 is the generalization of Proposition 2 in 2D and its geometric interpretation is similar. That is to say, the constraint lines of the signals and the occlusion boundary become constraint planes. For instance, the frequencies $(N\mathbf{k}_1, -\mathbf{v}_1^T N\mathbf{k}_1)$ and $(N\mathbf{k}_2, -\mathbf{v}_2^T N\mathbf{k}_2)$ fit the constraint planes of the occluding and occluded signals, defined as $\mathbf{k}_1^T \mathbf{v}_1 + \omega = 0$ and $\mathbf{k}^T \mathbf{v}_2 = 0$. In the distortion term, the arguments of the Dirac δ functions $\mathbf{k}^T \mathbf{v}_1 + \omega - \Delta \mathbf{v}^T N\mathbf{k}_2$ and $\mathbf{k}^T \mathbf{v}_1 + \omega$ represent a set of planes parallel to the constraint plane of the occluding signal $\mathbf{k}^T \mathbf{v}_1 + \omega = 0$. That is to say, for every discrete frequency $N\mathbf{k}_1$ and $N\mathbf{k}_2$ exhibited by both signals, there is a frequency spectrum fitting the planes given by $\mathbf{k}^T \mathbf{v}_1 + \omega - \Delta \mathbf{v}^T N\mathbf{k}_2 = 0$ and $\mathbf{k}^T \mathbf{v}_1 + \omega = 0$. The magnitudes of these planar spectra are determined by their corresponding scaling functions $c_{1\mathbf{n}}[(\mathbf{k} - N\mathbf{k}_1)^T \bar{\eta}]^{-1}$ and $c_{2\mathbf{n}}[(\mathbf{k} - N\mathbf{k}_2)^T \bar{\eta}]^{-1}$. Hence, Proposition 3 reveals useful constraint planes, as the power spectra of both signals peak within planes $\mathbf{k}^T\mathbf{v}_1 + \omega = 0$ and $\mathbf{k}^T\mathbf{v}_2 + \omega = 0$ and the constraint planes arising from the distortion are parallel to the spectrum of the occluding signal $\mathbf{I}_1(\mathbf{x}, t)$.

4 Numerical experiments

Aside from deriving formal proofs[2], several experiments were performed in support of the Propositions. The Fourier spectra obtained with both a standard FFT algorithm and those predicted by the theory were compared.

In order to verify the propositions, two 1-d signals which respectively act as occluding and occluded surfaces were used. Expression (6) is used with $\mathbf{I}_1(x - v_1t) = c_1\cos(k_1x - v_1t)$ and $\mathbf{I}_2(x - v_2t) = c_2\cos(k_2x - v_2t)$, where $\mathbf{I}_1$ and $\mathbf{I}_2$ are the occluding and the occluded surfaces with respective frequencies $k_1 = \frac{2\pi}{16}$ and $k_2 = \frac{2\pi}{8}$. Constants c_1 and c_2 correspond to signal amplitudes. To limit boundary conditions when numerically computing Fourier transforms, the signal was windowed with a Gaussian envelope. The discrete Fourier transform of the

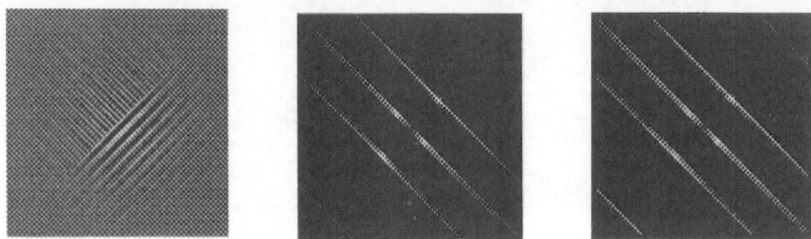

Figure 2: **a) (left):** Gaussian-windowed signal with sinusoidals acting as occluding and occluded surfaces. The occluding signal has frequency $k_1 = \frac{2\pi}{16}$ and velocity $v_1 = 1$. The occluded signal has frequency $k_2 = \frac{2\pi}{8}$ and velocity $v_2 = -1$. **b) (middle):** Fourier spectrum generated with a standard FFT algorithm. **c) (right):** Fourier spectrum predicted by theory.

windowed signal obtained with a standard FFT algorithm is shown in Figure 2b, where the peaks associated with both sinusoidals and the distortion lines are clearly visible. A discretized version of proposition 1, which models aliasing effects is shown in Figure 2c for the same frequencies and velocities as in Figure 2b: The spectra obtained with both a standard FFT algorithm and the theoretical results are essentially identical.

---

[2]The formal proofs of Propositions 1, 2 and 3 are found in [3]

5 Conclusion

Under a minimal set of hypotheses, such as locally constant velocity and intensity profiles satisfying Dirichlet conditions, we have shown the Fourier structure of occlusion and translucency phenomena in both 1 and 2D and outlined various interesting geometrical properties. For instance, the constraint lines or planes cast by the occlusion boundary have been characterized: In a multiple motion situation, their presence indicates an occlusion while their absence indicates a translucency phenomenon.

When a multiple motion situation is caused by an occlusion, the parallelism between the the distortion cast by the occluding boundary and the Fourier spectrum of the occluding signal differentiates the velocity of the occluding signal from the velocity of the occluded signal.

This analysis forms a basis for a class of constraint-grouping algorithms capable of distinguishing occlusion from translucency and identifying occluded and occluding surfaces, along with their respective velocities. In addition, the inclusion of the occlusion boundary distortions in models of multiple motions is likely to result in further improvements of signal-to-noise ratios. The results of this theory have been extended to linear models of optical flow and signal degeneracy caused by the aperture problem [4].

References

[1] G. Adiv. Determining three-dimensional motion and structure from optical flow generated by several moving objects. *IEEE PAMI*, 7(4):384–401, 1985.

[2] S. S. Beauchemin and J. L. Barron. The computation of optical flow. *ACM Computing Surveys*, 27(3):433–467, 1995.

[3] S. S. Beauchemin and J. L. Barron. A theory of occlusion. Technical Report TR-449, Dept. of Computer Science, Univ. of Western Ontario, March 1995.

[4] S. S. Beauchemin, A. Chalifour, and J. L. Barron. Discontinuous optical flow: Recent theoretical results. In *Vision Interface*, pages 57–64, Kelowna, Canada, May 1997.

[5] J. R. Bergen, P. J. Burt, R. Hingorani, and S. Peleg. Three-frame algorithm for estimating two-component image motion. *IEEE PAMI*, 14(9):886–896, 1992.

[6] M. J. Black and P. Anandan. A model for the detection of motion over time. In *Proceedings of ICCV*, pages 33–37, Osaka, Japan, December 1990.

[7] T. Darrell and A. Pentland. Robust estimation of a multi-layered motion representation. In *IEEE Proceedings of Workshop on Visual Motion*, pages 173–178, Princeton, New Jersey, October 1991.

[8] D. J. Fleet. *Measurement of Image Velocity*. Kluwer Academic Publishers, Norwell, 1992.

[9] B. K. P. Horn and B. G. Schunck. Determining optical flow. *Artificial Intelligence*, 17:185–204, 1981.

[10] M. Irani, B. Rousso, and S. Peleg. Computing occluding and transparent motions. *IJCV*, 12(1):5–16, 1994.

[11] A. D. Jepson and M. Black. Mixture models for optical flow computation. In *IEEE Proceedings of CVPR*, pages 760–761, New York, New York, June 1993.

[12] D. Marr and S. Ullman. Directional selectivity and its use in early visual processing. *Proceedings of Royal Society London*, B 211:151–180, 1981.

[13] H.-H. Nagel. Displacement vectors derived from second-order intensity variations in image sequences. *CVGIP*, 21:85–117, 1983.

[14] C. Schnorr. Computation of discontinuous optical flow by domain decomposition. *IEEE PAMI*, 8(2):153–165, 1992.

[15] B. G. Schunck. Image flow segmentation and estimation by constraint line clustering. *IEEE PAMI*, 11(10):1010–1027, 1989.

[16] M. Shizawa and K. Mase. Principle of superposition: A common computational framework for analysis of multiple motion. In *IEEE Proceedings of Workshop on Visual Motion*, pages 164–172, Princeton, New Jersey, October 1991.

[17] P. Toh and A. K. Forrest. Occlusion detection in early vision. In *ICCV*, pages 126–132. IEEE, 1990.

Algebraic method for solution of some best matching problems

Michail Schlesinger

1. Formulation and discussion of the problem

1.1. Introductory notions

Let V be a finite alphabet of signals, V^* be the set of strings, which are composed of signals from V, L be a subset in V^* and, finally, $d:V^* \times V^* \to R$ be a distinction function.

The best matching problem is meant as a calculation of the value

$$D(\bar{u}) = \min_{\bar{v} \in L} d(\bar{v}, \bar{u}) \tag{1}$$

for the given string $\bar{u}$ and the given subset L of strings.

In this article the special case of the problem is discussed and solved, when L is a regular language and d is a distinction function by Levenstein [1]. Let us turn into consideration the notions, which the regular languages and the distinctions by Levenstein will be defined by.

1.2. Regular languages

Let S be a finite set of states; V, as before, is a finite set of signal values. Let $B:S \to \{0,\infty\}$, $T:S \times V \times S \to \{0,\infty\}$ and $E:S \to \{0,\infty\}$ be three functions.

Definition 1. A string $(\bar{v}, s)$, $\bar{v} \in V^*$, $s \in S$ is allowable by functions B and T, if:

1. $\bar{v}$ is an empty string and $B(s) = 0$;

or

2. $\bar{v} = (\bar{v}', v)$, $\bar{v}' \in V^*$, $v \in V$, and there exists a state $s' \in S$, such that the string $(\bar{v}', s')$ is allowable and $T(s', v, s) = 0$.

Definition 2. A string $\bar{v}$ is allowable by the functions B, T, E, if there exists a state $s \in S$, such that the string $(\bar{v}, s)$ is allowable by functions B, T and $E(s) = 0$.

The set of allowable strings will be designated by $L_{B,T,E}$. Evidently, $L_{B,T,E}$ is a regular language [2]. It is also not difficult to prove that any regular language can be performed as a set of type $L_{B,T,E}$.

1.3. Distinction by Levenstein

Let us consider the operations of the folowing three types over the strings and define their costs.

An operation "to change" transforms a string of type $(\bar{v}, v, \bar{v}')$, $\bar{v} \in V^*$, $v \in V$, $\bar{v}' \in V^*$, into another one $(\bar{v}, u, \bar{v}')$, $u \in V$. Costs of such operations are defined by some function $CH{:}V \times V \rightarrow R$.

An operation "to delete" transforms a string of type $(\bar{v}, v, \bar{v}')$ into new one $(\bar{v}, \bar{v}')$. Costs of such type operations are defined by some function $DE{:}V \rightarrow R$.

An operation "to insert" transforms $(\bar{v}, \bar{v}')$ into $(\bar{v}, v, \bar{v}')$. Its cost is defined by a function $IN{:}V \rightarrow R$.

Let some chain $\bar{v}_1, \bar{v}_2, ..., \bar{v}_n$ of strings be such that every string $\bar{v}_i$, $i \neq 1$ can be obtained from the string $\bar{v}_{i-1}$ by an operation c_i , every c_i being an operation of above mentioned type. Then we will say that this chain is a path from $\bar{v}_1$ to $\bar{v}_n$ and that this path costs $\sum_{i=2}^{n} \varphi(c_i)$, where $\varphi(c_i)$ is a cost of the operation c_i .

Definition 3. A distinction by Levenstein of a string $\bar{v}$ from a string $\bar{u}$ is the cost of the cheapest path from $\bar{v}$ to $\bar{u}$.

So defined distinction function depends on the functions CH, IN and DE . It will be designated by $d_{IN,CH,DE}$. Note that , in general, this function does not posses the properties of a distance function, i.e. the triangle inequality etc.

1.4. Formulation of the problem

It is necessary to construct the algorithm, that for every six-tuple B, T, E, CH, DE, IN of functions and for every string $\bar{u}$ calculates a value

$$D(\bar{u}) = \min_{\bar{v} \in L_{B,T,E}} d_{IN,CH,DE}(\bar{v}, \bar{u}) \; . \qquad\qquad (2)$$

1.5. Discussion of the problem

Though some special cases of the above formulated problem are already solved [4], the problem in its full generality seems to be not very easy. First of all, though the expression (2) defines the value to be calculated quite unambiguously, this value is defined not explicitly, but through the minimization procedure. Moreover, the function $d_{IN,CH,DE}$ under minimization in its turn is also defined not explicitly, but as a solution of the certain minimization problem [3]. These difficulties, however, are already overcome [4] for the special case, when the distinction function has a property of distance, i.e. it is symmetric non-negative function etc. In general, when a distinction function is not obligatory a distance function, one must not overlook lot of trifles to construct a convincing and faultless algorithm for efficient calculation of (2).

Let us consider, for example, the simplest case of calculation of the distinction of the string, that consists of the single signal v , from the empty string. The cost of such transformation does not obligatory equal $DE(v)$, because it is possible at first to convert the signal v into another signal u and after that to delete the signal u . Really, the sum $CH(v, u) + DE(u)$ may be less than $DE(v)$, in general. Moreover, the cheapest way of converting the signal v into u may consist not only of one single change, but of the certain chain of changes. Thus a necessity of solution of some optimization problem arises even in this simplest situation. Truth to tell, this specific problem is not too difficult, but number of such small snares is too large, and when the algorithm for calculation of (2) is based only on the common sense, it is highly probable that some of such small snares will be overlooked. The algorithm for such puzzling problems is to be developed inside the certain formal framework, which should be more rigorous than reasonable verbal considerations.

An analysis and solution of the problem are based in this article on the well-known fact [e.g. 5], that a set of positive numbers with minimization and addition forms a semi-ring. On this base the function (2) for $D(u)$ can be performed by the specific algebraic expression, which can be equivalently transformed in a such way, that finally an expression is obtained, whose calculation provides no difficulties. Though the chain of such transformations is not too short, every link of the chain can be formally checked up, that makes the algorithm clear and valid.

2. Formulation of main results

Let the functions B, T, E define the language $L_{B,T,E}$ and let the functions IN, CH, DE define the Levenstein's distinction $d_{IN,CH,DE}$, as it was defined above. The following theorem is valid [6].

Theorem. *For any six-tuple B, T, E, CH, IN, DE of functions there exist such three functions $b{:}S \rightarrow R$, $f{:}S \times V \times S \rightarrow R$ and $e{:}S \rightarrow R$, that the equality*

$$D(u) = \min_{\bar{v} \in L_{B,T,E}} d_{IN,CH,DE} \left(\bar{v}, \bar{u}\right) =$$

$$= \min_{s_0, s_1, \dots, s_n} \left[b(s_0) + \sum_{i=1}^{n} f(s_{i-1}, u_i, s_i) + e(s_n) \right] \tag{3}$$

is valid for every string $\bar{u} = (u_1, u_2, \dots, u_n)$, $u_i \in V$.

Through the theorem the problem solution for every given language and every given distinction function consists of two steps. On the first step the functions B, T, E, IN, CH, DE are being converted into the functions b, f, e, whose properties and existence are stated by the theorem. The string $\bar{u}$ under analysis is not used on this step. On the second step value $D(\bar{u})$ is calculated, using the expression in the right side of (3). These calculations are to be fulfilled in the following way.

Let $f_0, f_1, \dots, f_n$ be some functions of type $S \rightarrow R$, n being length of the string $\bar{u}$ under analysis. These functions are defined by the following expressions:

$$f_0(s) = b(s), \ s \in S;$$

$$\tag{4}$$

$$f_i(s) = \min_{s' \in S} \left[f_{i-1}(s') + f(s', u_i, s) \right], \ s \in S, \ i = 1, \dots, n.$$

Then the value $\min_{s \in S} \left[f_n(s) + e(s) \right]$ is the solution of the problem, i.e.

$D(\bar{u})$. One can see, that this way of computation has a complexity of order $k^2 \times n$, k being the amount of states in S.

In the next section it is described without proof, how to transform the initial data about the language $L_{B,T,E}$ and the distinction function $d_{IN,CH,DE}$ into the functions b, f and e, which are necessary for computations (4) on the second step. Necessary proofs are described in [6,7].

3. Generalized convolutions and equivalent transformation of minimization problems

3.1. Generalized convolutions

Let W be a set of non-negative numbers, $\oplus$ and $\otimes$ being two operations of type $W \times W \to W$, such that for any $x \in W, y \in W$, $x \oplus y = \min(x,y)$ and $x \otimes y = x + y$. A triple $(W, \oplus, \otimes)$ forms a semi-ring [5,8], and so allows to construct convolutions of functions, which take their values from W.

Let X, Y, Z be some three sets, $f_1 : X \times Y \to W$ and $f_2 : Y \times Z \to W$ be two functions. These functions at whole, which are meant as mappings, will be designated by $f_1[x,y]$ and $f_2[y,z]$, where x, y, z are identifiers of variables, which the functions depend on. The values, which the functions take for some values of variables, for example, when $x = a$, $y = b$, $z = c$, will be denoted by $f_1(a,b)$ and $f_2(b,c)$.

Definition 4. *The function* $f[x,z] : X \times Z \to W$, *whose values are defined by the expression*

$$f(x,y) = \bigoplus_{y} (f_1(x,y) \otimes f_2(y,z)),\qquad(5)$$

will be referred as a convolution of the functions $f_1[x,y]$ *and* $f_2[y,z]$ *by variable* y. *This convolution will be denoted by the expression*

$$f[x,z] = f_1[x,y] \underset{y}{\otimes} f_2[y,z].\qquad(6)$$

The identifiers x,y and z in (5) and (6) are to be understood not only as the designators of a single variable, but also as the designators of the sequence of variables, maybe empty. So $f_1[x,y] \underset{y}{\otimes} f_2[y]$ is a function of x, $f_1[x] \otimes f_2[y]$ is a function of x and y, and $f_1[x] \underset{x}{\otimes} f_2[x]$ is no function, but a value from W.

Let some function $f[x,y]$ is of the type $X \times X \to W$, i.e. both variables take values from the same set X. The notion $\delta[x,y]$ will be used for such function $X \times X \to W$, that $\delta[x,y] = 0$, if $x = y$, and $\delta[x,y] = \infty$, if $x \neq y$. For any function f the denotion

f^i, $i = 0, 1, ..., i, ..., \infty$, will mean, that $f^0 = \delta$ and $f^i[x,z] = f^{i-1}[x,y] \underset{y}{\otimes} f[y,z]$. It is known [6,7], that when the set X

consists of finite number k of elements, then $\overset{\infty}{\underset{i=0}{\oplus}} f^i = (\delta + f)^{k-1}$, and

calculation of this infinite sum has a complexity of order k^3 [9]. For any function $f: X \times X \to R$ a designation f^* will be used for the sum

$\overset{\infty}{\underset{i=0}{\oplus}} f^i$.

3.2. Convolution representation of the minimization problem and its equivalent transformations

Let $F: V^* \to \{0, \infty\}$ be the function, such that $F(\bar{v}) = 0$, if $\bar{v} \in L_{B,T,E}$, and $F(\bar{v}) = \infty$, if $\bar{v} \notin L_{B,T,E}$. Then the function $D: V^* \to R$, which was above defined by (2), is the following convolution

$$D[\bar{u}] = F[\bar{v}] \underset{\bar{v}}{\otimes} d_{IN,CH,DE}[\bar{v},\bar{u}] . \tag{7}$$

Due to the definitions 1 and 2 the function $F: V^* \to \{0, \infty\}$ can be expressed by the convolution too,

$$F[\bar{v}] = B[s_0] \underset{s_0}{\otimes} T[s_0, v_1, s_1] \underset{s_1}{\otimes} T[s_1, v_2, s_2] \underset{s_2}{\otimes} \cdots \underset{s_{n-1}}{\otimes} T[s_{n-1}, v_n, s_n] \underset{s_n}{\otimes} E[s_n] . \tag{8}$$

The function $d_{IN,CH,DE}$ can be expressed as a convolution of three more simpler functions

$$d_{IN,CH,DE}[\bar{v},\bar{u}] = d_{IN}[\bar{v},\bar{u}_1] \underset{\bar{u}_1}{\otimes} d_{CH}[\bar{u}_1,\bar{u}_2] \underset{\bar{u}_2}{\otimes} d_{DE}[\bar{u}_2,u] , \tag{9}$$

where $d_{IN}(\bar{v},\bar{u}_1)$ is a cost of the cheapest chain of insertions, that transforms $\bar{v}$ into $\bar{u}_1$, $d_{CH}(\bar{u}_1,\bar{u}_2)$ is a cost of the cheapest chain of changes, that transforms $\bar{u}_1$ into $\bar{u}_2$ and $d_{DE}(\bar{u}_2,\bar{u})$ is a cost of the cheapest chain of deletions, which transforms $\bar{u}_2$ into $\bar{u}$.
So the function D , which was above expressed by (2) and (7), can be expressed by more detailed construction

$$D[\bar{u}] = F[\bar{v}] \underset{\bar{v}}{\otimes} d_{IN}[\bar{v},\bar{u}_1] \underset{\bar{u}_1}{\otimes} d_{CH}[\bar{u}_1,\bar{u}_2] \underset{\bar{u}_2}{\otimes} d_{DE}[\bar{u}_2,\bar{u}] \ . \tag{10}$$

The convolution $F[\bar{v}] \underset{\bar{v}}{\otimes} d_{IN}[\bar{v},\bar{u}_1]$ of the two leftmost factors in (10) is a function of the string $\bar{u}_1 = (u_{11},u_{12},...,u_{1n_1})$. This function will be denoted by F_{IN} . It has been proved [6,7], that this convolution can be expressed in the form

$$F_{IN}[\bar{u}_1] = F[\bar{v}] \underset{\bar{v}}{\otimes} d_{IN}[\bar{v},\bar{u}_1] =$$

$$= B[s_0] \underset{s_0}{\otimes} f_{in}[s_0,u_{11},s_1] \underset{s_1}{\otimes} f_{in}[s_1,u_{12},s_2] \underset{s_2}{\otimes} \cdots \underset{s_{n_1-1}}{\otimes} f_{in}[s_{n_1-1},u_{n_1},s_{n_1}] \underset{s_{n_1}}{\otimes} E[s_{n_1}] \ ,$$

$$\tag{11}$$

where the function $f_{in}[s,u,s'] : S \times V \times S \to W$ is to be constructed in accordance with the expression

$$f_{in}[s,u,s'] = T[s,u,s'] \oplus (\delta[s',s] \otimes IN[u]) \ . \tag{12}$$

So the new representation

$$D[\bar{u}] = F_{IN}[\bar{u}_1] \underset{\bar{u}_1}{\otimes} D_{CH}[\bar{u}_1,\bar{u}_2] \underset{\bar{u}_2}{\otimes} d_{DE}[\bar{u}_2,\bar{u}] \tag{13}$$

is obtained for the function $D[\bar{u}]$, which was previously expressed dy (2), (7) and (10).

The convolution $F_{IN}[\bar{u}_1] \underset{\bar{u}_1}{\otimes} d_{CH}[\bar{u}_1,\bar{u}_2]$ of the two leftmost factors in (13) is a function of the string $\bar{u}_2 = (u_{21},u_{22},...,u_{2n_2})$. This function will be denoted by $F_{IN,CH}$. Taking on account representation (11) for F_{IN} it is possible to represent the convolution $F_{IN}[\bar{u}_1] \underset{\bar{u}_1}{\otimes} d_{CH}[\bar{u}_1,\bar{u}_2]$ in the form

$$F_{IN,CH}[\bar{u}_2] = F_{IN}[\bar{u}_1] \underset{\bar{u}_1}{\otimes} d_{CH}[\bar{u}_1,\bar{u}_2] =$$

$$= B[s_0] \underset{s_0}{\otimes} f_{in,ch}[s_0,u_{21},s_1] \underset{s_1}{\otimes} f_{in,ch}[s_1,u_{22},s_2] \underset{s_2}{\otimes} \cdots$$

$$\cdots \underset{s_{n_2-1}}{\otimes} f_{in,ch}[s_{n_2-1},u_{2n_2},s_{n_2}] \underset{s_{n_2}}{\otimes} E[s_{n_2}] \ . \tag{14}$$

A function $f_{in,ch}[s,u,s'] : S \times V \times S \to W$ in (14) shall be constructed in accordance with the expression

$$f_{in,ch}[s,u,s'] = f_{in}[s,v,s'] \underset{v}{\otimes} CH^*[v,u] \ , \tag{15}$$

where CH^* is a function $\overset{\infty}{\underset{i=0}{\oplus}} CH^i$.

So the function $D[u]$, which was before expressed by (2), (7), (10) and (13), can be now expressed in the form

$$D[\bar{u}] = F_{IN,CH}[\bar{u}_2] \underset{\bar{u}_2}{\otimes} d_{DE}[\bar{u}_2,\bar{u}] \ . \tag{16}$$

This convolution has been proved [6,7] to have a form

$$D[\bar{u}] = D[u_1,u_2,...,u_n] =$$

$$b[s_0] \underset{s_0}{\otimes} f[s_0,u_1,s_1] \underset{s_1}{\otimes} f[s_1,u_2,s_2] \underset{s_2}{\otimes} \ \cdots \ \underset{s_{n-1}}{\otimes} f[s_{n-1},u_n,s_n] \underset{s_n}{\otimes} e[s_n] \ , \tag{17}$$

which is equal to expression (3) in the formulation of the theorem. The function b in (17) equals B , and the functions $f[s,u,s'] : S \times V \times S \to W$ and $e[s] : S \to W$ are to be constructed in the following way. An auxiliary function $\varphi : S \times S \to R$ is to be constructed by the convolution

$$\varphi[s,s'] = f_{in,ch}[s,v,s'] \underset{v}{\otimes} DE[v] \ , \tag{18}$$

and then

$$f[s,u,s'] = \varphi^*[s,s''] \underset{s''}{\otimes} f_{in,ch}[s'',u,s'] \ , \tag{19}$$

$$e[s] = \varphi[s,s'] \underset{s'}{\otimes} E[s] \ . \tag{20}$$

The expressions (12), (15), (18), (19), (20) show directly, how one must obtain the functions b, f, e , whose existence was stated by the theorem and which allow to represent the initial problem in the form (3).

References:

[1] Левенштейн В.И. Двоичные коды с исправлением выпадений, вставок и замещений символов // Докл. АН СССР.- 1965.-163, № 4. - С. 840-850.

[2] Ахо А., Ульман Дж. Теория синтаксического анализа, перевода и компиляция.- М. : Мир, 1978.- Т. 1.

[3] Wagner, R. A., and Fischer, M. J. The string-to-string correction problem. J. ACM 21, 1 (Jan. 1974), 168-173.

[4] Wagner, R. A., and Seiferas, J. I. Correcting counter-automaton-recognizable languages. SIAM. J. Comput. 7, 3 (1978), 357-375.

[5] Aho, A. V., Hopcroft, J. E., and Ullman, J. D. The Design and Analysis of Computer Algorithms. Addison-Wesley, Reading, Mass., 1975.

[6] Schlesinger, M. I. Systeme von Funktionsoperationen angewendet auf eine Aufgabe der besten Uebereinstimmung. //ISSN 0863-0798/Wissenschaftliche Beitraege zur Informatik - Fakultaet Informatik TU Dresden/7(1994) Heft 3.- S. 62-79.

[7] Шлезингер М.И. Обобщенные свертки функций и их применение для синтаксического анализа искаженных последовательностей //Проблемы управления и информатики, Киев, 1995 г, № 2.- С. 67-81.

[8] Фрид, Элементарное введение в абстрактную алгебру.-М. : Мир,1978.- 260 с. (A Russian translation of "Absztrakt algebra - elemi ueton" by E.Fried, Budapest, Mueszaki Koenyvkiadoe, 1972.

[9] Floyd, R. W. (1962), Algorithm 97; Shortest path, Comm. ACM 5, № 6, 345.

Determining the attitude of planar objects with general curved contours from a single perspective view

Michael Schubert and Klaus Voss

1   Introduction

In 3D-scene analysis, the monocular 3D-pose estimation represents a relatively restricted part. The goal is to determine the location and orientation of modelled objects in a threedimensional scene by a single perspective view. The need for a model description restricts these methods mainly to technical objects.

The known methods of monocular pose estimation request that correspondences of geometric primitives the model object and image object are known and the parameters of these primitives can be determined exactly in the image. Such primitives are points, line segments, circular arcs etc. ([6, 7, 2, 4, 12]). The methods based on primitives fail in the case of general curved surface contours.

In [5] invariants derived from canonical frames are used for the detection of objects with general curved contours. The canonical frames are computed using local features of the contour. In [16] this concept is expanded to perspective invariant canonical frames. But the canonical frames are also computed using local features of the contour. The local features they use for the computation of canonical frames and for pose estimation are mainly the contact points of bitangents with the contour and points of inflection. For the purpose of pose estimation, the detection of such local features of curved contours in noisy images is relatively instable.

The new method explained in this paper (see also [17]) allows to determine the spatial attitude of planar objects with general curved contours using area moments and canonical frames derived from them (see [9, 11, 13, 8]). The only model data we use are the area moments of the object (up to the third or fourth moments), which can be computed from any representation of the object contour.

2   Approximation of the perspective transformation

For a planar object O, the area moments are defined as follows:

$$m_{ij} = \int\limits_{-\infty}^{\infty} \int\limits_{-\infty}^{\infty} x^i y^j f(x,y)dxdy = \iint\limits_{O} x^i y^j dxdy \quad , \tag{1}$$

with the indicator function $f(x,y)$ taking inside the object O the value 1 and outside the object the value 0.

These area moments we can compute both for the model object from the model data and for the image object from the contour detected in the image.

The perspective mapping of a planar object into the image plane of a camera is a perspective 2D-transformation. If the depth extension of the object is small compared with the distance between object and camera, this perspective transformation can be approximated by an affine transformation. The moments of the image object than can be expressed as a function of the transformation parameters a_{kl} and the moments of the model object. Therefore we obtain the equation system

$$m_{ij}^{[B]} = f_{ij}(a_{kl}, m_{mn}^{[M]}) \quad , \quad (2)$$

where the transformation parameters a_{kl} are unknown. This equation system is nonlinear.

A solution strategy for this nonlinear equation is given by the concept of canonical frames. We determine an affine transformation into a canonical frame by stepwise normalization of certain moments. In [9, 11, 13] some canonical frames are proposed, which are characterized by the normalization rules ($m_{20} = 1; m_{11} = 0; m_{02} = 1; m_{30} + m_{12} = 0$) or ($m_{30} = 0; m_{11} = 0; m_{20} = 1; m_{02} = 1$) or ($m_{31} = 0; m_{13} = 0; m_{20} = 1; m_{02} = 1$). The canonical frames are affine invariant, i.e. if the normalization procedure is realized for an affine copy of the object, the same canonical frame is obtained. Therefore, from the transformations of the model object and the image object into the canonical frame, we can determine the direct affine transformation between model and image object (see figure 1).

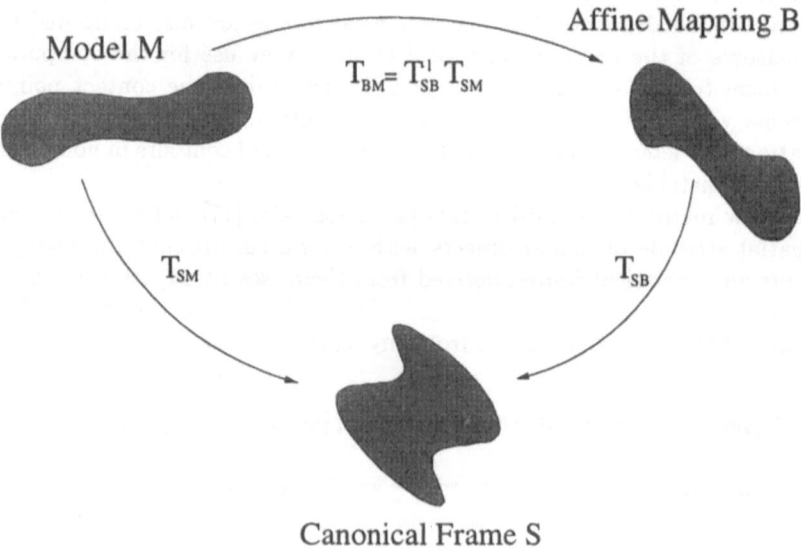

Fig. 1. Determination of an affine transformation using canonical frames

Actually the image object B is just nearly an affine mapping of the model object M because of perspective distortions and other disturbances (noise). Thats why the canonical frames are not exactly identic (see figure 2) and we obtain with $\mathbf{T}_{BM}$ just an approximation of the real transformation between model and image object.

The canonical frames are ambiguous, because the normalized moments of the canonical frames are not changed by reflections and rotations by multiples of $\frac{\pi}{4}$. Other ambiguities comes up, if the objects transformed into their canonical frames are symmetric. Therefore we have to examine all possible transformations $\mathbf{T}_{BM}^{(i)}$ corresponding with these ambiguities. For the first case, a decision can be made comparing the moments of the model object transformed with $\mathbf{T}_{BM}^{(i)}$ and the moments of the image object or by directly comparing the transformed model contour with the image contour. If the normalized objects are symmetric, there remain of course ambiguities.

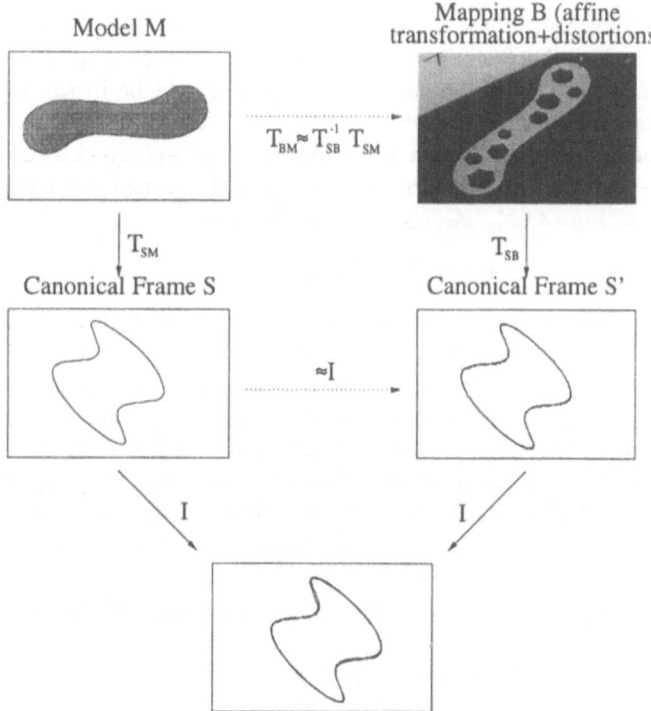

Fig. 2. Approximating a perspective transformation using canonical frames

Figure 3 shows the result of the approximation at the example of a model object and its mapping into the image plane of a simulated camera. The small deviations perceptible in figure 3 are caused by perspective distortions.

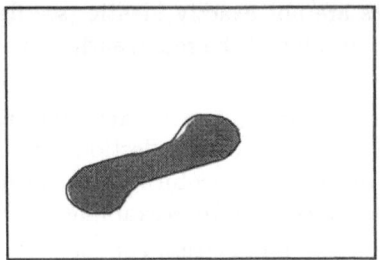

Fig. 3. Affine Approximation of a
perspectively mapped object

3 Reconstruction of the object position

The position of an object is described by an Euclidean Transformation (translation and rotation) between a model coordinate system Σ_M and the world coordinate system Σ_W. The planar model object should be in the x-y-plane of the model coordinate system.

The perspective mapping of a point $\mathbf{p}_M = (x_M, y_M, z_M, 1)^T$ given in the coordinate system Σ_M by the camera $\mathbf{A}_{BW}$ into the image point $\mathbf{p}_B$ with homogeneous coordinates $(x'_B, y'_B, z'_B)^T$ is described by

$$\mathbf{p}_B = \mathbf{A}_{BW}\mathbf{T}_{WM}\mathbf{p}_M \qquad . \tag{3}$$

$\mathbf{T}_{WM}$ is the unknown Euclidean transformation describing the position of the model object relating to the world coordinate system. The parameters of the camera $\mathbf{A}_{BW}$ are known from a calibration procedure. For any points of the x-y-plane of Σ_M, the perspective mapping with $\mathbf{A}_{BW}\mathbf{T}_{WM}$ into the image plane is approximated by the affine transformation $\mathbf{T}_{BM}$ which we obtained using the moments. Now, we can select three arbitrary points $\mathbf{p}_{Mi} = (x_{Mi}, y_{Mi}, 0, 1)^T$ of the x-y-plane of Σ_M, which must not be collinear, and compute the affine mappings $\mathbf{p}_{Bi} = \mathbf{T}_{BM} \cdot (x_{Mi}, y_{Mi}, 1)^T$. Note, that these three pairs of points are an equivalent description of the affine transformation $\mathbf{T}_{BM}$. Therefore, the points $\mathbf{p}_{Bi}$ are approximations of the real perspective mappings of the corresponding object points:

$$\mathbf{p}_{Bi} \approx \mathbf{A}_{BW}\mathbf{T}_{WM}\mathbf{p}_{Mi} \qquad i = 1, 2, 3 \quad . \tag{4}$$

Equation (4) is a formulation of the triangle pose reconstruction problem, which can be solved analytically (see for example [12, 3]). In the most cases we obtain two solutions for the position of the model coordinate system Σ_M relating to the world coordinate system Σ_W.

4 Approximation errors

In the pairs of corresponding points $(\mathbf{p}_{Mi}, \mathbf{p}_{Bi})$ used for the triangle pose reconstruction, the image points $\mathbf{p}_{Bi}$ are more or less disturbed because we use

T_{BM} instead of $A_{BW}T_{WM}$ to generate them. In the following, we will examine these errors. In [15] are analyzed approximation errors of other affine invariants (length and area relations for example) but this is not directly transferable to our case.

The perspective 2D-transformation between model and image point is exactly described by the equations

$$x_B = \frac{x'_B}{z'_B} = \frac{a_{00}x_M + a_{01}y_M + a_{02}}{a_{20}x_M + a_{21}y_M + a_{22}} \; ; \quad y_B = \frac{y'_B}{z'_B} = \frac{a_{10}x_M + a_{11}y_M + a_{12}}{a_{20}x_M + a_{21}y_M + a_{22}} \quad (5)$$

and approximated by an affine transformation of the form

$$x_B = b_{00}x_M + b_{01}y_M + b_{02} \; ; \quad y_B = b_{10}x_M + b_{11}y_M + b_{12} \quad . \quad (6)$$

The approximation errors are locally variable. Therefore we should select such points with small errors. At first, we want to analyse the existence of points, where the approximation and the exact transformation are equal.

If we substitute in the equations (5) and (6) the linear expressions $a_{00}x_M + a_{01}y_M + a_{02} = u$ and $a_{20}x_M + a_{21}y_M + a_{22} = v$, with the new parameters c_{ij} and d_{ij} we obtain $a_{10}x_M + a_{11}y_M + a_{12} = c_{10}u + c_{11}v + c_{12}$, $b_{00}x_M + b_{01}y_M + b_{02} = d_{00}u + d_{01}v + d_{02}$ and $b_{10}x_M + b_{11}y_M + b_{12} = d_{10}u + d_{11}v + d_{12}$. Equating the right hand sides of the equations (5) and (6), we obtain

$$\frac{u}{v} = d_{00}u + d_{01}v + d_{02}$$
$$\frac{c_{10}u + c_{11}v + c_{12}}{v} = d_{10}u + d_{11}v + d_{12} \quad (7)$$

and with some conversions the 3rd degree polynom for v

$$(d_{10}d_{01} - d_{11}d_{00})v^3 + (c_{11}d_{00} - c_{10}d_{01} + d_{10}d_{02} - d_{12}d_{00} + d_{11})v^2 +$$
$$+ (c_{12}d_{00} - c_{10}d_{02} - c_{11} + d_{12})v - c_{12} = 0 \quad (8)$$

with one or three real solutions for v and accordingly for the points (x_M, y_M), whose affine and perspective mappings are equal. However, we can't compute the coordinates of these points in a practical application.

For illustration, the approximation errors are visualized for some simulated examples. In Figure 4 model objects with the given 3D-position T_{WM} are mapped into the image plane of a virtual camera A_{BW}. The affine transformation T_{BM} between the model and image object was computed using the moments and canonical frames. For all image points we can now compute the corresponding model point by the inverse perspective transformation, and then map it back to the image plane with the affine approximated transformation. The distance between these two points is interpreted as the approximation error and visualized as grey value of the original image point. For better orientation, the contours of the mapped model objects are marked in the images.

At the triangle the approximation error disappears in the corners, because any triangle can be affinely mapped into any other triangle, i.e. also into the

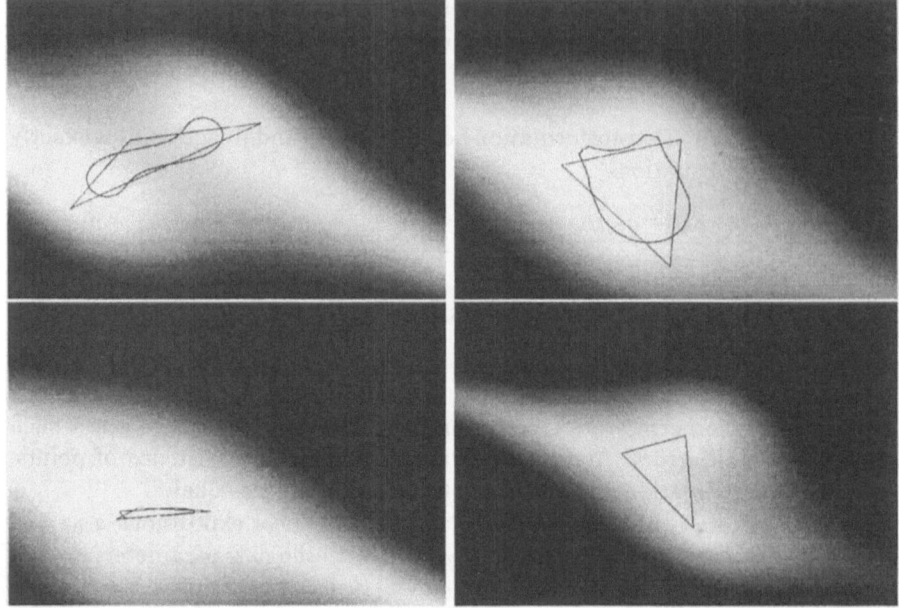

Fig. 4. Approximation errors

perspectively mapped one. For the other model objects in figure 4 the approximation error is smallest near that parts of objects, which are far from the center of gravity (see figure 4, particularly the upper left image). The reason is, that the object points far from the center of gravity have a larger weight in the computation of the moments.

To keep the influence of approximation errors on the reconstruction accuracy small, there should be selected points with large distances from the center of gravity. On the other hand, the points should have large distances between each other, because reconstruction errors with disturbed points become as smaller, as more distant they are. To fulfill these demands, we have fitted a triangle to the model object and use the corners for reconstruction. The corner points of the fitted triangle we obtain by transforming the corner points of a triangle in the canonical frame with $\mathbf{T}_{SM}^{-1}$ ([10, 14]). The fitted triangles are also marked in figure 4.

5 Modified ICP-algorithm

Mapping the model contour into the image plane using the reconstructed position, there occurs deviations from the contour of the image object (see figure 5). To minimize these deviations, the both solutions for the object positions are used as starting solutions for a modified ICP-algorithm (see [1]) shortly outlined in the following.

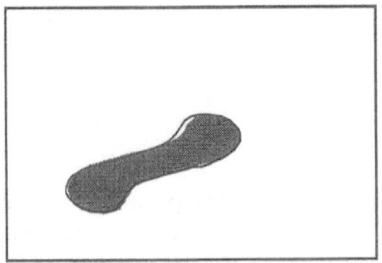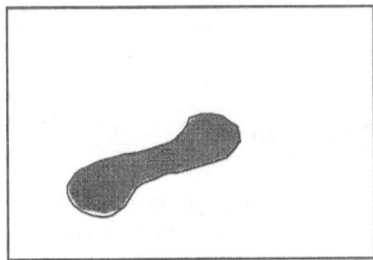

Fig. 5. Position estimation using the affine transformation from figure 3

1. Determination of an initial position estimation $\mathbf{T}_{WM}^{(0)}$.
2. Selection of a set of points P situated at the contour of the model object (for example approximately equidistant points).
3. For all points $\mathbf{p}_i \in P$, the corresponding image point $\mathbf{p}_{Bi} = \left(\frac{\xi_i'}{\tau_i}, \frac{\eta_i'}{\tau_i}\right)$ is computed according to

$$\begin{pmatrix} \xi_i' \\ \eta_i' \\ \tau_i \end{pmatrix} = \mathbf{A}_{BW}\,\mathbf{T}_{WM}^{(k)}\mathbf{p}_i \tag{9}$$

and the nearest point $\mathbf{q}_i$ of the image object contour is searched, i.e. $\|\mathbf{q}_i - \mathbf{p}_{Bi}\| \rightarrow Min$.
4. Using the pairs of points $(\mathbf{p}_i, \mathbf{q}_i)$, a new position estimation $\mathbf{T}_{WM}^{(k+1)}$ is computed by minimization of

$$\sum \|\mathbf{A}_{BW}\mathbf{T}_{WM}^{(k+1)}\mathbf{p}_i - \mathbf{q}_i\| \quad . \tag{10}$$

5. If any distance between $\mathbf{T}_{WM}^{(k)}$ and $\mathbf{T}_{WM}^{(k+1)}$ is less than a given value, the iteration is finished, else continue with 3.

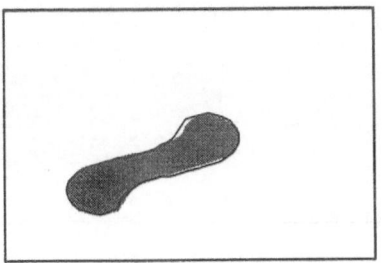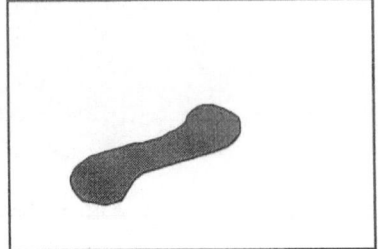

Fig. 6. Position estimation by modified ICP algorithm using the results of figure 5 as starting solutions

The figure 6 shows the results of this iteration for the two starting solutions from figure 5. The solution according to the right image meets exactly the real object position though the starting solution differs some millimeters from this position.

6   Example

In an experiment (figures 7 and 8), the pose of an working piece was estimated using the contour detected in the image of a real scene. In figure 7, for the two reconstruction solutions, the model contours are mapped into the image. Figure 8 shows analogous the results of the following iteration with the modified ICP algorithm.

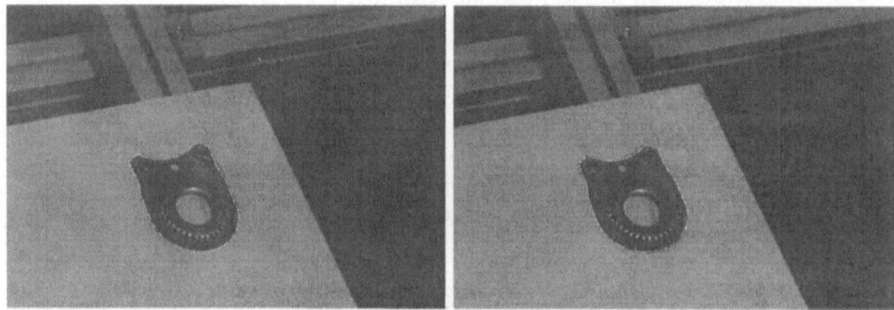

Fig. 7. Initial position estimation ($\mathbf{T}_{WM}^{(0)}$)using moments

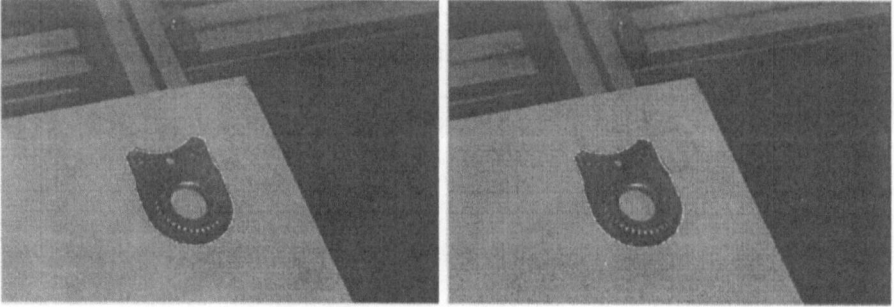

Fig. 8. Results of iteration

Obviously, one of the two solutions (solution 2 in table 1) is nearly identical with the reference measurement. The other solution differs noticeable from the actual position. However, the mappings of the model object for both solutions have just small deviations to the image object. Therefore, in many practical cases it will be impossible to verify the solutions using these deviations alone. For this

Table 1. Normal vector n and translation vector t of the object position

	Solution 1		Solution 2	
	n	t	n	t
Reference measurement	0.00	30.0	0.00	30.0
	-1.00	-36.0	-1.00	-36.0
	0.00	57.0	0.00	57.0
Reconstruction using	-0.72	51.1	-0.01	33.6
moments	-0.34	0.2	-1.00	-33.1
	-0.61	76.8	-0.04	58.1
Iteration	-0.69	41.6	0.00	30.0
	-0.40	-18.7	-1.00	-39.0
	-0.61	66.8	-0.04	56.9

verification should be used additional information like the normal vector of the plane, the planar object is lying on. For three dimensional objects, such parts of the object could be used for verification, which are outside the plane defined by the surface used for the pose reconstruction.

The precision of the pose reconstruction depends strongly on the precision of contour detection. There were particularly notable deviations in translation, if the detected image contour runs partially along the boundaries of the upper and the lower surfaces of the object, because the lateral surfaces of flat objects often are not recognizable.

7 Conclusion

The proposed algorithm allows the model based monocular pose reconstruction of planar objects or surfaces with general curved contours. It uses global object features and is thereby robust according noise. On the other hand, it needs the whole object or surface to be seen. Reconstruction errors, which occurs because of an approximation of the perspective transformation by an affine transformation, are minimized by a following Iteration.

Note, that by analogy the correspondence problem of unordered point sets can be solved under the condition, that the point sets contain mainly corresponding points and one point set is nearly an affine transformation of the other, i.e the deviations from an affine transformation are small in relation to the distance of the points between each other. An affine transformation can be determined using the geometrical moments of the point sets. By transforming the points of one set and searching the nearest point of the other set, the corresponding point is found.

References

[1] P.J. Besl, N.D. McKay, "A Method for registration of 3D-Shapes", IEEE Trans. Pattern Analysis and Machine Intelligence, vol. 14, pp. 239-256, 1992

[2] N. Daucher, M. Dhome, J.T. Lapreste, G. Rives, "Modelled object pose estimation and tracking by monocular vision", Proc. 4. BMVC, Guildford 1993, pp. 249-258

[3] M. Dhome, M. Richetin, J.T. Lapreste, G. Rives, "Determination of the attitude of 3D-objects from a single perspective view", IEEE Trans. Pattern Analysis and Machine Intelligence, vol. 11, pp. 1265-1278, 1989

[4] R. Kumar, A.R. Hanson, "Robust methods for estimating pose and sensitivity analysis", CVGIP-IU 60, pp. 313-342, 1994

[5] Y. Lamdan, J.T. Schwartz, H.J. Wolfson, "Object recognition by affine invariant matching", Proc. CVPR, 1988, p. 335-344

[6] S. Linnainmaa, D. Harwood, L.S. Davis: Pose determination of a three-dimensional object using triangle pairs. IEEE Trans. Pattern Analysis and Machine Intelligence, vol. 10, pp. 634-647, 1988

[7] Y. Liu, T.S. Huang, O.D. Faugeras, "Determination of camera location from 2D to 3D line and point correspondences", Proc. IEEE Conf. on Computer Vision and Pattern Recognition 1988, pp. 82-89

[8] I. Rothe, H. Süße, K. Voss, "The method of normalization to determine invariants", IEEE Trans. Pattern Analysis and Machine Intelligence, vol. 18, pp. 366-376, 1995

[9] H. Süße, K. Voss, "Affine Standardlagen und Separationsmethode", Proc. 16. DAGM-Symp., Wien 1994, pp. 409-416

[10] H. Süße, K. Voss, "Fitting von Objekten durch Superquadriken", Proc. 18. DAGM-Symp., Heidelberg 1996, pp. 29-36

[11] K. Voss, H. Süße, "Adaptive Modelle und Invarianten für zweidimensionale Bilder", Aachen: Verlag Shaker, 1995

[12] K. Voss, R. Neubauer, M. Schubert, "Monokulare Rekonstruktion für Robotvision", Aachen: Verlag Shaker, 1995

[13] K. Voss, H. Süße, I. Rothe, "Affine normalization of planar regions by moments using a new separation method", Proc. Europe-China Workshop on Geometrical Modeling and Invariants for Computer Vision. Xian, China 1995, pp. 356-359

[14] K.Voss, H. Suesse, "Invariant fitting of planar objects by primitives", IEEE Trans. Pattern Analysis and Machine Intelligence, vol. 19, pp. 80-84, 1997

[15] Yu Cheng, "Analysis of affine invariants as approximate perspective invariants", CVIU-63, pp. 197-207, 1996

[16] A. Zissermann, D.A. Forsyth, J.L. Mundy, C.A. Rothwell, "Recognizing general curved objects efficiently", In: J.L. Mundy, A. Zissermann (eds.), "Geometric Invariance in Computer Vision", Cambridge, Massachusetts: The MIT Press, 1992, pp. 228-251

[17] M. Schubert, K. Voss, "Monokulare Lagerekonstruktion für beliebig geformte planare Objekte", Proc. 18. DAGM-Symp., Heidelberg 1996, pp. 29-36

CAD based 3d object recognition on range images

Björn Krebs and Friedrich M. Wahl

1   Introduction

In industrial manufacturing the production process still is separated from the design level. But, the growing need for a higher standard of quality, a higher variety of products and a more flexible production forces to bring the separated fields together. Only a broad communication between all levels can guarantee that the causes for malfunctions are eliminated early and quickly. Thus, it is desirable to use general CAD descriptions at all levels of manufacturing. One step towards this direction is the new field called *CAD Based Vision* (CBV) introducing usual CAD object representations into the computer vision community (e. g. [7, 13, 16]).

In this paper we propose a new contribution to CBV. Model based object recognition is widely accepted as a robust method because meaningful a priori knowledge of objects can be incorporated into the recognition process itself. Section 2 describes new techniques to extract discriminative features from range data. A feature extraction from arbitrary CAD models allows to compute initial matching proposals (section 3). A procedure to improve a primary estimation of an object location is the ICP (Iterative Closest Point) algorithm proposed by Besl and McKay which computes a transformation to map a point set onto any CAD model by minimizing the distance between corresponding points [1]. Nevertheless, the algorithm is not able to provide a proper segmentation of the data. Hence, the ICP algorithm is applied mostly for object matching or tracking of single objects (e. g. [8, 17]) or to compute camera movements (e. g. [14, 23]).

In section 4 we propose a *Fuzzy ICP* algorithm which separates adjacent objects properly. In section 5 we show how the results of the Fuzzy ICP are used to determine the best match via an *evidence of reference*. Our objects have been designed with AUTOCAD and subsequently have been produced with a three axis NC milling machine. Experimental results with these objects are shown in section 6.

2   3d approximation of planar patches from range images

The sensor data is acquired by a range sensor based on the coded light approach (CLA) proposed by Wahl [20]. To achieve a complete measurement of the work space we use a depths-eye-in-hand configuration [18].

Since the data is noisy, sparse and contains many outliers we propose a fast and robust 3d approximation technique of planar patches which give an estimation of the object's surfaces. Subsequently, a set of features has to be computed from the extracted planar patches to generate initial matching proposals.

To compute the approximating planar patch through a set of points we have to look at the following minimization problem: the sum of the errors ε_i of each point P_i to the approximating planar patch has to be minimized:

$$\varepsilon(\alpha, \beta, d_h) = \sum_{i=1}^{n}(x_i \cos\alpha \cos\beta + z_i \sin\alpha \cos\beta + y_i \sin\beta - d_h)^2 \quad \to min \quad (1)$$

The minimum of the error function is found by computing the zero-values of the partial derivatives:

$$\beta = \frac{1}{2}arctan2(-D, \frac{1}{2}E) \quad (2)$$

$$C = (\bar{x}, \bar{y}, \bar{z}) \quad (3)$$

The values $\bar{x}$, $\bar{y}$ and $\bar{z}$ are means of the respective coordinates. Thus the centroid $C = (\bar{x}, \bar{y}, \bar{z})$ lies in the planar patch. A planar patch $[\mathcal{N}, \mathcal{C}]$ is defined by the patch normal $\mathcal{N} = [\cos(\alpha)\cos(\beta), \sin(\beta), \sin(\alpha)\cos(\beta)]$ and a point on the patch, i.e. $\mathcal{C}$.

$$d = \sum_{i=1}^{n} y_i z_i + \frac{\sum_{i=1}^{n} y_i \sum_{i=1}^{n} z_i}{n}$$

$$e = \sum_{i=1}^{n} x_i y_i + \frac{\sum_{i=1}^{n} x_i \sum_{i=1}^{n} y_i}{n}$$

$$f = \sum_{i=1}^{n} x_i^2 - \frac{\sum_{i=1}^{n} x_i \sum_{i=1}^{n} x_i}{n}$$

$$g = \sum_{i=1}^{n} z_i^2 - \frac{\sum_{i=1}^{n} z_i \sum_{i=1}^{n} z_i}{n}$$

$$h = \sum_{i=1}^{n} y_i^2 - \frac{\sum_{i=1}^{n} y_i \sum_{i=1}^{n} y_i}{n}$$

$$D = e\cos(\alpha) + d\sin(\alpha)$$

$$E = h - f\cos^2(\alpha) - g\sin^2(\alpha) - 2a\sin(\alpha)\cos(\alpha)$$

The values a, d, e, f, g, h are terms of the coordinates and D, E are functions of α. Thus, the partial solution for β depends on the angle α which is a orthographic projection onto the x-z-plane. Therefore, the angle α can be computed prior to the angle β by projecting the data orthographically onto the x-z-plane and computing a polygonal approximation of the projected data.

But, we still face the problem to find a proper segmentation of the range data.

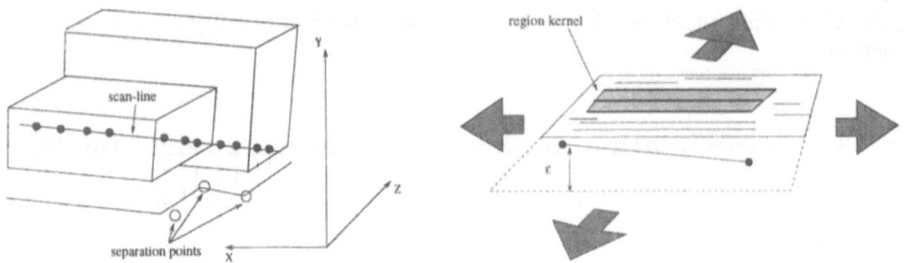

Figure 1: Computation a linear approximation of the scan-lines and subsequently planar region growing as an approximation of the object's surfaces

The process of a 3d approximation can be speed up by using the image order for an image segmentation [10, 15]. In [3] we have shown that the image order provide topological information of the 3d points as well: All points belonging to a row j in the image lie in a *plane of camera projection* P_c defined by the image row j and the focal point F. The plane of camera projection intersects the object's surface in a *scan-line*. By choosing the z-axis perpendicular to the image plane, the x-z-plane and all planes of camera projection belong to the same pencil of planes. Projecting the 3d scan-line orthographically onto the x-z-plane the scan-line is mapped into a 2d curve. The normal $N_{xz} = [\cos(\alpha), 0, \sin(\alpha)]$ at a point of the curve is an orthographic projection of the surface normal $\mathcal{N}$. The angle α can be found by the polygonal approximation of the projected scan-line:

$$\varepsilon(\alpha, d_{h_{xz}}) = \sum_{i=1}^{n} (x_i \cos(\alpha) + z_i \sin(\alpha) - d_{h_{xz}})^2 \quad \rightarrow min \qquad (4)$$

Setting the partial derivatives to zero yields a solution for the angle α:

$$\alpha = \frac{1}{2} arctan2(-a, \frac{1}{2}b) \qquad (5)$$

a and b are terms of the x and z-coordinates of the space points:

$$a = \sum_{i=1}^{n} x_i z_i + \frac{\sum_{i=1}^{n} x_i \sum_{i=1}^{n} z_i}{n} \qquad b = \sum_{i=1}^{n} z_i^2 - \sum_{i=1}^{n} x_i^2 + \frac{(\sum_{i=1}^{n} x_i)^2 - (\sum_{i=1}^{n} z_i)^2}{n}$$

A proper segmentation of a noisy and sparse set of 3d points into a set of planar patches can be computed by a two step algorithm: In the first step line segments are approximated within the x-z-plane of the projected scan-lines by a bisection algorithm for each row j of the image (see Figure 1, left). A second step builds planar patch segments with a region growing algorithm (see Figure 1, right). The new 3d approximation technique computes a set of planar patches from a 512×512 range image within one second on a Sun Sparc V workstation. Since different surfaces are separated properly, the approximation gives a robust segmentation of the sensor data (see Figure 2). A set of three adjacent patches intersecting at one point determine the six degrees of freedom of an object. Thus, it is very easy to extract initial locations for objects in scenes. Curved surfaces are approximated by several planar patches (see example in Figure 3). As we will see, the planar approximation is sufficient for feature matching; no extraction of higher order surfaces is necessary. Furthermore, the planar patches have well defined geometrical properties which allow to build a world map of the observed scene using Kalman filter techniques to combine the planar patches of all acquired views *(view fusion)*. This even allows to compute features of patches retrieved from different views.

3   Feature extraction from CAD models

Arbitrary CAD models consist of various different types of object definitions, e. g. free-form surfaces like rational/non-rational Bezier, B-spline or NURBS patches (e. g. [4, 5]). A feature extraction has to cope with all these different types of object descriptions. A feature which is extracted from a geometric

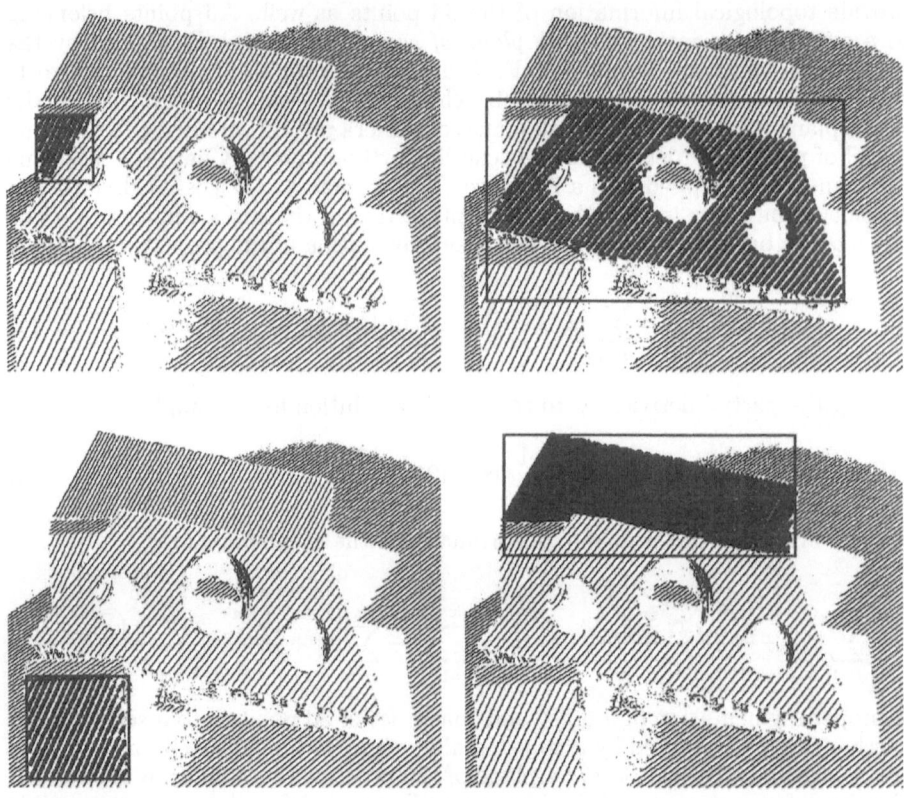

Figure 2: Results of planar patch segmentation of an example scene

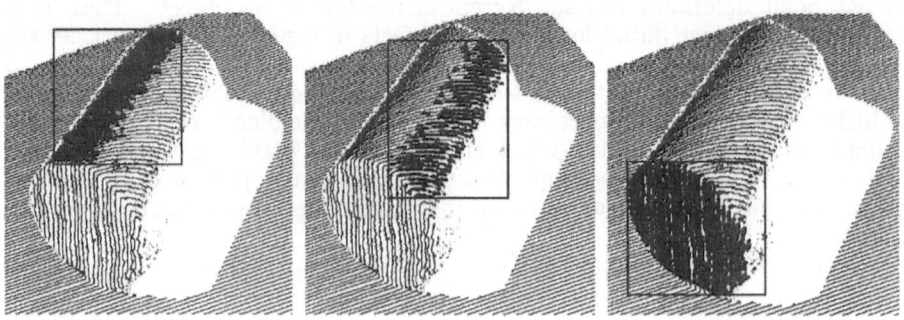

Figure 3: A curved surface is approximated by several planar patches.

model should have a strong geometric meaning. Furthermore, it should bind all degrees of freedom to allow efficient computation of an object's location. In real world scenes objects overlap generally. Hence, a feature has to be derived from a local portion of an object's surface. This so called *local feature focus* has been proved to be a robust method in several applications (e. g. [6, 19]). A feature

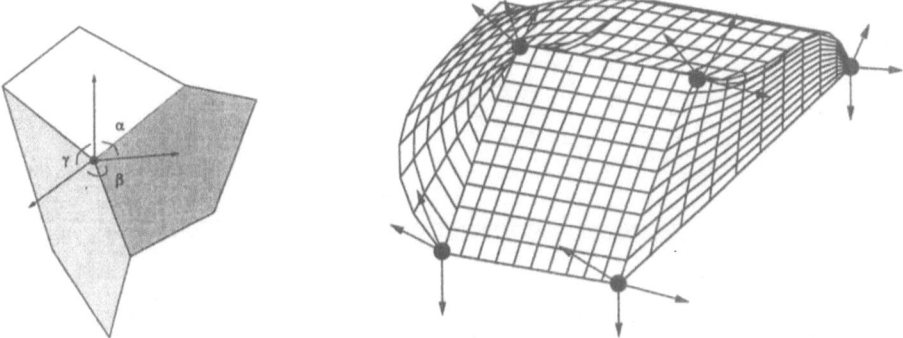

Figure 4: A feature point is defined by three adjacent surfaces.

should help to identify an object and therefore, should mark only a prominent surface part. In industrial applications objects have several corners, edges and rims. The feature extraction exploits these properties to enable simple and fast matching. Hence, *feature points* are extracted from a CAD model where three adjacent surfaces touch only with a C^0-continuity, i. e. at a corner (see Figure 4). Only border points and surface normals have to be derived from the CAD descriptions. At each feature point the normals of the adjacent surfaces define a local coordinate system. Therefore, it is easy to compute a transformation which describes the object's location with computed features from sensor data. Furthermore, the angles between the normals provide a characteristic measure to distinguish different object types.

in addition to this, surface parts with maxima / minima or significant changes of the surface curvature characterize prominent feature points as well. Such feature points can be computed by a polygonal approximation of a free-form object (see example in Figure 5). Each free-form surface is subdivided until the bounding box converges to a plane using a subdivision method [5]. Adjacent planar patches intersect at a point which provides an approximation of the surface location where the surface curvature is changing significantly. To allow efficient matching all feature points and their associated transformations are stored in a hash-table. A hash-key is computed from the angles between surface normals. Thus, leading to an efficient and robust matching algorithm calculating initial matching proposals from extracted sensor data. Furthermore, a simple preprocessing can build the hash-tables off-line.

4   The fuzzy ICP algorithm

Having computed a set of matching proposals which describe possible locations of objects in an observed scene, we now have to determine which of the proposals

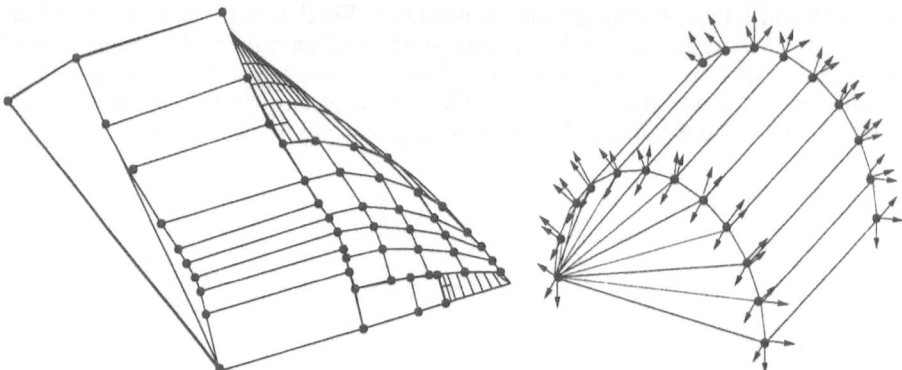

Figure 5: A planar approximation of object surfaces defines further feature points.

lead to correct matches. Given an initial transformation (rotation R^0, translation t^0) of a data shape, i. e. a point set $P = \{p_1, \ldots, p_N\} \subset \Re^3$ to a model shape X_m. In the k-th iteration the ICP algorithm computes a *corresponding point set* $X^k = \{x_1^k, \ldots, x_N^k\} \subset \Re^3$. Using X^k the transformation (R^k, t^k) is updated until the change in the average distance falls below a threshold ε_{icp}, i. e. terminates in the k_t-th iteration [1]:

1. Set $Q^0 = \{q_i^0 \mid q_i^0 = R^0 p_i + t^0, p_i \in P\}$
2. Compute $x_i^k \in X^k$ that $\|x_i^k - q_i^k\|^2 \to min$
3. Compute R^k and t^k that $\sum_{\forall i} \|R^k p_i + t^k - x_i^k\|^2 \to min$
4. Set $Q^{k+1} = \{q_i^{k+1} \mid q_i^{k+1} = R^k p_i + t^k, p_i \in P\}$
5. $\bar{d}^{k+1} = \frac{1}{N} \sum_{i=1}^{N} d_i^{k+1}$, with $d_i^{k+1} = \|q_i^{k+1} - x_i^k\|$
6. Repeat from step 2 until $(\Delta\bar{d} = |\bar{d}^{k+1} - \bar{d}^k|) < \varepsilon_{icp}$

The translation t and the Rotation R are computed by a least square registration minimizing the average distance

$$\bar{d} = \frac{1}{N} \sum_{i=1}^{N} d_i \qquad (6)$$

described by Horn [9]. This method defines the transformation with respect to the centroids $\bar{p}$, $\bar{x}$ and the matrix Σ_{px}:

$$\bar{p} = \frac{1}{N} \sum_{i=1}^{N} p_i, \qquad \bar{x} = \frac{1}{N} \sum_{i=1}^{N} x_i, \qquad (7)$$

$$\Sigma_{px} = \frac{1}{N} \sum_{i=1}^{N} (p_i - \bar{p})(x_i - \bar{x})^T \qquad (8)$$

The algorithm always converges monotonically to a local minimum [1]. But, the algorithm fails if only a subset of the data shape matches with a part of the model shape. Zhang proposes a method to discard points from the iteration set Q^k [23]:

$$Q^{k+1} = Q^k - \{q_i^k \mid q_i^k < d_{max}\} \tag{9}$$

$$\begin{array}{ll} \mu < D & d_{max} = \sigma + 3\mu \\ \mu < 3D & d_{max} = \sigma + 2\mu \\ \mu < 6D & d_{max} = \sigma + \mu \\ \text{else} & d_{max} = \mu \end{array} \qquad \text{with} \quad \mu = \frac{1}{N}\sum_{i=1}^{N} d_i^k,$$

$$\sigma = \sqrt{\frac{1}{N}\sum_{i=1}^{N}(d_i^k - \mu)^2}.$$

This is only reasonable if the distance of an outlier significantly differs from a point belonging to the object. However, it is impossible to decide at each iteration level which points really belong to the object. Hence, the ICP is not able to provide a segmentation of the data.

To model imprecise properties of varying degree Zadeh introduced *fuzzy sets* ([21, 22]). To model the uncertain membership we expand the iteration set Q^k to a fuzzy set $F^k = (Q^k, \mu_X)$, defined by a membership function μ_X. There are various membership functions applied in fuzzy clustering (e. g. [2, 11, 12]). But we achieved sufficient results with a simple linear membership function:

$$w_i^k = \mu_X(q_i^k) = \begin{cases} 1 - \frac{d_i^k}{d_{max}} & d_i^k < d_{max} \\ 0 & d_i^k \geq d_{max} \end{cases} \tag{10}$$

The membership function μ_X provides a weight w_i^k for each point $q_i^k \in Q^k$. The mean distance from (6) has to be changed to:

$$\bar{d} = \frac{\sum_{i=1}^{n} w_i^k d_i}{\sum_{i=1}^{n} w_i^k} \tag{11}$$

To integrate the concept of fuzzy sets into the ICP algorithm we only have to change (7) and (8) to:

$$\bar{p} = \frac{1}{N_{value}}\sum_{i=1}^{N} w_i^k p_i, \qquad \bar{x} = \frac{1}{N_{value}}\sum_{i=1}^{N} w_i^k x_i, \tag{12}$$

$$\Sigma_{px} = \frac{1}{N_{value}}\sum_{i=1}^{N} w_i^k (p_i - \bar{p})(x_i - \bar{x})^T, N_{value} = \sum_{i=1}^{N} w_i^k. \tag{13}$$

To guarantee stability in the transformation we defuzzify Q^k after each iteration and update with:

$$Q^{k+1} = Q^k - \{q_i^k \mid \mu_X^k(q_i^k) < \kappa_0\}, \quad \kappa_0 \in [0,1] \tag{14}$$

Furthermore, this will speed up the computation, especially if many objects are present. So, if the first estimation is good enough, points with a very small membership value can be discarded like Zhang proposed. Now, we are able to provide a proper 3d segmentation of the data samples. The experiments show that the transformation computed with the fuzzy ICP fits the data better than the crisp ICP (see section 6). The mean distance after termination $\bar{d}^{k_t}$ indicates how good the set Q^{k_t} fits the model shape.

5   Evidence for correct matching

After applying the Fuzzy ICP algorithm we still face the problem whether X_m of the model base $B_M = \{X_1, \ldots, X_M\}$ is the correct model to describe P. The resulting iteration set Q^{k_t} of the Fuzzy ICP algorithm is defuzzified with (14) providing the set Q^* of *verified inliers*. Now, we have to determine how much of the model surface is referenced by the used part of the point set P, i.e Q^*. For each model X_m a *set of representative points* $S = \{s_1, \ldots, s_n\}$ is referenced with Q^*. To guarantee reasonable results and to be independent of the point density, all points in S must be spaced almost equidistantly:

$$\forall s \in S \, \neg \exists \, \acute{s} \in S \quad \|s - \acute{s}\| < d_a \tag{15}$$

d_a should be small enough to represent the surface correctly.
The degree of how much X_m is referenced by Q^* is defined by the set:

$$C_R = \{(s_i, q_j^*) \mid s_i \in S, q_j^* \in Q^*, \|s_i - q_j^*\| < d_a\} \tag{16}$$

A value to validate the reference is given by the *reference evidence*:

$$e_{C_R} = \frac{|C_R|}{|S|} \tag{17}$$

The following algorithm computes the reference evidence e_{C_R} for a point set P and a model shape X_m, given the set of representatives S of X_m and $m = |S|$:

1. For each point $s_i \in S$ compute the closest point $q_j \in Q^*$
2. Count the number n of points q_j with $\|q_j - s_i\| < d_a$
3. The reference evidence is given by $e_{C_R} = \frac{n}{m} * 100\%$

6   Experimental results and conclusions

In the example scene of Figure 6a an initial transformation for the polyhedral object is improved by the Fuzzy ICP to a location shown in Figure 6b. The crisp and the fuzzy evaluation have been applied for comparison purposes. The crisp ICP can't separate the objects correctly, many points from other objects are still considered to be inliers (see Figure 6c). Furthermore, the calculated transformation is not correct. The Fuzzy ICP detects all proper inliers and calculates a transformation which fits the data very well (see Figure 6d). As a result of the better transformation, the mean distance achieved by the Fuzzy ICP ($\bar{d} = 0.496$) is far lower than the one achieved by the crisp ICP ($\bar{d} = 7.431$). In the scene of Figure 6 we look for the best match of the polyhedral object. Several matching proposals with different estimations of the location and orientation of the object are tested. The fuzzy ICP and the evidence accumulation algorithm are applied for each matching proposal. Only the simultaneous consideration of the reference evidence and the mean distance makes a reliable decision possible. The best match has a low average distance and a high reference evidence. If the reference evidence of an incorrect match is high the mean distance is high, too. But if the mean distance is low for an incorrect match then the referenced surface is quite small. Thus, the correct match can be distinguished from the wrong matches

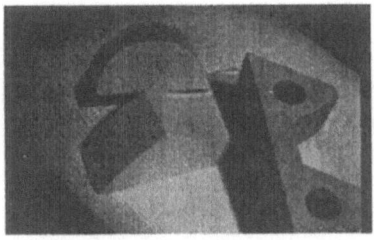 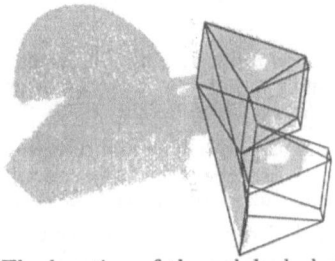

a.) A scene with overlapping objects   b.) The location of the polyhedral object

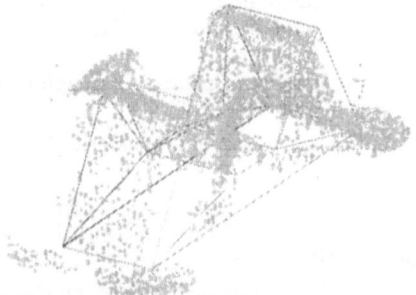 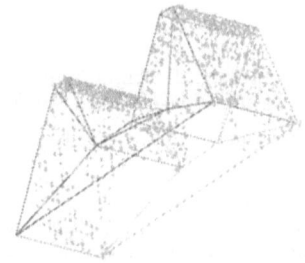

c.) The inliers of the crisp valuation   d.) The inliers of the fuzzy valuation

Figure 6: The Fuzzy ICP gives a proper segmentation of complex scenes.

quite clearly.

In this paper we have proposed new methods incorporating CAD object descriptions in 3d object recognition. An efficient and robust matching algorithm calculates initial matching proposals from extracted sensor data using hash-tables for storing feature points. The hash-tables are constructed off-line in a simple preprocessing. A new approach for 3d matching which allows extensive use of free form object models determines the correct match from the set of initial matching proposals. The introduced *Fuzzy ICP* algorithm can separate data from overlapping objects. Furthermore, we proposed an evidence accumulation, which determines how good the sensor data references a model shape.

References

[1] P. J. Besl and N. D. McKay. A method for registration of 3-d shapes. *IEEE Transactions on Pattern Analysis and Machine Intelligence*, 12(2):239–256, 1992.

[2] J. C. Bezdek and S. K. Pal. *Fuzzy Models For Pattern Recognition*. IEEE Press, New York, 1992.

[3] B.Krebs and F. M. Wahl. Efficient planar patch segmentation of range images via 3d approximation. Technical Report 12-94-1, Institute of Robotics and Computer Control, TU Braunschweig, 1994.

[4] W. Boehm, W. Farin, and G. Kaufmann. A survey of curve and surface methods in cagd. *Computer Aided Geometric Design*, 1:1–60, 1984.

[5] G. E. Farin. *Curves and Surfaces for Computer Aided Geometric Design, a Practical Guide 3rd. ed.* Academic Press, New York, 1993.

[6] P. J. Flynn and A. K. Jain. 3d object recognition using invariant feature indexing of interpretation tables. *Computer Vision, Graphics, and Image Processing*, 55(2):119–129, 1992.

[7] L. Grewe and A. Kak. Interactive learning of a multiple-attributed hash table classifier for fast object recognition. *Int. J. of Computer Vision and Image Understanding*, 61(3):387–416, 1995.

[8] K. Higuchi, M. Hebert, and K. Ikeuchi. Bulding 3-d models from unregisterd range images. In *Proc. IEEE International Conference on Robotics and Automation, San Diego, California*, pages 2248–2253, 1994.

[9] B. K. P. Horn. Closed-form solution of absolute orientation using unit quaternions. *J. Opt. Soc. of America*, 4(4):629–642, 1987.

[10] X. Y. Jiang and H. Bunke. Fast segmentation of range images into planar regions by scan line grouping. *I. J. of Machine Visions and Applications*, 7(2):115–122, 1994.

[11] R. Krishnapuram, H.Frigui, and O. Nasraoi. Surface approximation through fuzzy shell clustering. *IEEE Trans. on Fuzzy Systems*, 1:98–110, 1993.

[12] R. Krishnapuram and J. M. Keller. A possibilistic approach to clustering. *IEEE Trans. on Fuzzy Systems*, 1(2):98–110, 1993.

[13] J. Mao, A. K. Jain, and P. J. Flynn. Integration of multiple feature groups and multiple views into an 3d object recognition system. In *Proc.CAD-Based Vision Workshop, Champion, Pennsylvania*, pages 184–192, 1994.

[14] T. Masuda and N. Yokova. A robust method for registration and segmentation of multiple range images. *Int. J. of Computer Vision and Image Understanding*, 61(3):295–307, 1995.

[15] T. Pavlidis. Segmentation of pictures and maps through functional approximation. *Computer Graphics Image Processing*, 1:360–372, 1976.

[16] L. G. Shapiro, S. L. Tanimoto, and J. F. Brinkley. A visual database system for data experiment management in model-based computer vision. In *Proc.CAD-Based Vision Workshop, Champion, Pennsylvania*, pages 64–74, 1994.

[17] D. A. Simon, M. Hebert, and T. Kanade. Real-time 3-d pose estimation using a high-speed range sensor. In *Proc. IEEE International Conference on Robotics and Automation, San Diego, California*, volume 3, pages 2235–2240, 1994.

[18] T. Stahs and F. Wahl. Fast and versatile range data acquisition in a robot work cell. In *Proc IEEE International Conference on Intelligent Robots and Systems, Raleigh, North Carolina*, pages 1169–1174, 1992.

[19] T. Stahs and F. M. Wahl. Object recognition and pose estimation with a fast and versatile 3d robot sensor. In *Proc. International Conference on Pattern Recognition, The Hague, Netherlands*, 1992.

[20] F. M. Wahl. A coded light approach for depth map aquisition. In G. Hartmann, editor, *8.DAGM-Symposium Paderborn*. Springer-Verlag, 1986.

[21] L. A. Zadeh. Fuzzy sets. *J. Inform. Control*, 8:338–353, 1965.

[22] L. A. Zadeh. Outline of a new approach to the analysis of complex systems and decision processes. *IEEE Trans. Syst, Man. ,Cybern*, SMC-3(1):28–44, 1973.

[23] Z. Zhang. Iterative point matching for registration of free-form curves and surfaces. *Int. J. of Computer Vision*, 13(2):119–152, 1994.

Dual quaternions for absolute orientation and hand-eye calibration

Konstantinos Daniilidis

1 Introduction

Many computer vision problems involving three dimensional motion necessitate an efficient representation for 3D displacement that enhances the understanding of the problem and facilitates linear solutions of low complexity. The most common representation is a rotation about an axis through the origin followed by a translation and represented by an orthogonal matrix and a vector, respectively. An alternative representation to orthogonal matrices are the unit quaternions already used in several vision algorithms [4] which still use the translation as a separate unknown. From Chasles' theorem [1] it is known that a rigid transformation can be modeled as a rotation about an axis not through the origin and a translation along this axis. This well known screw transformation can be algebraically modeled using dual vectors, matrices or quaternions [5].

We first give an exposition on the properties of dual numbers and dual quaternions. Then we describe how a line transformation is expressed with dual quaternions and how we obtain a dual quaternion from the $(\boldsymbol{R}, \vec{\boldsymbol{t}})$-representation. The dual quaternion is given as a function of the screw parameters.

The estimation of *absolute orientation* involves the computation of the relative displacement between two 3D coordinate systems given correspondences of 3D-features measured in these systems. Measurements may be reconstructed features in stereoscopic systems or range sensors. Plenty of algorithms exist for the computation of absolute orientation from point and line segments correspondences (refer to [12] for a survey). Dual quaternions were used in case of given both line and point correspondences in [15] and in the exterior orientation or pose estimation in [11]. We propose a new linear absolute orientation algorithm with the screw parameters as unknowns.

The second accomplishment of this paper is a new modeling and solution for the hand-eye calibration problem. Hand-eye calibration is called the computation of the relative position and orientation between the robot gripper and a camera mounted rigidly on the gripper. This problem concerns also all sensors that are rigidly mounted on mechanical links, like a camera mounted on a binocular head with mechanical degrees of freedom as well as a camera mounted on a vehicle. Many algorithms using traditional displacement representations were already proposed [13, 14]. Based on the insight of Chen [2] we prove algebraically that hand-eye calibration is independent of the angle and pitch of the camera and motor displacements. Furthermore, we show that hand-eye calibration can be reduced to the problem of absolute orientation from line correspondences. We find the simultaneous solution for translation and rotation [6], however, using only the relevant information (screw axes) and, even more important, avoiding a nonlinear minimization.

2   Dual quaternions

This section outlines briefly the dual quaternions. First quaternions are explained followed by a short description of dual numbers. Finally, the dual quaternions and their relevant properties are introduced.

Quaternions are an extension of the complex numbers to $\mathbb{R}^4$. Among other formalisms one definition of quaternions is as pairs $(s, \vec{q})$ where $s \in \mathbb{R}$ and $\vec{q} \in \mathbb{R}^3$. The following operations

$$q_1 + q_2 = (s_1 + s_2, \vec{q}_1 + \vec{q}_2) \tag{1}$$

$$\lambda(s, \vec{q}) = (\lambda s, \lambda \vec{q}), \tag{2}$$

where $\lambda \in \mathbb{R}$ make the quaternions a vector space over the reals - we will call $\mathbb{H}$ - with the zero element $(0,0)$. The multiplication between quaternions defined as

$$q_1 q_2 = (s_1 s_2 - \vec{q}_1^T \vec{q}_2, s_1 \vec{q}_2 + s_2 \vec{q}_1 + \vec{q}_1 \times \vec{q}_2) \tag{3}$$

has a unit element $(1, 0)$ and is associative but not commutative. Therefore the quaternions are an associative algebra and since they do not contain zero-divisors they are a division algebra. The norm of a quaternion is defined as $\|q\|^2 = q\bar{q}$ where $\bar{q}$ is the conjugate quaternion $(s, -\vec{q})$. A subgroup of $\mathbb{H}$ regarding only the multiplication operation are the unit quaternions with norm equal one. For every rotation (element of SO(3)) about an axis $\vec{n}$ ($\|\vec{n}\| = 1$) with an angle θ a corresponding unit quaternion $q = (\cos\frac{\theta}{2}, \sin\frac{\theta}{2}\vec{n})$ exists that maps a vector $\vec{x} \in \mathbb{R}^3$ to the vector $q(0, \vec{x})\bar{q}$.

A *dual number* [1] is defined as

$$\check{z} = a + \epsilon b \quad \text{with} \quad \epsilon^2 = 0 \tag{4}$$

The operations addition and multiplication make them an abelian ring called Δ but not a field because only dual numbers with real part not zero possess an inverse element. An important property is associated with the derivatives of functions with dual arguments. Since all powers greater equal two of ϵ vanish a Taylor expansion yields always

$$f(a + \epsilon b) = f(a) + \epsilon b f'(a). \tag{5}$$

Dual vectors are defined in Δ^3 and with the addition and the external multiplication with a dual number make a module over the ring Δ. Dual vectors with orthogonal real and dual parts are a representation of lines in $\mathbb{R}^3$ known as Plücker coordinates. The real part is the direction of the line and the dual part is its moment. The inner product between two such dual vectors is equal the cosine of a dual angle $\check{\theta} = \theta + \epsilon d$ which has a nice geometric interpretation: θ is the angle between the two space lines and d is their distance.

Dual quaternions are defined in a similar way like real quaternions as $(\check{s}, \check{\vec{q}})$ where $\check{s}$ a dual number and $\check{\vec{q}}$ a dual vector. The operations have the same definitions

$$\check{q}_1 + \check{q}_2 = (\check{s}_1 + \check{s}_2, \check{\vec{q}}_1 + \check{\vec{q}}_2) \tag{6}$$

$$\check{\lambda}(\check{s}, \check{\vec{q}}) = (\check{\lambda}\check{s}, \check{\lambda}\check{\vec{q}}) \tag{7}$$

$$\check{q}_1 \check{q}_2 = (\check{s}_1 \check{s}_2 - \check{\vec{q}}_1^T \check{\vec{q}}_2, \check{s}_1 \check{\vec{q}}_2 + \check{s}_2 \check{\vec{q}}_1 + \check{\vec{q}}_1 \times \check{\vec{q}}_2). \tag{8}$$

The first two (6) and (7) make the dual quaternions a Δ-module. Addition (6) and multiplication (8) make them a non-abelian ring with unit element $(1, 0)$. All three operations make them an associative algebra. Dual vectors $\check{\vec{q}}$ can be written as dual quaternions $(0, \check{\vec{q}})$ and their multiplication possesses the nice property

$$(0, \check{\vec{q}}_1)(0, \check{\vec{q}}_2) = (-\check{\vec{q}}_1^T \check{\vec{q}}_2, \check{\vec{q}}_1 \times \check{\vec{q}}_2). \tag{9}$$

The norm of a dual quaternion is defined as $\|\check{q}\|^2 = \check{q}\bar{\check{q}}$ and is a dual number with positive real part. If the norm has a non vanishing real part than the dual quaternion has an inverse $\check{q}^{-1} = \|\check{q}\|^{-1}\bar{\check{q}}$. If the norm is equal one then an inverse element exists and is equal to the conjugate quaternion. If $\check{q} = q + \epsilon q'$ then the unity condition $\check{q}\bar{\check{q}} = 1$ can be written

$$q\bar{q} = 1 \quad \text{and} \quad \bar{q}q' + \bar{q}'q = 0. \tag{10}$$

As we shall describe in the following unit dual quaternions represent general motions of lines and the expression $\check{q}\check{x}\bar{\check{q}}$ valid for rotation of points in case of real quaternions is also true for general motion of lines in case of dual quaternions.

3 Line transformations with unit dual quaternions

As already known the rotation of a point $\vec{p}_b$ to a point $\vec{p}_a$ can be written by means of a unit quaternion q as the product $\vec{p}_a = q\vec{p}_b\bar{q}$. This form allows the concatenation of rotations to be represented by a simple quaternion product. Unfortunately, no such quaternion representation exists for a general rigid transformation including translation. We will describe in this section that the introduction of dual quaternions allows a rigid transformation rule as simple as the one for pure rotations, however, not for a point but for a line.

A line in space with direction $\vec{l}$ through a point $\vec{p}$ can be represented with the 6-tuple $(\vec{l}, \vec{m})$ where $\vec{m}$ is called the line moment and is equal to $\vec{p} \times \vec{l}$. The line moment is normal to the plane through the line and the origin with magnitude equal to the distance from the line to the origin. The constraints $\|\vec{l}\| = 1$ and $\vec{l}^T \vec{m} = 0$ guarantee that the degrees of freedom of an arbitrary line in space are four.

We next give an answer to the following problem:

> A line given by its dual quaternion $\check{l}_a = l_a + \epsilon m_a$ is transformed with $(R, \vec{t})$ into a line $\check{l}_b$. Show that a unit dual quaternion exists such that $\check{l}_a = \check{q}\check{l}_b\bar{\check{q}}$.

Applying a rotation R and a translation $\vec{t}$ to a line $(\vec{l}_b, \vec{m}_b)$ we obtain the transformed line $(\vec{l}_a, \vec{m}_a)$

$$\vec{l}_a = R\vec{l}_b \tag{11}$$

$$\begin{aligned} \vec{m}_a &= \vec{p}_a \times \vec{l}_a = (R\vec{p}_b + \vec{t}) \times R\vec{l}_b \\ &= R(\vec{p}_b \times \vec{l}_b) + \vec{t} \times R\vec{l}_b = R\vec{m}_b + \vec{t} \times R\vec{l}_b. \end{aligned} \tag{12}$$

If we summarize the Plücker vectors $(\vec{l}, \vec{m})$ into a dual vector $\check{l}$ we obtain the matrix-vector dual representation [10, 8]

$$\check{l}_a = \check{R}\check{l}_b \qquad where \qquad \check{R} = R + \epsilon[\vec{t}]_{\times}R$$

with $[\vec{t}]_{\times}$ the antisymmetric matrix of translation.

We now change from vector to quaternion notation which means that the vector $\vec{l}$ is represented by a quaternion with zero scalar part $l = (0, \vec{l})$. The terms containing rotation can be easily written with quaternions. The difficulty with the cross-product is tackled with the identity

$$(0, \vec{t} \times \vec{q}) = \frac{1}{2}(q\bar{t} + tq) \tag{13}$$

where t is the translation quaternion $(0, \vec{t})$ and q the rotation quaternion $(0, \vec{q})$. Using the identity (13) we obtain

$$\begin{aligned} l_a &= ql_b\bar{q} \\ m_a &= qm_b\bar{q} + \frac{1}{2}(ql_b\bar{q}\bar{t} + tql_b\bar{q}). \end{aligned} \tag{14}$$

We define a new quaternion $q' = \frac{1}{2}tq$ and a dual quaternion $\check{q} = q + \epsilon q'$. It can be easily shown that (14) is equivalent to

$$l_a + \epsilon m_a = (q + \epsilon q')(l_b + \epsilon m_b)(\bar{q} + \epsilon\bar{q}'). \tag{15}$$

Denoting also the lines by dual quaternions $\check{l}_a$ and $\check{l}_b$ we obtain

$$\check{l}_a = \check{q}\check{l}_b\bar{\check{q}}.$$

It should be emphasized that the resulting dual quaternion is a unit dual quaternion:

$$|\check{q}|^2 = \check{q}\bar{\check{q}} = q\bar{q} + \epsilon(q\bar{q}' + q'\bar{q}) = q\bar{q} + \epsilon/2(q\bar{q}\bar{t} + tq\bar{q}) = 1.$$

Given $\vec{q}$ the dual part can be computed as $q' = \frac{1}{2}tq$. Reversely, the translation t can be recovered from the dual quaternion as $t = 2q'\bar{q}$.

3.1 Absolute orientation algorithm

Based on eq. (14) we propose an algorithm for the absolute orientation problem stated as follows:

> Given N 3D-line correspondences $((\vec{l}_a, \vec{m}_a), (\vec{l}_b, \vec{m}_b))$ find the relative displacement expressed as (q, q') between the coordinate systems a and b.

We split eq. (15) in its non-dual

$$l_a = ql_b\bar{q} \tag{16}$$

and dual part:

$$m_a = q l_b \bar{q}' + q m_b \bar{q} + q' l_b \bar{q}. \tag{17}$$

Multiplying both equations on the right with q and applying the identity $\bar{q} q' + \bar{q}' q = 0$ in the first term of the right hand side of the second equation we obtain

$$l_a q = q l_b$$
$$m_a q = -l_a q' + q m_b + q' l_b.$$

The scalar parts of all line quaternions are zero, hence each of the above equations consists actually of three scalar equations. We introduce again the direction and moment vectors of the lines and we rewrite the above equations into a homogeneous linear system

$$\begin{pmatrix} \vec{l}_a - \vec{l}_b & [\vec{l}_a + \vec{l}_b]_\times & 0_{3\times 1} & 0_{3\times 3} \\ \vec{m}_a - \vec{m}_b & [\vec{m}_a + \vec{m}_b]_\times & \vec{l}_a - \vec{l}_b & [\vec{l}_a + \vec{l}_b]_\times \end{pmatrix} \begin{pmatrix} q \\ q' \end{pmatrix} = 0 \tag{18}$$

where the matrix - we will call S - is a 6×8 matrix and the vector of unknowns (q^T, q'^T) is 8-dimensional.

Recall that we have two constraints on the unknowns so that the result is a unit dual quaternion

$$q^T q = 1 \quad \text{and} \quad q^T q' = 0. \tag{19}$$

Unfortunately, the six equations are dependent because the vectors $\vec{l}_a$ and $\vec{l}_b$ are unit vectors and the vectors $\vec{m}_a$ and $\vec{m}_b$ are perpendicular to $\vec{l}_a$ and $\vec{l}_b$, respectively, so that two equations are redundant. As already known [12, 7] we need two non-parallel lines correspondences to solve the absolute orientation problem.

Suppose now that $N \geq 2$ correspondences are given. We construct the $6n \times 8$ matrix

$$T = (\begin{array}{cccc} S_1^T & S_2^T & \cdots & S_n^T \end{array})^T \tag{20}$$

which in the noise-free case has rank 6. Since in the noise-free case the equations arise from natural constraints the null-space contains at least the actual solution (q, q'). It is trivial to see that an additional orthogonal solution is $(0_{4\times 1}, q)$. Hence, the matrix is maximally of rank 6.

We compute the Singular Value Decomposition (SVD) $T = U \Sigma V^T$ where Σ is a diagonal matrix with the singular values, the columns of U are the left singular vectors, and the columns of V are the right singular vectors. If the rank is 6 than the last two right singular vectors $\vec{v}_7$ and $\vec{v}_8$ - corresponding to the two vanishing singular values - span the nullspace of T. We write them as composed of two 4×1 vectors $\vec{v}_7^T = (\vec{u}_1^T, \vec{v}_1^T)$ and $\vec{v}_8^T = (\vec{u}_2^T, \vec{v}_2^T)$. A vector (q^T, q'^T) satisfying $T(q^T, q'^T)^T = 0$ must be a linear combination of $\vec{v}_7$ and $\vec{v}_8$, hence

$$\begin{pmatrix} q \\ q' \end{pmatrix} = \lambda_1 \begin{pmatrix} \vec{u}_1 \\ \vec{v}_1 \end{pmatrix} + \lambda_2 \begin{pmatrix} \vec{u}_2 \\ \vec{v}_2 \end{pmatrix}.$$

The two degrees of freedom are fixed by the constraints (19) which imply two quadratic equations in λ_1 and λ_2. Because the second constraint of (19) is homogeneous in λ_1 and λ_2 the solution can be obtained avoiding a quartic equation.

4   Unit dual quaternions and screws

This section shows that the scalar and the vector part of the dual quaternion have a specific meaning which relates them to the kinematic notion of a screw. According to Chasles' theorem [2] a rigid transformation can be modeled as a rotation about an axis not through the origin and a translation along this axis. As the screw axis is a line in space it depends on four parameters which together with the rotation angle θ and the translation along the axis d (pitch) constitute the six degrees of freedom of a rigid transformation.
In the following we will solve the problem

> *Compute d as well as the screw axis given by its direction and moment pair $(\vec{l}, \vec{m})$ from $\boldsymbol{R}$ and $\vec{t}$.*

The direction $\vec{l}$ is parallel to the rotation axis. The pitch d is the projection of translation on the rotation axis, therefore equal $\vec{t}^T \vec{l}$. In order to recover the moment $\vec{m}$ we introduce a point $\vec{c}$ on the screw axis being the projection of the origin on the axis (Fig. 1).

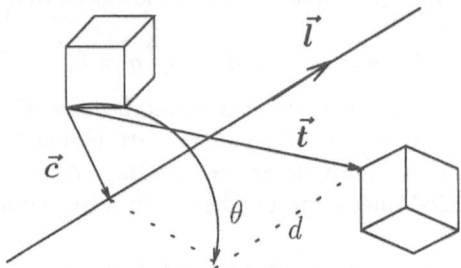

Figure 1: The geometry of a screw: Every motion can be modeled as a rotation with angle θ about an axis at $\vec{c}$ with direction $\vec{l}$ and a subsequent translation d along the axis.

The coordinate system is shifted to this point and then transformed. The resulting translation is then $d\vec{l} + (I - \boldsymbol{R})\vec{c}$. The so called pitch $d = \vec{l}^T \vec{t}$. Using the Rodrigues formula

$$\boldsymbol{R}\vec{c} = \vec{c} + \sin(\theta)\vec{l} \times \vec{c} + (1 - \cos\theta)\vec{l} \times (\vec{l} \times \vec{c})$$

and $\vec{c}^T \vec{l} = 0$ it follows that

$$\vec{c} = \frac{1}{2}(\vec{t} - (\vec{t}^T \vec{l})\vec{l} + \cot\frac{\theta}{2}\vec{l} \times \vec{t}). \tag{21}$$

This point and hence the screw axis is not defined if the angle θ is either 0 or 180. Otherwise the moment vector reads then

$$\vec{m} = \vec{c} \times \vec{l} = \frac{1}{2}(\vec{t} \times \vec{l} + \vec{l} \times (\vec{t} \times \vec{l})\cot\frac{\theta}{2}). \tag{22}$$

We proceed then with the computation of the corresponding quaternion:

Given the screw parameters $(\theta, d, \vec{l}, \vec{m})$ *compute the corresponding dual quaternion* $\breve{q}$.

The quaternion derived from the rotation matrix $\boldsymbol{R}$ reads

$$(q_0, \vec{q}) = (\cos\frac{\theta}{2}, \sin\frac{\theta}{2}\vec{l}) \tag{23}$$

hence the moment equation (22) can be written

$$\sin\frac{\theta}{2}\vec{m} = \frac{1}{2}(\vec{t}\times\vec{q} + q_0\vec{t} - \cos\frac{\theta}{2}(\vec{l}^T\vec{t})\vec{l}).$$

Using $(\vec{l}^T\vec{t}) = d$ and rewriting

$$\sin\frac{\theta}{2}\vec{m} + \frac{d}{2}\cos\frac{\theta}{2}\vec{l} = \frac{1}{2}(\vec{t}\times\vec{q} + q_0\vec{t})$$

which is the vector part of the dual part q' of the dual quaternion $\breve{q}$. Applying (23) and $q' = \frac{1}{2}tq$ we obtain

$$\breve{q} = \begin{pmatrix} q_0 \\ \vec{q} \end{pmatrix} + \epsilon \begin{pmatrix} -\frac{1}{2}\vec{q}^T\vec{t} \\ \frac{1}{2}(q_0\vec{t} + \vec{t}\times\vec{q}) \end{pmatrix} = \begin{pmatrix} \cos\frac{\theta}{2} \\ \sin\frac{\theta}{2}\vec{l} \end{pmatrix} + \epsilon \begin{pmatrix} -\frac{d}{2}\sin\frac{\theta}{2} \\ \sin\frac{\theta}{2}\vec{m} + \frac{d}{2}\cos\frac{\theta}{2}\vec{l} \end{pmatrix}. \tag{24}$$

Every function f of dual numbers obeys the rule $f(a+\epsilon b) = f(a) + \epsilon b f'(a)$ hence

$$\cos(\frac{\theta + \epsilon d}{2}) = \cos\frac{\theta}{2} - \epsilon\frac{d}{2}\sin\frac{\theta}{2} \quad \text{and} \quad \sin(\frac{\theta + \epsilon d}{2}) = \sin\frac{\theta}{2} + \epsilon\frac{d}{2}\cos\frac{\theta}{2}.$$

It is now straightforward to see that a dual quaternion can also be written as

$$\breve{q} = \begin{pmatrix} \cos(\frac{\theta + \epsilon d}{2}) \\ \sin(\frac{\theta + \epsilon d}{2})(\vec{l} + \epsilon\vec{m}) \end{pmatrix}. \tag{25}$$

This representation is very powerful since first it algebraically separates the angle and pitch information from the line information characterizing the pose of the screw axis. Second writing the dual angle $\breve{\theta} = \theta + \epsilon d$ and the dual vector $\vec{\breve{l}} = \vec{l} + \epsilon\vec{m}$ equation (25) becomes equivalent to the pure rotation non-dual equation (23). We can easily verify that

$$\breve{q} = (\cos\breve{\theta}/2, \vec{\breve{l}}\sin\breve{\theta}/2)$$

is a unit quaternion $\breve{q}\bar{\breve{q}} = 1$.

5 Hand-eye transformation with unit dual quaternions

The usual way to describe the hand-eye calibration is by means of homogeneous transformation matrices. We denote by $\boldsymbol{X}$ the transformation from camera to gripper, by A_i the transformation matrix from the camera to the world coordinate system and by B_i the transformation matrix from the robot base to the gripper at the i-th pose. The camera-world transformation A_i is obtained with the extrinsic calibration techniques. The robot base to gripper transformation B_i is given by the direct kinematic chain from the joint angle readings. We see that for one pose we have two transformations as unknowns: robot base to world and the camera to gripper X. In order to eliminate the base to world transformation we need one motion (two poses) which yields the well known hand-eye equation [13, 14]:

$$AX = XB \qquad (26)$$

where $A = A_1 A_2^{-1}$ and $B = B_1 B_2^{-1}$. It follows one matrix and one vector equation

$$R_A R_X = R_X R_B \qquad (27)$$
$$(R_A - I)\vec{t}_X = R_X \vec{t}_B - \vec{t}_A \qquad (28)$$

The majority of the approaches regards the rotation estimation in (27) decoupled from translation estimation, the latter following the former. At least two rotations containing motions with not parallel rotation axes are required to solve the problem [14, 13, 3, 16].

The concatenation of two rigid displacements or screws can be written as the product of two dual quaternions. Let $\breve{a}$ denote the screw of a camera motion and $\breve{b}$ denote the screw of the motor motion. Motor (hand) and camera (eye) are rigidly attached to each other. The rigid transformation between them is unknown and it will be denoted by the unit dual quaternion $\breve{q}$. The screw concatenation yields then

$$\breve{a} = \breve{q}\breve{b}\bar{\breve{q}} \qquad (29)$$

which is the most compact equation for the hand-eye relation since the dual quaternion components are eight and not twelve like in the homogeneous matrices of (26). The scalar part of a dual quaternion $\breve{a}$ is $(\breve{a} + \bar{\breve{a}})/2$, hence

$$Sc(\breve{a}) = \frac{1}{2}(\breve{a} + \bar{\breve{a}}) = \frac{1}{2}(\breve{q}\breve{b}\bar{\breve{q}} + \breve{q}\bar{\breve{b}}\bar{\breve{q}}) = \frac{1}{2}\breve{q}(\breve{b} + \bar{\breve{b}})\bar{\breve{q}} = \breve{q}Sc(\breve{b})\bar{\breve{q}} = Sc(\breve{b})\,\breve{q}\bar{\breve{q}} = Sc(\breve{b}). \qquad (30)$$

According to (25) the scalar parts are equal to the cosine of the respective dual angles, i.e. $\breve{\theta}$:

$$\cos \frac{(\theta_a + \epsilon d_a)}{2} = \cos \frac{(\theta_b + \epsilon d_b)}{2}.$$

which is equivalent to $\cos \frac{\theta_a}{2} = \cos \frac{\theta_b}{2}$ and $d_a \sin \frac{\theta_a}{2} = d_b \sin \frac{\theta_b}{2}$. Hence, the angle and the pitch of the motor screw is equal to the angle and the pitch of the camera screw, or the angle and the pitch remain invariant under coordinate transformations (Screw Congruence Theorem [2]).

The fundamental equation $\breve{a} = \breve{q}\breve{b}\bar{\breve{q}}$ consists of four dual equations. Since the scalar parts are equal only the vector components contribute to the computation of the unknown $\breve{q}$:

$$\sin \frac{\breve{\theta}_a}{2}(0, \vec{\breve{a}}) = \breve{q}(0, \sin \frac{\breve{\theta}_b}{2}\vec{\breve{b}})\bar{\breve{q}} = \sin \frac{\breve{\theta}_b}{2}\breve{q}(0, \vec{\breve{b}})\bar{\breve{q}}.$$

If the angles $\theta_{a,b}$ are not 0 or 360 degrees the sines can be simplified yielding

$$(0, \breve{\vec{a}}) = \breve{q}(0, \breve{\vec{b}})\breve{\bar{q}} \tag{31}$$

which is nothing else then the motion of the lines of the screw axes. Thus,

1. The hand-eye estimation is independent of the angle and the pitch of the camera and the motor motions.

2. The hand-eye calibration is equivalent to the 3D motion estimation problem from 3D-line correspondences where the lines are the screw axes of the motors and the cameras.

We should note here that all other hand-eye calibration methods make use of the rotation angle and the pitch at least at the translation estimation step (28) which turns out in (31) to be unnecessary. Having shown that the problem is equivalent to the 3D-motion problem we can imply from last section that the minimum requirement are two motions with non parallel screw axes. The same linear solution as in Sec. 3.1 can be applied on eq. (31).

Acknowledgements

I want to thank Thomas Bülow for his help with the final revision of the page layout.

References

[1] O. Bottema and B. Roth. *Theoretical Kinematics*. North-Holland Publishing Company, Amsterdam New York London, 1979.

[2] H. Chen. A screw motion approach to uniqueness analysis of head-eye geometry. In *IEEE Conf. Computer Vision and Pattern Recognition*, pages 145–151, Maui, Hawaii, June 3-6, 1991.

[3] J.C.K. Chou and M. Kamel. Finding the position and orientation of a sensor on a robot manipulator using quaternions. *Intern. Journal of Robotics Research*, 10(3):240–254, 1991.

[4] O. Faugeras. *Three-dimensional Computer Vision*. MIT-Press, Cambridge, MA, 1993.

[5] J. Funda and R.P. Paul. A computational analysis of screw transformations in robotics. *IEEE Trans. Robotics and Automation*, 6:348–356, 1990.

[6] R. Horaud and F. Dornaika. Hand-eye calibration. *Intern. Journal of Robotics Research*, 14:195–210, 1995.

[7] B.K.P. Horn. *Robot Vision*. MIT Press, Cambridge, MA, 1986.

[8] J. Kim and V.R. Kumar. Kinematics of robot manipulators via line transformations. *Journal of Robotic Systems*, 7:649–674, 1990.

[9] M. Li and D. Betsis. Hand-eye calibration. In *Proc. Int. Conf. on Computer Vision*, pages 40–46. Boston, MA, June 20-23, 1995.

[10] J.M. McCarthy. Dual orthogonal matrices in manipulator kinematics. *Intern. Journal of Robotics Research*, 5(2):45–51, 1986.

[11] T.Q. Phong, R. Horaud, A. Yassine, , and D.T. Pham. Optimal estimation of object pose from a single perspective view. In *Proc. Int. Conf. on Computer Vision*, pages 534–539. Berlin, Germany, May 11-14, 1993.

[12] B. Sabata and J.K. Aggarwal. Estimation of motion from a pair of range images: a review. *CVGIP: Image Understanding*, 54:309–324, 1991.

[13] Y.C. Shiu and S. Ahmad. Calibration of wrist-mounted robotic sensors by solving homogeneous transform equations of the form $ax = xb$. *IEEE Trans. Robotics and Automation*, 5:16–27, 1989.

[14] R.Y. Tsai and R.K. Lenz. A new technique for fully autonomous and efficient 3d robotics hand/eye calibration. *IEEE Trans. Robotics and Automation*, 5:345–358, 1989.

[15] M.W. Walker. Manipulator kinematics and the epsilon algebra. *IEEE Journal of Robotics and Automation*, 4:186–192, 1988.

[16] C.C. Wang. Extrinsic calibration of a vision sensor mounted on a robot. *IEEE Trans. Robotics and Automation*, 8:161–175, 1992.

Segmentation of behavioral spaces for navigation tasks

Ruzena Bajcsy, Henrik I. Christensen & Jana Košecká

1 Introduction

From the very beginning, the forefathers of the Artificial Intelligence field (Mc-Carthy, Minsky, Newel and Simon) have emphasized the importance of the internal representation of an agent, whether artificial or biological. The issue that has been debated for the last 30 years is what the exact form of this representation is. In fact some philosophers, such as Dreyfus [5], even doubt whether this internal representation can ever be formalized. In this paper we shall assume such a formalism exists and do our part to address the long-debated question of what it is or what it should be.

Past researchers who have addressed the representation problem can generally be divided into three distinct categories: (1) those who adhered to symbolic or discrete representations, where the formalism was logic based (e.g., McCarthy, Minsky, Newel and Simon, and their disciples [12, 13, 14, 16]); (2) those who adhered to a behavior-based approach, which takes its formalism from adaptive systems and control engineering (e.g., Arbib and Ashby [1, 2]), based on continuous differential equations, and (3) the more recent connectionists (e.g., Smolensky and many others [20]). It is clear to us that agents functioning in a physical environment and communicating with each other need both continuous/signal based and discrete/symbol based representations, i.e., *hybrid* representations. Recently, researchers such as Brockett [3], Murray, Li and Sastry [15], and Ramadge and Wonham [17] have been developing suitable mathematics to account for these hybrid phenomena. Our work is based on this latter research, where we examine the appropriateness of and the transformations from signal to symbol to signal.

2 The problem

To examine the appropriateness of different representations, one must answer the following questions: (1) What is the alphabet into which signal(s) should be partitioned/segmented? (2) Is there a natural way, predicated on physics (nature) of the problem, to determine this partitioning? (3) Can we separate the problems where the partitioning depends not on physics but on social/cultural/economic laws? (4) How does the task, context and environment determine and/or constrain this partitioning? and (5) How does the agent's prior experience in a given task influence this partitioning?

The assumptions under which we shall examine these questions follow. The agent is a mobile platform with three degrees of freedom of motion. It can move back and forth and turn. The physical agent is shown in Figure 1 and is equipped with a positioning device, i.e., an odometer and a set of visual cameras that can detect obstacles versus free space and the target, place and/or goal of its destination. The obstacle avoidance is implemented by a stereo pair of

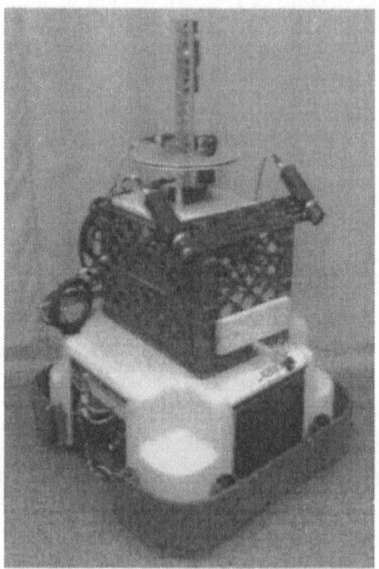

Figure 1: The mobile agent.

cameras and a procedure called *inverse perspective transformation*. The places are recognized by another camera positioned on a turntable. For complete details of this process, see [9]. The environment is indoors, specifically the GRASP Laboratory, with flat floors, walls, doors, and furniture is present. A typical task is to navigate from an initial position to a final destination while avoiding obstacles, going through narrow passages, and following another agent.

3 Choosing the alphabet/symbol

We must first recognize that the symbols and, more importantly, their interpretation will depend upon the space in which we shall cast our navigation problem. As usual, one has several choices:

Geometric representation of the environment. In this case it is assumed that the environment is static and the complete geometry is known. One can then compute the optimal path of the trajectory for the agent from the initial position to the goal position. In turn, the agent executes this trajectory. Here the symbols would stand for the initial and final place. The remaining path can be continuously controlled, assuming that the agent possesses the capability to move along the prescribed path. See [10, 19] for more details.

Configuration space representation. Configuration space represents the agent's degrees of freedom of motion (kinematics only) in a given environment. In other words, this representation will account not only for the geometry of the environment but also for the motion capabilities of the agent. See [11] for details.

Potential fields. The advantage of the potential field representation is·that it is *reactive* as opposed to the previous two representations which are global and assume complete knowledge of the environment ahead of time. In the potential field method one computes from the sensors the free space and the obstacles and navigates accordingly. The disadvantage is that one gets into local minima, since one does not have global knowledge about the environment! See [6, 7] for details.

State space representation. The advantage of this systems approach is that the space has well-defined continuous space state parameters as well as discrete states, and it is relatively easy to go from one to the other provided that the designer has done the partitioning. See [15] for details.

Behavioral space. Brooks introduced the space of behaviors, recognizing that one must tightly connect perception and action into a behavior [4]. Each elementary behavior can be a continuous feedback system, modeling some motion, communication process or other activity of an agent. One can then compose several of these behaviors into more complex behaviors [9]. The outstanding problem here is still what should be the choice of elementary behaviors.

Dynamic systems. The dynamic systems approach to the navigation problem introduces behavioral variables and phase space representation, which is a natural consequence of the dynamics theory. Here the selection of behavioral variables is the key. This approach is again *reactive* and has all the advantages and disadvantages of reactive control. See [18] for details.

The lesson to be learned is that whatever space of representation one selects, the outstanding problem still exists – how does one partition it!

For this paper, we have chosen the behavioral space of representation with some modifications to account for discrete states. Elementary behaviors are modeled by simple linear differential equations. Examples include GoTo, Track, Stop, Avoid Obstacles and so on. These differential equations are derived from the Lagrange formulation of motion:

$$F(q_i) = M(q_i)\ddot{q}_i + C(q_i, \dot{q}_i) + G(q_i)$$

where $i = 1 \ldots n$ denotes the number of degrees of freedom of the system, F is the force exerted on the system necessary to perform the motion, M is the inertia matrix, C is the coriolis and centrifugal force, G is the gravitational force, and q denotes the generalized matrix.

The natural partitioning of the behavioral space comes about from: (1) control of different degrees of freedom of the agent (e.g., the difference between GoTo and Track); (2) place-based navigation, which involves looking and recognizing a place; and (3) different control strategies based on an external stimulus, such as obstacle avoidance or cooperative marching.

244

4 An example of place-based navigation

Our framework combines the geometry of the environment and control of the mobile robot in such a manner that global navigation is robust and reliable. We formulate the global navigation as a sequence of relative positioning problems accomplished via by a sensory based closed-loop strategy with respect to the environment. We use visual sensing to derive such strategies and partition the model of the environment in such manner that there exists an appropriate strategy for every configuration of the mobile robot [9].

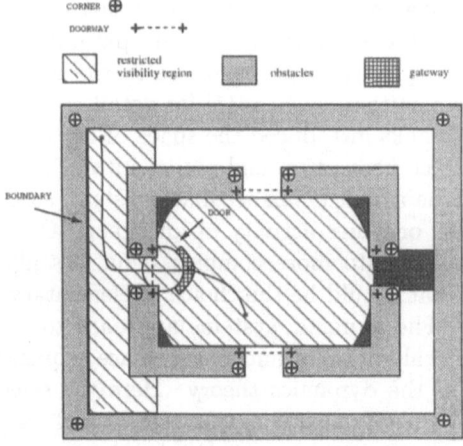

Figure 2: Landmarks chosen from the 2-D map of the laboratory. The initial configuration of the mobile base is in the visibility region of the doorway. After accomplishing the relative positioning task, a wall following strategy is invoked.

By choosing distinctive landmarks in the environment and geometric features associated with them, the environment is partitioned into a set of places. Within these places the mobile robot can either be reliably positioned with respect to a set of visible landmarks or can follow a boundary visible from a given place leading to a landmark. The spatial relationship between places is represented by a "place graph." The goals of the mobile robot are specified in terms of places, and a particular sequence of places which need to be visited while moving from one location to another results from the search of the place graph.

The mobile robot is modeled as a single point in the two dimensional configuration space $\mathcal{C}$. The environment is partitioned into a family of subsets, called *places*, such that the subsets form a cover of $\mathcal{C}$. Places are characterized by visibility constraints, and can be partitioned into two different categories: (1) visibility regions associated with landmarks, and (2) visibility regions associated with boundaries leading to landmarks. The first type of place (visibility region) associated with landmarks is defined as a set of points in a free space, such that from any point in the place there exists a path to any other point in the place, such that along the path the landmark is visible at all times. Landmarks are defined as a set of naturally occurring features, which are visually distinctive and recognizable. We assume that the set of landmarks and their relative relationships is determined ahead of time by the designer. Since in our case the landmark is composed from various features, we need to take into account the limited field of view of the camera, which restricts the points from which all features can be seen simultaneously. Thus, we define the visibility region of a landmark as a set of points from which all features belonging to a landmark are visible under the limited field of view assumption. The visibility region associated with a boundary leading to a landmark is called an *approachability region*. A landmark is approachable from a given point if there is a visible boundary of an obstacle which can be followed to approach the landmark.

By selecting naturally occurring features in office environments as a set of landmarks and computing the associated visibility region with each landmark and boundary leading to a landmark, we obtain a partitioning of the environment in terms of places. Two landmarks are in the neighborhood of each other if their associated place overlap. The regions where places overlap are referred to as *gateways* [21]. (See Figure 2 for an example.) For successful navigation between places we choose the setpoints of the elementary servoing strategies such that they will bring the camera frame to a gateway region of two landmarks [9].

To facilitate global navigation the neighborhood relationships between landmarks, (such as the gateways shown in Figure 3) are represented in a *place graph* (such as that shown in Figure 4). Individual nodes in the place graph represent the intersections of the visibility regions of specified landmarks or boundaries leading to landmarks. The edges coming out of the node correspond to the possible servoing strategies that can be applied from a given place. A node is characterized by a set of visible or approachable landmarks, i.e., set of landmarks with respect to which the mobile robot can be positioned. In the case every point in the free 2-D configuration space belongs to a certain place, the place graph is fully connected. By first determining the initial and goal location of the mobile base within a place graph in terms of places, the overall plan can be constructed as a result of a graph search.

5   Task description language

In the design of autonomous agents, there is always the question of how to communicate the task to such agents. This leads to the design of a task description language, i.e., a linguistic expression/command language that automatically translates into correct behaviors. We have implemented such a language, and the composition operators are given below, where P, R and S range over the set of processes.

Sequential composition. $P = R$; S. Process P behaves like R until R terminates and then behaves like S. P terminates when S terminates and has the same termination status as S.

Concurrent composition. $P = R \parallel S$. Process P behaves like R and S running in parallel. P terminates with the termination and status of the last

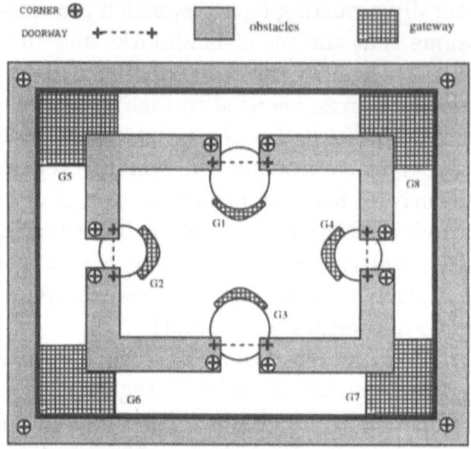

Figure 3: The gateway regions corresponding to the nodes of the place graph.

terminated process.

Conditional composition. $P = R : S$. Process P behaves like R until R terminates successfully computing v which is then used to initialize process S. If R fails the composition fails.

Disabling composition. $P = R \sharp S$. Disabling composition is similar to concurrent but if one of the processes terminates the other process is immediately terminated as well.

Synchronous recurrent composition. $P = R :; S$ is recursively defined as $R :; S = R : (S ; (R :; S))$. This composition terminates with the failure of process R.

Asynchronous recurrent composition. $P = R :: S$ is recursively defined as $R :; S = R : (S \| (R :: S))$. This composition terminates with the failure of process R.

The syntax of this language is such that it generates a finite state machine with states that are recognized via the perceptual apparatus of the agent. The novelty of our implementation is that in the semantics of each behavior there is a provision made for interruptions and errors (see, for example, Figure 5).

6 Prior knowledge

In our problem definition, we have asked what is the difference in the representation between the (expert) agents who know, let us say, the environment in which they are navigating and the (novice) agents who do not know anything about the environment except for some basic physical knowledge, such as the fact that they navigate in an indoor or outdoor environment. In other words, what is the instruction that an expert versus a novice must receive to successfully accomplish a navigation task? With a little bit of introspection, it is clear that the expert

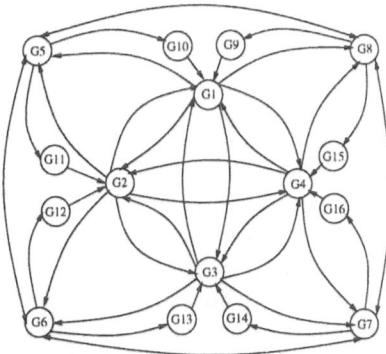

Figure 4: Place graph corresponding to a set of landmarks chosen in our laboratory. $G2$ corresponds to the gateway between the door and the boundary of the wall leading to two corner landmarks.

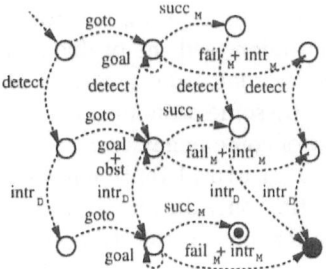

Figure 5: An example of parallel composition for the navigational task of the mobile base going to desired location (x_d, y_d) while avoiding obstacles. Process Navigate can be specified as: Navigate := GoTo(x_d, y_d) ‖ Detect where the processes GoTo and Detect are the elementary processes.

needs only information regarding the initial starting point and final destination because the intermediate path can be generated from previous knowledge, while the novice must receive rather detailed instructions regarding places and motion directions. This implies that in the case of the expert, the intermediate path can be carried out by a controller implemented via a continuous differential equation, unless some environmental events require a change in the smooth path following strategy, such as the occurrence of obstacles, icy surfaces, staircases, etc. On the other hand, the novice must translate all the commands and the particular places into discrete strategies; the continuous controller will function only between different places as prescribed in the task. This is also the case when one reports dynamic scene events, such as occur in traffic scenes [8]. These reports typically contain detailed linguistic descriptions of motion, relationships of the agents on the road and places. Hence, there is a need for detail representations similar to the novice agent.

7   Conclusion

In this paper, we began with the assumption that autonomous agents who live and act in a real physical environment need hybrid representations, accounting both for signal/continuous and discrete/symbol information and their mutual transformation. The difficult problem is this transformation! We have posed and tried to answer the question of how to segment/partition the space of all behaviors that correspond to some physical or logical principles. We have shown that in the task of navigation, in a relatively constrained environment, one can partition elementary behaviors based on the degrees of freedom of motion of the agents, or on different control strategies invoked by the task and/or by the environment. We have further shown that these elementary behaviors can be logically composed into more complex behaviors, expressed in a formal task description language. This language then can be automatically compiled into finite state machines, which further invoke appropriate control strategies of motion during task execution. We have not addressed the problem of how to prioritize some of the behaviors based principles that are other than physical. Examples of such prioritization schema would be some economical, social or other human-imposed hierarchies in the execution of some behaviors.

It is rather clear to us that an hybrid representation has an advantage over a strictly symbolic representation only on the grounds of combinatorial explosion. The continuous representation of control strategies is a more compact representation and generates a continuous path. On the other hand, one needs, as was shown, to have different control strategies depending on different physical demands. One needs as well a discretization of the space into some places. Furthermore, one needs a mechanism to switch amongst the differing control strategies. This is accomplished by the finite state machine formalism. The issue here is how to keep this part of the representation as compact as possible, i.e., the as yet unaddressed matter of representation granularity. This is our future work.

8   Acknowledgments

This material is based upon work supported by, or in part by, Army Research Office grants DAAH04-96-1-0429 and DAAH04-96-1-0007, Defense Advanced Research Projects Agency grant N00014-92-J-1647 and National Science Foundation grants IRI93-07126 and SBR89-20230.

References

[1] Arbib, M.A.: The Metaphorical Brain. New York: Wiley-Interscience 1972.

[2] Ashby, W.R.: Design for a Brain. London: Chapman & Hall and Science Paperbacks 1952.

[3] Brockett, R.: Hybrid Models for Motion Control Systems. In: Trentelman, H.L. and Willens, J.C. (eds.): Essays on Control: Perspectives in the Theory and its Applications. Boston: Birkhauser 1993.

[4] Brooks, R.: Intelligence without Representation. Artificial Intelligence, 47(1-3) (January 1991).

[5] Dreyfus, H.L.: What Computers Can't Do: A Critique of Artificial Reason. New York: Harper & Row 1972.

[6] Khatib, O.: Real-time Obstacle Avoidance for Manipulators and Mobile Robots. International Journal of Robotics Research, 5(1), 90-98 (1986).

[7] Koditschek, D.: Robot Planning and Control via Potential Functions. Robotics Review (1992).

[8] Kollnig, H., Nagel, H.-H., Otte, M.: Association of Motion Verbs with Vehicle Movements Extracted from Dense Optical Flow Fields. In: Eklundh, J.-O. (ed.): Proc. 3rd European Conf. on Computer Vision, Vol. II. Berlin Heidelberg New York: Springer-Verlag 1994 (Lecture Notes in Computer Science, vol. 801, pp. 338-347)

[9] Košecká, J.: A Framework for Modeling and Verifying Visually-Guided Agents: Design, Analysis and Experiments. Ph.D. thesis, Computer & Information Science Dept., University of Pennsylvania, Philadelphia, PA, 1996.

[10] Latombe, J.C.: Robot Motion Planning. Boston: Kluwer Academic 1991.

[11] Lozano-Perez, T.: Spatial Planning: A Configuration Space Approach. IEEE Transactions on Computers, C-32,2 (February 1983).

[12] McCarthy, J.: Programs with Common Sense. In: Proceedings of the Teddington Conference on the Mechanization of Thought Processes. London: Her Majesty's Stationary Office 1959.

[13] McCarthy, J.: Generality in Artificial Intelligence. Communications of the ACM, 30(12) 1030-1035 (1987).

[14] Minsky, M.: A Framework for Representing Knowledge. In: Winston P.H. (ed.): The Psychology of Computer Vision. New York: McGraw-Hill 1975.

[15] Murray, M., Li, Z., Sastry, S.S.: A Mathematical Introduction to Robotic Manipulation. Boca Raton, FL: CRC Press 1994.

[16] Newell, A., Simon, H.A.: Computer Science as Empirical Inquiry and Search. Communications of the ACM, 19(3), 113-126 (1976).

[17] Ramadge, P.J., Wonham, W.M.: The Control of Discrete Event Systems. Proceedings of the IEEE, 77(1), 81-97 (January 1989).

[18] Schöner, G., Dose, M.: A Dynamical System Approach to Task-level System Integration Used to Plan and Control Autonomous Vehicle Motion. Robotics and Autonomous Systems, 10, 253-267 (1992).

[19] Schwartz, J.T., Sharir M., Hopcroft, J. (eds.): Planning, Geometry and Complexity of Robot Motion. Norwood, NJ: Ablex Publishing 1987.

[20] Smolensky, P.: On the Proper Treatment of Connectionism. Behavioral and Brain Sciences, 11, 1-74 (1988).

[21] Taylor, C.J., Kriegman, D.J.: Vision-Based Motion Planning and Exploration Algorithms for Mobile Robots. Proceedings of the Workshop on the Algorithmic Foundations of Robotics, 1994.

Geometric algebra as a framework for the perception–action cycle

Gerald Sommer, Eduardo Bayro–Corrochano, Thomas Bülow

1   Introduction

In this paper we will present a mathematical framework for embedding the realization of technical systems which are designed on principles of the perception–action cycle (PAC). The use of PAC as a design principle of systems which should have both capabilities of perception and action is motivated by ethology and has its theoretical roots in the theory of non–linear dynamic systems. PAC is the frame of autonomous behavior. It relates perception and action in a purposive manner. The global competence of such systems results from cooperation and competition of a set of behaviors, each as an observable manifestation of a certain kind of competence. If both acquired skill and experience are the sources to yield competence, there is hope also to gain such attractive system properties like robustness and adaptivity. The essence behind this extension of the active vision paradigm is a certain kind of equivalence between visual perception and action. That means both perceptual categories and those of actions are mutually supported and have to be mutually verified. Perception and action constitute the afferent and efferent interfaces of the agent to its environment. Using them in a mature stage the active agent stabilizes its relation to the environment by equalizing categories of perception with those of action. The first ones are defined by the experience that similar patterns cause similar actions (or reactions) and the second ones correspond to the skill that similar actions cause similar patterns.

Following that line it should be possible to design both technical visual systems with support of active components of movement and seeing robots. This necessitates the fusion of computer vision (as active vision), robotics, signal processing, and neural computation. It becomes obvious that representations will take on central importance. They have to relate the agent with the environment in Euclidean space–time. Evaluating the actual situation with respect to the representation problem we have to state both serious shortcomings within the disciplines and gaps between them.

In order to overcome these problems the time is ripe to identify the deep reasons for this situation. Our hypothesis is the following: Linear algebra of vector spaces on real or complex numbers is a too poor language for representing phenomena of the world as complete and effective as necessary. This results in limited capabilities of reconstruction of complex objects from projected patterns in the approach of explicit representation of structure and slow learning rates of higher order correlations which are responsible for the structure of complex objects within an implicit representation approach of neural nets. Even if the ultimate goal of an agent is not visual reconstruction of the world, it has to find out the mapping rules between visual percepts and the world they stand for, constrained by its relations to that world.

What we need is a language which expresses a lot of group theoretical constrained geometric isomorphisms within the agent's mind. This has to be a rich algebraically structured geometry or a geometrically interpretable rich structured algebra. We may only refer to some of the serious limitations of linear algebra. In vector spaces of real numbers intrinsic representations are limited to zero order geometric entities (points) without any symmetry. Geometric transforms are restricted to translation. Lines and planes as geometric entities are no intrinsic conceptions of linear vector spaces but result from a process of construction using points and translation operations. Endowing vector spaces with complex numbers results in representations of first order entities (lines) with even/odd symmetry. Geometric transformations are enriched by rotation in the complex plane. In both cases the scalar product enables only to model bilinear relations between two vectors with an outcome as scalar. This poverty of operations hinders recognition of intrinsic dimensionality or reconstruction of higher order entities which constitute the perceivable world. Only by using richer numbers than real or complex ones, respectively by enabling richer symmetry conceptions, vector spaces can be modeled from subspaces which stand for irreducible invariants as members of a basis system of structure of higher order then zero or one.

Our conception of the theory for PAC consists of two parts. First part is the so–called geometric or Clifford algebra as the global frame for representations of actions or patterns [1, 2, 3, 5, 7, 14]. To sketch out the basic conceptions and to demonstrate some first results is the topic of this article. The second part concerns the use of Lie algebra as local frame for both differential generation or recognition of patterns (see e.g. [15]). In such frame a unified architecture of a PAC system for the task of perception projects local patterns to the set of irreducible invariants in the frame of geometric algebra and successively from these projections complex patterns are constructed. Vice versa also local patterns of actions are generated from such set to construct from them complex patterns of motion and action. This algebraic constrained local approach also could be helpful to overcome the contemporary gap between geometric entities in Computer Vision and structural primitives in signal theory and thus to realize Faugeras' stratification approach [9] of vision on the signal level.

2 Geometric algebra of vector spaces

What we need is a more general mathematics for easier modeling of both structures (perceived and generated) and operations. This mathematics has been formulated in the last century by W. K. Clifford (1876) as an algebra of directed numbers with both quantitative and operational interpretations. Clifford algebra (see [16] for a modern survey) can be seen as result of the unification of H. Grassmann's algebra of extensions (1844), which concerns the quantitative interpretation of numbers, with the algebra of quaternions, introduced by W. R. Hamilton (1844) as an operational interpretation of numbers. With this interpretation of the relations between the mentioned algebras we follow the ideas of David Hestenes [13] who presented Clifford algebra as a "unified language for mathematics and physics" [10] and named it geometric algebra (GA) as Clifford did. It is his great merit to reformulate and to work out Clifford algebra from a geometrical point of view as a framework for describing physical processes in the world. Thus, he also decided not to care about the long lasting debate of pure mathematicians on the priority of Grassmann's or Clifford's algebra in establishing a universal geometric algebra [8]. Indeed, Clifford algebra contains Grassmann algebra as a subalgebra.

Also the perception–action cycle concerns physical phenomena of the real world and some problems in modern physics are indeed comparable to those of computer vision, robotics or neural computation.

A geometric algebra G_n results from providing an n–dimensional vector space V_n in addition to vector addition and scalar multiplication with a non–commutative product. The geometric product is associative and distributive with respect to addition. The geometric product of two vectors $\mathbf{a}$, $\mathbf{b}$ is written $\mathbf{ab}$ and can be understood according

$$\mathbf{ab} = \mathbf{a} \cdot \mathbf{b} + \mathbf{a} \wedge \mathbf{b}$$

as the sum of a symmetric inner product $\alpha = \mathbf{a} \cdot \mathbf{b}$ and an antisymmetric outer product $\mathbf{B} = \mathbf{a} \wedge \mathbf{b}$. In case that $\mathbf{a}$, $\mathbf{b}$ are vectors — we say of grade one — the inner product corresponds to the scalar product — its result is a scalar (of grade zero), but the result of the outer product is a new entity of grade two. This is called a bivector. That means, in contrast to the scalar product of vector algebra, the geometric product of geometric algebra results in both contraction (inner product) and expansion (outer product) of the grade of entities. As a consequence we get from the product of n vectors $\mathbf{a}_1, \ldots, \mathbf{a}_n$ a multivector

$$\mathbf{A} = \langle \mathbf{A} \rangle_0 + \langle \mathbf{A} \rangle_1 + \ldots + \langle \mathbf{A} \rangle_n \quad ,$$

which is a mixture of multivector parts $\langle \mathbf{A} \rangle_r$ of grade r. Any multivector $\mathbf{A}_r = \langle \mathbf{A} \rangle_r$ is called homogeneous of grade r or r–vector. Only if such r–vector can be factored according

$$\mathbf{A}_r = \mathbf{a}_1 \mathbf{a}_2 \cdots \mathbf{a}_r$$

it is called an r–blade. The geometric product of any two homogeneous multivectors $\mathbf{A}_r, \mathbf{B}_s$ results in a spectrum of multivectors of different grade

$$\mathbf{A}_r \mathbf{B}_s = \langle \mathbf{A}_r \mathbf{B}_s \rangle_{|r-s|} + \langle \mathbf{A}_r \mathbf{B}_s \rangle_{|r-s|+2} + \ldots + \langle \mathbf{A}_r \mathbf{B}_s \rangle_{r+s} \quad ,$$

ranging from pure inner product $\langle \mathbf{A} \rangle_r \cdot \langle \mathbf{B} \rangle_s = \langle \mathbf{A}_r \mathbf{B}_s \rangle_{|r-s|}$ to pure outer product $\langle \mathbf{A} \rangle_r \wedge \langle \mathbf{B} \rangle_s = \langle \mathbf{A}_r \mathbf{B}_s \rangle_{r+s}$.

Thus, an n–dimensional vector space V_n uniquely determines a geometric algebra $G(\mathbf{A}) = G_n$ which itself spans a linear space of dimension 2^n. From a given set of n linearly independent vectors spanning V_n we get $\binom{n}{r}$ linear independent r–blades. These r–blades themselves constitute a basis of the linear subspaces $G_r(\mathbf{A})$ of dimension $\binom{n}{r}$ of all r–vectors in G_n. Each such r–blade $\mathbf{A}_r \in G_r(\mathbf{A})$ has a geometric interpretation as an uniquely oriented r–dimensional vector space $V_r = G_1(\mathbf{A}_r)$, consisting of all vectors $\mathbf{a}$ which satisfy

$\mathbf{a} \wedge \mathbf{A}_r = 0$, as subspace of $V_n = G_1(\mathbf{A})$. Thus, any r–vector part $\langle \mathbf{A} \rangle_r$ can be understood as a projection of $\mathbf{A}$ into the space $G_r(V_n)$ and any r–vector $\mathbf{A}_r$ can be formulated as a sum of r–blades. Since V_n is the vector space of $\mathbf{A}_n$, it follows $\mathbf{a} \wedge \mathbf{A}_n = 0$ and $\mathbf{a}_1 \wedge \mathbf{a}_2 \wedge \ldots \wedge \mathbf{a}_n = \lambda I$ with I as unit pseudoscalar or direction of V_n. From the existence of such pseudoscalar follows the important intrinsic duality principle of geometric algebra which results from any unit r–blade and unit $(n - r)$–blade in $I_r I_{n-r} = I$. As a result of this the relation

$$\mathbf{A}^* = \mathbf{A}I^{-1}$$

defines a dual $\mathbf{A}^*$ of an r–vector $\mathbf{A} = \langle \mathbf{A} \rangle_r$ with respect to the unit pseudoscalar I. The grade of $\mathbf{A}^*$ is $(n - r)$ due to $\mathbf{A}I^{-1} = \mathbf{A} \cdot I^{-1}$. In case that $\mathbf{A}$ is an r–vector and $\mathbf{B}$ is an s–vector, it results the duality of inner and outer product corresponding to

$$\mathbf{A} \cdot \mathbf{B}^* = (\mathbf{A} \wedge \mathbf{B})^*$$

If $r + s = n$, then $\mathbf{A} \wedge \mathbf{B}$ equals a pseudoscalar $P = \lambda I$, and because $II^{-1} = 1$, it follows

$$[P] = [\mathbf{A} \wedge \mathbf{B}] = (\mathbf{A} \wedge \mathbf{B})I^{-1} = \mathbf{A} \cdot \mathbf{B}^* \quad .$$

Here $[P] \equiv \lambda$ is the bracket of the pseudoscalar P as used in Grassmann–Cayley algebra (see chapter 4). Because the sign of the bracket is independent of the signature or metric of G_n it is possible to define for that algebra also two qualitative operations. For any linear independent r–vector $\mathbf{A}$ and s–vector $\mathbf{B}$

$$\mathbf{C} = \mathbf{A} \wedge \mathbf{B}$$

is the join (or union) of both. Thus $\mathbf{C}$ is of grade $r + s$. On the other hand, if $\mathbf{A}$ and $\mathbf{B}$ are not linearly independent, the join represents the subspace which they span. As another qualitative operation the meet (or intersection) of $\mathbf{C} = \mathbf{A} \vee \mathbf{B}$ is indirectly defined with respect to the join as

$$\mathbf{C}^* = (\mathbf{A} \vee \mathbf{B})^* = \mathbf{A}^* \wedge \mathbf{B}^* \quad .$$

For $r + s = n$ the join will span the whole space and the meet as a multivector of grade $|r - s|$ will be easily computed as

$$\mathbf{C} = \pm(\mathbf{A}^* \cdot \mathbf{B}) \quad .$$

Both operations are of fundamental importance due to their constructive properties for instance in projective geometry (see chapter 4).

3 Geometric algebra of euclidean 3D–space

The perception–action cycle takes place in Euclidean space–time where the agent is interested in recognizing and organizing processes in such world, even if for some tasks only projective or affine constraints of Euclidean space are used. In chapter 4 problems of projective geometry and kinematics are presented briefly.

Following the facts of chapter 2, the geometric algebra of Euclidean 3D–space is 8–dimensional. Much higher–dimensional spaces result if geometric algebra is applied to manifolds, as in chapter 5.

An n–dimensional vector space endowed with an orthogonal basis $\{\sigma_l\}, l = 1, \ldots, n$, and a bilinear form such that $\sigma_l \cdot \sigma_k = \delta_{lk}$ results in a basis of the geometric algebra G_n:

$$1, \{\sigma_l\}, \{\sigma_l\sigma_k\}, \{\sigma_l\sigma_k\sigma_m\}, \ldots, \sigma_1\sigma_2 \ldots \sigma_n \quad .$$

Thus, the basis of $G_3 = G(E_3)$ is composed of the following components

$$1, \{\sigma_1, \sigma_2, \sigma_3\}, \{\sigma_1\sigma_2 = i_1, \sigma_2\sigma_3 = i_2, \sigma_3\sigma_1 = i_3\}, \sigma_1\sigma_2\sigma_3 = i \quad ,$$

which themselves constitute the basis vectors of the subspaces $G_r \subseteq G_3$. In this way i is the unit trivector or unit pseudoscalar of E_3 with $i^2 = -1$, and $i_l, l = 1, 2, 3$ are the unit bivectors which are the basis vectors of the quaternion algebra. Any multivector $\mathbf{A} \in G_3$, $\mathbf{A} = \alpha + \mathbf{a} + \mathbf{B} + \mathbf{T}$ is component wise composed of multiples of these unit vectors of geometric algebra. However, due to the duality principle, we can change the basis of any r–vector part by its dual basis, e.g.

$$\mathbf{B} = B_1 i_1 + B_2 i_2 + B_3 i_3, \quad i_1 i_2 i_3 = 1$$

or

$$\mathbf{B} = i\mathbf{b} \quad \text{with} \quad \mathbf{b} = B_1\sigma_1 + B_2\sigma_2 + B_3\sigma_3 \quad .$$

This will be useful if consideration of different interpretations of any multivector is of interest.

Any r–vector of G_3 can get an interpretation as geometric entity. Both points and lines are represented by vectors and planes are represented by bivectors. The relation of a line $\mathbf{a}$ with respect to a plane $\mathbf{B}$ is given by the geometric product $\mathbf{aB} = \mathbf{a} \cdot \mathbf{B} + \mathbf{a} \wedge \mathbf{B}$. If the line is on the plane we get $\mathbf{a} \wedge \mathbf{B} = 0$ whereas $\mathbf{a} \cdot \mathbf{B} = 0$ corresponds to a line perpendicular to the plane.

An operational interpretation of multivectors results by considering the 4–dimensional even subalgebra G_3^+. Any multivector $\mathbf{A} \in G_3^+$, $\mathbf{A} = \langle \mathbf{A} \rangle_0 + \langle \mathbf{A} \rangle_2 \equiv \alpha + \mathbf{B}$ is representing a spinor if $\mathbf{B} = i\mathbf{b}$ is used. A spinor stands for a rotation–dilation (not only in E_3). Indeed, the rotation component, represented by the rotor $\mathbf{R} = \pm e^{\mathbf{B}/2}$ with the rotation plane represented by the bivector $\mathbf{B}$, is a much more general way of expressing rotations then using matrix operations or using the frame of quaternions. The rotation $\mathbf{B}_r = \mathbf{R}\mathbf{A}_r\tilde{\mathbf{R}}$, where $\tilde{\mathbf{R}}$ stands for the conjugate of $\mathbf{R}$ and thus $\mathbf{R}\tilde{\mathbf{R}} = \tilde{\mathbf{R}}\mathbf{R} = 1$, of any r–vector $\mathbf{A}_r$ works for all spaces of any dimension on any type of objects, whatever grade. Moreover, it works without the use of external coordinates.

4   Geometric algebra of 4D–space

The contemporary knowledge does not allow to work out the complete theory of perception of spatio–temporal equivalence classes in the frame of stratified space–time. This theory would permit to model projective, affine, or metric perception of structure from differential motion in space. Instead, the visual interpretation of the world from image sequences is treated either as stationary n–views problem of structure from motion with limited information capacity. By abandoning conceptions of time, kinematics often is considered as spatial transformation or rigid displacement in Euclidean space.

In this chapter we will show the use of geometric algebra for either problems of projective geometry or kinematics by embedding both tasks in different algebraic frames.

For the sake of generality, in the characterization of the geometric algebra the signature of G_n has to be considered. Writing $G_{p,q,r}$ instead, where $n = p+q+r$, refers to the number of basis elements which square to 1 for p, -1 for q, and zero for r. For example, $G_{3,0,0} = G(E_3)$ stands for $\sigma_l^2 = 1$, $l = 1, 2, 3$.

As has been shown by Hestenes [11], geometric algebra is well suited to deal with problems of projective geometry. Because the projective space P_3 is a non–metric one, it has to be extended to an associated 4–dimensional vector space R_4 with the basis vectors γ_l, $l = 1, 2, 3, 4$. To become consistent with the signature of G_3 for the geometric algebra of the Euclidean space, the geometric algebra of R_4 has to be $G_{1,3,0}$ [14]. The correspondence between both spaces is given by $\sigma_i \equiv \gamma_i\gamma_4$, $i = 1, 2, 3$. This 16–dimensional space is spanned by the basis

$$1, \{\gamma_l\}, \{\gamma_4\gamma_k, i\gamma_4\gamma_k\}, \{i\gamma_l\}, i \quad ,$$

with $l = 1, 2, 3, 4$, $k = 1, 2, 3$, $\gamma_4^2 = 1$, $\gamma_k^2 = -1$, $i = \gamma_1\gamma_2\gamma_3\gamma_4$, and $i^2 = -1$. Here γ_4 plays the role of a selected direction. By computing the projective split of a vector $\mathbf{X} = X_1\gamma_1 + X_2\gamma_2 + X_3\gamma_3 + X_4\gamma_4$

$$\mathbf{X}\gamma_4 = \mathbf{X} \cdot \gamma_4 + \mathbf{X} \wedge \gamma_4 = X_4\left(1 + \frac{\mathbf{X} \wedge \gamma_4}{X_4}\right) \equiv X_4(1 + \mathbf{x})$$

any vector $\mathbf{X} \in R_4$ may be related to a vector $\mathbf{x} \in E_3$ and vice versa by

$$\frac{\mathbf{X} \wedge \gamma_4}{X_4} = \frac{X_1}{X_4}\gamma_1\gamma_4 + \frac{X_2}{X_4}\gamma_2\gamma_4 + \frac{X_3}{X_4}\gamma_3\gamma_4 \equiv x_1\sigma_1 + x_2\sigma_2 + x_3\sigma_3 = \mathbf{x}$$

it may be recognized that X_i represent the homogeneous coordinates of $\mathbf{x}$. The projective split [12] is a very powerful tool for any mapping of entities between spaces of different dimension [2, 4, 14]. In this way vectors, bivectors, and trivectors in $G_{1,3,0}$ correspond to points, lines, and planes in E_3. Using the join between any non–collinear points $\mathbf{x}_1, \mathbf{x}_2, \mathbf{x}_3 \in E_3$, respectively $\mathbf{X}_1, \mathbf{X}_2, \mathbf{X}_3 \in R_4$, a plane $\Pi \in G_{1,3,0}$ passing these points is represented by

$$\Pi = \mathbf{X}_1 \wedge \mathbf{X}_2 \wedge \mathbf{X}_3 = L \wedge \mathbf{X}_3$$

with $L = \mathbf{X}_1 \wedge \mathbf{X}_2$. As an example for the meet of entities in geometric algebra we consider the intersection $L \vee \Phi$ of the above defined line L with the plane $\Phi = \mathbf{Y}_1 \wedge \mathbf{Y}_2 \wedge \mathbf{Y}_3$. After using some algebra [2] the intersection point $\mathbf{Z} \in R_4$ is given by

$$\mathbf{Z} = L \vee \Phi = [X_1X_2Y_2Y_3]\mathbf{Y}_1 + [X_1X_2Y_3Y_1]\mathbf{Y}_2 + [X_1X_2Y_1Y_2]\mathbf{Y}_3 \quad .$$

In [14] the framework of geometric algebra has been applied for computing $3D$ projective invariants. In [2] geometric algebra has been used to compute point correspondences between n cameras and invariant projective depth by taking into account n–linear constraints. It has been shown that geometric algebra is superior to the recently used Grassmann–Cayley or Double algebra with respect to both elegance of derivations and gain of geometric insight of operations.

Besides, geometric algebra is not special to problems of projective geometry. This has been shown in [7], [4]. There the hand–eye calibration in visual robotics could be solved as a linear problem. The simultaneous estimation of translation and rotation is a nonlinear problem by itself. However, choosen a dual quaternion or motor algebra this becomes a linear problem.

Dual quaternions belong to the general class of composed numbers $a = b + \omega c$, where the algebraic operator ω specifies complex numbers for $\omega^2 = -1$, double numbers for $\omega^2 = 1$ and dual numbers for $\omega^2 = 0$. In the last case the term b is called the real part and c corresponds to the dual part of a.

Clifford [6] recognized that dual quaternions are representations of a so–called screw motion, which can be understood as a rigid motion (that means coupled rotation and translation) of lines in E_3. He introduced the dual quaternions with the name motors as abbreviation of "moment and vector". Motors are the multivectors of the even 8–dimensional subalgebra $G_{0,3,1}^+$ of $G_{0,3,1}$, which is the geometric algebra of a 4–dimensional vector space R_4 with a pseudomet-ric $\gamma_4^2 = 0$, $\gamma_l^2 = -1$, $l = 1,2,3$. In accordance to the requirement of the algebraic operator of dual numbers $G_{0,3,1}$ is endowed with a unit pseudoscalar $i = \gamma_1\gamma_2\gamma_3\gamma_4$ which squares $i^2 = 0$. The basis of the degenerated algebra $G_{0,3,1}^+$ is $(1, \{\gamma_4\gamma_l\}, \{i\gamma_4\gamma_l\}, i)$, where $\{\gamma_4\gamma_l\}$ define the basis of the real part and $\{i\gamma_4\gamma_l\}$ define the basis of the dual part of motors [4].

The basic geometric interpretation of a motor $\mathbf{M}$ corresponds to the sum of two non–coplanar lines, represented in the dual basis of $G_{0,3,1}^+$, i.e.

$$
\begin{aligned}
\mathbf{M} &= \mathbf{X_1X_2 + X_3X_4} \\
&= (a_0 + a_1\gamma_4\gamma_1 + a_2\gamma_4\gamma_2 + a_3\gamma_4\gamma_3) \\
&\quad + i(b_0 + b_1\gamma_4\gamma_1 + b_2\gamma_4\gamma_2 + b_3\gamma_4\gamma_3) \\
&= \mathbf{R} + i\mathbf{R'} \quad .
\end{aligned}
$$

A motor therefore can be represented as a dual rotor. On the other hand a motor is a coupled translation–rotation, i.e.

$$
\mathbf{M} = \mathbf{TR} = \left(1 + i\frac{\mathbf{t}}{2}\right)\mathbf{R} \quad .
$$

Here the term $\mathbf{T}$ defines a so–called translator as a rotation plane displaced from the origin of reference by vector $\mathbf{t}$ and with the same orientation of that vector. By augmenting the space E_3 by using R_4 instead, rigid displacements of lines is a very attractive alternative of that of points. In dual number representation a line $\mathbf{l}_d$,

$$
\mathbf{l}_d = \mathbf{n} + i\mathbf{n} \wedge \mathbf{p} = \mathbf{n} + i\mathbf{m}, \quad i^2 = 0 \quad ,
$$

represents by its real part the line direction **n** and by its dual part the moment **m** which results from vector **n** and any vector **p** touching the line. Its motion in terms of motors reads

$$l'_d = \mathbf{M}l_d\tilde{\mathbf{M}} = \mathbf{Rn\tilde{R}} + i(\mathbf{Rn\tilde{R}'} + \mathbf{R'n\tilde{R}} + \mathbf{Rm\tilde{R}})$$

Of course also the other entities exist in the augmented space R_4 but their use in tasks of rigid transformations is limited in comparison to those of lines.

It seems that unrestricted merging of projective and kinematic tasks in the frame of geometric algebra would be possible if the Euclidean space E_3 would be algebraically extended to R_5.

5 Geometric algebra of manifolds

Because geometric algebra plays the role of a very general scheme of embedding any task of the PAC, it will be important also for analysis of multi–dimensional signals and for (neural) mapping of perceived signals onto those of motor control. ¿From the last problem follows the necessity to reconsider the role of the linear associator in neural nets and to enrich it with the capability to process multivectors. This topic [3] should be passed over here. Instead, we will consider some problems of multi–dimensional signal processing, mentioned in the introduction, with strong relevance to early visual processing.

The well known Fourier transform hitherto is inable to provide us with possibilities of representing real multi–dimensional signals. That means it is only limited to the separable case. This is strongly related with its linear nature. On the other side real multi–dimensional structures are constituted in a non–linear manner from one–dimensional basis functions. To become adequate for multi–dimensional signals and simultaneously keeping its linear structure, a multi–dimensional Fourier transform has to be algebraically extended to the requested dimension. In [5] a Clifford Fourier transform (CFT) $F^c(\mathbf{u})$ of an n–dimensional signal $f(\mathbf{x})$

$$F^c(\mathbf{u}) = \int \cdots \int f(\mathbf{x}) Q_{\mathbf{u}}(\mathbf{x}) d^n\mathbf{x}$$

has been introduced by defining its basis functions as

$$Q_{\mathbf{u}}(\mathbf{x}) = \prod_{k=1}^{n} e^{-j_k 2\pi u_k x_k} \quad .$$

In contrast to the classic approach each one–dimensional component transforms to its own complex domain, indicated by the n different imaginaries j_k. From this follows that the quaternionic Fourier transform (QFT), which is adequate to two–dimensional signals, splits such signal into four components in the quaternionic Fourier domain. Therefore not only more symmetry conceptions result but also only on this way a multi–dimensional phase can be defined.

Another topic of future importance will be the design of local operators which in the linear vector space of signals represent non–linear operators but in contrary to this in the multivector space of geometric algebra represent linear ones. This problem is related to the problem of estimation of higher order correlations of signals within the operator support. In principle each pixel of that domain contributes with one dimension to the signal space and consequently very high–order relations may be estimated. But this is hindered by the computational complexity of the nonlinear nature of operators. By using Volterra series approach for the local estimation of signal structure and by embedding the task in the frame of geometric algebra, the estimation problems become linear ones in the corresponding multivector subspace of geometric algebra.

6 Conclusion

We presented Clifford or geometric algebra as a powerful and general scheme of embedding any problem of perception–action cycle, ranging from kinematics via projective geometry to signal theory. The paper summarizes some key ideas of the algebra in relation to different applications in the mentioned fields. Although the development of methodology is in its infancy yet, its potential becomes visible. Both reformulations of well known approaches and extension to new approaches will result in overcoming of existing limitations in the design of technical systems which might be able to perform perception–action cycles in real–time.

References

[1] Bayro–Corrochano, E., Sommer, G.: Object modeling and collision avoidance using Clifford algebra. In: Hlavac V., Sara R. (eds.): Computer Analysis of Images and Patterns, Proc. CAIP'95, Prague 1995. Berlin Heidelberg New York Tokyo: Springer 1995 (Lecture Notes in Computer Science, vol. 970, pp. 669–704).

[2] Bayro–Corrochano, E., Lasenby, J., Sommer, G.: Geometric Algebra: A framework for computing point and line correspondences and projective structure using n uncalibrated cameras. In: Proc. ICPR, Vienna, 1996, Vol. A. Los Alamitos: IEEE Computer Society Press 1996, pp. 334-338.

[3] Bayro–Corrochano, E., Buchholz, S., Sommer, G.: A new self–organizing neural network using geometric algebra. In: Proc. ICPR, Vienna, 1996, Vol. D. Los Alamitos: IEEE Computer Society Press 1996, pp. 555–559.

[4] Bayro–Corrochano, E., Daniilides, K., Sommer, G.: Hand–eye calibration in terms of motion of lines using geometric algebra. In: Proc. SCIA'97, The 10th Scand. Conf. on Image Analysis, Lappeenranta, 1997, pp. 397–404.

[5] Bülow, Th., Sommer, G.: Algebraically extended representations of multi-dimensional signals. In: Proc. SCIA'97, The 10th Scand. Conf. on Image Analysis, Lappeenranta, 1997, pp. 559–566.

[6] Clifford, W.K.: Preliminary sketch of bi–quaternions. Proc. London Math. Soc. 4, 381–395 (1873).

[7] Daniilidis, K., Bayro–Corrochano, E.: The dual quaternion approach to hand–eye calibration. In: Proc. ICPR, Vienna, 1996, Vol. A. Los Alamitos: IEEE Computer Society Press 1996, pp. 318–322.

[8] Doran, C., Hestenes, D., et al.: Lie groups as spin groups. J. Math. Phys. 34, 3642–3669 (1993).

[9] Faugeras, O.: Stratification of three–dimensional vision: projective, affine, and metric representations. J. Opt. Soc. Am. A 12, 465–485, 1995.

[10] Hestenes, D., G. Sobczyk: Clifford Algebra to Geometric Calculus. Dordrecht: D. Reidel Publ. Comp. 1984.

[11] Hestenes, D., Ziegler, R.: Projective Geometry with Clifford algebra. Acta Applicandae Mathematicae 23, 25–63 (1991).

[12] Hestenes, D.: The design of linear algebra and geometry. Acta Applicandae Mathematicae 23, 65–93 (1991).

[13] Hestenes, D.: New Foundations for Classical Mechanics. Dortrecht: Kluwer Academic Publ. 1993.

[14] Lasenby, J., Bayro–Corrochano, E., Lasenby, A.N., and Sommer, G.: A new methodology for computing invariants in computer vision. In: Proc. ICPR, Vienna, 1996, Vol. A. Los Alamitos: IEEE Computer Society Press, 1996, pp 393–397.

[15] Michaelis, M., Sommer, G.: A Lie group approach to steerable filters. Patt. Recogn. Lett. 16, 1165–1174 (1995).

[16] Porteous, I.R.: Clifford Algebras and the Classical Groups. Cambridge: Cambridge University Press 1995.

List of contributors

Ruzena Bajcsy
GRASP Laboratory, Computer and Information Science Department
University of Pennsylvania
Philadelphia, PA 19104, USA
bajcsy@cis.upenn.edu

Eduardo Bayro-Corrochano
Christian–Albrechts-Universität zu Kiel
Institut für Informatik und Praktische Mathematik
Lehrstuhl für Kognitive Systeme
Preußerstraße 1–9, 24105 Kiel, Germany
edb@informatik.uni-kiel.de

John L. Barron
Department of Computer Science
University of Western Ontario
London, Ontario, Canada, N6A 5B7
barron@csd.uwo.ca

Steven S. Beauchemin
Department of Computer Science
University of Western Ontario
London, Ontario, Canada, N6A 5B7
beau@csd.uwo.ca

Brahim Benhamouda
Faculty of Mathematics
Technical University Chemnitz-Zwickau
Reichenhainer Str. 41, 09107 Chemnitz, Germany
brahim@mathematik.tu-chemnitz.de

Souheil Ben-Yacoub
IDIAP, CP 592
1920 Martigny, Switzerland
sby@idiap.ch

Thomas Bülow
Christian–Albrechts-Universität zu Kiel
Institut für Informatik und Praktische Mathematik
Lehrstuhl für Kognitive Systeme
Preußerstraße 1–9, 24105 Kiel, Germany
tbl@informatik.uni-kiel.de

262

Dmitry Chetverikov
Computer and Automation Research Institute
Kende u. 13–17, 1111 Budapest, Hungary
mitya@leader.ipan.sztaki.hu

Henrik I. Christensen
Centre for Autonomous Systems, CVAP/NADA
Royal Institute of Technology
Stockholm, Sweden
hic@nada.kth.se

Konstantinos Daniilidis
Christian–Albrechts-Universität zu Kiel
Institut für Informatik und Praktische Mathematik
Lehrstuhl für Kognitive Systeme
Preußerstraße 1–9, 24105 Kiel, Germany
kd@informatik.uni-kiel.de

Vito Di Gesú
University of Palermo
Dipartimento di Matematica ed Applicazioni
Via Arvhirafi 34, 90123 Palermo, Italy
digesu@dipmat.math.unipa.it

Christophe Duperthuy
Laboratoire Reconnaissance de Formes et Vision
Bât 403, INSA de Lyon
20, Avenue Albert Einstein, 69621 Villeurbanne Cedex, France
cduper@rfv.insa-lyon.fr

Roy Eagleson
Department of Electrical Engineering
University of Western Ontario
London, Ontario, Canada, N6A 5B9
eagleson@uwo.ca

Ulrich Eckhardt
Institut für Angewandte Mathematik
Universität Hamburg
Bundesstraße 55, 20146 Hamburg, Germany
Eckhardt@math.uni-hamburg.de

Georgy L. Gimel'Farb
Division of Science and Technology, Tamaki Campus
University of Auckland
Private Bag 92019, 1005 Auckland, New Zealand
georgy@cs.auckland.ac.nz

Eckart Hundt
Siemens Research Laboratories
Otto-Hahn-Ring 6, 81739 München, Germany
Eckart.Hundt@mchp.siemens.de

Atsushi Imiya
Department of Information and Computer Sciences
Chiba University
1–33 Yayoi-cho, Inage-ku, Chiba 263, Japan
imiya@ics.tj.chiba-u.ac.jp

Herbert Jahn
Institut für Weltraumsensorik
Deutsche Forschungsanstalt für Luft- und Raumfahrt e. V. (DLR)
Rudower Chaussee 5, 12484 Berlin, Germany
herbert.jahn@dlr.de

Jean-Michel Jolion
Laboratoire Reconnaissance de Formes et Vision
Bât 403, INSA de Lyon
20, Avenue Albert Einstein, 69621 Villeurbanne Cedex, France
jolion@rfv.insa-lyon.fr

Reinhard Klette
Computing and Information Technology Research – CITR
Computer Science Department, Tamaki Campus
University of Auckland
Private Bag 92019, 1005 Auckland, New Zealand
rklette@cs.auckland.ac.nz

Andreas Koschan
Department of Computer Science, FR 3–11
Technical University of Berlin
Franklinstr. 28–29, 10587 Berlin, Germany
koschan@cs.tu-berlin.de

Jana Košecká
Robotics & Intelligent Machines Laboratory
Electrical Engineering and Computer Sciences Department
University of California, Berkeley
Berkeley, CA 94720, USA
janka@robotics.eecs.berkeley.edu

Matevž Kovačič
University of Ljubljana
Faculty of Computer and Information Science
Tržaška c. 25, 1000 Ljubljana, Slovenia
matevz.kovacic@fri.uni-lj.si

Vladimir A. Kovalevsky
Technische Fachhochschule Berlin, FB 13
Luxemburger Straße 10, 13353 Berlin, Germany

Ryszard Kozera
Department of Computer Science
University of Western Australia
Nedlands, WA 6907, Australia
ryszard@cs.uwa.edu.au

Björn Krebs
Institute for Robotics and Computer Control
Technical University Braunschweig
Hamburger Str. 267, 38114 Braunschweig, Germany
B.Krebs@tu-bs.de

Walter G. Kropatsch
Vienna University of Technology
Institute of Automation / Pattern Recognition and Image Processing
Treitlstr. 3, 1832 Vienna, Austria
krw@prip.tuwien.ac.at

Bojan Kverh
University of Ljubljana
Faculty of Computer and Information Science
Tržaška c. 25, 1000 Ljubljana, Slovenia
bojan.kverh@fri.uni-lj.si

Arnold Meijster
Institute for Mathematics and Computing Science
University of Groningen
P.O. Box 800, 9700 AV Groningen, The Netherlands
arnold@cs.rug.nl

Jos B.T.M. Roerdink
Institute for Mathematics and Computing Science
University of Groningen
P.O. Box 800, 9700 AV Groningen, The Netherlands
roe@cs.rug.nl

Volker Rodehorst
Photogrammetry and Cartography, EB 9
Technical University of Berlin
Strasse des 17. Juni 135, 10623 Berlin, Germany
vr@fpk.tu-berlin.de

Michail Schlesinger
Institute of Cybernetics
Ukrainian Academy of Sciences
40, Prospect Akademika Glushkova, 252022 Kiev, Ukraine
schles%image.kiev.ua@ts.kiev.ua

Karsten Schlüns
Computing and Information Technology Research – CITR
Computer Science Department, Tamaki Campus
University of Auckland
Private Bag 92019, 1005 Auckland, New Zealand
karsten@cs.auckland.ac.nz

Michael Schubert
Friedrich-Schiller-University Jena
Institute of Computer Science
07740 Jena, Germany
michael.schubert@uni-jena.de

Wladyslaw Skarbek
Institute of Radioelectronics
Warsaw University of Technology
Nowowiejska 15/19, 00-665 Warszawa, Poland
Skarbek@ire.pw.edu.pl

Franc Solina
University of Ljubljana
Faculty of Computer and Information Science
Tržaška c. 25, 1000 Ljubljana, Slovenia
franc.solina@fri.uni-lj.si

Gerald Sommer
Christian–Albrechts-Universität zu Kiel
Institut für Informatik und Praktische Mathematik
Lehrstuhl für Kognitive Systeme
Preußerstraße 1–9, 24105 Kiel, Germany
gs@informatik.uni-kiel.de

Cesare Valenti
University of Palermo
Dipartimento di Matematica ed Applicazioni
Via Arvhirafi 34, 90123 Palermo, Italy
cvalenti@ipamat.math.unipa.it

Klaus Voss
Friedrich-Schiller-University Jena
Institute of Computer Science
07740 Jena, Germany
klaus.voss@uni-jena.de

Friedrich M. Wahl
Institute for Robotics and Computer Control
Technical University Braunschweig
Hamburger Str. 267, 38114 Braunschweig, Germany
F.Wahl@tu-bs.de

Joachim Weickert
Department of Computer Science
University of Copenhagen
Universitetsparken 1, 2100 Copenhagen East, Denmark
joachim@diku.dk

SpringerComputerScience

C. Brink, W. Kahl, G. Schmidt (eds.)

Relational Methods in Computer Science

1997. 30 figures. XV, 272 pages.
Soft cover DM 69,–, öS 485,–. ISBN 3-211-82971-7
Advances in Computing Science

The calculus of relations turned into an important conceptual and methodological tool in computer science. The methods presented in this book include questions of relational databases, applications to program specification, resource-conscious linear logic, semantic and refinement consideration, nonclassical logics for reasoning about programs, tabular methods in software construction, algorithm development, linguistic problems, followed by a comprehensive bibliography. The reader gets an overview of the wide-ranging applicability of relational methods in computer science.

Contents:
- Introduction: Background Material.
- Algebras: Relation Algebras. - Heterogeneous Relation Algebra. - Fork Algebras.
- Logics: Relation Algebra and Modal Logics. - Relational Formalisation of Nonclassical Logics. - Linear Logic.
- Programs: Relational Semantics of Functional Programs. - Algorithms from Relational Specifications. - Programs and Datatypes. - Refinement and Demonic Semantics. - Tabular Representations in Relational Documents.
- Other Applications Areas: Databases. - Logic, Language, and Information. – Natural Language.

SpringerWienNewYork

Sachsenplatz 4-6, P.O.Box 89, A-1201 Wien, Fax +43-1-330 24 26
e-mail: order@springer.at, Internet: http://www.springer.at
New York, NY 10010, 175 Fifth Avenue • D-14197 Berlin, Heidelberger Platz 3
Tokyo 113, 3-13, Hongo 3-chome, Bunkyo-ku

Springer-Verlag
and the Environment

WE AT SPRINGER-VERLAG FIRMLY BELIEVE THAT AN international science publisher has a special obligation to the environment, and our corporate policies consistently reflect this conviction.

WE ALSO EXPECT OUR BUSINESS PARTNERS – PRINTERS, paper mills, packaging manufacturers, etc. – to commit themselves to using environmentally friendly materials and production processes.

THE PAPER IN THIS BOOK IS MADE FROM NO-CHLORINE pulp and is acid free, in conformance with international standards for paper permanency.